Marriage and Family Therapy (MFT) National Exam

Eli A. Karam, PhD, LMFT, is a full professor and former acting director of the Couple and Family Therapy program at the University of Louisville's Kent School of Social Work and Family Science. He has been a practicing therapist in both community and private practice settings since 2001. His leadership in the marriage and family therapy (MFT) profession includes service as president of the Kentucky Association for Marriage and Family Therapy (KAMFT) and as a board member of the American Association of Marriage and Family Therapy (AAMFT). Dr. Karam is the recipient of several prestigious awards from the AAMFT, including the Dissertation Award, Training Award, Divisional Contribution Award, and Media Award. He is also host and co-executive producer of the award-winning AAMFT podcast.

Marriage and Family Therapy (MFT) National Exam

Your Study Guide for Success

Eli A. Karam, PhD, LMFT

SPRINGER PUBLISHING

Springer Publishing Company, LLC
11 West 42nd Street, New York, NY 10036
www.springerpub.com
connect.springerpub.com/
examprepconnect.springerpub.com

Acquisitions Editor: Rhonda Dearborn
Compositor: diacriTech

ISBN: 9780826186775
ebook ISBN: 9780826186782
DOI: 10.1891/9780826186782

24 25 / 6 5

LCCN: 2022942110

Printed in the United States of America by Gasch Printing.

This book is dedicated to the memory of Marian F. Cona—a great aunt, saintly woman, and believer in the power of education. What she did for me cannot be adequately expressed in words. I eagerly anticipate the chance to honor her spirit and pay it forward to those close to me in the future!

Contents

Foreword

It is an honor to write the foreword to this extremely important book, which targets the newly graduated marriage and family therapist. After enduring the stress of a family therapy training program, the new graduate has to immediately pivot to beginning a career. Becoming licensed is a key step in that process, as one is not truly independent or graduated until the license to practice independently is achieved. An important step in the licensing process is completing and passing the licensure examination. Although one would expect a graduate program to fully equip its students to easily pass the examination, this is rarely the case. We have all heard multiple stories of exam takers who have failed at least once, some multiple times. This is not a reflection of their skills as a therapist, but rather of their preparation to take a test under stress. The program they graduated from may have been excellent, but may have underemphasized learning components that appear on the licensure exam. This is because few faculty in family therapy training programs are aware of the content that is on the licensing examination and as a result, many do not actively teach to this content. Most faculty tend to spend more time on their favored theoretical approaches.

In Marriage and Family Therapy (MFT) National Exam: Your Study Guide for Success, Eli A. Karam provides a service to the new marriage and family therapy professional. Preparation for success in the national examination is made easier through use of this book that is filled with the knowledge and guidance needed to maximize results in studying and preparing for the examination. This guidance from an expert in the field of marriage and family therapy will prove to be invaluable. This book provides the reader with an overview of the testing process, in-depth learning of the six domains of the licensing examination, and a review of the key knowledge areas included on the examination. In addition, the book provides practical wisdom on best strategies to prepare and take the examination so as to maximize success. Although the book does not guarantee a passing score, I strongly believe that it will enhance the success of those taking the examination. This book offers tools new graduates can use to be more successful in preparing and passing the examination, which will allow them to practice independently in a shorter period of time. For those preparing to take the examination, this book is an essential resource.

Adrian Blow, PhD
Department of Human Development
and Family Studies
East Lansing, Michigan

Preface

Behind every book there is a story. This exam-prep book is no exception. The story is simple. Some years ago, I was asked by my state association of family therapists to put together a "model review" course for those prelicensed individuals getting ready to sit for the national examination. That request corresponded with me taking on the task of teaching a professional development course in my accredited training program that was designed to prepare students for life after graduation while on the road to licensure. The feedback I received for these endeavors was positive, so when Springer asked whether I wanted to take that knowledge and develop materials to reach a larger audience, the answer was simple—YES!

Most professions require some type of state or national examination before formal entrance into the respective field can occur. Marriage and family therapy (MFT) is no different. Before one can practice MFT independently, the Association of Marriage & Family Therapy Regulatory Boards (AMFTRB) Marital and Family Therapy National Examination must be passed. The AMFTRB exam is a 180-question test that focuses on six domains and assesses the individual's depth and breadth of knowledge to ensure the therapist has the skills required to successfully function in professional practice.

In the 20 years or so since I took this test, the AMFTRB has evolved the focus of the exam. Although it was once an evaluation of basic knowledge of MFT theories and interventions, it now measures one's ability to apply what was learned in training in an ethical, systemic way to a host of vignettes and clinical scenarios. The examination does not encompass all that an effective systemic therapist should know; it tests only a mere sampling. The AMFTRB exam is arguably one of the most anxiety-provoking milestones associated with becoming a licensed marriage and family therapist (LMFT). Failing to pass the examination delays one's entry into the profession, leading to uncertainty, potential financial strain, and, for some, thoughts of inadequacy and a myriad of negative emotions. Therefore, the anxiety surrounding the exam is understandable. The best way to maximize your chances of passing the examination on the first attempt is to prepare adequately. *Marriage and Family Therapy (MFT) National Exam: Your Study Guide for Success* provides a comprehensive review of core exam content and includes over 360 sample test questions.

Despite the students' best efforts to review for the AMFTRB examination, they can encounter difficulties answering questions correctly that can jeopardize their chances of passing. If you are someone who struggles with standardized test taking or has failed the AMFTRB exam before, you need a resource like this book to identify mistakes and to offer strategies for correcting these errors. This book is going to become your new best friend and you can use it in a variety of ways. I believe it can serve as a vital text used to support traditional systematic study methods or as a stand-alone resource for those who are not able to invest in a formalized study program. Many students will find the textbook format useful as a primer at the beginning of their individualized study process or as a thorough review at its end. Questions found at the end of each chapter can serve as a gauge for successful review of the chapter material and the full mock exam at the end of the book offers a cumulative review as you prepare for test day. Regardless of how you use *Marriage and Family Therapy (MFT) National Exam: Your Study Guide for Success*, I wish you tremendous success with the exam and in your future career as an LMFT. Passing the AMFTRB exam will be one of the most memorable stages of your professional life. I am delighted and privileged to play a small role in that process.

In partnership,

Eli A. Karam
info@elikaram.com
www.elikaram.com

List of Podcasts

All podcasts recorded by Eli A. Karam.

Acknowledgments

I am forever indebted to the field of family therapy for bringing me a professional lifetime of joy and stimulation. I was lucky enough to find something that was both a calling for me and offered connection. From the first time I stepped foot in a therapy room as a master's-level intern to this very moment as I write these words, I have had a love affair with this profession. They say that if you love your job, you never work a day in your life. I have never worked a day in my life!

In writing this book, I am indebted to my teachers, colleagues, students, and clients, both past and present. They are too numerous to name individually. Some have been especially helpful in my formation as a marriage and family therapist, however. I am eternally grateful to those who lit the systemic spark in me back at the Family Institute at Northwestern University, and during my doctoral training at Purdue University.

I am also indebted to my wife, Tracy, and our children, Charlie and Molly. They made many sacrifices, but never complained during the writing process that took me away from family time. Finally, I appreciate the fine professionals at Springer Publishing Company, especially Rhonda Dearborn and Kirsten Elmer, who made this publication possible.

Pass Guarantee

If you use this resource to prepare for your exam and you do not pass, you may return it for a refund of your full purchase price. To receive a refund, you must return your product along with a copy of your original receipt and exam score report. Product must be returned and received within 180 days of the original purchase date. This excludes tax, shipping, and handling. One offer per person and address. Refunds will be issued within 8 weeks from acceptance and approval. This offer is valid for U.S. residents only. Void where prohibited. To initiate a refund, please contact customer service at CS@springerpub.com.

PART I

Marriage and Family Therapy Exam-Prep Overview

How to Use This Book: The Association of Marital and Family Therapy Regulatory Boards Exam Makeup

1

LEARNING OBJECTIVES

After reading this chapter, you should be able to:

1. Describe the testing protocol for the Association of Marital and Family Therapy Regulatory Boards (AMFTRB) examination
2. Outline the purpose and structure of this book
3. Identify the six domains of the AMFTRB examination
4. Review the knowledge areas that are included on AMFTRB examination

INTRODUCTION

Welcome to this important part of your burgeoning career as a marriage and family therapist! The preparation and dedication needed to pass the AMFTRB Marital and Family Therapy National Examination is substantial. Assessing whether you have the basic knowledge necessary to safely and ethically practice, the examination helps measure that you are competent to independently provide systemic services to individuals, couples, and families. While passing this exam is only one step on the road to becoming a licensed marriage and family therapist (LMFT), for many it is the most difficult, anxiety-provoking milestone in the journey toward licensure. This guide aims to assist you through the exam-prep process in several fundamental ways. It will help you to:

1. *Compare and contrast various models of marriage and family therapy (MFT) regarding theory, treatment planning, and practice.*
2. *Assess, diagnose, and monitor therapy progress using a variety of theories and model specific, systemic orientations.*
3. *Review knowledge of the primary, legal, and ethical aspects of MFT, including the management of crisis situations.*
4. *Cultivate specific test-taking strategies surrounding the AMFTRB MFT National Examination.*

The purpose of this book is to allow examination candidates, students, and others who wish to update their knowledge to review the fundamental concepts and practices of MFT. This book allows individuals to identify areas of strength and deficit in that knowledge. It provides summaries of various major MFT models and theoretical perspectives and is intended to represent the depth and breadth of knowledge that applicants should consider as they prepare for the national exam.

What this exam-prep book does well is (a) filter all that information down to its most essential elements, and (b) organize it in such a way that it is easier to remember so as to be useful on the exam. Although it is true that the necessary knowledge can come from textbooks used in graduate programs, it is also true that success in testing relies at least in part on good test-taking skills. Although it is not produced by or affiliated with AMFTRB in any way and does not guarantee a passing score on the exam, this book is designed using test-taking strategies and practice items that complement the relevant exam content. These strategies are so helpful in passing the exam because the skills that it takes to be a good marriage and family therapist in practice can be very different than the skills that it takes to pass the examination.

Any exam-preparation book is only as good as its practice questions and answers, and that is another strength of this text. The book supplies a myriad of test questions (both a pretest and full mock exam) that prepare the candidate for what to expect on the actual MFT exam. Each answer is explained in depth to make the principles and reasoning behind it understandable.

Part I (Chapter 1) provides both an overview to this book and the specific makeup of the AMFTRB MFT National Examination. This exam allows state licensing boards to use a uniform standard whereby they can evaluate the knowledge of applicants for licensure. We outline the six practice domains that provide the overall structure both for the exam and this book.

Part II (Chapters 2–11) is dedicated to the practice of systemic therapy and designing/conducting treatment using the major models and theories of MFT, including

- *Historical and conceptual foundations of MFT;*
- *Strategic family therapy;*
- *Structural family therapy;*
- *Experiential family therapy;*
- *Behavioral and cognitive behavioral MFT approaches;*
- *Transgenerational family therapy;*
- *Psychoanalytic family therapy;*
- *Postmodernism, social constructionism, and the feminist critique;*
- *Solution-focused therapy; and*
- *Narrative therapy.*

Each chapter in Part II is designed to include information specific to the model, including description of key figures, techniques/interventions, and other important theoretical contributions. There is a glossary of key terms and a quiz at the end of each chapter.

Part III (Chapters 12–13) centers around assessment and diagnosis in systemic therapy. Chapter 12 outlines many of the important domains used for systemic assessment, including the presenting problem, family life cycle stage, presence of violence, and substance abuse. In addition to informal interview techniques, the chapter also explores the use of formal assessment tools in family therapy. Chapter 13 reviews the diagnostic criteria of the major disorders listed within the *Diagnostic and Statistical Manual of Mental Disorders* (5th ed.; *DSM-5*; American Psychiatric Association [APA], 2013), as well as the etiology underlying these disorders. There is a glossary of key terms and a quiz at the end of both chapters in this section.

Part IV (Chapter 14) focuses on tasks related to continuously evaluating the therapeutic process and incorporating feedback into the course of treatment, as well as planning for termination. Part V (Chapter 15) examines tasks related to assessing and managing emergency situations and intervening when clinically indicated and/or legally mandated. It also includes practice strategies that beginning therapists often struggle with as they encounter the challenges of working with clients with substance abuse, the potential for self-harm, interpersonal violence, and family secrets. Part VI (Chapter 16) explores both ethical issues and legal considerations based on the 2015 American Association for Marriage and Family Therapy (AAMFT; 2015) *Code of Ethics*. The focus is on tasks related to ongoing adherence to ethical codes, treatment agreements, professionalism, and maintaining competency in the field. Again, a glossary of key terms and a quiz are provided at the end of each chapter in Parts IV through VI.

This book concludes with Part VII (Chapters 17–19), three chapters designed to complete your preparation for the AMFTRB examination. Chapter 17 orients the reader to both question types and answering strategies, whereas Chapter 18 outlines how to get ready and what to expect on test day. The guide ends with a full, 180-item mock exam that tests not only one's awareness of MFT therapy concepts, models, and knowledge domains, but also requires the candidate to be able to apply their knowledge to the entry-level, direct practice of MFT.

AMFTRB EXAM

The MFT National Examination is sponsored by the AMFTRB. As marriage and family therapists begin their preparation for the AMFTRB exam, they are anxious not only about knowing the test content, but also about the format of the exam itself. You will be allowed to sit for the examination only after your credentials have been reviewed and are found to meet the education and experience requirements for licensure in your chosen state. The examination is designed to assess a broad, basic knowledge through questions focused on the tasks that an entry-level marriage and family therapist should be able to perform, and the knowledge required to perform those tasks successfully. The AMFTRB contends candidates who have completed the required academic and experiential preparation and who have developed the level of competence necessary for entry-level professional practice in MFT should be able to pass the test. Becoming familiar with the exam structure will reduce your anxiety about the unknown as you prepare for test day.

TOP 10 THINGS TO KNOW

1. AMFTRB, with the advice and assistance of the Professional Testing Corporation, prepares the examination. The questions for the examination are written by MFT experts and are reviewed for construction, accuracy, and appropriateness by the AMFTRB. There are 180 multiple-choice questions, and you will have 4 hours to answer them.
2. As there is no additional penalty for incorrect answers, it is to your advantage to answer each item even when you are uncertain of the correct response. You do not want to leave any questions blank; answer all 180 questions in the 4 hours. Each item has four answer options, only one of which is correct. You should choose the single best answer to each item, as no credit is given for items in which more than one response is selected.
3. The exam covers six content areas and will be weighted in approximately the following manner (Table 1.1):

Table 1.1 Exam Domains

Domains of Practice	Percentage of Examination	Number of Items
Domain 1—The Practice of Systemic Therapy	23.33	42
Domain 2—Assessing, Hypothesizing, and Diagnosing	13.82	25
Domain 3—Designing and Conducting Treatment	12.14	22
Domain 4—Evaluating Ongoing Process and Terminating Treatment	17.51	31
Domain 5—Managing Crisis Situations	14.44	26
Domain 6—Maintaining Ethical, Legal, and Professional Standards	18.76	34

The exam also may include items derived from the following knowledge areas:

- Foundations of the discipline of marital, couple, and family therapy
- Models of marital, couple, and family therapy
- Development and evolution of the practice of systemic therapy
- Family studies and science
- Marital studies and science
- Couple/relationship studies and science
- General systems theory
- Clinical application of couple and family therapy models
- Evidence-based approaches to couples and family therapy
- Individually based theory and therapy models
- Impact of couple dynamics on the system
- Family belief systems and their impact on problem formation and treatment
- Family homeostasis as it relates to problem formation and maintenance
- Family life cycle stages and their impact on problem formation and treatment
- Human development throughout the life span
- Diverse family patterns
- Strength-based resilience across the life span
- Theories of personality
- Psychopathology across the life span
- Impact of developmental disorders on system dynamics
- Trauma and vicarious trauma
- Bias and discrimination
- Risk factors, indicators, and impact of abuse and patterns of endangerment across the life span
- Risk factors, indicators, and impact of loss and grief across the life span
- Behaviors, psychological features, or physical symptoms that indicate a need for medical, educational, psychiatric, or psychological evaluation
- Diagnostic interviewing techniques
- *DSM-5*
- Standardized psychological assessment tests
- Nonstandardized assessment tests (e.g., genograms, family maps, and scaling questions)
- Relational diagnostic tests
- Dynamics of and strategies for managing transference and countertransference
- Stages of acculturation, multiethnic identities, and multicultural identities
- Effect of immigration or refugee/asylum status
- Implications of human diversity factors on client systems
- Reference materials regarding purpose, use, side effects, and classification of medications
- Effects of nonprescription substance use on the client system
- Effects of substance abuse and dependency on individual and family functioning
- Effects of addictive behaviors on the client system
- Addiction treatment modalities
- Principles and elements of recovery-oriented systems of care for addiction and substance abuse
- Divorce and its impact on the client system
- Child custody and its impact on the client system
- Infertility and its impact on the client system
- Adoption and foster care and its impact on the client system
- Infidelity and its impact on the client system

- Trauma intervention models
- Crisis intervention models
- Sex therapy
- Human sexual anatomy, physiology, and development
- Sexual behavior and maladaptive sexual behavior
- Sexual orientation and gender identity
- Sexual abuse treatment for victims, perpetrators, and their families
- Spiritual and religious beliefs and their impact on the client system
- Physical and mental health status, and experience of acute and chronic illness and disability and their impact on the client system
- Impact of client system's use of resources
- Current research literature and methodology, including quantitative and qualitative methods, sufficient to critically evaluate assessment tools and therapy models
- Methodologies for developing and evaluating educational support groups
- Applicable statutes, case law, and regulations regarding the practice of therapy
- Codes of ethics
- Business practices (e.g., storage and disposal of records, referrals, advertising)
- Implications of the use of technology in business practice by therapists and office staff
- Impact of technology on the client system
- Training and practice of teletherapy and telesupervision
- Impact of social stratification, social privilege, and social oppression on the client system
- Influence of prevailing sociological climate on the therapeutic relationship
- Impact of economic stressors on presenting problems and treatment
- Community systems (e.g., schools and human service agencies)
- Mandated group treatment programs
- Group treatment, education, and supprt programs
- Supervision issues and their impact on supervisee and supervisor relationship

Although it is impossible to identify the information that will be tested in your examination, the AMFTRB provides the practice domains, task statements, and knowledge statements on which the examination is based in their annual *Handbook for Candidates* (AMFTRB, 2022; available at amftrb.org).

4. Although the exam covers the six content domains and you may structure your studying to learn all the related material, the questions on the test occur in random order and skip across the different domains. For example, there is no separate section of questions labeled "The Practice of Systemic Therapy, Managing Crisis Situations," and so on. You may have an assessment question followed by one on ethics, so you really need to reset mentally between questions and avoid trying to relate them to one another in any way.
5. You probably want to know how many of the 180 questions you need to answer correctly to pass the exam. Although this sounds like an easy question, it is not! All items are counted in computing your score. The reported score equals the total number of correct responses: Using an "anchor examination," the passing score is established by a panel of expert judges. This exam becomes the standard of knowledge to which all future forms of the examination are compared. Some forms of the examination will contain individual items that may differ in difficulty than items on other forms. To compensate for these variations, test forms are compared using a psychometric process called *equating*. This equating process accounts for the varying item difficulties and adjusts the passing score up or down accordingly.
6. The examination is computerized but requires no specialized computer knowledge. There is a brief computer tutorial that will assist you when you first sit down and look at

the screen, and spending time getting to feel comfortable with the device at that time is a good idea, because it will not count toward your 4-hour time limit.

7. You will be taking your examination at a testing center with others who are being tested in different disciplines whose examinations may take longer or shorter to complete than yours, so do not compare yourself to other test takers or be concerned if they finish before or after you.
8. Testing-center activities are closely monitored, and you will need to leave all of your belongings, including your watch, in a provided locker. You may ask for scrap paper or a pencil but you will not be able to bring anything into the room with you. All testing accommodations related to documented disabilities must be approved by your state licensing board and arranged in advance with AMFTRB. You may take a brief restroom break or stand to stretch, but the clock does not stop, and these activities will be included in your 4-hour limit, so you want to manage your time carefully. Visit www.prometric.com for more information about what to expect on test day.
9. You will leave the testing center without knowing the results of your exam. Your results on the domains and on the total examination are sent to your state licensing board and to you via email within 20 business days following the close of the testing period. This is necessary to allow for the psychometric review and administration time required to ensure accurate and reliable scores. These results will be available online only for 60 days, so be sure to save a copy of your score report in your permanent files.
10. You can take the exam during 1 week of each month at testing locations offered through Prometric. Although this may vary by state, traditionally you may take the examination no more than three times in any 12-month period. Should you not pass the exam, the next available testing period would be in approximately 3 months. For example, if you take the exam in January and are unsuccessful, because it would be too late to register for the February or March testing period, you could next register for the April test period.

CONCLUSION

After reading this brief overview, you are now ready to start studying the content for the AMFTRB exam. At the end of the book, we revisit essential exam information by reviewing specific test-taking strategies and describing how to prepare for exam day. In addition to this book, remember to visit www.amftrb.org for all relevant and up-to-date exam information.

Although there are numerous test-preparation materials on the market to help you prepare for the AMFTRB exam, all materials are not created equal. This book was developed by an award-winning AAMFT professor and LMFT who has spent the past 20 years helping his students get ready for this important milestone. Individuals who are studying for the MFT licensing examination don't want to waste their precious time tracking down multiple materials; rather, they want to focus their energy on actual study time. This book provides relevant exam content in a single, manageable, easy-to-use guide. Best wishes as you begin your study . . . stay systemic, my friends!

REFERENCES

American Psychiatric Association. (2013). *Diagnostic and statistical manual of mental disorders.* (5th ed.).

American Association for Marriage and Family Therapy. (2015). *Code of ethics*. AAMFT.

Association of Marital & Family Therapy Regulatory Boards. (2022). *Handbook for candidates.* Professional Examination Service.

PART II

The Practice of Systemic Therapy: Designing and Conducting Treatment Using the Major Models and Theories of Marriage and Family Therapy (Domains 1-3)

2

Historical and Conceptual Foundations of Marriage and Family Therapy

LEARNING OBJECTIVES

After reading this chapter, you should be able to:

1. Identify the major personalities who pioneered family therapy
2. Explain key developments in the historical roots of family therapy
3. Distinguish the main tenets of cybernetics
4. Describe the main concepts of systems theory

RELEVANT EXAM DOMAINS

- *Domain 1—The Practice of Systemic Therapy*

Explores tasks related to incorporating systemic theory and perspectives into practice activities and establishing and maintaining ongoing therapeutic relationships with the client system.

INTRODUCTION

During the first half of the 20th century, psychotherapy, most often in the form of classical psychoanalysis, tended to focus on the inner experience and the client's intrapsychic world, even as family relationships clearly were impacting the individual. Tired of the traditional way of viewing people and their problems, the earliest systemic-thinking pioneers broke away from the establishment and the status quo. The shift away from focusing on the individual to the family system brought many new approaches to psychotherapeutic theory and clinical practice. One such new approach, vital to the history of family therapy, was the theory of cybernetics—the science of communications and automatic control systems in both machines and living things. Concerned with patterns and processes, the family systems perspective proposes use of a cybernetic framework as an alternative to the old ways of knowing and thinking.

MODEL DEVELOPERS AND SIGNIGIFICANT CONTRIBUTORS

NATHAN ACKERMAN

Nathan Ackerman led the charge for psychiatrists to go beyond using traditional analytic techniques to explore the role of family dynamics in the etiology of mental illness. A pioneer in the field of family therapy, Ackerman who was also a co-founder of *Family Process*, a journal that focuses on family studies.

GREGORY BATESON

Gregory Bateson was interested in communication patterns in families with individuals who had been diagnosed with schizophrenia. After obtaining several government grants for study, Bateson, along with Jay Haley, John Weakland, and eventually Don Jackson, formulated a controversial theory of dysfunctional communication called the *double bind*. Although this theory regarding the origin of schizophrenia later proved to be incomplete, if not inaccurate, its effort to look beyond the symptomatic person to family interactions was revolutionary. Bateson also introduced the notion that a family might be analogous to a cybernetic system in its use of self-regulating feedback mechanisms to maintain balance and constancy (Bateson, 1972).

LUDWIG VON BERTALANFFY

Ludwig von Bertalanffy is considered one of the founders of general systems theory (GST). He provided a model for understanding living systems that is focused on how apparently unrelated events or phenomena can be seen as interrelated parts or components of a larger whole or system. Individuals are seen in the context of a bigger, dynamic system that can evolve, adapt to environmental stimuli, and engage in self-preservation (Nichols, 2013).

THEODORE LIDZ

Theodore Lidz argued that a family-oriented perspective could contribute to a needed overhauling of psychoanalytic theory, particularly refuting the singling out of rejecting mothers by calling attention to the father's possibly destructive role in those diagnosed with schizophrenia. He introduced the concepts of *schism*, the division of the family into two antagonistic and competing groups; and *skew*, whereby one partner in the marriage dominates the family to a striking degree, because of serious personality disorder (Nichols, 2013).

LYMAN WYNNE

Lyman Wynne observed that schizophrenic families deal with emotions, both positive and negative, in false and unreal ways. Wynne termed these patterns *pseudomutuality* and *pseudohostility*. He labeled the shifting boundaries surrounding these families the *rubber fence* as they allow some outside information to be introduced and what is deemed unacceptable to be kept out (Nichols, 2013).

THE RISE OF FAMILY THERAPY

Five independent scientific and clinical developments that occurred during the decade following World War II helped set the stage for the emergence of family therapy. These are described in the text that follows.

THE INVESTIGATION OF THE FAMILY'S ROLE IN THE DEVELOPMENT OF SCHIZOPHRENIA

Frieda Fromm-Reichmann (1948) postulated that maternal rejection was responsible for the development of schizophrenia. She introduced the term *schizophrenogenic mother* to denote a domineering, cold, rejecting, possessive, guilt-producing person, who, in combination with a passive, detached, and ineffectual father, causes her offspring to feel confused and inadequate and ultimately to become schizophrenic.

In 1954, after receiving a 2-year grant from the Macy Foundation to study schizophrenic communication patterns, Gregory Bateson began collaborating with Don Jackson. Interested in developing an interactional theory to understand this disorder, their research group began to study the possible link between pathological communication patterns within a family and the emergence and maintenance of schizophrenic behavior in a family member.

First, at the Menninger Foundation in Topeka, Kansas, in the early 1950s and later at the National Institute of Mental Health (NIMH) near Washington, DC, Murray Bowen, a psychiatrist, broke new ground in the study of schizophrenia. In a dramatic experiment conducted at NIMH, Bowen arranged for mothers to move into cottages on clinic grounds near their hospitalized, schizophrenic children for several months. He was especially interested in identifying unresolved symbiotic mother–child interactions. When Bowen moved on to Georgetown Medical School in 1956, Lyman Wynne succeeded him as head of the family studies section at NIMH. Wynne's research centered on the blurred, ambiguous, and confused communication patterns that occur in families with schizophrenic members.

Although these initial efforts to link schizophrenia to family life were groundbreaking at the time, they were ultimately disavowed. Researchers today no longer look for a culpable, pathologizing parent and a victimized child, but more often search for biological or genetic markers in trying to understand the disorder's origins. Nevertheless, studying schizophrenic communication patterns in family systems remains historically important in the evolution of family therapy because it brought attention to dysfunctional interactions occurring within a family context and shared by all family members.

THE EVOLUTION OF MARITAL AND PREMARITAL COUNSELING

Focusing on issues surrounding dyads, early marital counselors, viewed as "experts," attempted to provide answers for people with sexual and other marital difficulties. These experts consisted of gynecologists and other physicians, lawyers, and college professors who were family-life specialists. Clergy were especially prominent in offering formal premarital counseling, often as part of an optional or mandatory preparation program pursued before a wedding. When they discussed their marital and family concerns, people usually confided in this group of paraprofessionals rather than with mental health professionals. These professionals knew the families in question well because they usually lived with them in a shared community over many years.

Beginning in 1939, the National Council on Family Relations and its journal, *Marriage and Family Living*, promoted research-based knowledge about family life throughout the United States. In 1941, largely through the guidance of family life educator Emily Mudd, the American Association of Marriage Counselors (AAMC) was formed. The AAMC brought together various professionals, primarily physicians, but also others concerned with the new interdisciplinary field of marriage counseling. This organization led the way in developing standards for training and practice, certifying marriage counseling centers, and establishing a professional code of ethics. The association later changed its name from the American Association of Marriage and Family Counselors to the American Association for Marriage and Family Therapy (AAMFT).

THE GROWTH OF THE CHILD GUIDANCE MOVEMENT

The child guidance movement, emerging early in the 20th century, posited that if emotional problems did indeed begin in childhood, then early identification and treatment of children could prevent later psychopathology. Alfred Adler helped found the child guidance movement in Vienna in the early 1900s, and although he did not work therapeutically with entire families, he did influence one of his disciples, Rudolf Dreikurs, who later emigrated to the United States, to expand child guidance centers into family counseling centers. Child guidance clinics now exist in almost every city in the United States. They provide major settings for identifying and treating childhood psychological disorders and are valuable in involving parents and attending to the larger social systems from which the presenting problem evolved.

ADVANCES IN GROUP DYNAMICS AND GROUP THERAPY

A group is a meaningful and functioning unit in and of itself, more than the sum of its parts, which is a collection of positions and roles and not of individuals. Group dynamics and the behavior of small groups served as models of family functioning for some early family therapists such as John Bell. Family therapy was considered a special subset of group therapy, except that the participants were not strangers. Calling this approach *family group therapy*, Bell believed the therapist's task was to promote interaction, facilitate communication, clarify the group process, and interpret interpersonal dynamics—as any group therapy leader would do.

BACKLASH TO PSYCHOANALYSIS AND BEHAVIORISM

The major psychological theories followed in the United States in the early part of the 20th century were psychoanalysis and behaviorism. Both were philosophically and clinically focused on dealing only with individual clients. Proponents of psychoanalysis, for instance, believed that dealing with more than one person at a time in therapy would constrain the transference process and keep depth analysis from occurring. Similarly, behaviorists stressed straightforward work with clients, usually in the form of conditioning and counterconditioning, which are linear in nature.

Rather than viewing a person's problems as originating solely within the individual, early systemic thinkers risked professional excommunication from their psychiatrist and behaviorist brethren by viewing these problems from a relational perspective. If a person was depressed, the therapist explored the person's relationships with friends and family in detail. If a child displayed problematic behavior, the psychiatrist involved the parents in problem-solving discussions rather than merely addressing the issues by medicating the child. As these renegade early family therapists understood more about human development, they invited other mental health professionals to view individual symptoms within an interpersonal context.

CYBERNETICS

The term *cybernetics* was coined by Norbert Weiner to describe systems that regulate themselves through means of feedback loops (Wiener, 1954). The family stabilizes or changes and maintains its homeostasis (state of equilibrium) through cybernetics. Cybernetics can refer to an inorganic system, such as a furnace, or an organic system, such as a family. A major difference between cybernetics and general systems theory is that cybernetics is more of a mechanical model. People are not like machines.

Historically, the science of cybernetics was born in the early 1940s during a series of wartime interdisciplinary conferences held in New York City, sponsored by the Josiah Macy Foundation, and attended by a cross-section of the leading scientists, engineers, mathematicians, and social scientists of the time. The conferees addressed, among other things, the study of communication in reference to regulation and control (e.g., the wartime problems of guided missiles and rockets) through the operation of feedback mechanisms.

Researchers from both the physical and social sciences began to explore how these systems, or cybernetics notions, could be applied to various fields in which both living and nonliving entities could be governed by self-regulating feedback loops that become activated to correct errors or deviations in the system and thus restore stability in the process of reaching a preprogrammed goal.

A major task for families is to maintain a balance between stability and change. This balance is regulated by feedback loops, or the cycles by which individuals influence one another's actions. The impact that a behavior has on the system and the response of the system to that behavior are viewed in terms of positive and negative feedback. Positive and negative have no valence here and are not value judgments about the behavior; rather they indicate whether a change has occurred in the system. A positive feedback loop reinforces itself. If a change has occurred and has been accepted by the system, a positive feedback loop has occurred. The status quo was not maintained, so the process is referred to as *positive feedback*. If left unchecked, the reinforcing effects of positive feedback tend to exacerbate a system's errors, leading to a runaway process. *Negative feedback*, on the other hand, can lead to nearly stable behavior with gentle fluctuations, like a thermostat that maintains a certain room temperature. The entire system is governed by feedback loops that regulate and control; negative feedback tends to stabilize systems, whereas positive feedback tends to destabilize systems. Positive feedback may give way to pronounced behavior escalation, whereas negative feedback counters the volatile change of positive feedback.

Beginning in the late 1970s, some family therapists began to pay attention to the theories of Chilean biologist Humberto Maturana, cognitive scientist Francisco Varela, and cyberneticist Heinz von Foerster. These systemic thinkers rallied against the traditional cybernetic notion that a living system could be observed, studied objectively, and changed from the outside. Although first-order cybernetics may well remain the primary focus for many therapists who see family systems as analogous to mechanical systems, these new-wave, second-order cyberneticists argue that living systems should not be seen as objects that can be programmed from the outside, but rather as self-creating, independent entities.

GENERAL SYSTEMS THEORY

From von Bertalanffy's work on general systems theory, social scientists conceptualized that all living systems, such as plants, animals, and even families, operate on a similar set of principles (von Bertalanffy, 1968):

1. The whole is greater than the sum of its parts.
2. A system is a compilation of subsystems arranged in a hierarchical structure.
3. Systems adapt self-stabilizing mechanisms to maintain homeostasis and equilibrium.
4. Systems have the capacity to adapt and change in response to environmental conditions.

Reductionism asks us to think about things mechanistically, breaking things down to their simplest form and individual parts. To understand families; however, we cannot reduce them down to their distinct parts or individual members. General systems theory focuses on the relationship and interaction between the objects in a system. It provides a model for understanding living systems that is focused on how apparently unrelated events or phenomena can be seen as interrelated parts or components of a larger whole or system.

Systems can be closed or open. Closed systems have no interchange with their environments. For example, machines are closed systems. They do not exchange energy with the environment. Open systems, on the other hand, exchange matter, energy, or information with their environments. Most biological and social systems are open systems. Families are an example of open systems.

Family systems are more complicated than linear causality can explain. There is no one cause behind a behavior and no one person to blame or praise when an interaction occurs the way it does. Although linear causality is a useful concept when two or more objects are linked together by interactions moving in one direction (A causes B, B causes C, and so forth), circular causality offers better insight into the nature of the complicated and interconnected dynamics of family systems. Family dynamics impact individuals, and individuals in turn impact the dynamics of the family in multiple dimensions (Watzlawick et al., 1967).

CONCLUSION

In this chapter, we reviewed the movements that gave rise to family therapy and the foundational concepts of family systems theory and cybernetics. The shift from an individual, linear perspective to a systemic perspective was groundbreaking, providing those who made the shift with a powerful tool for understanding families and communication. Five seemingly independent scientific and clinical developments together set the stage for the emergence of family therapy: (a) the study of schizophrenia, (b) the marriage counseling movement, (c) the child guidance movement, (d) the study of group dynamics, and (e) the backlash to psychoanalysis and behaviorism. Cybernetics, applied to families, is the study of how feedback is used to regulate systems. According to family systems theory, it is impossible to understand the behavior of individual family members without considering how the family system operates as a whole. To do so it may be necessary to look at process (how family members interact) and structure (how the family is organized).

KEY TERMS

Analogic communication: Communication not with words, but via nonverbal, paraverbal, and contextual aspects of interaction. In family therapy, it refers to the process of communication, rather than its content.

Autopoietic: Refers to systems that are self-organizing and self-maintaining, such as biological and human systems.

Black-box concept: The idea that because the mind is so complex, it is better to study people's input and output (behavior, communication) than to speculate about what goes on in their minds.

Boundary: Emotional and physical barriers that protect and enhance the integrity of individuals, subsystems, and families.

Circular causality: The idea that actions are related through a series of recursive loops or repeating cycles.

Closed system: A functionally related group of elements regarded as forming a collective entity that does not interact with the surrounding environment.

Complementarity: Refers to the reciprocity that is the defining feature of every relationship in which the qualities of one make up for deficits in the other.

Conjoint therapy: This type of therapy involves two or more family members and was introduced by Mental Research Institute (MRI) psychiatrist, Don Jackson.

Content: The actual ideas and facts discussed in a therapy session and/or the words used between therapist and clients. Content is the material, or the "what" of counseling, and is the opposite of process.

Cybernetics: The science of feedback; how information, especially positive and negative feedback loops, can help self-regulate a system.

Digital communication: A verbal mode of communication that takes place via spoken or written words.

Double bind: A hypothesis of Gregory Bateson's research group regarding the origin of schizophrenia. The theory states that two seemingly contradictory messages may exist at the same time on different levels and lead to confusion, if not schizophrenic behavior, on the part of an individual who cannot comment on or escape from the relationship in which this is occurring. For example, a mother may tell her child that she loves them while discouraging or rejecting any show of affection from the child.

Ecosystemic approach: This approach looks at the family's relationship to other larger systems, such as community, school, and work.

Entropy: The tendency of a system to become disorganized.

Equifinality: The ability of complex systems to reach a given final goal in a variety of different ways.

Family system: A conception of the family as a collective whole entity made up of individual parts plus the way the parts function together.

Feedback loop: The return of a portion of the output of a system, especially when used to maintain the output within predetermined limits (negative feedback), or to signal a need to modify the system (positive feedback).

First-order change: Temporary or superficial change within a system that does not alter the basic organization of the system itself.

First-order cybernetics: The idea that an outside observer can study and make changes in a system while remaining separate and independent of that system.

General systems theory: Developed by Ludwig von Bertalanffy, this biological model proposes that living systems are whole entities that maintain themselves through continuous input and output from the environment.

Homeostasis: Refers to a balanced steady state of equilibrium.

Identified patient: The family member with the presenting symptom; thus, the person who initially seeks treatment or for whom treatment is sought.

Interlocking pathology: A term created by Nathan Ackerman to explain how families and certain family members remain dysfunctional. In an interlocking pathology, an unconscious process between family members keeps them stuck together in an unhealthy relationship.

Linear causality: Refers to the idea that one event is the cause of an action and another is the effect; in behavior, it is the idea that one behavior is a stimulus, the other a response.

Marital schism: A disturbed marital situation characterized by family disharmony, self-preoccupation, the undermining of the spouse, and frequent threats of divorce by one or both partners.

Marital skew: A disturbed marital situation in which one partner dominates the family to an extreme degree and in which the marriage is maintained at the expense of the distortion of reality.

Metacommunication: The implied message within a message typically conveyed in a nonverbal manner.

Morphogenesis: The process by which a system changes its structure to adapt to new contexts, usually requiring a second-order change rather than a first-order change.

Morphostasis: The tendency of a person or system to resist change and remain the same.

Negative feedback: Information that signals a system to correct a deviation and restore the status quo.

Open system: A set of interrelated elements that exchange information, energy, and material with the surrounding environment.

Positive feedback: Information that confirms and reinforces the direction a system is taking.

Pseudohostility: As proposed by Wynne, a process by which families employ bickering and turmoil to maintain their relationship, avoiding tenderness and covering up deeper feelings, often of greater underlying hostility.

Pseudomutuality: As proposed by Wynne, a homeostasis-seeking relationship between and among family members that gives the surface appearance of being open, mutually understanding, and satisfying, when in fact it is not.

Reductionism: A procedure that reduces complex data to simple terms and is a powerful tool for understanding reality by breaking complex identities down into constituent parts, allowing significant insight into how things work.

Rubber fence: As proposed by Wynne, a shifting boundary around a family, intended to protect them from outside contact, arbitrarily permitting certain acceptable bits of information to penetrate but not others.

Runaway: Unchecked positive feedback that causes a family or system to get out of control.

Schizophrenogenic mother: Frieda Fromm Reichmann's term for aggressive, domineering mothers once thought to precipitate schizophrenia in their offspring.

Second-order change: Basic change in the structure and functioning of a system.

Subsystem: Refers to smaller units in families, determined by generation, sex, or function.

Symmetrical relationship: Refers to equality or parallel form in relationships.

System: A group of interrelated elements plus the way they function together.

Systems theory: A generic term that refers to the study of a group of related elements that interact as a whole entity; it encompasses general systems theory and cybernetics.

KNOWLEDGE CHECK: CHAPTER 2

1. Systemic approaches conceptualize an individual's symptoms as originating ________________.

   A. In the unconscious mind
   B. From social construction
   C. From faulty schemas
   D. Within family and relational dynamics

2. The concept of homeostasis, as it pertains to family systems, can be thought of as ____________.

   A. Havoc that creates instability for the family
   B. A resistance to new behaviors intended to create stability for the family
   C. A lack of movement intended to create healthy boundaries and new behaviors for the family
   D. A set of behaviors that forces the family to change

3. ____________ is analogous to a thermostat, whereas ________________ may be experienced by a family as an escalation in behavior or more extreme reactions by each member in the system.

   A. Positive feedback; negative feedback
   B. Universal feedback; positive feedback
   C. Negative feedback; positive feedback
   D. General feedback; positive feedback

4. ________________ refers to shifts in family interactions during the beginning stages of therapy, which may seem like real change, but in reality, the underlying family rules and structure remain the same.

   A. False self-phenomenon
   B. The rubber fence
   C. First-order change
   D. Second-order change

5. When a marriage and family therapist views the family as a system, they believe that ______________________.

   A. One cannot not communicate
   B. The whole is greater than the sum of its parts
   C. One member of the system is usually the problem
   D. People possess the ability to self correct

(*See answers next page.*)

1. D) Within family and relational dynamics

As opposed to psychodynamic or cognitive models, systemic approaches view the individual's problems as embedded within family and other close, interpersonal relationships.

2. B) A resistance to new behaviors intended to create stability for the family

Within family systems, *homeostasis* refers to unique behavioral, emotional, and interactional patterns developed and maintained by systems to enhance stability. Homeostasis is not a fixed process. Instead, systems constantly use feedback, or information about the system, to monitor and self-correct.

3. C) Negative feedback; positive feedback

There are two types of feedback loops: positive and negative. Positive feedback amplifies system output, resulting in growth or decline. Negative feedback dampers output stabilizes the system around an equilibrium point. Positive feedback loops are effective for creating change, but generally result in negative consequences if not moderated by negative feedback loops.

4. C) First-order change

First-order change is change that occurs on the behavioral level without impacting the operating rules of the system. These changes are considered more superficial and less sustainable than second-order changes, but these first-order changes can create a temporary shift in systemic dynamics that can set the stage for more sustainable second-order changes.

5. B) The whole is greater than the sum of its parts

Although all these statements are true, family systems theory hinges on nonsummativity, or the idea that the family as a whole is greater than the sum of its parts.

6. Systemic therapists view _____________ as playing a role in maintaining relational homeostasis and stability in family life.

A. Dysfunction
B. Symptoms
C. Defenses
D. Parents

7. Many early family therapists rejected the notion of __________.

A. Circular causality
B. Systems
C. Intrapsychic dynamics
D. Homeostasis

8. Group-oriented therapists who inspired the marriage family therapy (MFT) profession promoted systemic thinking by concentrating on ______ rather than ______.

A. Process; content
B. Solutions; problems
C. The system; the individual
D. Positive feedback loops; negative feedback loops

(*See answers next page.*)

6. B) Symptoms

Early family theorists believed that the identified patient's symptoms serve to maintain family homeostasis, thus having a function in the system. For example, when parents who are distant and about to separate come together to take care of their depressed teenager. The teen's depression functions to maintain family homeostasis.

7. C) Intrapsychic dynamics

Rather than viewing a person's problems as originating solely within the individual, early systemic thinkers rejected intrapsychic dynamics in favor of more systemic concepts like options (A) circular causality, (B) systems, and (D) homeostasis.

8. A) Process; content

The content/process distinction present in group dynamics that gave rise to family therapy posits that how things are communicated and discussed (the process) can be more impactful than what is being said (the content).

AUDIO PODCAST 2.1
Marriage and Family Therapy Origins
Eli A. Karam
https://bcove.video/3CGjVhD

AUDIO PODCAST 2.2
Cybernetic Concepts
Eli A. Karam
https://bcove.video/3CJuFLQ

REFERENCES

Bateson, G. (1972). *Steps to an ecology of mind*. Ballantine.

Nichols, M. P. (2013). *Family therapy: Concepts and methods* (10th ed.). Pearson.

von Bertalanffy, L. (1968). *General systems theory: Foundations, development, applications*. George Braziller.

Watzlawick, P., Beavin, J. H., & Jackson, D. D. (1967). *Pragmatics of human communication*. W. W. Norton.

Wiener, N. (1954). *The human use of human beings: Cybernetics and society*. Avon.

Strategic Family Therapy

3

LEARNING OBJECTIVES

After reading this chapter, you should be able to:

1. Identify model developers and other key figures associated with strategic family therapy
2. Describe the assessment process in strategic family therapy
3. Review the main interventions/techniques of strategic family therapy
4. Identify goals of strategic family therapy
5. Develop the role of the therapist in strategic family therapy

RELEVANT EXAM DOMAINS

- *Domain 1—The Practice of Systemic Therapy*
  Includes tasks related to incorporating systemic theory and perspectives into practice activities and establishing and maintaining ongoing therapeutic relationships with the client system.
- *Domain 2—Assessing, Hypothesizing, and Diagnosing*
  Includes tasks related to assessing the various dimensions of the client system, forming and reformulating hypotheses, and diagnosing the client and family system in order to guide therapeutic activities.
- *Domain 3—Designing and Conducting Treatment*
  Includes tasks related to developing and implementing interventions with the client system.

INTRODUCTION

This chapter presents the main concepts and clinical techniques associated with strategic family therapy. Strategic therapies originate from the research projects on family communication around schizophrenia initiated by the Palo Alto Bateson group. Building on the application of cybernetics and systems theory, strategic approaches offer direct, straightforward as well as indirect, paradoxical interventions aimed at reducing or eliminating the presenting family problems or behavioral symptoms. Less focused on the meaning or the origin of the symptom, strategic therapists intervene to change repetitive interactive sequences in order to disrupt family homeostasis.

MODEL DEVELOPERS AND SIGNIFICANT CONTRIBUTORS

The development of strategic family therapy by Jay Haley and others was strongly influenced by Gregory Bateson. Bateson, a research anthropologist, was studying patterns of communication and cybernetic systems at the Palo Alto Veterans Affairs Hospital when he was joined by Jay Haley, John Weakland, and William Fry, Richard Fisch, Jules Riskin, and Paul Watzlawick. Concurrently, at the same institution, Don Jackson was beginning his work with people who have schizophrenia. Jackson's collaborations with the Bateson project led to many significant contributions, including the double-bind theory of schizophrenia (Bateson et al., 1956; Haley, 1976). This Mental Research Institute (MRI) group collaboration was significant because it provided the conceptual base for strategic therapy and led to the integration of communications theory and systems theory.

Milton Erickson was another major figure whose work helped shape the development of strategic therapy. Haley and Weakland were strongly influenced by Erickson's hypnotic and paradoxical techniques. Much of Haley's early therapeutic work is derived from Erickson's and is outlined in Haley's (1973) book *Uncommon Therapy: The Psychiatric Techniques of Milton H. Erickson, M.D.* This text provides a comprehensive examination of Dr. Erickson's theories and techniques and their application to various cases at different stages of the family life cycle.

After collaborating with Sal Minuchin in Philadelphia, Jay Haley and Cloé Madanes blended structural and strategic techniques together to form the Family Therapy Institute of Washington, D.C.

The Milan Group's (Luigi Boscolo, Gianfranco Cecchin, Mara Selvini Palazzoli, and Giuliana Prata) approach was an outgrowth of the MRI model. It expanded the network of people involved in maintaining problems but still concentrated on interrupting destructive family games. Theirs differed from other strategic schools in being less problem focused and more interested in changing family members' beliefs about covert collusions and the motives for problematic behavior (Palazzoli, 1986).

MODEL OVERVIEW

The primary objective of strategic therapy is behavior change around the presenting problem. Strategic therapy emphasizes short-term treatment lasting about 10 sessions, with particular focus on the first session. Often, strategic therapies are characterized as brief therapies. Rather than thinking in terms of time, brief therapy has to do more with gaining clarity about what needs to be changed.

Strategic therapists assume circular causality and studied patterns of communications linked together, forming chains of negative and positive feedback loops. When the response to a family member's problematic behavior exacerbates the problem and homeostasis cannot be maintained, that chain is seen as a positive feedback loop. Insight is not a prerequisite for change. Problems cannot be alleviated through understanding alone because they persist through ongoing, interactional processes and feedback loops.

Haley views families as being "stuck" at a particular stage within the family life cycle (i.e., family members have difficulty making the transition from each stage of the family life cycle to the next). Madanes and Haley's aim is often to structurally reorganize the family, particularly its hierarchy and generational boundaries. Unlike in structural family therapy, however, these structural goals are always directly related to the presenting problem.

The strategic model follows a six-step treatment procedure (Haley, 1963):

1. Introduction to the treatment/social stage
2. Inquiry and definition of the problem
3. Estimation of the behavior maintaining the problem

4. Setting goals for treatment
5. Selecting and making behavioral interventions
6. Termination of treatment

SYMPTOMS

Symptoms characterize the ways family members relate to each other. A symptom is a communicative act that sends a message that serves as a contract between two or more members of the family system. It is a label for a nonlinear set of behaviors within a social organization. A symptom usually occurs when a system member is stuck in a particular situation and cannot find a nonsymptomatic way of getting out of it.

According to communications theory, the essential function of symptoms is to maintain the homeostatic equilibrium of family systems. Symptomatic families are trapped in dysfunctional, homeostatic patterns of interaction. These families cling to their rigid ways and respond to signs of change as negative feedback. That is, change is treated not as an opportunity for growth but as a threat to family homeostasis (Weakland et al., 1974). Symptoms can be a way of communicating metaphorically within the family. For example, a woman's depression may be a way of conveying her unhappiness in her marriage.

POWER AND HIERARCHY

Haley (1976) believes that any relationship is a power struggle. Any message has elements of both "command" and "report." When a father says to his son, "It's raining. Your bicycle is outside," he is reporting on the weather and the location of the bicycle, and he is also commanding his son to get the bicycle out of the rain. If the son brings the bicycle inside, he is allowing the father to remain in charge at the top of the hierarchy. If he refuses to bring the bicycle in or gets his siblings to bring in the bicycle, then he is engaging in a power struggle with the father.

The major focus of strategic therapy has been to arrange the hierarchy so that parents are in a position superior to their children. Parents are encouraged to state rules concretely to increase the likelihood that they will be followed. Rules must be practical, and there should be consequences if the rules are not followed. When the child obeys rules, then the child is placing the parents in a superior position in the hierarchy. However, when the child refuses to obey the rules, then the child is in a position of superior power (Haley, 1976; Minuchin, 1974).

Symptoms can be conceptualized through hierarchically structured power. The parent should have power in the family system and thus be at the top of the hierarchy. However, in some cases children may develop a symptom (e.g., using drugs or running away) to change the power relationship.

ASSESSMENT

Therapists get a clear description of the presenting problem from each member of the family system before identifying the behavioral sequences and feedback loops maintaining homeostasis.

INTERVENTIONS AND TECHNIQUES

Given that the primary focus of strategic family therapy surrounds the symptom or the presenting problem, therapists are concerned primarily with those techniques that change the sequence of interaction that is maintaining the problems. Techniques are tailored to alter repetitive sequences that govern family rules and lead to the presenting problems.

The strategic therapist maintains control of therapy through the use of tasks or directives. A *directive* is an instruction from a family therapist for a family to behave differently. Tasks can be either explicit (e.g., telling a family member what to do) or implicit (e.g., verbal intonation or silence). Before selecting a task, the therapist will often determine whether the family is resistant to change. If the family is not resistant, the therapist will choose a straightforward task, which the therapist expects the family to complete. When the family is resistant to change, the therapist will design paradoxical directives to override resistance. Straightforward tasks attempt to change the sequences of interaction in the family. They may help a family to become more organized, establish operational boundaries, set rules, or establish family goals (Haley, 1963).

When therapists attempt to change the family member's problem, however, they are threatening the family's homeostasis and thus will encounter the family's resistance to change. Whereas straightforward directives are successful for family members who do what the therapist asks, paradoxical directives are more effective for members who resist completing tasks. Resistance typically takes the form of failure to complete homework assignments. "Prescribing the symptom," a type of paradoxical directive, encourages the family system to continue what it has been doing because to change would result in the loss of benefits to the family. If the family follows the therapist's directive, it is allowing the therapist to take control by continuing its symptomatic behavior. Compliance also implies that the symptomatic behavior is amenable to change. If the family defies the therapist's directive, however, it must discontinue the symptomatic behavior. Either compliance or defiance creates change in the family system (Watzlawick et al., 1974).

The ordeals technique involves helping the client to give up symptoms that are more troublesome to maintain than they are worth. In this method, the therapist assigns a family or family member(s) the task of "performing an ordeal" in order to eliminate a symptom. The ordeal is a constructive or neutral behavior that must be performed before engaging in the undesirable behavior. For example, an ordeal might be to exercise before engaging in playing video games. In essence, the ordeal is always healthy, but it is not an activity that those directed to do it want to engage in immediately. The hope is that those involved in doing the ordeal will give up or modify actions or symptoms in order to avoid performing the ordeal, or constructive behavior (Haley, 1984).

In the pretend technique, originated by Cloé Madanes, the therapist asks family members to pretend to engage in a troublesome behavior, such as having a fight, or to imagine some disconnect so they do not have to respond to a stimulus. Overall, the act of pretending to fight helps individuals change through experiencing control of a previously involuntary action (Madanes, 1981).

Strategic family therapists generally attribute positive motives to clients' problematic actions and behaviors. Problem behaviors are often relabeled by the Milan group to have more positive meaning. They refer to their technique as *positive connotation* and believe that all observable family behaviors appear to be inspired by the common goal of preserving the cohesion of the family. For example, a positive label for *jealousy* could be *caring*, and *anger* could be relabeled as *desiring attention*. New labels often provide family members with a new way of viewing the problem so that it can be resolved.

Hypothesizing is central to the Milan approach. It refers to a formulation created by a therapist based on information the therapist possesses about a family and involves a meeting of treatment team members before the arrival of a family for therapy to formulate a plan and discuss aspects of the family's situation that could be generating a symptom. During this presession, the team members attempt to prepare themselves to treat the family. Their belief is that they must come up with ideas about how a particular family operates or the family will define the problem and its treatment in a faulty way. Hypotheses are modified as treatment continues.

Circular questioning focuses attention on family connections by framing every question so that it addresses differences in perception by family members about events or relationships.

Family members might be asked to state how they perceived the family dealing with a crisis situation. The intent is to highlight information, differences, and circular processes within the family system. It gives the family clear information while breaking down the idea of individual causes and helping family members raise questions.

An *invariant prescription* involves a specific kind of ritual and it is given to parents with children who are psychotic or anorexic to break up the family's dirty game, that is, the power struggle between generations that is sustained by symptomatic behaviors. The parents go out together for varying periods of time (some of them quite long) without telling their children where they are going or when they will return. This mysterious type of behavior unites parents in a new way and gives them an opportunity to observe and discuss the family's reactions. In the process, changes within the parents themselves and the family as a whole are noted. Constructive changes are preserved in this Milan Group intervention (Palazzoli et al., 1978).

ROLE OF THE THERAPIST

As the expert responsible for change, it is the therapist's job to plan strategies to resolve family problems. Therapists often proceed quickly and specifically in their focus on resolving presenting problems and virtually ignore family histories or any *Diagnostic and Statistical Manual of Mental Disorders* (5th ed.; *DSM-5*; American Psychiatric Association, 2013) diagnoses. Strategic family therapists try to use presenting problems as ways to bring about change in families by giving them tasks that are usually carried out between sessions in the form of homework.

ORIENTATION IN TIME

Strategic family therapy focuses on the present. Family members' history is not as relevant as the present situation because dysfunctional behavior is maintained by current interactions. Past patterns are not emphasized. Treatment should be pragmatic and short-term.

PROCESS AND GOALS OF THERAPY

Goals include the family system experiencing symptom relief and the resolution of the client-identified presenting problem. Insight and history are not a part of the model. Emphasis is on process, not content. Family members give up outdated ideas. Change focuses on breaking up maladaptive feedback loops and vicious cycles of interaction and replacing them with more adaptive cycles.

CONCLUSION

Communication theories emerged from the MRI in Palo Alto in the 1950s to impact the family therapy field by framing family problems as interactional, rule governed, and maintained by feedback mechanisms. Negative feedback accounts for the stability of normal families and the inflexibility of dysfunctional ones. If families don't have adequate positive feedback mechanisms, they have difficulty adjusting to changing circumstances. This MRI group collaboration laid the foundation for what would eventually be known as *strategic family therapy*. The model uses therapeutic double binds, or paradoxical techniques, to change family rules and disrupt homeostasis. "Prescribing the symptom" is a paradoxical technique used to undermine resistance to change by rendering it unnecessary.

Strategic schools vary in some of the techniques used, but share a problem-centered, therapist-as-expert core that focuses on highlighting and changing behavioral sequences. The MRI model is strictly interactional by observing and intervening in behavioral sequences of interaction that surround a problem rather than venturing into the black box and speculating about the thoughts and feelings of the client system.

Haley and Madanes, on the other hand, are interested in motives: Haley is focused mainly on the desire to control others and Madanes in the desire to love and be loved. Their version of strategic family therapy focuses on parental hierarchy; transitions in the family life cycle; and Madanes's nonconfrontational interventions directed at achieving change without inviting resistance, known as *pretend techniques*.

The Milan team's version of strategic family therapy focused on hypothesizing, circular questioning, and therapist neutrality as guidelines for conducting sessions. Positive connotations and the use of prescribed rituals are other signature techniques of the Milan model, which tried to understand the elaborate multigenerational games that surrounded symptoms in the family system. Although it was thought to be creative and innovative by many at the time of its development, this model has not aged well. Many therapists now view the approach as deceptive, controlling, and manipulative to client systems.

KEY TERMS

Circular questioning: A method of interviewing developed by the Milan Associates in which questions are asked that highlight differences among family members.

Communications theory: The study of relationships in terms of the exchange of verbal and nonverbal messages.

Complementary: A type of dyadic transaction or communication pattern in which inequality and the maximization of differences exist (e.g., dominant/submissive) and in which each participant's response provokes or enhances a counterresponse in the other in a continuing loop.

Directives: Homework assignments designed to help families interrupt homeostatic patterns of problem-maintaining behavior.

Family ritual: Technique used by Selvini Palazzoli and her Milan Associates that prescribes a specific act for family members to perform that is designed to change the family system's rules.

Function of the symptom: The idea that symptoms are often ways to distract or otherwise protect family members from threatening conflicts.

Family rules: A descriptive term for redundant behavioral patterns.

Greek chorus: As observers/consultants of a family session, the chorus members debate the merits of what a therapist is doing to bring about change. They send messages about the process to the therapist and family.

Invariant prescription: A technique developed by Selvini Palazzoli that requires parents to mysteriously sneak away together and to unite so that children cannot manipulate them.

Metaphor: A therapeutic analogy used to characterize family relationships; or a condition, such as a symptom, that represents another condition by analogy.

Negative cooperative tasks: Tasks that family members agree to complete but that the therapist expects the family not to accomplish.

Neutrality: The Milan Group's term for balanced acceptance of family members.

Ordeal: Paradoxical intervention in which the client is directed to do something that is more of a hardship to perform than the symptom.

Paradoxical directive: Request by the therapist that the family member or members continue behaving in a symptomatic manner, thus exposing the secondary gain produced by the symptom. If they conform, they admit control and expose secondary gain; if they rebel, they give up their symptoms.

Positive connotation: Selvini Palazzoli's technique of ascribing positive motives to family behavior in order to promote family cohesion and avoid resistance to therapy.

Positive cooperative tasks: Tasks that family members agree to complete and that the therapist anticipates they will perform.

Prescribing the symptom: A paradoxical directive that forces a client to either give up a symptom or admit that it is under voluntary control.

Pretend techniques: Madanes's playful paradoxical intervention in which family members are asked to pretend to engage in symptomatic behavior. The paradox is if they are pretending to have a symptom, the symptom cannot be real.

Restraining: A strategic technique used to overcome resistance by suggesting that a family not change.

Rituals: A set of prescribed actions designed to change a family system's rules.

Straightforward tasks: Tasks that the family is intended to accept and perform as stated.

Symptom: Behavior of a family member that indicates dysfunction in the family.

Symmetrical: A type of dyadic transaction or communication pattern characterized by equality and the minimization of differences; each participant's response provokes a similar response in the other, sometimes in a competitive fashion.

KNOWLEDGE CHECK: CHAPTER 3

1. A family comes to therapy because their 12-year-old son is stealing money from them. After three sessions, the stealing stops, and the family decides to terminate therapy. A strategic family therapist would ________.

   A. Agree with the family's decision to terminate because the presenting problem appears to have been resolved
   B. Ask the family to rate on a scale of 1–10 how they feel the problem is now, compared to when they originally came in
   C. Ask the parents to write a new narrative of their son's behavior
   D. Assume the family is avoiding conflict and design the proper paradoxical intervention

2. Strategic therapists believe ________.

   A. Intrapsychic mechanisms strongly influence behavior between family members
   B. Family rules govern family interactions
   C. The locus of pathology resides within the individual in the family system
   D. Feedback loops help therapists uncover client thoughts and feelings inside of the black box

3. Which of the following is not a related theory complementing the strategic approach to family therapy?

   A. General systems theory
   B. Communications theory
   C. Humanistic theory
   D. Cybernetics

4. In the Mental Research Institute (MRI) version of family therapy, it is essential to ________.

   A. Assess the hierarchical disorder
   B. Identify the disabling sequence of which the symptom is a vital part
   C. Always intervene paradoxically to use the system's resistance against itself
   D. Acknowledge the therapist's own role in maintaining the family symptom

5. The major characteristic of strategic family therapy is that the therapist ________.

   A. Plans a strategy for solving the presenting problems
   B. Remains passive throughout treatment
   C. Follows the family's lead because the clients know what's best for them
   D. Provides the family with the necessary insight to change targeted behaviors

(*See answers next page.*)

1. A) Agree with the family's decision to terminate because the presenting problem appears to have been resolved

Strategic therapy ends when the presenting problem (determined by the family) is resolved. Option B refers to solution-focused therapy and option C alludes to narrative therapy.

2. B) Family rules govern family interactions

Strategic models are strictly interactional—they are used to observe and intervene in sequences of interaction surrounding the family rules that govern the presenting problem in order to disrupt family homeostasis.

3. C) Humanistic theory

Humanistic theory would go on to influence experiential models of family therapy. General systems theory, communications theory, and cybernetics all influenced strategic family therapy.

4. B) Identify the disabling sequence of which the symptom is a vital part

MRI therapists identified the feedback loop and studied the rules governing it before changing the loops and rules. Hierarchy was not important to MRI, and although they did sometimes use paradox to break up dysfunctional sequences, they also utilized many straightforward directives to initiate change.

5. A) Plans a strategy for solving the presenting problems

Strategic therapists are directive by nature, believing that the family cannot change without intervention by the therapist. They believed that by attempting first-order change, or change in the behavior, second-order change, or change in the system's structure, could be achieved. Clients do not need insight as to why they have problems, nor do they need to understand why the change in behavior is needed. They simply need to act differently and see for themselves that the family's rules for problem-solving can be more flexible. These therapists try to keep resistance low and motivation high.

6. Many of the underlying assumptions and interventions used by strategic therapists are based on the earlier work of __________.

A. Erik Erikson
B. Milton Erickson
C. Sigmund Freud
D. Braulio Montalvo

7. A paradoxical technique that forces a client to either give up a symptom or admit that it is under voluntary control is known as ______.

A. A positive re-storying
B. Scapegoating
C. A crucible
D. An ordeal

8. Strategic therapy is an outgrowth of _______ theory.

A. Cognitive
B. Psychodynamic
C. Postmodern
D. Communications

9. The central intervention within the original Milan model consisted of either a ritual or a _________.

A. Family sculpting
B. Positive connotation
C. Therapeutic double bind
D. Family crucible

10. Strategic therapy has been used to develop all of the following approaches *except*:

A. Multisystemic family therapy (MST)
B. Brief Strategic family therapy (BSFT)
C. Multidimensional family therapy (MDFT)
D. Emotionally focused therapy (EFT)

11. A Milan-systemic therapist would define the purpose of circular questioning as:

A. To distract the identified patient
B. To expand on the notion of a reframe
C. Used to learn more about differences in family members' perceptions of their relationships
D. As an individualized prescription of an action or series of actions designed to alter the family's roles

(*See answers next page.*)

6. B) Milton Erickson

Milton Erickson, MD, is most well-known for his brilliance in the art of medical hypnosis. His ability to heal his patients by accessing their unconscious minds with the use of trance has inspired many generations of therapists, most notably Jay Haley.

7. D) An ordeal

Ordeals are directives that are aimed at making the symptom harder to keep than give up. The ordeal requires the clients to do something they do not want to do but is something that would benefit them in some way. Options A, B, and C are not related to strategic therapy.

8. D) Communications

Communications theorists, like Gregory Bateson, didn't look for underlying motives; instead, they assumed circular causality and analyzed patterns of communications linked together in chains of stimulus and response as feedback loops.

9. B) Positive connotation

A distinguishing characteristic of the Milan Group is the use of positive connotation, in which therapists abstain from criticizing anyone in the family and highlight the commendable aspects of the symptomatic behavior of both the identified patient and the other family members. Positive connotation is often used as an antecedent to the paradoxical prescription that the family continue its current functioning.

10. D) Emotionally focused therapy (EFT)

Although EFT is experiential and attachment based, MST, BSFT, and MDFT are all evidenced-based, third-wave family therapies that have strong ties to classic structural and strategic models.

11. C) Used to learn more about differences in family members' perceptions of their relationships

Unlike linear questions, which are ideal for eliciting definitive facts and content and determining information about the situation, circular questioning, pioneered by the Milan team, encourages reflection and exploration regarding how the issue relates to others within the family.

12. A strategic therapist asks a couple to fake being in love for an evening. This technique is called ________.

   A. A pretend technique
   B. Ordeal therapy
   C. A metaphorical task
   D. A straightforward directive

13. Each session of Milan systemic therapy is divided into the following five segments:

   A. Preassessment, session, intersession, reframe, discussion
   B. Presession, session, intervention, intersession, discussion
   C. Presession, discussion, session, intervention, intersession
   D. Presession, session, intersession, intervention, postsession discussion

14. The therapeutic stance of the Milan team can be described in one word:

   A. Logic
   B. Neutrality
   C. Action
   D. Balance

15. Mental Research Institute (MRI) therapists view the presenting problem as ____________________.

   A. An individual problem
   B. A linear problem
   C. An interactional problem
   D. A transgenerational problem

(*See answers next page.*)

12. A) A pretend technique

Developed by Madanes, pretend techniques encourage the family to act "as if"—or to imagine another set of circumstances to act differently than they normally would.

13. D) Pre-session, session, intersession, intervention, post-session discussion

The original Milan model was highly scripted. Families were treated by male–female co-therapists and observed by other members of the team. The standard format had five parts: presession, session, intersession, intervention, and postsession discussion. During the presession, the team came up with an initial hypothesis about the family's presenting problem. During the session itself, the team members would validate, modify, or change the hypothesis. After about 40 minutes, the entire team would meet alone to discuss the hypothesis and arrive at an intervention. The treating therapists would then go back to deliver the intervention to the family, either by positively connoting the problem situation or assigning a ritual to be performed by the family; the ritual commented on the problem situation and was designed to introduce change. Finally, the team would meet for a postsession discussion to analyze the family's reactions and to plan for the next session.

14. B) Neutrality

The Milan team originally saw therapy as a power struggle between therapists and families. The team's main advice to therapists was to remain neutral in the sense of avoiding the appearance of taking sides. This neutrality often manifested as distance, so that therapists delivered their dramatic pronouncements while acting aloof; not surprising, many families found it hard to engage with this style.

15. C) An interactional problem

MRI's interactional view assumes that problems can best be understood by examining clients' (often dysfunctional) interactions with others and their resulting problems. Strategic therapy is a form of interactional therapy because it does not focus on the root causes of the client's problems, but instead tries to increase competency and develop problem-solving skills that will help the client in their interactions with others.

AUDIO PODCAST 3.1
Strategic Family Therapy Overview
Eli A. Karam
https://bcove.video/3e3np3r

REFERENCES

American Psychiatric Association. (2013). *Diagnostic and statistical manual of mental disorders.* (5th ed.).

Bateson, G., Jackson, D. D., Haley, J., & Weakland, J. H. (1956). Toward a theory of schizophrenia. *Behavioral Science, 1,* 251–261. https://doi.org/10.1002/bs.3830010402

Haley, J. (1963). *Strategies of psychotherapy.* Grune & Stratton.

Haley, J. (1973). *Uncommon therapy: The psychiatric techniques of Milton H.* W. W. Norton.

Haley, J. (1976). *Problem-solving therapy.* Jossey-Bass.

Haley, J. (1984). *Ordeal therapy.* Jossey-Bass.

Madanes, C. (1981). *Strategic family therapy.* Jossey-Bass.

Minuchin, S. (1974). *Families and family therapy.* Harvard University Press.

Palazzoli, M. (1986). Towards a general model of psychotic games. *Journal of Marital and Family Therapy, 12,* 339–349. https://doi.org/10.1111/j.1752-0606.1986.tb00665.x

Palazzoli, M., Boscolo, L., Cecchin, G., & Prata, G. (1978). *Paradox and counterparadox.* Aronson.

Watzlawick, P., Weakland, J., & Fisch, R. (1974). *Change: Principles of problem formation and problem resolution.* W. W. Norton.

Weakland, J. B., Fisch, R., Watzlawick, P., & Bodin, A. M. (1974). Brief therapy: Focused problem resolution. *Family Process, 13,* 141–168. https://doi.org/10.1111/j.1545-5300.1974.00141.x

Structural Family Therapy

4

LEARNING OBJECTIVES

After reading this chapter, you should be able to:

1. **Identify model developers and other key figures associated with structural family therapy**
2. **Describe the assessment process in structural family therapy**
3. **Review the main interventions/techniques of structural family therapy**
4. **Identify the goals of structural family therapy**
5. **Develop the role of the therapist in structural family therapy**

RELEVANT EXAM DOMAINS

- *Domain 1—The Practice of Systemic Therapy*
  Involves tasks related to incorporating systemic theory and perspectives into practice activities and establishing and maintaining ongoing therapeutic relationships with the client system.
- *Domain 2—Assessing, Hypothesizing, and Diagnosing*
  Involves tasks related to assessing the various dimensions of the client system, forming and reformulating hypotheses, and diagnosing the client and family system to guide therapeutic activities.
- *Domain 3—Designing and Conducting Treatment*
  Involves tasks related to developing and implementing interventions with the client system.

INTRODUCTION

The structural approach to family therapy is primarily associated with Salvador Minuchin, who first pioneered this model at the Wiltwyck School and later at the Philadelphia Child Guidance Center. Among the most popular and enduring of all family therapy models, structural family therapy contends that every family has a structure composed of subsystems, roles, and boundaries. Subsystems are units of the family based on function and regulated by interpersonal boundaries. In healthy families, boundaries are clear enough to protect independence and permeable enough to allow mutual support. Structural family therapists join with each member of the family system before conducting a structural assessment and using restructuring techniques to realign inverted hierarchies and restore healthy boundaries.

MODEL DEVELOPERS AND SIGNIFICANT CONTRIBUTORS

Salvador Minuchin was born in Argentina to Russian Jewish emigrants. After completing a medical degree in Argentina and participating in the Israeli Army, he studied psychoanalysis in New York, where he met Nathan Ackerman (Ackerman, 1958). Later he served as the medical director of the Wiltwyck School, before eventually taking over the leadership of the Philadelphia Child Guidance Clinic. One of the most innovative ideas he had while there was to pioneer a training program for community paraprofessionals; this program proved to be highly effective in providing mental health services to the poor. In Philadelphia, Minuchin worked closely with Braulio Montalvo and Jay Haley, whom he hired from California. Several other prominent theorists contributed to the development of structural family therapy, including Bernice Rosman, Harry Aponte, and Charles Fishman.

MODEL OVERVIEW

One of the primary premises underlying structural family therapy is that every family has a family structure that is revealed only when the family is interacting. In some families, structure is well organized in a hierarchical pattern, and members easily relate to each other. In others, there is little structure, and few arrangements are provided by which family members can easily and meaningfully interact.

Subsystems are smaller units of the system as a whole. They exist to carry out various family tasks. Without subsystems, the overall family system would not function. They are best defined by the boundaries and rules connected with them. Subsystems are formed when family members join together to perform various functions. When subsystems are disrupted, stress and increased emotional reactivity may result. Of particular significance are the spousal, parental, and sibling subsystems. The spousal subsystem may consist of a single parent, a gay or lesbian couple, or a heterosexual couple. Spousal subsystems work best when there is complementarity of functions. The parental subsystem may include a single parent, two grandparents, two biological parents, a biological parent and a stepparent, and so forth. Referred to as the *executive subsystem*, the parental subsystem is responsible for the care, protection, and socialization of children (Minuchin, 1984). The sibling subsystem is that unit within the family whose members are of the same generation. In some families, the sibling subsystem is composed of those born of the same parents. In other families, such as blended or stepfamilies, the sibling subsystem consists of children unrelated by blood.

Minuchin (1984) categorized the structure of families by thinking about them along a continuum from distance to closeness. The first is to do with their emotional closeness. In disengaged families, emotional connection is loose. Minuchin thought these kinds of families were more likely to have problems with young people who might distance themselves from their families while engaging in risky behavior. At the other extreme are enmeshed families. Here, family members struggle to develop a life outside the family and sometimes appear to be overinvolved with each other's needs. Minuchin thought these kinds of families were more likely to have young people who had psychosomatic problems and difficulty separating from their parents (Minuchin, 1974; Minuchin et al., 1978).

Boundaries are the physical and psychological factors that separate people from one another. There are three major types of boundaries (Figure 4.1):

- Clear, represented by a broken horizontal line (---)
- Rigid, represented by a solid line (—)
- Diffuse, represented by a dotted line (. . .)

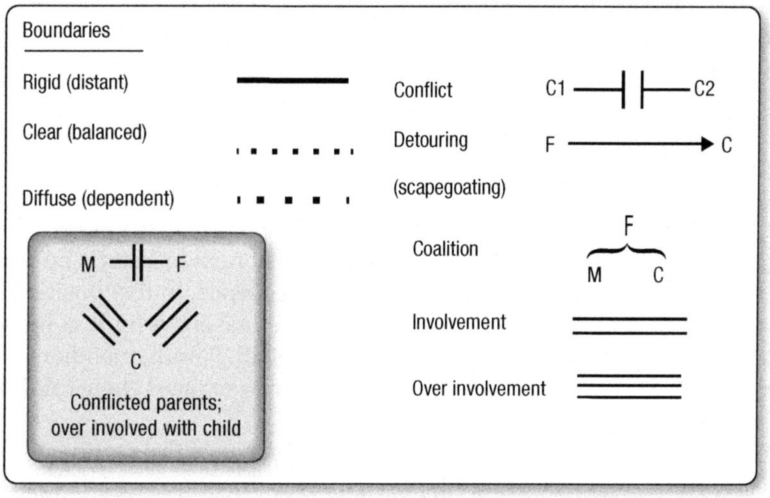

Figure 4.1 Types of boundaries.

Source: Adapted from Minuchin, S. (1967). ***Families of the slums: An exploration of their structure and treatment.*** Basic Books.

Clear boundaries consist of rules and habits that allow family members to enhance their communication and relationships with one another because they encourage dialogue. Rigid boundaries are inflexible and are characterized by power struggles. In families with rigid boundaries, members experience difficulty relating in an intimate way to one another, and therefore individuals become emotionally detached or cut off from other family members. In the case of diffuse boundaries, there is not enough separation between family members. Instead of creating independence and autonomy within individuals, as with clear boundaries, diffuse boundaries encourage dependence.

ASSESSMENT

Given that problems are a function of the entire family, structural family therapists need to see all members of the family system in order to make an accurate assessment. This assessment process relies on here-and-now observations and enactments to gauge boundaries, complementarity, hierarchy, and family roles. The therapist begins by asking questions about the presenting problem until family members begin to see that the problem goes beyond the identified patient to include the entire family. This is followed by a brief exploration of the past, focusing on how the parents in the family came to develop the perspectives that now influence their problematic interactions. Throughout the assessment process, structural family therapists help family members see how their interactions may inadvertently be perpetuating the presenting problem (Minuchin et al., 2007).

INTERVENTIONS AND TECHNIQUES

In order to build the therapeutic alliance, the structural family therapist makes contact with each individual family member through a process known as joining. During this process, the therapist allies with family members through expressing interest in them as individuals and working with and for them. Tracking is a technique used to gain an understanding of the interactive patterns in which a presenting situation is embedded. The therapist "tracks" or follows the content of the family by asking clarifying questions and encouraging communication. In mimesis, the therapist becomes like the family by emulating the manner or content of the family's communications in order to gain acceptance with the system (Minuchin & Fishman, 1981).

The technique of reframing involves changing a perception by explaining a situation from a different context. In this activity, the facts of an event do not change, but the meaning of the situation is examined from a new perspective.

Unbalancing is a procedure by which the structural therapist supports an individual or subsystem against the rest of the family. A therapist may sit next to a son who is being accused of not living up to the family's standard of academic excellence. In this position, the therapist can also take up for the son against the family and give reasons why it is important for the son to create new ways of showing his competence and skill. Family members are then forced to act differently with the person or subsystem in order to expand their roles and functions (Minuchin et al., 2006).

An enactment occurs when the therapist directs members of the family system to interact directly with each other, therefore bringing problematic behavioral sequences into the session. First, the therapist encourages the family to replay the same behaviors and patterns that they engage in at home. During this phase, the therapist looks to see what is maintaining a problematic pattern and what kind of intervention would help the family change that pattern. Next, the therapist intervenes to help the family change the pattern in a more fruitful way. Finally, the therapist debriefs the family and works out how the members can keep the "new" pattern going at home rather than resort to the old negative ways of communicating (Minuchin et al., 2014).

A boundary is an invisible line that psychologically separates people or subsystems from each other. In boundary making, part of the therapeutic task is to help the family define, redefine, or change the boundaries within the family. The therapist also helps the family to either strengthen or loosen boundaries, depending on the family's situation.

Intensity is the structural technique of changing maladaptive transactions by using strong affect, repeated intervention, or prolonged pressure. The tone, volume, pacing, and choice of words used by a therapist can raise the affective intensity of statements. If done correctly, this technique breaks down family homeostasis and challenges the family's perception of reality. The use of intensity is the most effective when the therapist speaks in a direct, unwavering, and goal-specific manner (Minuchin et al., 2014).

Restructuring involves changing the makeup and organization of the family. The rationale behind restructuring is to make the family more functional by altering the existing hierarchy and interaction patterns so that problems are not maintained. The structural family therapist rearranges the hierarchy of the family so that the executive subsystem is firmly in charge. Restructuring is completed through the structural techniques of enactment, unbalancing, directives, and boundary making (Minuchin & Nichols, 1993).

In the process of shaping competence, structural family therapists help system members become more functional by highlighting positive behaviors. Therapists reinforce family members for doing things right or making their own appropriate decisions. Therapists may praise parents in session who make their children behave, even if their success is short lived (Fishman, 1993).

ROLE OF THE THERAPIST

Highly influential in the change process, the structural family therapist is both an observer of family process and an expert who is active in the process of family restructuring. To be effective in this model requires high energy and precise timing so that in-session enactments lead to new family organization. The therapist must be active and creative (Aponte, 1994).

ORIENTATION IN TIME

Structural family therapy focuses on the present. Past patterns and history are not emphasized. Ignoring historical data, structural family therapists map the present configuration of the family rather than pay attention to the developmental milestones of the family over time.

PROCESS AND GOALS OF THERAPY

Structural therapy is divided into three phases: (a) joining and accommodating, (b) mapping the family structure, and (c) intervening. Action is emphasized over insight, with the therapist using specific techniques to help family members interact in new ways. Family members are given homework to do outside of therapy sessions. The overall goals of this model are to reorganize and restructure the family system to improve problem-solving capabilities, strengthen the executive subsystem, and promote clear boundaries between all subsystems and members of the family system.

CONCLUSION

In structural family therapy, behavior, including the presenting problem, is considered within the context of the family. Dysfunctional structures point to the covert rules governing family transactions. In particular, the family's subsystems, boundaries, alignments, and coalitions are assessed to understand its structure. Structural family therapy is present focused and requires an active therapist who is responsible for creating change. To achieve such change, the therapist helps to renegotiate dysfunctional family rules and to seek greater boundary clarity. After joining with each member of the family system, the structural therapist engages in techniques, such as family mapping, enactment, boundary making, and reframing, to help transform family structure. The ultimate goal is to restructure the family's transactional rules by developing more appropriate boundaries between subsystems and strengthening the family's hierarchy and executive subsystem.

KEY TERMS

Accommodation: Elements of a system automatically adjust to coordinate their functioning; accommodation is a therapeutic tactic, used primarily by structural family therapists, whereby the therapist attempts to make personal adjustments to adapt to the family's style in an effort to build a therapeutic alliance with the family.

Boundary making: A technique used by structural family therapists aimed at realigning boundaries within a family by changing the psychological proximity (closer or farther apart) between family subsystems.

Coalition: An alliance between two persons against a third member of a system. A *stable coalition* is a fixed and inflexible union (such as a mother and son) that becomes a dominant part of the family's everyday functioning. A *detouring coalition* is one in which the pair holds a third family member responsible for their difficulties or conflicts with one another, thus decreasing the stress on themselves or their relationship.

Cross-generational coalition: An inappropriate alliance between a parent and child, who side together against a third member of the family.

Disengagement: Psychological isolation that results from overly rigid boundaries around individuals and subsystems in a family.

Enactment: An interaction stimulated in structural family therapy in order to observe and then change interactions that make up family structure.
Enmeshment: Loss of autonomy due to a blurring of physical and psychological boundaries.
Family structure: The functional organization of families that determines how family members interact.
Hierarchical structure: Family functioning based on clear generational boundaries in which the parents maintain control and authority.
Intensity: Minuchin's term for changing maladaptive transactions by using strong affect, repeated intervention, or prolonged pressure.
Joining: A structural family therapy term for accepting and accommodating families to win their confidence and circumvent resistance.
Mimesis: A tactic used by structural family therapists in which one attempts to copy or mimic a family's communication and behavioral patterns in order to gain acceptance by the family members.
Parentified child: One who is given privileges and responsibilities that exceed what would be considered developmentally consistent with the child's age.
Shaping competence: A process in which one encourages and reinforces productive behavior rather than criticizing dysfunctional behavior.
Tracking: A therapeutic tactic associated with structural family therapy in which the therapist deliberately attends to the symbols, style, language, and values of the family, using them to influence the family's transactional patterns.
Unbalancing: A therapeutic technique used to alter the hierarchy of the family whereby the therapist forms a coalition with one or more members.

KNOWLEDGE CHECK: CHAPTER 4

1. Minuchin was director of the _____________ .

   A. Chicago Family Institute
   B. Walton Institute for Boys
   C. Eastern Pennsylvania Psychiatric Institute
   D. Philadelphia Child Guidance Clinic

2. A structural family therapist would believe that dysfunctional families require ________.

   A. A change in the covert rules that govern family rules and boundaries
   B. Resolving problems with each parent's family of origin
   C. Increased togetherness
   D. Indirect approaches to minimize their resistance

3. To assess functioning in structural family therapy, each of the following subsystems is most important *except*:

   A. Spousal
   B. Friend
   C. Parental
   D. Sibling

4. Members of enmeshed families run the risk of overemphasizing __________.

   A. Family belongingness
   B. The need for independence
   C. Individual differentiation
   D. The need for natural consequences

5. In structural family therapy, interference with a parental subsystem's functioning __________.

   A. Is an example of a system in "runaway"
   B. Leads to accommodation
   C. Occurs naturally at developmental nodal points
   D. Can result in symptomatic behaviors

6. Boundaries are ___________________ in disengaged families.

   A Inappropriately rigid
   B Easily crossed
   C Poorly differentiated
   D Clear

(*See answers next page.*)

1. D) Philadelphia Child Guidance Clinic

The Child Guidance Clinic was located in South Philadelphia next door to Children's Hospital of Philadelphia, both moved to a new building in the University of Pennsylvania Medical complex in 1974. The 7 years between Minuchin's arrival in Philadelphia and the Clinic's move to its new location were the most fruitful in developing the theories, practice, and research of structural family therapy. The 7 years following the move allowed for some elaboration, but more important, these were the years the ideas and practices of the therapy were disseminated through practice, workshops, and internships.

2. A) A change in the covert rules that govern family rules and boundaries

Modifications in structure are required when a family or one of its members encounters external pressures and when developmental transitions are reached. Healthy families accommodate to changed circumstances; dysfunctional families increase the rigidity of structures that are no longer working. Option A is the only one of the four choices that uses structural language. (B) is talking about Bowen, (C) is referencing an experiential model, and (D) is talking about a psychodynamic framework.

3. B) Friend

The friend subsystem is not real. *Family subsystems* refer to the specific subgroupings within a family. These groupings are made based on gender, age, or interest. Common subsystems include *parental* (can include any caregiver taking care of the children), *spousal* (may include a single parent or couple), and *sibling* (includes any biological, adopted, or stepsibling pairs).

4. A) Family belongingness

In an enmeshed family, there are no boundaries between the family members. Instead of the strong bonds that signal a well-functioning family unit, family members are joined together in unhealthy ways. Parents become over-reliant on their children, and children are not allowed to individuate, or to separate from their parents and form their own identity.

5. D) Can result in symptomatic behaviors

Parental hierarchies can be rigid and unfair or weak and ineffective. When they are disrupted, problems develop throughout the entire family system.

6. A) Inappropriately rigid

Rigid boundaries are restrictive and permit little contact with outside subsystems, resulting in disengagement. Disengaged subsystems are independent but isolated. On the plus side, this fosters autonomy. On the other hand, disengagement limits affection and support. Disengaged families must come under extreme stress before they mobilize assistance.

7. All of the concepts are associated with structural family therapy *except*:

A. Accommodation
B. Enactment
C. Boundaries
D. Sculpting

8. ________________ describes a relationship between two persons against a third.

A. An alliance
B. A coalition
C. A triad
D. A complementary relationship

9. Structural family therapists map boundaries, hierarchies, and subsystems, which are all part of ______________________.

A. The internal family system
B. Family structure
C. Family differentiation
D. Linear family patterns

10. Minuchin created ______________ to see the family in action rather than simply relying on members talking about their interactions.

A. Reframes
B. Boundaries
C. Enactments
D. One-way mirrors

11. All of the following are goals of structural family therapy *except*:

A. Establishing clear boundaries between subsystems
B. Promoting parents as head of the hierarchy
C. Distinguishing between the marital/couple subsystem and the parental subsystem
D. Reducing family fusion in the system

(*See answers next page.*)

7. **D) Sculpting**

Options A, B, and C are all relevant to structural family therapy, leaving sculpting (derived from experiential family therapy) as the only remaining viable option.

8. **B) A coalition**

Coalitions usually form across generational boundaries between one parent and child against the other parent or against another child. Coalitions create power blocks in families, which serve either to balance another coalition or establish control.

9. **B) Family structure**

Structural family therapy relies on a technique known as *family mapping* to uncover and understand patterns of behavior and family interactions. During this process, the therapist creates a visual representation that identifies the family's problems and how those issues are maintained through family dynamics. This map diagrams the basic structure of the family, including the members of the family unit, their ages, genders, and relationships to one another. Aspects of the family observed during this process include family rules, patterns of behavior, and hierarchies.

10. **C) Enactments**

In an enactment, family members are asked to talk with each other rather than to the therapist. This serves the dual purpose of allowing the therapist to see firsthand how clients interact, instead of relying on their descriptions, and having clients experience different ways of interacting.

11. **D) Reducing family fusion in the system**

All of these terms come from structural family therapy except *fusion*, which comes from Bowen family systems. Be careful not to confuse the concepts of enmeshment and fusion. *Fusion* refers to individual behavior that takes place in a system, and *enmeshment* refers to a systemic behavior involving individuals. The difference is slight—just one of perspective, functioning, and how to intervene.

AUDIO PODCAST 4.1
Structural Family Therapy Overview
Eli A. Karam
https://bcove.video/3KqY93h

AUDIO PODCAST 4.2
Structural Interventions
Eli A. Karam
https://bcove.video/3TkmfjY

REFERENCES

Ackerman, N. (1958). *The psychodynamics of family life*. Basic Books.

Aponte, H. J. (1994). How personal can training get? *Journal of Marital and Family Therapy, 20*, 3–15.

Fishman, H. C. (1993). *Intensive structural therapy: Treating families in their social context*. Basic Books.

Minuchin, S. (1974). *Families and family therapy*. Tavistock Publications.

Minuchin, S. (1984). *Family kaleidoscope*. Harvard University Press.

Minuchin, S., & Fishman, H. C. (1981). *Family therapy techniques*. Harvard University Press.

Minuchin, S., Lee, W.-Y., & Simon, G. (2006). *Mastering family therapy*. John Wiley & Sons.

Minuchin, S., Montalvo, B., Guerney, B., Rosman, B., & Schumer, F. (1967). *Families of the slums: An exploration of their structure and treatment*. Basic Books.

Minuchin, S., & Nichols, M. P. (1993). *Family healing: Tales of hope and renewal from family therapy*. Free Press.

Minuchin, S., Nichols, M., & Lee, W.-Y. (2007). *Assessing families and couples: From symptom to system*. Pearson Education.

Minuchin, S., Reiter, M., & Borda, C. (2014). *The craft of family therapy*. Routledge.

Minuchin, S., Rosman, B., & Baker, L. (1978). *Psychosomatic families*. Harvard University Press.

Experiential Family Therapy

5

LEARNING OBJECTIVES

After reading this chapter, you should be able to

1. Identify model developers and other key figures associated with experiential family therapy
2. Describe the assessment process in experiential family therapy
3. Review the main interventions/techniques of experiential family therapy
4. Identify goals of experiential family therapy
5. Develop the role of the therapist in experiential family therapy

RELEVANT EXAM DOMAINS

- *Domain 1—The Practice of Systemic Therapy*
  Includes tasks related to incorporating systemic theory and perspectives into practice activities and establishing and maintaining ongoing therapeutic relationships with the client system.
- *Domain 2—Assessing, Hypothesizing, and Diagnosing*
  Includes tasks related to assessing the various dimensions of the client system, forming and reformulating hypotheses, and diagnosing the client and family system in order to guide therapeutic activities.
- *Domain 3—Designing and Conducting Treatment*
  Includes tasks related to developing and implementing interventions with the client system.

INTRODUCTION

Experiential family therapy is an outgrowth of Gestalt therapy and Rogerian client-centered therapy. The work of first-generation experiential family therapists, like Virginia Satir and Carl Whitaker, evolved from psychodynamic, existential, and humanistic approaches to psychotherapy. Prioritizing experience, confrontation, intuition, spontaneity, and living in the here-and-now, these therapists tend to minimize theory as a therapeutic hindrance and argue that change resides in having authentic emotional experiences that establish the conditions for personal growth and unblock family interaction. They are not particularly interested in client insight into the origins of their problems. It is the relationship between the family and an involved therapist in a therapeutic process that catalyzes the growth of individual family members as well as the family system as a whole. Expanding experiences, unblocking suppressed impulses and feelings, developing greater sensitivity, and learning to recognize and express emotions are some of the goals of experiential therapy. More recently, Susan Johnson's emotionally focused therapy (EFT) and Dick Schwartz's internal family systems (IFS) have taken over for Satir and Whitaker as next-generation experiential marriage and family therapy (MFT) models.

MODEL DEVELOPERS AND SIGNIFICANT CONTRIBUTORS

VIRGINIA SATIR

A pioneer in family therapy, Virginia Satir focused on building self-esteem and self-worth in people within families through clear communication. Satir's method revolved around family reconstruction, through which she attempted to guide families through a process of engaging in positive change using experiential interventions from guided fantasy, psychodrama, family sculpting, parts parties, and role-playing.

CARL WHITAKER

A maverick whose symbolic-experiential therapy approach challenged families to look at the absurdity of their situations, Whitaker emphasized uncovering and using the unconscious lives of families to bring emotions to the surface.

RICHARD SCHWARTZ

Trained as a classic structural/strategic family therapist at Purdue University and firmly grounded in systems thinking, Dick Schwartz developed internal family systems (IFS) therapy in an effort to help clients heal themselves. IFS is a non-pathologizing technique that is based on compassion, trust, honesty, and encouragement and invites clients to acknowledge each unique part of themselves and to recognize the strengths and weaknesses within them and how they influence behaviors and emotions.

SUE JOHNSON

Sue Johnson is a scientist-practitioner and a leading innovator in the field of couple therapy and adult attachment. She is the primary developer of emotionally focused therapy (EFT), which has demonstrated its effectiveness in over 30 years of peer-reviewed clinical research.

MODEL OVERVIEW

SATIR GROWTH MODEL/HUMAN VALIDATION PROCESS MODEL

Satir held four assumptions: (a) All people await the potential of growth and are capable of transformation, (b) people contain all the resources they need for growth and development, (c) families are systems wherein everyone and everything impacts and is impacted by everyone and everything else, and (d) the beliefs of the therapist are more important than the techniques used (Satir & Baldwin, 1987).

Not relying on theory, Satir suggests that much of the therapeutic language is sterile and technical and often keeps distance between the therapist and client. Experiential family therapists focus on being fully present with the family to help them handle problems. With theory deemphasized in experiential family therapy, the conceptual focus is on individuality, freedom of choice, emotional expression, and personal growth.

Dysfunctional families are characterized by interactional rigidity and emotional deadness. These conditions often produce symptoms in one or more family members. In healthy families; however, individual members are encouraged to express themselves freely. Family members tend to listen to one another and accept one another's feelings. In this way, family members may develop appropriate ways for expressing their emotions. Satir suggests that when family members are free to express themselves, they feel valued and loved. Moreover, such freedom of expression allows family members the important opportunity to nurture each other (Satir, 1988).

SYMBOLIC-EXPERIENTIAL THERAPY

The classic experiential family therapy models developed by Satir and Whitaker do not rely primarily on theory. Carl Whitaker suggests that therapists are more effective when they are being themselves. Whereas theory may be necessary for the beginner, the creative therapist is open and spontaneous in this approach. Experiential family therapists are concerned primarily with the perceptions, meanings, and values of individual family members. Experiential therapists emphasize the subjective experience of the individual rather than observable behavior (Kempler, 1991).

The healthy family continues to grow under stress. In functional families, problems are used to increase family experience and growth. When problems arise, family members are free to play various roles and thereby expand their experience. In dysfunctional families, roles are bound by myths and customs, and change is not permitted. In such families, problems become symptoms.

Experiential family therapists focus on personal growth rather than the removal of symptomatic behaviors. To the experiential family therapist, growth is a continuous process. Change requires that family members continue to challenge their beliefs and open themselves to new experiences. The therapist often grows and changes as family members change. Thus, experience in therapy can mean personal growth for all participants.

Thus, the effectiveness of experiential family therapy depends not on therapeutic technique but on the therapist. The personhood of the therapist is the crucial variable in the treatment of the family. Therapists must be genuine, open, and trusting before they can expect family members to be the same with each other.

EMOTIONALLY FOCUSED THERAPY

Emotionally focused therapy (EFT) uses a structured approach; it was originally developed for couple therapy and is based on attachment science. Interventions in EFT integrate a humanistic, experiential approach to restructuring emotional experience and a systemic, structural approach to restructuring interactions (Johnson & Whiffen, 2003).

EFT helps clients learn to communicate the softer primary emotions (vulnerability, fear, sadness) that always lie underneath the secondary emotions, which are more on the surface (anger, frustration, and defensiveness), and that keeps couples in a negative cycle of conflict and disconnection.

EFT is composed of three stages and nine steps (Johnson, 1996):

- Stage 1: De-Escalation
    - Step 1: Create alliance and delineate conflict issues in the core attachment struggle.
    - Step 2: Identify the couple's negative interaction cycle.
    - Step 3: Access unacknowledged emotions underlying interactional positions.
    - Step 4: Reframe the problem in terms of the negative cycle, underlying emotions, and attachment needs.

- Stage 2: Changing Interactional Patterns
  - Step 5: Promote identification of disowned emotions, needs, aspects of self, and integrate these into relationship interactions.
  - Step 6: Promote acceptance of partner's experience and new interactional responses.
  - Step 7: Facilitate expression of needs and wants, creating emotional engagement and bonding events that redefine attachment.
- Stage 3: Consolidation
  - Step 8: Facilitate emergence of new solutions to apply to old relationship problems.
  - Step 9: Consolidate new positions and new cycles of attachment behaviors.

INTERNAL FAMILY SYSTEMS

Internal family systems (IFS) is a powerfully transformative, evidence-based model of psychotherapy. It is the nature of the mind to be subdivided into an indeterminate number of subpersonalities, or parts. Everyone has a Self, and the Self can and should lead the individual's internal system. The non-extreme intention of each part is something positive for the individual. There are no "bad" parts, and the goal of therapy is not to eliminate parts, but instead to help them find their nonextreme roles. As we develop, our parts develop and form a complex system of interactions among themselves; therefore, systems theory can be applied to the internal system. When the system is reorganized, parts can change rapidly. Changes in the internal system will cause changes in the external system and vice versa (Schwartz, 1995).

Parts refer to aspects of one's personality that interact internally in sequences and styles that are similar to the ways in which people interact. They may be experienced in any number of ways—as thoughts, feelings, sensations, images, and more. All parts want something positive for the individual and use a variety of strategies to gain influence within the internal system. Parts develop a complex system of interactions among themselves. Polarizations develop as parts try to gain influence within the system. Parts that become extreme are carrying "burdens"—energies that are not inherent to the function of the part and don't belong to the nature of the part, such as extreme beliefs, emotions, or fantasies. Parts that have lost trust in the leadership of the Self will "blend" with or take over the Self. Parts can be helped to "unburden" and return to their natural balance (Schwartz, 1995).

1. *Exiles* are young parts that have experienced trauma and often become isolated from the rest of the system in an effort to protect the individual from feeling the pain, terror, fear, and so on, of these parts. An exiled part can become increasingly extreme and desperate in an effort to be cared for and tell its story, leaving the individual feeling fragile and vulnerable.
2. *Managers* are parts that run the day-to-day life of the individual. They attempt to keep the individual in control of every situation and relationship in an effort to protect parts from feeling any hurt or rejection.
3. *Firefighters* are a group of parts that react when exiles are activated in an effort to control and extinguish their feelings. They manifest themselves in any number of ways, including drug or alcohol use, self-mutilation (cutting), binge eating, gambling, and acting out sexually. Although they have the same goals as managers, they use different strategies to keep exiles away.

The Self can and should lead the internal system and is in the center of the "you" that the parts are talking to. When differentiated, the Self is competent, secure, self-assured, relaxed, and able to listen and respond to feedback. An empowering aspect of this model is that everyone has a Self.

ASSESSMENT

SATIR GROWTH MODEL/HUMAN VALIDATION PROCESS MODEL

In addition to exploring the family system's symptomatic behavior, Satir assessed family communication styles. People's communication styles generally fall into four types: placater, blamer, computer, and distracter. Although individuals may be able to communicate with integrity in nonemotional situations, in stress situations involving our self-esteem, Satir posited that most family members adopt one of these four communication styles to hide their feelings (Satir, 1983).

1. *Placater:* Is apologetic and eager to please (hides fear)
2. *Blamer:* Finds fault and is critical (hides pain)
3. *Computer:* Is super-reasonable, prefers the theoretical (afraid of feelings)
4. *Distracter:* Is irrelevant and talkative (afraid of reality)

Satir believed that learning to replace these four positions with a more authentic style can improve family communication.

SYMBOLIC-EXPERIENTIAL THERAPY

Whitaker required the whole family be present for the initial interview in order to win the battle for structure so that he could assess the internal worlds of each individual family member and their transgenerational belief system. The battle for structure is the decision over who will attend the therapy session. For assessment purposes, it is important in this model to meet everyone in the family system at the onset of therapy (Neill & Kniskern, 1982).

EMOTIONALLY FOCUSED THERAPY

Assessment is more of a dialogue than a series of questions and answers in EFT. The therapist seeks to enter the experience of each partner, to understand how each person constructs their understanding of the relationship, and to track the recurring emotional sequences of interactions that perpetuate the couple's distress, as well any positive cycles of interaction in which they are able to reach for and respond to one another's needs for support and comfort. In tracking the cycle, the therapist is assessing both the secondary emotions as well as the primary emotions that lie underneath the surface (Johnson, 1996).

INTERNAL FAMILY SYSTEMS

An IFS therapist begins by introducing the language of the model before assessing clients' external context and constraints to doing this work. The therapist then proceeds by checking for the individual's awareness of parts by asking how the individual experiences the part: as thoughts, feelings, sensations, images, and so on. By creating a therapeutic contract, the therapist reaches an agreement with the client on initial goals of therapy in terms of the internal system. Next, the IFS therapist must assess the fears of manager parts and value the roles of the managers while providing reassurance that the therapy can work without the feared outcomes of the managers happening. Also in the assessment phase, the therapist must take an inventory of dangerous firefighters, and work with managers' fears about triggering firefighters (Schwartz, 1995).

INTERVENTIONS AND TECHNIQUES

SATIR GROWTH MODEL/HUMAN VALIDATION PROCESS MODEL

Satir has popularized the technique of sculpting the family structure. Family sculpture may be used throughout the therapeutic process to increase family members' awareness of perceptions and thereby alter family relationships. In implementing the technique, Satir physically positions each family member in a composite living sculpture to represent the way the other family members see this person. Each family member's position is spatially related to the role the member occupies in the family. It is very common for Satir to have a dependent member on their knees holding another member, or a peripheral parent standing in the corner. Space then becomes a metaphor for closeness or distance, symbolizing the boundaries of the system. Satir also asks family members to express emotions through exaggerated facial expressions such as extreme smiling or frowning at each other. In such a sculpture, members of the family can express the way things are or the way they would like them to be (Satir, 1983).

One of Satir's hallmarks is the use of touch. She often began sessions by making physical contact with each member of the family system before teaching parents how to use the healing power of physical touch with their children.

The "Parts Party" was an experiential method Satir developed to help clients experience the different parts of their personalities. The family member directs others to act out the specific parts, fostering new personal experience, and insight (Satir & Baldwin, 1983).

The Temperature Reading was a task Satir asked of families in which time is set aside each day for family members to connect with each other by expressing appreciation, talking about achievements, asking questions, sharing feelings, and talking about hopes and wishes for the future (Satir & Baldwin, 1983).

SYMBOLIC-EXPERIENTIAL THERAPY

Whitaker does not offer a well-defined set of techniques. Most experiential therapists who followed Whitaker use techniques that are an extension of their own personalities. The personal encounter between the therapist and the family allows the therapist to become an important member of the family. When the therapist becomes a member of the family, the therapist experiences the same joy, sadness, and helplessness that other members of the family experience. Experiential family therapists argue that technique evolves naturally out of each unique family relationship (Roberto, 1991).

Whitaker typically employs a co-therapist to share the emotional involvement of the therapeutic process. The personal involvement of the treatment process often produces countertransference reactions in the therapist. Countertransference reactions operate at an unconscious level. The co-therapist can observe and help to extract the therapist from the emotional entanglements of countertransference. The co-therapist can also provide an opportunity for each therapist to reflect on the relationship and focus on specific members or subsystems of the family (Napier & Whitaker, 1978).

Whitaker would often act unconventionally and say absurd things to family members. However, experiential family therapists accept absurdity as a necessary tool in challenging the family's definition of a symptom. This capacity to say and do the unconventional can be seen in the experiential therapist's use of fantasy as technique. By suggesting that the family can tolerate the fantasy discussion, the therapists expand the family's emotional life without real violence or acting out. The consideration of fantasy alternatives offers the family new freedom to communicate about frightening ideas (Whitaker & Bumberry, 1988; Whitaker & Ryan, 1989).

The therapist confronts the family with their subjective emotional experience of the family. If a therapist is experiencing boredom, they might yawn and tell the family that "you are putting me to sleep." A therapist who feels angry might choose to express that anger at a family member. Such emotional expressions are short-lived and often have dramatic impact.

EMOTIONALLY FOCUSED THERAPY

Validation is performed using the RISSSC mnemonic (Johnson, 1996):

R: Therapist intentionally REPEATS key words and phrases that highlight primary emotion.
I: Therapist uses IMAGES that evoke emotions.
S: Therapist uses SIMPLE and concise phrases.
S: Therapist will SLOW speech to enable a client to deepen emotional expression.
S: Therapist will use a SOFT and soothing tone of voice.
C: Therapist uses CLIENT words and phrases.

In a core EFT intervention known as *heightening*, the therapist highlights specific responses to intensify a client's emotional experience. The EFT therapist tracks, reflects, and often heightens emotion, moving partners from secondary emotions such as irritation/anger to more primary, underlying emotions such as fear and sadness. This skill also involves repeating, re-enacting, or using images and metaphors to enliven an experience. *Evocative responding* involves asking open-ended questions about tentative, unclear, or emerging aspects of experience, and helps partners expand and deepen their experience. These questions call up client's primary emotions and their related habitual ways of signaling to and engaging with their spouse. The therapist asks when, what, where, and how, focusing on specific elements of the client's experience (Johnson, 1996).

Empathetic conjectures involve making inferences by drawing on therapist experience of the couple's cycle. Conjectures must be offered tentatively and are informed by fears of engulfment, rejection, and abandonment. These exploratory responses are made for the purpose of enhancing clients' attention to and engagement with primary emotion. They are not cognitive interpretations, but empathic responses based on empathic immersion in the client's world of experience and on an understanding of attachment processes (Johnson, 1996, 2002).

In an enactment, the therapist gives directions for one partner to talk directly to the other. The experience brings partners into direct contact with each other in the immediate moment. The focus is on owning and disclosing experience, not discussing it. The aim is to promote responsive contact, not a longer discussion. In the beginning of therapy, enactments are used to help partners see the negative cycle more clearly (Johnson, 1996, 2002).

INTERNAL FAMILY SYSTEMS

IFS therapists begin by separating the client's various parts by walking through the 6Fs: *find, focus, flesh out, feel toward, (be)friend,* and *fear* (Schwartz, 1995).

SIX F'S OF INTERNAL FAMILY SYSTEMS INTERVENTION TO HELP PROTECTIVE PARTS DIFFERENTIATE FROM THE SELF

1. *Find a Part*—Who needs your attention right now? Where do you notice it?
2. *Focus on the Target Part*—Turn your attention inside.

3. *Flesh out*—Learn more about the part in a way that supports the separation between part and Self.
4. *Feelings Toward the Part*—Reactive parts often need to feel heard and validated. Stay with them until they are willing to let us get to know the target part. Once they agree, we ask the client, "How do you feel toward the (target) part now?"
5. *(Be)Friend the Part*—This involves learning about the target part and developing a friendly relationship with it. This builds relationships internally (Self to part) and externally (part to therapist). The therapist asks, "How did it get this job? How effective is the job? If it didn't have to do this job, what would it rather do? How old is it? How old does it think you are? What else does it want you to know?"
6. *Fears of the Part*—The therapist asks, "What does it want for you? What would happen if it stopped doing this job?"

It is important to develop an alliance with protective parts, and work with them first. In building this relationship, the IFS therapist may need to negotiate the pace of work by giving the part an opportunity to talk about concerns. In order to respect the concerns for the protective part, the therapist must work out a system for the part to let the therapist know when things are moving too fast.

The Unburdening Process (Schwartz, 1995)

1. *Contacting the Exile:* Establishes a connection between the Self and exile in which the Self can be present with the experience of the exile.
2. *Witnessing the Exile:* Invites the exile to show anything it wants to show so it can be seen, felt, and understood in what happened in the past and how that made it feel.
3. *Reparenting the Exile:* Allows the exile to have a new experience—either by remembering the past or experienced in the present.
4. *Retrieving the Exile*: Frees the exile from the situation of the past and brings it into a better situation in imagination or the present.
5. *Unburdening the Exile:* Holds a ritual in which the exile can let go of the burdens it has been holding.
6. *Integrating the Exile and the Protector:* Finds a good place for both exile and protector to coexist harmoniously in the system.

ROLE OF THE THERAPIST

In addition to the teaching/modeling role, the experiential family therapist becomes a facilitator in the therapeutic process. The therapist's use of questions, empathic responses, clarification, and directives facilitates effective communication in the family. The experiential therapist shares their own emotional reactions in an authentic way with clients in the family system.

ORIENTATION IN TIME

SATIR GROWTH MODEL/HUMAN VALIDATION PROCESS MODEL

Satir stays in the here-and-now to develop congruence and authentic emotional expression in her work with family systems.

SYMBOLIC-EXPERIENTIAL THERAPY

Whitaker saw the problems that families brought to therapy as failures to adapt together to common problems of life and the here-and-now as the necessary moment for creative intervention and change.

EMOTIONALLY FOCUSED THERAPY

Although EFT is primarily present focused, the therapy may explore how early attachment wounds in childhood in the infant/caregiver relationship are manifested in the adult romantic relationship.

INTERNAL FAMILY SYSTEMS

This is a model that moves fluidly from a present focus when working with manager parts to a more early, primitive time in a client's life when working with young, exiled parts. Unburdening the exile from the situation of the past brings the focus of therapy back to the here-and-now and sets the stage for a healthy future in which the Self is in the lead (Schwartz, 1995).

PROCESS AND GOALS OF THERAPY

SATIR GROWTH MODEL/HUMAN VALIDATION PROCESS MODEL

The Satir Growth Model embraces four universal meta-goals as the focus of therapy (Satir, 1983):

1. *Raising self-esteem*: Self-esteem is how people experience and judge themselves in the present. People who have high self-esteem experience themselves through their spiritual Life Energy, or Self.
2. *Becoming a choice maker*: When one is living from the level of Self, one's choices are to move toward freedom. One's choices are in the direction of health, happiness, peace, and love. One feels empowered to choose wisely.
3. *Becoming responsible*: When one is living from the level of Self, one is conscious of their internal experiences and is responsible for all feelings, perceptions, expectations, and yearnings as well as one's behavior. Satir reminds us that all our internal experiences belong to us. The Self is greater than all feelings, greater than all thoughts, greater than all unmet expectations. When we become responsible for our internal world, we experience the vastness of our Being. We then become responsible for our own growth toward becoming more fully human.
4. *Becoming congruent*: Congruence is a deeply imbedded concept and goal of the Satir Growth Model. In her early communication model, Satir encouraged people to be "straight"—to say what they meant and do what they said. However, congruence as a meta-goal implies that people can grow to be in harmony with their own Life Energy and to experience the peace, joy, love, and connection that exist there. When one is more congruent, one is free from negative experiences of the past as one is now living in the present at the level of Being. Other ways of describing congruence might include being integrated, real, genuine, or authentic. In the Satir Growth Model there is an expectation that therapists have attained a high level of congruence in their lives and can be congruent while working with their clients.

SYMBOLIC-EXPERIENTIAL THERAPY

According to Whitaker, therapy occurs in several phases. In the beginning phase, therapy is quite structured. The co-therapy team must battle for "structure" and "initiative." In the battle for structure, the therapists want the family to know who is in charge of therapy. Although the battle for initiative involves getting the family to take responsibility for its decisions, the therapists try to gain therapeutic leverage by first insisting that all family members attend the first session. In the end phase, the family becomes more independent, and the therapist begins to disengage from the family. The family members become less dependent on the therapist and more involved with each other. Goals for therapy include an increased sense of belonging and encouraging freedom of individuation. Individuals are encouraged to grow in ways congruent to their authentic selves (Napier & Whitaker, 1978).

EMOTIONALLY FOCUSED THERAPY

The goals of EFT are to (a) expand and reorganize key emotional responses and, in the process, the organization of self; (b) create a positive shift in couple interactional positions and patterns; and (c) foster the creation of a secure bond between partners (Johnson, 1996).

INTERNAL FAMILY SYSTEMS

The goals of IFS are to (a) achieve balance and harmony within the internal system and (b) differentiate and elevate the Self so it can be an effective leader in the system. When the Self is in the lead, the parts provide input to the Self but will respect the leadership and ultimate decision-making of the Self. All parts exist and lend talents that reflect their nonextreme intentions (Schwartz, 1995).

CONCLUSION

As a contrast to other classic family therapy models that emphasized problem-solving, experiential family therapy is dedicated to emotional well-being. Experiential family therapists use the immediacy of the therapeutic encounter with the family system and the associated here-and-now emotional experiencing to help target the family's natural tendency toward growth and the fulfillment of individual members' potentials. Early experiential approaches were signified by their ahistorical, nontheoretical approach stressing action over insight, primarily by providing a growth-enhancing experience through the family–therapist encounter. Personal integrity and self-fulfillment are seen as innate human capacities that will emerge spontaneously once defensiveness is overcome. To challenge the familiar and enhance experience, therapists use their own lively personalities as well as a host of expressive techniques. Techniques like role-playing and emotional confrontation, and other expressive methods, such as family sculpting and family drawing, are hallmarks of early experiential family therapy. With the passing of one-of-a-kind, experiential family therapy pioneers, Virginia Satir and Carl Whitaker, these methods have taken a back seat to more contemporary models like EFT and IFS. These approaches have successfully integrated an experiential focus on the individual with a more sophisticated understanding of family systems.

KEY TERMS

Attachment: The emotional bond between a mother and child or between two adults in an intimate relationship.

Attachment needs: The need of children and adults to be involved in relationships that provide safety, security, and satisfaction.

Attachment style: There are four attachment styles and most parent–child or marital relationships fall into one of these four categories: secure, insecure-ambivalent, insecure-avoidant, and disorganized.

Avanta Network: Virginia Satir's original network, which revolved around teaching therapists and social workers her approach to working with individuals, groups, and families; now known as the *Virginia Satir Global Network.*

Avoider: A Satir communication style in which the family member tends to distract others from potential conflict by acting helpless, weak, and lacking an understanding.

Battle for initiative: A process by which a therapist gets a client system to become motivated to make changes by stressing the need and urgency for doing so. If therapy is to be effective, clients must win the battle for initiative.

Battle for structure: The struggle to establish the parameters under which therapy is conducted. Therapists must win the battle for structure if therapy is to be effective.

Blamer: One of Satir's communication styles; this type of family member judges and complains, often for the purpose of bullying others into accepting their preferences.

Blending: This occurs when the feelings and beliefs of one part merge with another part or with the Self in IFS.

Burdens: In IFS, extreme ideas or feelings that are carried by parts and that govern their lives. Parts accrue burdens from exposure to an external person or event.

Choreography: A process in which clients symbolically enact a pattern or a sequence involving a relationship, often with family members.

Communication stance: One of Virginia Satir's experiential and humanistic family therapy procedures in which family members are asked to exaggerate the physical positions of their roles, such as blaming others for everything that has gone wrong in their lives by pointing a finger at them.

Computer: According to Virginia Satir's theory, a person who interacts in a family primarily on a cognitive, super-rational, and intellectual level.

Degrees of craziness: Whitaker's term for being driven crazy, going crazy, and acting crazy.

Disorganized attachment: Children with this attachment style following separation show aspects of both avoidant and ambivalent patterns. Disorganized attachment is a common correlate of child abuse and neglect and early parental bereavement. Marital and family relationships are characterized by approach-avoidance conflicts, clinging, and sulking.

Distracter: Satir's term for a nonadaptive communication style used consistently to avoid rather than resolve conflict that is characterized by changing the subject, being quiet, feigning helplessness, or pretending to misunderstand.

Empathic attunement: The EFT therapist communicates that they are tracking with the client's experience. Often these are short utterances and body language that mimic what the client is feeling in the moment; may also expand into restating and mirroring client communication.

Empathic conjecture: A tentative interpretation of client's experience seen through the attachment lens offered by the EFT therapist to facilitate a more intense experiencing from which new meanings may arise with an expanded awareness.

Empty-chair technique: A Gestalt therapy technique designed to help clients deal with their emotions and unresolved relationships through role-plays and speaking to people with whom the client has unfinished business.

Evocative responding: The EFT therapist elicits and captures the implicit aspects of a client's emotional world in a tentative manner by asking questions about a client's present experience, including internal responses and reactions to in-session dynamics.

Exiles: In IFS, parts that have been sequestered within a system for their own protection or for the protection of the system.

Experiential symbolic family therapy: An approach to working with families developed by Carl Whitaker that posits individuals in families are not aware of their emotions. Therapists emphasize expressing feelings in the here and now, and use their own personalities, spontaneity, and creativity during treatment to promote change.

Family drawing: An experiential therapy technique in which family members are asked to draw their ideas about how the family is organized.

Family map: Virginia Satir's family reconstruction technique of producing a visual representation of the structure of three generations of the family using adjectives to describe each family member's personality.

Family sculpting: A nonverbal experiential technique in which family members are placed in a tableau that reveals significant aspects of their perceptions and feelings.

Family reconstruction: A therapeutic innovation developed by Virginia Satir to help family members discover dysfunctional patterns in their lives stemming from their family of origin.

Filial therapy: Serving as both a therapeutic intervention and a preventive approach, in this model, developed by Bernard and Louise Guerney, parents function as experiential play therapists for their children.

Firefighters: In IFS, these are parts that go into action after the exiles have been activated in order to calm the exiles or distract the system from them.

Flight toward health: This refers to a family abruptly stopping treatment, which Whitaker believed was a positive sign indicating the family experienced sudden and profound growth and no longer requires therapeutic support.

Insecure-ambivalent attachment: Children with this attachment style seek contact with their parents following separation but are unable to derive comfort from it. They cling and cry or have tantrums. Marital partners with this attachment style tend to be overly close but dissatisfied. Families characterized by insecure-ambivalent relationships tend to be enmeshed and to have blurred boundaries.

Insecure-avoidant attachment: Children with this attachment style avoid contact with their parents after separation. Marital partners with this attachment style tend to be distant and dissatisfied. Families characterized by insecure-avoidant relationships tend to be disengaged and to have impermeable boundaries.

Managers: In IFS, this refers to parts that try to run a system in ways that minimize the activation of exiles.

Multiplicity paradigm: In IFS, the recognition that the human mind is not unitary, but instead is subdivided into a multitude of subpersonalities.

Parts: The term used in IFS for a person's subpersonalities. Parts are best considered internal people of different ages, talents, and temperaments.

Parts Party: This therapeutic technique from Satir helps clients experience the different parts of their personalities. The family member directs others to act out the specific parts, fostering new personal experience and insight.

Personal growth: The primary goal of experiential therapies is personal growth, which includes increasing self-awareness, self-esteem, self-responsibility, and self-actualization. Solving the presenting problem is secondary to this primary goal.

Placater: Per Virginia Satir, this is one of four roles that a person takes when not communicating clearly and directly. Avoiding conflict at the cost of integrity, a placater may ingratiate, apologize, or avoid disagreement when the opposite behavior is called for.

Primary emotions: In EFT, the underlying emotions that occur in immediate response to unmet attachment needs, such as emotional hurt, loss, sadness, and loneliness. Facilitating the expression of these emotions is essential to creating connection and promoting therapeutic change in EFT.

Secondary emotions: In EFT, these are emotions that occur as a reaction to primary emotional responses when attachment needs are triggered. They include anger, hostility, revenge, and frustration. Preventing the full expression of these emotions and promoting the expression of primary emotional responses are necessary to create connection and promote therapeutic change.

Secure attachment: The healthiest form of attachment, it describes an attachment where a child feels comforted by the presence of their caregiver or a spouse feels comforted by their partner.

Secure base: In secure attachment relationships, the parent or partner is viewed as a secure base from which to explore the world.

Self: In IFS, this refers to the core of a person, which contains leadership qualities such as compassion, perspective, curiosity, and confidence. The Self is best equipped to lead the internal family system.

Self-actualization: Realizing one's full human potential; integrating disowned aspects of experience into the self; resolving unfinished business; being fully aware of moment-to-moment experiences; and communicating in a congruent, authentic, clear, and direct way.

Self-leadership: Leadership in IFS characterized by compassion, calmness, clarity, curiosity, confidence, courage, creativity, and connectedness.

Temperature reading: Satir's term for the family task of setting aside time each day to connect with each other by expressing appreciation, talking about achievements, asking questions, making complaints, solving problems, and talking about hopes and wishes for the future.

Therapy of the absurd: Symbolic-experiential therapy may be referred to as absurd due to its unrecognizable structure, spontaneous process, and therapist transparency.

KNOWLEDGE CHECK: CHAPTER 5

1. The experiential model that integrates experiential, systemic, and attachment theories is known as _______.

   A. Satir Growth Model
   B. Symbolic-experiential therapy
   C. Emotionally focused therapy (EFT)
   D. Internal family systems (IFS)

2. Instead of observing behavioral interactional sequences, experiential therapists choose to focus more on the __________ components of family interactions.

   A. Emotional
   B. Internal
   C. Unconscious
   D. Cognitive

3. Experiential family therapists can be associated with all of the following terms *except*:

   A. Repressed emotion
   B. Encounter
   C. Unconscious
   D. Individual growth

4. A therapist using the Satir Growth Model would help the client system _________.

   A. Learn self-soothing techniques
   B. Create a sense of curiosity for interpersonal learning
   C. Foster individual growth as well as improving family interactions
   D. Express their true feelings through provocation and confrontation

5. A therapist who has been influenced by symbolic-experiential family therapy will use techniques to create ________to break family systems out of their rigid interaction patterns.

   A. Confusion and disorganization
   B. Hear-and-now experiencing
   C. Physical movement
   D. Empathy and validation

6. Each of the following models fall into the category of experiential family therapies *except*:

   A. Satir Growth Model
   B. Symbolic-experiential therapy
   C. Emotionally focused therapy (EFT)
   D. External family systems

(*See answers next page.*)

1. C) Emotionally focused therapy (EFT)
EFT is used to improve attachment and bonding in adult relationships. Although often used for couples, it has also been adapted for use with families. This treatment can help couples and family members form a more secure emotional bond, which can result in stronger relationships and improved communication.

2. A) Emotional
In experiential therapies, individuals directly experience their emotions, and the focus is on the experience, understanding, and reconceptualizing of one's emotions and how they affect one's behavior.

3. C) Unconscious
Unconscious is associated with psychodynamic models, whereas experiential models bring emotions and feelings into the here-and-now conscious awareness and experience.

4. C) Foster individual growth as well as improving family interactions
Satir's model was designed to foster individual growth while improving relationships and communication within the family structure by addressing a person's actions, emotions, and perceptions as they relate to that person's dynamic within the family unit.

5. A) Confusion and disorganization
Carl Whitaker's therapy of the absurd is a tongue-in-cheek style that inverts common therapeutic methods and produces dramatic results. Although sharing the same objectives as other experiential therapists, he uses sharply different approaches. His model confuses clients, confronts, and cajoles them into change.

6. D) External family systems
The correct name of the Dick Schwartz's experiential model is internal family systems (IFS).

7. Unlike Bowenians, experiential therapists strive to_______________, then behave in alternately provocative and supportive ways in order to help families learn to express honest emotion.

   A. Encourage development of transference
   B. Discourage development of transference
   C. Raise the level of anxiety in the family
   D. Lower the level of anxiety in the family

8. What is the heart of relational goals in Satir's approach?

   A. Restructuring the family boundaries
   B. Reconfiguring the family's interaction sequences
   C. Congruent communication for all family members
   D. Reducing emotional reactivity through detriangulation

9. Family reconstruction, as used by Virginia Satir, was a form of ________.

   A. Paradoxical intention
   B. Genogram
   C. Structural diagram
   D. Family sculpting

10. Each of the following statements is true of internal family systems (IFS) *except*:

    A. Each person's inner life has multiple parts that form a system that functions like a family system
    B. Each person's inner world is characterized as having various parts that interrelate as a coherent system with the same dynamics one would see in a family
    C. IFS therapists see some parts of the system as good and others as bad
    D. Each person has a Self that is its core and is distinct from parts that have vision, compassion, and confidence; the goal of therapy is to have this Self provide inner leadership to the various parts

11. Exiles are best described as ____________.

    A. Parts used to keep managers locked up so they cannot take control
    B. Parts of self that forcefully keep firefighters in check
    C. An oppressed group kept from the conscious mind at any cost
    D. Helpers used to keep the Self in control

12. In internal family systems (IFS), the controller, the perfectionist, the dependent one, the passive pessimist, and the worrier are all examples of which subpersonality?

    A. The Self
    B. Exiles
    C. Firefighters
    D. Managers

(*See answers next page.*)

7. C) Raise the level of anxiety in the family

An experiential therapist like Whitaker feels comfortable and justified in raising anxiety by pushing the family due to the innate belief that the family has unlimited potential to grow. The therapist is very straightforward and direct with his responses and often confronts members of the family to tap into emotion and expose truths.

8. C) Congruent communication for all family members

Virginia Satir used her communication categories to help individual family members become aware of their incongruent behavior. Incongruent behavior occurs when your mind thinks one thing, but your body does another.

9. D) Family sculpting

Sculpting is a technique in family therapy in which the therapist asks one or more members of the family to arrange the other members (and lastly themselves) in relation to one another in terms of posture, space, and attitude so as to portray the arranger's perception of the family, either in general or with regard to a particular situation or conflict. This technique often reveals family dynamics visually in a way that may not be adequately captured in verbal descriptions by family members.

10. C) IFS therapists see some parts of the system as good and others as bad

A core tenet of IFS is that every part has a positive intent for the person, even if its actions or effects are counterproductive or cause dysfunction. This means that there is never any reason to fight with, coerce, or try to eliminate a part; the IFS method promotes internal connection and harmony.

11. C) An oppressed group kept from the conscious mind at any cost

Exiles are parts that are in pain, shame, fear, or trauma, usually from childhood. Managers and firefighters try to block these parts from consciousness, to prevent this pain from coming to the surface.

12. D) Managers

IFS calls the protective parts that are responsible for our day-to-day safety, the *managers*. Managers are the parts that want to control everything. They try to control relationships and the environment, so the person is never in a position to be humiliated, abandoned, rejected, attacked, or anything else unexpected and harmful.

13. *Primary emotions* refer to emotions that stem from attachment fears and needs. What do secondary emotions stem from?

A. The individual's own insecurities
B. Unmet attachment needs such as anger, frustration, and withdrawal
C. The innate need of all individuals to feel a sense of belonging
D. Poor attachment in previous influential relationships such as parents or siblings

14. The most common negative interaction cycle according to emotionally focused therapy (EFT) is ______________.

A. Withdraw/withdraw
B. Attack/attack
C. Pursue/withdraw
D. Report/command

15. When an emotionally focused therapy (EFT) therapist is in the assessment phase and discovers instances in which one partner was in a moment of high need or vulnerability and the other partner failed to offer the needed support or nurturance, the therapist might identify this as ____________.

A. An attachment injury
B. An attack
C. A normal couple process
D. An impasse in therapy

(*See answers next page.*)

13. B) Unmet attachment needs such as anger, frustration, and withdrawal
Secondary reactive emotions are "reactions to reactions" and perpetuate the negative interactional cycles couples may develop. Emotionally focused therapy (EFT) therapists strive to help the couple become aware of the secondary reactive emotions that trigger their negative relational patterns. Secondary emotions are unconscious attempts to avoid experiencing the more vulnerable feelings activated by a comment or situation.

14. C) Pursue/withdraw
Couples are often caught in the same fight over and over, but the content of the fight changes. The conflict is a dance, a self-perpetuating cycle. Couples become hopeless in finding the exit to these typical, negative cycles. In the pursue–withdraw cycle, the critical, demanding pursuits of a more anxious pursuer triggers avoidance and distancing in the anxious avoidant withdrawer partner. The distancing and avoidance of one partner creates more anxiety in the other and that partner becomes more critical in their pursuit. Over time, the cycle can change and the pursuer becomes burned out in their pursuing of the other and essentially stops trying. The withdrawer may then panic because of fear of losing the other and become more of a pursuer in the relationship.

15. A) An attachment injury
An attachment injury occurs when one partner violates the expectation that the other will offer comfort and caring in times of danger or distress. This incident becomes a clinically recurring theme and creates an impasse that blocks relationship repair in couple therapy. An attachment injury is characterized by an abandonment or a betrayal of trust during a critical moment of need. The injurious incident defines the relationship as insecure and maintains the relationship distress because it is continually used as a standard for the dependability of the offending partner.

AUDIO PODCAST 5.1
Satir & Whitaker
Eli A. Karam
https://bcove.video/3wyS27e

AUDIO PODCAST 5.2
Experiential Family Therapy
Eli A. Karam
https://bcove.video/3PTVb8q

AUDIO PODCAST 5.3
Internal Family Systems
Eli A. Karam
https://bcove.video/3pLdNgi

REFERENCES

Johnson, S. (1996). *The practice of emotionally focused marital therapy: Creating connection.* Brunner Mazel.

Johnson, S. (2002). *Emotionally focused couple therapy with trauma survivors: Strengthening attachment bonds.* Guilford Press.

Johnson, S., & Whiffen, V. (2003). *Attachment processes in couple and family therapy.* Guilford Press.

Kempler, W. (1991). *Experiential psychotherapy within families.* Kempler Institute.

Napier, A., & Whitaker, C. (1978). *The family crucible.* Harper & Row.

Neill, J., & Kniskern, D. (1982). *From psyche to system: The evolving therapy of Carl Whitaker.* Guilford Press.

Roberto, G. (1991). Symbolic-experiential family therapy. In A. Gurman & D. Kniskern (Eds.), *Handbook of family therapy* (Vol. 11, pp. 444–478). Brunner Mazel.

Satir, V. (1983). *Conjoint family therapy.* Science and Behavior Books.

Satir, V. (1988). *The new peoplemaking.* Science and Behavior Books.

Satir, V., & Baldwin, M. (1983). *Satir step-by-step: A guide to creating change in families.* Science and Behavior Books.

Satir, V., & Baldwin, M. (1987). *The use of self in therapy.* Haworth.

Schwartz, R. C. (1995). *Internal family systems therapy.* Guilford Press.

Whitaker, C., & Bumberry, W. (1988). *Dancing with the family. A symbolic-experiential approach.* Brunner Mazel.

Whitaker, C., & Ryan, M. (1989). *Midnight musings of a family therapist.* W. W. Norton.

Behavioral and Cognitive Behavioral Marriage and Family Therapy Approaches

6

LEARNING OBJECTIVES

After reading this chapter, you should be able to:

1. Identify developers of models using behavioral and cognitive behavioral approaches
2. Develop the theories underlying behavioral and cognitive behavioral approaches to marriage and family therapy (MFT)
3. Describe assessment strategies associated with various behavioral and cognitive behavioral approaches to MFT
4. Distinguish the main interventions/techniques of behavioral and cognitive behavioral approaches to MFT
5. Identify goals of behavioral and cognitive behavioral approaches to MFT

RELEVANT EXAM DOMAINS

- *Domain 1—The Practice of Systemic Therapy*
  Includes tasks related to incorporating systemic theory and perspectives into practice activities, and establishing and maintaining ongoing therapeutic relationships with the client system.
- *Domain 2—Assessing, Hypothesizing, and Diagnosing*
  Includes tasks related to assessing the various dimensions of the client system, forming and reformulating hypotheses, and diagnosing the client and family system in order to guide therapeutic activities.
- *Domain 3—Designing and Conducting Treatment*
  Includes tasks related to developing and implementing interventions with the client system.

INTRODUCTION

When they first began working with families, behavior therapists applied learning theory to train parents in behavior modification and to teach communication skills to couples. Although these approaches were effective with simple problems and well-motivated individuals, behaviorists had little appreciation of how misbehavior and poor communication were embedded in family systems. Since that time, however, behavioral couple and family therapy has evolved to become more systemic with increasing use of cognitive principles and attention to family dynamics.

MODEL DEVELOPERS AND SIGNIFICANT CONTRIBUTORS

INDIVIDUAL BEHAVIORISTS AND COGNITIVE BEHAVIORAL THERAPISTS

Albert Bandura, the founder of social learning theory, is best known for his emphasis on modeling as a way of learning. He contends that most people learn by imitating others through observation (Bandura, 1969).

Aaron Beck developed a cognitive behavioral therapy (CBT) approach to mental disorders. Over the past several decades, CBT has become by far the world's most extensively studied form of psychotherapy (Beck, 1976).

Albert Ellis is the founder of rational emotive behavior therapy, which was originally called *rational emotive therapy*. Ellis believed that to function in a healthy way, it is important to modify thoughts so that they are rational (Ellis, 1962).

B. F. Skinner is the originator of operant conditioning and the Skinner Box and was a champion at applying the principles of behaviorism to human society (Bjork, 1997).

COUPLE AND FAMILY COGNITIVE BEHAVIORAL THERAPISTS

Don Baucom and Norm Epstein are the founders and two of the most prolific researchers to study cognitive behavioral couple therapy (Epstein & Baucom, 2002). Baucom also created a useful method that integrates cognitive behavioral and insight-oriented couple therapy to help couples deal with infidelity.

As a leading expert in cognitive behavioral therapy with families, Frank Datillio adapted therapeutic techniques originally designed for individuals for use with family systems struggling with a wide range of relationship problems and stressful life transitions (Datillio, 2010).

Renowned for his work on marital stability and divorce prediction, John Gottman conducted over four decades of breakthrough research with thousands of couples. He and his wife, Julie Gottman, created The Gottman Method, an approach to couples therapy that includes a thorough assessment of the couple's relationship and integrates research-based interventions based on the Sound Relationship House theory (Gottman, 1999, 2002).

Neil Jacobson and Andrew Christensen devoted their careers to the advancement of evidence-based treatments for couples in distress. Jacobson was a pioneer of traditional behavioral couples therapy (TBCT). Along with Christensen, he developed integrative behavioral couple therapy (IBCT), an empirically supported treatment for couples that emphasizes acceptance- and tolerance-building techniques (Christensen et al., 2015; Jacobson & Christensen, 1996).

SEX THERAPISTS

William H. Masters and Virginia E. Johnson pioneered research into the nature of human sexual response and the diagnosis and behavioral treatment (sensate focus) of sexual disorders and dysfunctions (Masters & Johnson, 1966).

Helen Singer Kaplan was an Austrian American sex therapist and the founder of the first clinic in the United States to treat sexual disorders; she developed the triphasic sexual response cycle to introduce the concept of sexual desire into the field of sex therapy (Kaplan, 2013).

Joseph LoPiccolo is an American psychologist and sex researcher who focused on female sexual response. He coauthored the self-help book *Becoming Orgasmic: A Sexual and Personal Growth Program for Women* (1988) with Julia Heiman.

David Schnarch, by combining sex therapy with a family systems approach in his Sexual Crucible model, helped couples improve their level of differentiation by focusing on self-validated intimacy as opposed to partner-validated intimacy (Schnarch, 1991).

MODEL OVERVIEW

PARENT TRAINING: DIFFERENCES BETWEEN TRADITIONAL BEHAVIORISM AND SYSTEMS THINKING

Behavioral family therapy is derived from Albert Bandura's social learning theory, which combines operant conditioning with social modeling. These techniques were traditionally used to treat individuals rather than families as systems. Behavioral family therapists have incorporated principles of systems theory, but they have done so within a linear structure. Family problems are seen as being caused by ineffective patterns of reinforcement between parents and children or between marital partners. Behavioral family therapists give little attention to the circular interactional patterns in the family system that may be maintaining the problem.

Behavioral family therapists concentrate on dyadic interactions (parent–child or spouse–spouse), whereas systems family therapists focus on triadic interactions (mother–father–child). Thus, behavioral family therapists focus primarily on the family member or members who administer consequences for the problem behavior (e.g., a mother who rewards a child's problem behavior), whereas systems family therapists center their attention on patterns of behavior within the entire family system.

Behavioral and family systems approaches also differ in their views of resistance to change. Behavior theorists, on the one hand, view failure to change as a result of either (a) the client's feeling that the short-term cost of change outweighs the perceived long-range benefits or (b) the therapist's failure to select the correct behavior or contingencies for change. Systems theorists, on the other hand, view resistance as a consequence of disrupting the homeostatic balance. They see resistance as the family's efforts to preserve its equilibrium or, in cybernetic terms, as negative feedback. Behavioral theorists view resistance as an obstacle to behavior change, whereas systems theorists often view resistance as a necessary step toward change.

As behavior therapists began to consider the cost-effectiveness of their treatment of children, they paid increased attention to employing the child's parents as the agents of change. Typically, treatment involved parent training in which parents were instructed to identify and record inappropriate behaviors of the child and then systematically intervene, using social learning principles (e.g., reinforcement, modeling, time out, and extinction) to eliminate the problem (Falloon, 1988).

TRADITIONAL BEHAVIORAL COUPLES THERAPY

In social exchange theory, the individual is seen as attempting to maximize "rewards" while minimizing "costs." A couple's relationship is viewed as satisfying to the degree that the partners provide one another with a high ratio of benefits to costs and that alternative relationships offer fewer comparative rewards and more costs. Any couple has a minimum reward/cost ratio that determines the success of the relationship; the ratio is unique to each couple.

When two people reward one another at an equitable rate, we refer to the nature of the exchange as *reciprocity*. Couple conflict may occur when there is a lack of reciprocity and either spouse attempts to control the partner's behavior with aversive stimuli. This attempt to control another person's behavior with negative reinforcement is referred to as *coercion*. Coercion often sets off a string of sequential interactions that, although unpleasant for both partners, becomes self-perpetuating.

TBCT, originally known as *behavioral marital therapy*, developed from the application of social exchange and social learning theories to the understanding and modification of couple interactions. TBCT, with its primary intervention components in (a) behavior exchange and

(b) communication and problem-solving training, was found to be both the most used and validated therapy modality by couple therapists (Jacobson & Margolin, 1979). TBCT, however, appeared to be limited in its ability to produce clinically meaningful change in severely distressed couples, older couples, and in emotionally disengaged couples. Hence, it became increasingly clear that TBCT's emphasis on promoting change seemed to be a poor fit for some couples and some problems. Additionally, results showed that 38% of the couples that received TBCT treatment had divorced during a 4-year follow-up period. These research findings resulted in Neil Jacobson's update of this model to a new approach known as *integrative behavioral couple therapy* (IBCT; Christensen et al., 2015; Jacobson & Christensen, 1996).

INTEGRATIVE BEHAVIORAL COUPLE THERAPY

The term *integrative* comes from the integration of change and acceptance into tradition behavioral couples therapy techniques. IBCT suggests that acceptance be promoted as an essential step toward improvement in couples with problems, whereas TBCT promotes behavior exchange and the development of effective communication skills as the path to solving difficulties.

Whereas the emphasis in TBCT is on the prescribed exchanging of desired behaviors in a way that promotes score keeping between couples, now the focus has moved to the partner's emotional response to their partner's non-prescribed, unsolicited actions. IBCT highlights the couple's natural behaviors so improvements are not due to something as artificial as therapist-driven rules for the relationship or contrived behavior exchanges (Christensen et al., 2015; Jacobson & Christensen, 1996).

COUPLE AND FAMILY COGNITIVE BEHAVIORAL THERAPY

According to cognitive behaviorists, the schemas that plague relationships are learned in the process of growing up and reinforced in current relationships with romantic partners and other family members. Some of these dysfunctional beliefs are assumptions about specific family roles, whereas others are about couple and family life in general. These schemas are the basis of biased assumptions that negatively influence relationships by distorting family members' responses to each other. The following is a list of some typical cognitive distortions (Beck, 2005):

1. *All-or-nothing thinking* is also known as *black and white thinking* or *polarized thinking*. This type of thinking involves viewing things in absolute terms: Situations are always black or white, everything or nothing, good or bad, success or failure.
2. *Overgeneralization* occurs when you make a rule after a single event or a series of coincidences.The words *always* or *never* frequently appear in the sentences. Because you have experience with one event playing out a certain way, you assume that all future events will have the same outcome.
3. A *mental filter* is the opposite of overgeneralization, but has the same negative outcome. Instead of taking one small event and generalizing it inappropriately, the mental filter takes one small event and focuses on it exclusively, filtering out anything else.
4. *Discounting the positive* is a cognitive distortion that involves ignoring or invalidating good things that have happened to you. It is like mental filtering, but instead of simply ignoring the positives, you are actively rejecting them.
5. *Mind reading* occurs when you think someone is going to react in a particular way, or you believe someone is thinking things that they aren't.
6. *Fortune telling* is when you predict events will unfold in a particular way, often to avoid trying something difficult.

7. *Magnification* refers to exaggerating the importance of shortcomings and problems while minimizing the importance of desirable qualities. Similar to mental filtering and discounting the positive, this cognitive distortion involves magnifying your negative qualities while minimizing your positive ones.
8. *Emotional reasoning* is a way of judging yourself or your circumstances based on your emotions. This type of reasoning assumes that because you are experiencing a negative emotion, it must be an accurate reflection of reality.
9. *Personalization* is a cognitive distortion whereby you entirely blame yourself, or someone else, for a situation that in reality involved many factors that were out of your control.
10. *Labeling* is a cognitive distortion that involves making a judgment about yourself or someone else as a person, rather than seeing the behavior as something the person did that does not define them as an individual.

THE GOTTMAN METHOD

John Gottman's original research was devoted to the discovery of reliable patterns in observational data, testing to see whether there were indeed patterns of behavior, or sequences of interactions, that could discriminate happy from unhappy couples (Gottman, 1999, 2002).

Gottman and his colleagues built an apartment laboratory at the University of Washington that was dubbed the "Love Lab" by the media. This is where they discovered the basis of friendship and intimacy and its relation to conflict in their Bids and Turning Coding System. With that work they discovered how couples create and maintain friendship and intimacy and how this is related to conflict.

Together with his wife, Julie, Gottman started building the Sound Relationship House theory. That theory became the basis of the design of clinical interventions for couples in John Gottman's 1999 book, *The Marriage Clinic: A Scientifically Based Marital Therapy*. In 1996, they founded The Gottman Institute to continue to develop evidence-based approaches to improving couples therapy outcomes.

One of Gottman's most clinically relevant research findings is the Four Horsemen of the Apocalypse—criticism, contempt, defensiveness, and stonewalling. Each of these behaviors can create major problems in a relationship.

Criticism is the first horseman. In a relationship, it is never helpful to criticize a partner's character. If a partner is unhappy with a specific thing their significant other did, it may be necessary to express the complaint, but it is important to do so without attacking the partner for who they are. Instead of criticizing the partner, complaints should be addressed by using "I" statements to talk about what is needed from the partner.

The second horseman, *contempt*, is perhaps the most corrosive for any relationship. When a partner expresses contempt in their communication style, they are assuming a morally superior position and a complete disavowal of their partner. This can manifest in ridiculing the partner, mocking them, or using sarcasm. Contempt is often fueled by unaddressed negative feelings toward the partner. Instead of approaching a conversation or a conflict with contempt, it is important to recall the qualities admired in a partner and to affirm positive things they do.

The third horseman is *defensiveness*, which is often a response to criticism. Being defensive often involves finding excuses and trying to reallocate blame, which is never constructive. The antidote to defensiveness is taking responsibility, accepting your partner's influence, and apologizing when appropriate.

The fourth horseman is *stonewalling*, which is normally a response to contempt. Stonewalling occurs when a partner completely shuts down and withdraws during a conversation. Stonewalling is a result of physiological flooding, making it virtually impossible to converse effectively while in this state. To avoid stonewalling during an argument, a partner should acknowledge that they are overwhelmed and move away from the topic until they are ready to talk about it rationally and productively.

Gottman discovered successful couples engage in a 5:1 ratio. This ratio represents the positive to negative interactions within the relationship. Therefore, this means that for every one negative interaction, there are five positive interactions. It is important to experience more positives than negatives in a relationship, as negative interactions are more powerful and partners tend to dwell on them.

SEX THERAPY

Sex therapy is a type of psychotherapy in which concerns about sexual function, feelings, health, and intimacy are discussed with a trained clinician. It focuses specialized clinical skills on helping men and women as individuals and/or as couples to deal more effectively with their sexual expression.

William Masters and Virginia Johnson proposed a four-stage "linear" model of human sexual response based on some 10,000 recordings of changes in participants' physiology during sexual activity. From these data, they identified four successive stages: (a) excitement, (b) plateau, (c) orgasm, and (d) resolution (Masters & Johnson, 1966).

Although Masters and Johnson's model was intentionally focused on physiological changes, it was nevertheless criticized for being too narrow in its conceptualization. Along with other developments, Helen Kaplan proposed a triphasic model of sexual functioning—consisting of (a) desire, (b) excitement, and (c) orgasm—the most significant contributions being the critical addition of *sexual desire* and recognizing the importance of psychological factors in sexual response. Kaplan viewed desire as a precondition for subsequent sexual excitement/arousal and orgasm, thereby maintaining the linearity of the sexual response cycle. An interest in sex was essential for the body to become physiologically aroused. But the concept of desire was also intended to encapsulate a range of psychological, emotional, and cognitive aspects of human sexual response (Kaplan, 2013).

ASSESSMENT

PARENT TRAINING

Assessment in behavioral parent training entails observing and recording the frequency of the behavior to be changed, as well as the events that precede it and those that follow. Interviews, usually with the mother, are designed to provide a definition of the problem and a list of potential reinforcers. Observations maybe conducted behind a one-way mirror or during home visits. Typically, parents are trained to pinpoint problem behavior, record its occurrence, and note various actions that might serve as stimuli and reinforcers. Checklists and questionnaires provide information that may have been overlooked in interviews (Falloon, 1988).

TRADITIONAL BEHAVIORAL COUPLES THERAPY

Assessment in TBCT involves a behavioral analysis of the couple's distress. This analysis is based on interviewing, administering self-report questionnaires, and making behavioral observations. Two major areas of inquiry must be answered during the assessment process: What are the problematic behaviors that each partner would like to change, and how are these problematic behaviors currently reinforced in the relationship? Assessments are designed to reveal strengths and weaknesses of a couple's relationship and the manner in which rewards and punishments are exchanged (Jacobson & Margolin, 1979).

INTEGRATIVE BEHAVIORAL COUPLE THERAPY

The first three sessions in IBCT are devoted to a clinical assessment of the couple, which leads to a case formulation of the couple. This involves conducting a DEEP (**d**ifferences, **e**motional sensitivities, **e**xternal stressors, and the **p**attern of interaction) assessment. An initial conjoint session focuses on the presenting problems of the couple and their relationship history. The second and third sessions are individual sessions with each partner in which information on the presenting complaints and an individual history of each spouse is obtained. In the fourth session, IBCT therapists share with the couple a formulation of their problems based on information obtained in the previous three sessions from the interviews and related questionnaires. One can think of this formulation as a new story written about the problem. Typically, a couple comes to therapy with two stories about the problem—one generated by each partner, who emphasizes the faults in the other. The formulation provides a single unified story that takes into account both partners' experiences and puts them together in a nonblaming framework (Christensen et al., 2015; Jacobson & Christensen, 1996).

COGNITIVE BEHAVIORAL THERAPY

The goals of a cognitive behavioral assessment are to (a) identify strengths and problems in individuals, the couple or family, and the environment; (b) place individual and family functioning in the context of developmental stages; and (c) identify cognitive, emotional, and behavioral aspects of family interaction that might be targeted for intervention. Among the family patterns of interaction therapists look for are the style and degree to which family members express their thoughts and feelings to each other, who interrupts whom, and who speaks for whom (Epstein & Baucom, 2002).

After collecting sufficient information from interviews, questionnaires, and behavioral observations, the therapist meets with the couple or family and offers a summary of the patterns that have emerged, including the family's strengths, major concerns, stressors, and patterns of interaction that seem to be influencing their present difficulties (Epstein & Baucom, 2002).

THE GOTTMAN METHOD

With this method, a conjoint session, followed by individual interviews with each partner, is conducted. Couples complete questionnaires and then receive detailed feedback on their relationship (Gottman, 1999).

SEX THERAPY

A physiological assessment by medical professionals is indicated in the assessment of sexual problems and is usually recommended prior to beginning therapy to rule out any physical causes of the problem.

Sex therapy usually begins with an evaluation and assessment of the particular sexual problem and its impact on the couple relationship. This assessment has historically included taking an extensive sexual history of both partners, interviewed separately. Masters and Johnson advocated the use of a semi-structured interview that typically lasted for several hours. However, as pointed out by LoPiccolo, the utility of this type of interview has not been empirically demonstrated and its application may not be the most efficient use of therapeutic time (LoPiccolo & Steger, 1974).

Paper-and-pencil questionnaires are also commonly used to assess sexual history and current sexual functioning. These questionnaires can provide valuable information to the therapist by identifying arousal deficits and problem behaviors that can be the focus of treatment. They are also useful tools for identifying significant discrepancies in thoughts, feelings, and behaviors reported by the partners.

Following these initial assessment procedures, the therapist presents a comprehensive formulation of the etiology and maintenance of the dysfunction to the couple. Their sex histories, family-of-origin dynamics, cognitive styles, current relationship structure, external reinforcers, and any organic factors are used in this formulation, and the couple is informed about how these factors have interacted to create and maintain their sexual problems. This presentation is useful in initiating change procedures and sometimes has positive effects on the sexual problem itself (Hertlein et al., 2009).

INTERVENTIONS AND TECHNIQUES

PARENT TRAINING

A contingency contract is a written document between the parent or parents and child. Contracting is an effective instrument when the parent is trying to get the child to take more responsibility for their behavior; that is, contracting is particularly useful for clients who are aware of the negative consequences of their behavior and would like to do something about it. The contract is the parent and child's commitment to change. Contracting is a form of structured bargaining that specifies clearly what is expected. The therapist facilitates mutual agreements between opposing parties about reciprocal exchanges of mutual behaviors, reinforcers, and punishers. This approach has been highly successful with parent–youth conflicts. Contracts usually specify that the child can engage in a high-preference activity, such as watching television, when the child has completed a low-preference activity, such as completing chores (the Premack Principle). This principle posits that more probable behaviors will reinforce less probable behaviors (Premack, 1965).

Although programs vary in content and method of teaching, their basic content includes the following elements (Falloon, 1988):

1. *Introduction to social learning theory.* Basic principles of reinforcement are generally covered in this phase.
2. *Identification of the problem behaviors and controlling conditions.* Parents are taught to define problems in specific behavioral terms so that they can be objectively measured. Parents are then taught to identify the antecedents and consequences of the problem behavior.
3. *Gathering a baseline of the problem behavior.* Parents are taught to record the frequency or duration (or both) of the problem behavior. Once parents have collected baseline data, they are taught to graph the behavior to assess progress.
4. *Stating rules or directions.* Parents are taught how to state rules. Rules should be specific and positive and should include a time (e.g., today, end of the week) when the rule should be followed.
5. *Positive reinforcement.* Teaching the use of positive reinforcement generally focuses on increasing the frequency and range of reinforcers used by parents. Parents are taught to praise their child, thus reinforcing desired behavior. Parents are also taught to selectively reinforce behaviors (e.g., playing quietly) that are incompatible with an undesirable target behavior (for example, fighting).

6. *Ignoring undesirable behaviors*. Parents are taught to ignore behaviors that they can tolerate and that are not harmful to the child. If parents cannot ignore undesirable behaviors, they are taught to give verbal reprimands. Verbal reprimands are effective in decreasing noncompliance, whereas simple repetition of a command may be ineffective (Forehand et al., 1979).
7. *Teaching new behaviors*. When certain behaviors do not exist in the child's repertoire, parents often use shaping, modeling, instructions, and prompting to assist the child in developing new behaviors.
8. *Time out or isolation*. If children are behaving in ways that are harmful to themselves or others (e.g., fighting), then time out is most effective. Time out involves isolating the child in a neutral area devoid of reinforcing persons or objects. Time out is effective only when used in conjunction with reinforcement techniques (i.e., a child must lose the opportunity to earn reinforcement when sent to take time out). In teaching the use of time out, therapists encourage parents to give a warning to the child before administering time out.

TRADITIONAL BEHAVIORAL COUPLES THERAPY

Overall, behavioral couple therapy typically includes three basic components (Jacobson & Margolin, 1979):

1. The establishment of positive reciprocity, that is, a mutual or cooperative exchange of rewarding and valued behaviors between partners.
2. Communication skills training: Here couples learn to use "I" statements to express their feelings. They also learn to stick to here-and-now problems rather than dwell on the past. Furthermore, they begin to describe their spouse's specific behavior rather than apply a label to it, such as *lazy, aloof*, or *frigid*. Finally, in communication skills training, an individual is taught how to provide positive feedback to their significant other in response to similar behavior from that person.
3. Training in problem-solving: This component of behavioral couple therapy helps equip couples with new problem-solving skills, such as specifying what they want, negotiating for it, and making a contract.

The behavioral exchange model relies on the principle of social exchange (reciprocity). Within this model, each partner "gives" in order to "get" an increase in desired behaviors from the other. Behavioral exchange appears to work best when both parties possess resources (i.e., have reinforcement potential that is valuable to each other). When both partners have equal or nearly equal resources, then it is likely they will be willing to compromise. But when one spouse has more resources than the other, negotiation and compromise appear unlikely. Spouses are encouraged to request change by directly identifying the specific behaviors they wish to see more frequently. The goal is to eliminate undesirable behaviors, replacing them with desirable behaviors. Behavioral exchange attempts to extinguish undesirable behaviors and increase desirable behaviors that are more rewarding to both partners in the relationship.

Another variation of the behavioral exchange procedure is the use of "caring days." On caring days, each partner makes a special effort to please the other by engaging in a significantly greater number of caring behaviors than the other spouse expects. Richard Stuart, innovator of this intervention, asks partners to request specific behaviors that they would like to receive from one another and to increase the number of requests they make each day. For example, a spouse may request a back rub or a special meal. The assumption is that caring behaviors will increase positive feelings between the two partners. Spouses also learn the importance of making requests rather than assuming that their partner knows what is wanted. This type of technique embodies the idea of a positive risk, which is a unilateral action that is not dependent on another for success (Stuart, 2003).

INTEGRATIVE BEHAVIORAL COUPLE THERAPY

The intervention in IBCT consists of the familiar TBCT (strategies for change) techniques and new, acceptance and tolerance-based techniques. The acceptance/tolerance strategies are used as tools to manage incompatibilities, the differences that seem irreconcilable or unsolvable problems (Christensen et al., 2015; Jacobson & Christensen, 1996).

- *Empathic joining* around the problem is one of the first acceptance steps. Therapists emphasize the pain and honest efforts made by each partner without accusation. The formulation itself becomes a central vehicle for this joining by casting the couple's dilemma as flowing from an honest difference that naturally leads to polarization and eventually alienation. Therapists emphasize using "soft" rather than "hard" emotion descriptions in their reflections, and they encourage the partners to do the same.
- Encouraging *unified detachment*, or making the problem an "it" follows from empathic joining. Rather than blaming each other, the problem is externalized and often given a metaphorical name as an "it."
- *Tolerance techniques* can facilitate the path to acceptance. The procedures to finding acceptance would be pointing out positive features in negative behavior, practicing negative behavior in the therapy session, faking negative behaviors at home between sessions, and promoting tolerance through self-care.

COGNITIVE BEHAVIORAL THERAPY

Cognitive interventions are designed to increase family members' skills at monitoring the validity of their own cognitions regarding their important interpersonal relationships. *Cognitive restructuring* refers to the process of challenging and changing irrational thoughts. Socratic questioning is one technique used to encourage this process. Therapists use verbal Socratic questioning by asking probing questions about their clients' irrational thoughts. As clients improve their awareness of irrational thoughts, they can begin to consciously question their own thoughts. Examples include: *Can you provide an example that supports what you are saying? Can we validate that evidence? Do we have all the information we need?*

To improve their skill in identifying automatic thoughts, clients are encouraged to keep a diary and jot down situations that provoke automatic thoughts and the resulting emotional responses. The therapist's role then is to ask a series of questions about these assumptions, rather than to challenge them directly (Beck, 2005).

- *Simple thought record thought-monitoring worksheet.* A simple thought record worksheet is a great way of introducing clients to the process of monitoring their thoughts. It contains space in which to record the situation where the thought occurred, how it made them feel, and the thought or image that went through their mind at that time. It is helpful to remind clients that they should carry the thought-monitoring worksheet with them so that they can make a note as soon as they practically can after they notice the thought. It is helpful to advise that the best time to complete a thought record worksheet is whenever a client notices a sudden change in how they are feeling.
- *CBT thought-challenging record worksheet.* Challenging negative automatic thoughts (NATs) about your significant other or family member is an essential cognitive restructuring

technique in couple and family cognitive behavioral therapy. Once clients have become adept at noticing and capturing their negative automatic thoughts, the next step is to examine how accurate they are and to learn to challenge unhelpful or inaccurate thoughts. A CBT thought record contains space in which to identify where and when a negative thought occurred, how it made you feel, and some details about the thought itself. The next steps encourage clients to identify all of the evidence that supports the truthfulness of the thought: *"What facts make you believe that thought is true?"* The next step requires clients to identify all of the evidence that might contradict the negative automatic thought; *"What facts make you think this thought might not be 100% true all of the time?"* Most clients find this step to be more difficult and may initially need more support. Once clients have identified as much contradictory evidence as they can, the final step is to generate a more balanced thought, which takes into account all of the evidence for and against the original negative automatic thought. This more balanced thought is often longer because it is more nuanced than the original NAT.

Frank Dattilio (1999) introduced the "pad-and-pencil" technique to help family members overcome the annoying habit of interrupting each other. Family members are given a pad and pencil and asked to record the automatic thoughts that go through their minds when someone else in the family is talking (Dattilio, 1999).

Recently, mindfulness meditation has been employed as an adjunct to cognitive behavioral therapy with couples and families. Mindfulness teaches open and receptive attention to the present moment, which in turn promotes a less reactive response to challenging emotions (Gehart, 2012).

THE GOTTMAN METHOD

Interventions are designed to help couples develop antidotes to the Four Horsemen and strengthen their relationships in three primary areas: friendship, conflict management, and creation of shared meaning. Couples learn to replace negative conflict patterns with positive interactions and to repair past hurts. Interventions designed to increase closeness and intimacy are used to improve friendship, deepen emotional connection, and create changes, which enhances the couples' shared goals. Relapse prevention is also addressed.

The Sound Relationship House theory is the foundation of the Gottman Method. It uses a house as a metaphor for a secure relationship. The theory identifies seven levels or "floors" of the relationship house that a couple can move through to improve their relationship, along with two "weight-bearing walls," which are essential to holding the couple together. These are as follows (Gottman, 1999, 2002):

1. *Build love maps:* This is the first level of the Sound Relationship House and involves couples getting to know one another's inner psychological worlds.
2. *Share fondness and admiration:* On this level, couples learn to overtly express appreciation and respect for each other to strengthen their bond.
3. *Turn toward, not away:* This level involves learning to notice when one's partner is seeking attention, affection, and comfort and responding accordingly.
4. *The positive perspective:* This level helps partners learn to see one another positively, enabling them to see errors as matters of circumstance, not failures of the individual.
5. *Manage conflict:* On this level, couples learn to manage conflict through a three-step process. First, partners take each other's feelings into account. Next, partners learn to discuss their problems. Finally, when a partner starts to feel overwhelmed during conflict, they learn techniques to self-soothe to keep their cool.
6. *Make life dreams come true:* The penultimate level centers on supporting and championing one's partner in their dreams and goals.

7. *Create shared meaning:* The top level of the house mirrors the first level in that it involves understanding an inner world, but in this case, it's the couple's inner world and entails uncovering the rituals and stories that have shared meaning for them.
8. *Trust and commitment:* The two weight-bearing walls of the Sound Relationship House help couples work through the seven levels. Trust enables couples to believe they can rely on one another and feel like they're a team, and commitment means couples have agreed to stick together and to improve their relationship.

SEX THERAPY

Sensate-focus techniques often are customized for individual couples, but they generally follow the four stages outlined below (Masters & Johnson, 1966):

Stage 1—Each partner spends about 30 minutes caressing the other's naked body, head to toe and front and back, except for the genitals and breasts. The emphasis is on the "giver" touching in a way that they enjoy. The aim is to focus on each sensation and the reaction to it. If this is too much too soon, couples can start by holding hands or giving back rubs.

Stage 2—The couple repeats the exercise from Stage 1, except this time the "receiver" tells the giver what kind of touching they want and give direction on what is most enjoyable.

Stage 3—The couple expands the exercise from Stage 2 to include touching of the genitals and breasts, but not exclusively. The focus remains concentrating on sensations and expressing wants and pleasures without the goal of orgasm.

Stage 4— The couple now may engage in mutual touching and stimulation to the point of orgasm, including intercourse if mutually desired.

ROLE OF THE THERAPIST

The role of the therapist in couple and family behavioral and cognitive behavioral models is one of teacher and coach; the coach psychoeducates and instructs clients to work through their maladaptive thoughts and behaviors.

ORIENTATION IN TIME

Behavioral and cognitive behavioral approaches to couple and family therapy focus on the present. Past patterns and history are not emphasized. Treatment should be time-limited.

PROCESS AND GOALS OF THERAPY

PARENT TRAINING

The goals of behavioral parent training are to eliminate undesirable behavior and substitute desirable behavior as defined by the parent or parents. If desired behaviors or goals are stated in vague or imprecise terms by the parents, the therapist should help transform them into specific, measurable goals. A parent may request help from the therapist in eliminating a problem behavior, such as temper tantrums or fighting, but may have given less thought to an alternative to fighting or tantrums. If parents wish to eliminate an undesirable attention-getting behavior, they must replace it with a desirable behavior that provides the child with an equal or greater amount of attention. The process of identifying desired behaviors or goals provides a standard by which the therapist can measure progress. The effectiveness of therapy is measured by whether or not the parent reaches the goal with the child (Falloon, 1988).

TRADITIONAL BEHAVIORAL COUPLES THERAPY

TBCT uses a broad range of social exchange and problem-solving techniques to change maladaptive behaviors, with the goal of therapy being to reinforce desirable behaviors and eliminate unwanted ones in the couple relationship (Jacobson & Margolin, 1979).

INTEGRATIVE BEHAVIORAL COUPLE THERAPY

The goal of IBCT is to increase partner acceptance of those problems and issues within the relationship that are not inherently solvable. Even though the focus is on acceptance, the IBCT therapist does not tell each partner what is acceptable. The therapist is trying to create conditions that will lead to greater acceptance. If these evocative strategies that focus on greater acceptance are not sufficient to bring about the desired increase in relationship satisfaction, the IBCT therapist may also use some of the well-known, change-oriented, prescriptive strategies of TBCT. IBCT therapists may teach the couple communication training or problem-solving to help them handle their problems more effectively and directly. As couples improve, the IBCT therapist may space out sessions for longer periods of time until they reach a termination session. This termination session often includes a repeat of the DEEP formulation but is enhanced with additional information gleaned over the course of therapy and emphasizing the positive changes that have occurred in the relationship (Christensen et al., 2015; Jacobson & Christensen, 1996).

THE GOTTMAN METHOD

By working through the levels of the Sound Relationship House, couples can learn to increase affection and intimacy, achieve greater levels of empathy and understanding, and more effectively solve problems. The goals of therapy include: (a) enhancing friendship, (b) modifying existing conflict, and (c) creating shared meaning (Gottman, 1999, 2002).

COGNITIVE BEHAVIORAL THERAPY

A major goal of the cognitive approach is to help clients learn to identify and successfully counter the automatic negative thoughts about their significant others and family members that flash through their minds (Epstein & Baucom, 2002).

SEX THERAPY

The goal of sex therapy is to empower couples to understand the nature and sources of their sexual problems, better express their sexual wants and needs, and broaden their menu of sensual and sexual expression. A frequent aim is to enhance the pleasure and intimacy of a couple's sexual activity without the pressure to always have intercourse or achieve orgasm (Hertlein et al., 2009).

CONCLUSION

Although behavior therapists have applied their techniques to parents and children prior to the rise of family therapy, their approach was linear in nature. Family symptoms are treated as learned responses, involuntarily acquired and reinforced. Based on social learning theory, problematic behavior is maintained by its consequences and can be modified by altering those consequences. This focus has been broadened considerably by the introduction of cognitive interventions to address unhelpful assumptions and distorted beliefs. Clients are taught general principles of behavior management along with methods for reevaluating automatic thoughts with an attempt to identify distortions and address misconceptions. The behaviorists' focus on modifying the consequences of problem behavior accounts for the strengths and weaknesses of this approach. Currently, cognitive and behavioral approaches are having a significant impact in distinct areas: behavioral parent training, TBCT, IBCT, couple CBT, the Gottman Method, and sex therapy.

KEY TERMS

Acceptance building: In integrative behavioral couple therapy (IBCT), *acceptance building* refers to strategies involving empathic joining around the couple problem, unified detachment from the problem, tolerance building, and self-care.

Active listening: A psychotherapeutic technique in which the therapist listens to a client closely and attentively, asking questions as needed, to fully understand the content of the message and the depth of the client's emotion. The therapist typically restates what has been said to ensure accurate understanding.

Assumptions: Beliefs about how people generally behave in family relationships.

Attributions: Explanations for specific actions or events. Attributions for the actions of family members may be classified as personal (where the person is blamed) or situational (where the circumstances are blamed).

Aversive control: Using punishment and criticism to eliminate undesirable responses; commonly used in dysfunctional families.

Backwards chaining: Shaping a complex behavioral response pattern by beginning with reinforcing the last step in the sequence and successively working backwards.

Baseline: A record, usually established through monitoring, of problematic and positive behaviors prior to intervention.

Behavior exchange theory: Explanation of behavior in relationships as maintained by a ratio of costs to benefits.

Behavioral rehearsal: Procedures that involve practicing a desired behavior until it is learned and performed the way one wishes, for example, asking for directions. The process consists of gradually shaping a behavior and getting corrective feedback.

Bridge maneuver: Intervention pioneered by Helen Singer Kaplan requiring manual stimulation or masturbation by the female in an effort to produce orgasm; use gradually decreases as treatment progresses and partner can begin to fill the role.

Caring days: In discordant couples, these days are used to increase the amount of noncontingent reinforcement within the relationship by inviting couples to concurrently increase the rate with which they engage in behaviors their spouse has identified as helpful or loving.

Classical conditioning: A form of respondent learning in which an unconditioned stimulus (UCS), such as food, which leads to an unconditioned response (UCR), such as salivation, is paired with a conditioned stimulus (CS), such as a bell, the result of which is that the CS begins to evoke the same response as the UCS; used in the behavioral treatment of anxiety disorders.

Coercion: A process in which the behaviors of two family members are maintained by mutual negative reinforcement.

Cognition: A thought, idea, or conscious intellectual process involved in knowing.

Cognitive behavioral therapy (CBT): Treatment that emphasizes attitude change as well as reinforcement of behavior.

Cognitive distortions: Pervasive and systematic errors in reasoning that are negative and inaccurate and can result in unhealthy misperceptions of events.

Cognitive restructuring: A cognitive therapeutic process for coping with stress that involves replacing stress-provoking or irrational thoughts with more constructive or rational thoughts, thus helping clients recognize and modify their inner dialogue and develop coping self-statements.

Coital alignment technique (CAT): An intervention used to increase mutual stimulation through full body contact during intercourse in which the male learns to position and maneuver on top of the female.

Contempt: Negative communication that attacks or tears down the partner's self-worth with the intention of insulting or psychologically abusing them; one of the behaviors in Gottman's Four Horsemen of the Apocalypse.

Contingency contracting: A behavior therapy technique whereby agreements are made between family members to exchange rewards for desired behavior.

Criticism: Negative communication that attacks or complains about a relational partner's personality or character rather than the behavior that bothers the other partner; one of the behaviors in Gottman's Four Horsemen of the Apocalypse.

Defensiveness: Negative behavior that occurs when a person starts to see themselves as the victim and denies responsibility; one of the behaviors in Gottman's Four Horsemen of the Apocalypse.

Directed masturbation training: LoPiccolo's technique for treating anorgasmic women that teaches a woman to touch herself, and then her partner, in various ways to trigger her orgasm.

Dysfunctional thoughts: Thoughts that are nonproductive and unrealistic.

Exposure and response prevention: A procedure whereby clients with obsessive-compulsive disorder are exposed to obsession- and anxiety-provoking stimuli and are prevented from engaging in anxiety-reducing compulsive rituals.

Extinction: Eliminating behavior by not reinforcing it.

Flooding: A procedure whereby phobic clients habituate to anxiety-provoking stimuli through sustained exposure to maximally anxiety-provoking stimuli.

Four Horsemen of the Apocalypse: The four negative partner-response behaviors (criticism, contempt, defensiveness, and stonewalling) described by John Gottman that are strong relationship dissolution warning signs.

Functional analysis of behavior: In operant behavior therapy, a study of a particular behavior, what elicits it, and what reinforces it.

Gunnysacking: The behavior of storing up a complaint and bringing it up as a surprise during a disagreement in order to provoke.

"I" statement: An expression of feelings and thoughts that uses the first-person singular "I" in a way that encourages others to express their personal opinions and beliefs as well as take responsibility for one's actions, emotions, or thoughts by using the pronoun "I" at the beginning of any statement.

Kitchen sinking: The behavior of rehashing old arguments or bringing up totally unrelated issues during a new argument.

Operant conditioning: A form of learning whereby a person or animal is rewarded for performing certain behaviors; the major approach in most forms of behavior therapy.

Partial reinforcement: Also known as *intermittent reinforcement*. A schedule of reinforcement used to maintain a behavior, once it is established, through continuous reinforcement. In partial reinforcement, a reward is given at intervals that vary but are frequent enough to maintain the client's interest.

Premack Principle: Using a high-probability behavior (preferred activities) to reinforce a low-probability behavior (nonpreferred activities).

Problem-solving skills training: Coaching couple clients through modeling and role-play to define large daunting problems as a series of small solvable problems; each problem is addressed through the same process: brainstorming possible solutions, evaluating the pros and cons of these, selecting one, jointly implementing it, reviewing progress, and modifying the selected solution if it is ineffective or celebrating success if the problem is resolved.

Punishment: The presentation of an aversive stimulus or the removal of a pleasant stimulus. Punishment decreases the frequency of the occurrence of some undesirable behavior.

Quid pro quo contract: A contingency contract for couples in which the consequences for both parties of engaging in target positive behaviors are specified and linked.

Reinforcement: An event, behavior, or object that increases the rate of a particular response. A positive reinforcer is an event whose contingent presentation increases the rate of responding; a negative reinforcer is an event whose contingent withdrawal increases the rate of responding.

Reinforcement reciprocity: The exchange of rewarding behaviors between family members.

Relaxation training: Training clients to reduce physiological arousal and anxiety by systematically tensing and relaxing all major muscle groups and visualizing a calming scene.

Schemas: Underlying core beliefs that an individual has developed about the world and how it functions.

Sensate focus: A sex therapy procedure devised by William H. Masters and Virginia E. Johnson to eliminate performance anxiety by instructing a couple to engage in nonerotic touching.

Shaping: An operant conditioning procedure that involves reinforcing responses that come successfully closer to the desired response; the process of learning in small gradual steps. Shaping is often referred to as *successive approximation*.

Social exchange theory: Thibaut and Kelley's theory according to which people strive to maximize rewards and minimize costs in a relationship.

Social learning theory: This theory uses understanding and treatment of behavior using principles from social and developmental psychology as well as from learning theory.

Spectatoring: Occurs when one gets distracted by performance anxiety and loses focus during sex rather than connecting with one's partner and enjoying the moment; focusing on a critical internal dialogue instead of allowing oneself to relax and focus purely on the feelings and sensations within the body.

Squeeze technique: A technique devised by Masters and Johnson for overcoming premature ejaculation: The penis is stimulated until the man is aroused, then the partner briefly squeezes the head of the penis where it joins the shaft. When the squeeze is released, a pause in stimulation is taken for 30 seconds to 1 minute. The squeeze and pause lower arousal, and stimulation is then resumed. After several stimulate–squeeze–pause–stimulate cycles, the man is stimulated to ejaculation. This procedure conditions the man to maintain an erection longer before ejaculation.

Standards: Beliefs about how people generally should behave in family relationships.

Star chart: A reward system in which a child receives a star on a wall chart each time they complete a target behavior. A collection of stars may be cashed in for a prize from a reinforcement menu.

Stonewalling: Negative behavior characterized by withdrawal from the interaction or, potentially, from the relationship to avoid conflict; one of the behaviors in Gottman's Four Horsemen of the Apocalypse.

Stop–start technique: A behavioral technique used to improve premature ejaculation in men, it builds confidence and bodily control by extending the amount of time men can last before orgasm.

Systematic desensitization: A counterconditioning process in which a person's dysfunctional anxiety is reduced or eliminated through pairing it with incompatible behavior, such as muscular or mental relaxation. This is a step-by-step gradual procedure in which events that produce increasingly higher levels of anxiety are treated by being paired with relaxation procedures and positive imagery one at a time.

Thought stopping: A cognitive behavioral theory technique in which clients are taught how to stop unproductive obsession about an event or person through overt and mental procedures.

Time out: A process that involves the removal of children from an environment in which they have been reinforced for certain actions. Isolation, or time out, from reinforcement for a limited amount of time results in cessation of the targeted behavior.

Token economy: A system of rewards using points that can be accumulated and exchanged for reinforcing items or behaviors.

Triphasic sexual response: Kaplan's conceptualization to better explain sexual intercourse, which includes sexual desire, excitement, and orgasm.

KNOWLEDGE CHECK: CHAPTER 6

1. Cognitive behavioral family therapists integrate systemic perspective into traditional cognitive behavioral therapy (CBT) methods by exploring how family members ___________ one another's behaviors to maintain ____________ and relational patterns.

   A. Control; symptoms
   B. Reinforce; symptoms
   C. Support; structure
   D. Observe; rewards

2. The major intent of behavioral exchange procedures is to help couples_________.

   A. Stop engaging in quid pro quo score keeping
   B. Increase the rate of rewarding interactions
   C. Resolve sexual arousal disorders
   D. Evaluate treatment outcome

3. One of the behavioral and cognitive behavioral approaches to couple therapy, _______is a scientifically based model derived from 30 years of research on the key differences between happy and unhappy marriages.

   A. Cognitive behavioral couple therapy
   B. Integrative behavioral couple therapy (IBCT)
   C. Gottman Method couple therapy
   D. Rational emotive couple therapy

4. The concept of personalization is a cognitive distortion that _______________.

   A. Focuses on the client's own contribution to the problem
   B. Emphasizes on one or two incidents to make global judgments about another's essential character
   C. Attributes external events to oneself
   D. Assigns blame to a person without proper evidence

(*See answers next page.*)

1. B) Reinforce; symptoms

Cognitive behavioral family therapy is an approach to family therapy that focuses on the use of principles of behavioral modification (namely, contingency contracting and negotiation strategies) and is designed to change the interactional patterns of family members, as well as the restructuring of distorted beliefs and perceptions that develop as a result of faulty interaction. There is also a heavy emphasis on schema, or what is otherwise known as *core beliefs* in an attempt to evaluate how these impinge on the emotions and behaviors of family members' interaction.

2. B) Increase the rate of rewarding interactions

Behavior exchange theory procedures are taught to increase the frequency of desired behavior. A typical device is to ask each partner to list three things they would like the other to do more often. While explicitly exchanging nice gestures in this way, couples are implicitly learning ways of influencing each other through positive reinforcement. Richard Stuart popularized couples "caring days," in which one partner demonstrates caring for the other partner in as many ways as possible.

3. C) Gottman Method couple therapy

Although both options A and B have empirical support, the Gottman Method, (developed by Dr. John Gottman and Dr. Julie Schwartz Gottman in the 1980s) is an evidence-based form of couples therapy that strives to assist couples in achieving a deeper sense of understanding, awareness, empathy, and connectedness within their relationships. By combining therapeutic interventions with couple exercises, this type of therapy helps couples identify and address the natural defenses that hinder effective communication and bonding. In the assessment phase, a joint session is followed by individual interviews with each partner. Couples complete questionnaires and then receive feedback on their relationship. Interventions are designed to help couples strengthen their relationships in three primary areas: friendship, conflict management, and creation of shared meaning. Couples learn to replace negative conflict patterns with positive interactions and to repair past hurts. Interventions designed to increase closeness and intimacy are used to improve friendship, deepen emotional connection, and create changes, which enhances the couple's shared goals. Relapse prevention is also addressed.

4. C) Attributes external events to oneself

Personalization is the belief that you are entirely to blame for something even though you had little or nothing to do with the outcome. In fact, the situation may not be connected to you in any way at all. It can also involve blaming someone else for something for which they have no responsibility. Although personalization and blame can vary from situation to situation, it always involves negative thinking and often hinges on negative self-talk. Some examples of symptoms include feeling like you are being intentionally excluded from a group when you see members interacting together without you, feeling that others are blaming you for something over which you had little or no control, and assuming that you have been targeted by someone's behavior when it actually has nothing to do with you.

5. In their assessment techniques, cognitive behavioral family therapists rely on _____.

A. Observable behaviors
B. Expressed emotions
C. Projective techniques
D. Transgenerational patterns

6. __________ developed the sensate focus technique.

A. Sigmund Freud
B. William Masters and Virginia Johnson
C. David Scnarch
D. Helen Kaplan

7. In contrast to traditional behavioral couples therapy (TBCT), integrative behavioral couple therapy (IBCT) emphasizes__________.

A. Insight
B. Emotional experiencing
C. Tolerance and acceptance
D. Increased focus on solving perpetual problems

8. Which clinical model posits that the thoughts, feelings, and behaviors of one member of the family influence, and are impacted by, other members in the family? Members of the family experience both individual and family-related schemas/core beliefs that influence family process:

A. Rational emotive therapy
B. Experiential family therapy
C. Cognitive behavioral family therapy
D. Dialectical behavior therapy

9. ___________ is an important intervention in cognitive behavioral therapy (CBT) that involves teaching clients psychological and relational principles about their problems and how best to handle them.

A. Psychoeducation
B. Psychoanalysis
C. Psychopharmacology
D. Biofeedback

(*See answers next page.*)

5. A) Observable behaviors

Cognitive behavioral therapy (CBT) practitioners rely on the ABC method to understand an observable behavior in their assessments. ABC is an acronym for antecedents, behavior, consequences. It is used as a tool for the assessment and formulation of problem behaviors and is useful when therapists want to understand the "active ingredients" of a problem behavior. It can be used to identify the triggers for a behavior by monitoring environmental and internal circumstances that occur before the behavior. Attention is also then drawn toward the consequences of the behavior: both short-term and long-term, intended and unintended. When working with clients who are able to engage with talking therapies and reflect on their behavior, the ABC Model is a helpful tool for building the client's awareness of the triggers for their behavior, and the consequences of their actions. When working more cognitively, some clinicians choose to adapt the model slightly to explore the sequence: antecedents > beliefs (Thoughts) > consequences.

6. B) William Masters and Virginia Johnson

Sensate focus is a technique used to improve intimacy and communication between partners around sex; reduce sexual performance anxiety; and shift away from ingrained, goal-oriented sexual patterns that may not be serving a couple. Dr. William H. Masters and Virginia E. Johnson developed this technique.

7. C) Tolerance and acceptance

IBCT assumes that relationship problems result not just from the egregious actions and inactions of partners, but also from their emotional reactivity to those behaviors. Therefore, IBCT focuses on the emotional context between partners and strives to achieve greater acceptance and tolerance between partners as well as make deliberate changes in target problems.

8. C) Cognitive behavioral family therapy

Cognitive behavioral family therapy is an approach that is conducted against the backdrop of systems theory and includes the premise that members of a family simultaneously influence and are influenced by each other. The focus of this approach is placed on thoughts and behaviors and how the behavior of one family member leads to behaviors, cognitions, and emotions in other family members. This, in turn, elicits cognitions, behaviors, and emotions in reciprocal response. As this cycle continues, the volatility of the family dynamics escalates, rendering family members vulnerable to a negative spiral of conflict. With this approach, restructuring distorted beliefs has a pivotal impact on regulating emotions and behaviors and vice versa.

9. A) Psychoeducation

For clients to use CBT effectively, they first need to have a strong understanding of the cognitive model. Psychoeducation usually begins in the first or second session and continues throughout treatment. Educating a client about psychological concepts is crucial when a client has a poor understanding of how their thoughts are linked to emotion and behavior.

10. In the Gottman Method, love maps are ______________.

A. A series of questions to help the couple understand what helps their partner feel loved
B. An outline of things that are hurtful to each partner in the couple
C. A series of questions to help the couple become more aware of the issues that are important to their partner
D. Directions to the Gottman Clinic in Washington

11. An enduring set of beliefs that organizes subsequent perceptions is known as _________.

A. Schemas
B. Automatic thoughts
C. Rituals
D. Attributions

12. Child management problems are frequently dealt with by behavior therapists using a _______________ model.

A. Social modification
B. Social stratification
C. Social adherence
D. Social learning

13. Contingency contracting is a behavioral procedure that is probably most useful with ___________.

A. Young children
B. Adolescents
C. College students
D. The older adults

(*See answers next page.*)

10. C) A series of questions to help the couple become more aware of the issues that are important to their partner

The Gottmans' research found that emotionally intelligent couples are intimately familiar with each other's worlds. This involves having a richly detailed *love map*: the term for that part of your brain where you store all the personally important information about your partner's life. These couples made plenty of cognitive room in their minds for their relationship. They remember the major events in each other's histories, and they keep updating their information as the facts and feelings of their spouse's world change. They know each other's goals in life, worries, and dreams. Without such a love map, you can't know your partner. Couples who have detailed love maps of each other's worlds are better prepared to cope with stressful events and conflict.

11. A) Schemas

Cognitive behavioral therapy (CBT) places a heavy emphasis on schemas, or what are otherwise known as *core beliefs*. The primary aim of the approach is to help family members recognize distortions in their thinking based on erroneous information and restructure their thinking and modify their behavior in order to improve their interactional patterns.

12. D) Social learning

Social learning theory proposes that the real-life experiences and exposures of children directly or indirectly shape their behavior. Children's strategies for managing emotions, resolving disputes, and engaging with others are learned from experience and carried forward across setting and time. For younger children especially, the primary source of these experiences is the parent–child and family relationship environment. Accordingly, interventions to improve child behavior have focused on altering the quality of parenting. Specific parenting behaviors targeted for assessment and treatment are positive attention and praise for the child's desirable behavior, contingency of parental response, as well as directions and instructions that are clear and set limits on undesirable behaviors.

13. B) Adolescents

Contingency contracting, best suited for teens or adolescents, involves the distribution of rewards, penalties, and punishments via a written contract constructed between two or more parties. Contracting is often used in family therapy as a vehicle for problem-solving, but is also an excellent way of providing rewards, penalties, and punishments in a structured and agreed-on format. After a specific behavior is defined as the presenting problem, each party (e.g., parent and adolescent) develops parameters to indicate how they would like the behavior defined and what consequences may follow its presence or absence. Contracting usually requires that each party negotiate behaviors of interest as well as acceptable consequences. Contracting typically begins with a mildly problematic behavior that is easily defined and amenable to placement in a contract. This is done to give the conflicting parties practice at the contracting process and to experience success in problem-solving. Subsequent contracts gradually become more detailed and complex and may involve multiple behaviors and consequences.

14. Dichotomous thinking is a cognitive distortion defined by __________.

A. Going to either extreme of overemphasizing or underemphasizing based on the facts
B. An all-or-nothing mentality
C. Generalizing one or two incidents to make a broad sweeping judgment about another's essential character
D. Focusing on one detail while ignoring the context and other obvious details

15. *When you have completed your homework, you may play your videogame.* In behavioral family therapy, this sentence is an example of a parent's use of ____________.

A. Counterconditioning
B. The Premack Principle
C. Social exchange
D. Shaping

(*See answers next page.*)

14. B) An all-or-nothing mentality

All-or-nothing thinking refers to thinking in extremes. You are either a success or a failure. Your performance was totally good or totally bad. If you are not perfect, then you are a failure. This binary way of thinking does not account for shades of gray, and can be responsible for a great deal of negative evaluations of yourself and others. All-or-nothing thinking often involves using absolute terms, such as *never* or *ever*. This type of faulty thinking can also include an inability to see the alternatives in a situation or solutions to a problem. If clients have anxiety or depression, this often means only seeing the downside of any given situation.

15. B) The Premack Principle

The Premack Principle is a theory of reinforcement that states that a less desired behavior can be reinforced by the opportunity to engage in a more desired behavior. The theory is named after its originator, psychologist David Premack.

AUDIO PODCAST 6.1
Cognitive Behavioral Therapy Overview
Eli A. Karam
https://bcove.video/3cpxWoZ

REFERENCES

Bandura, A. (1969). *Principles of behavior modification*. Holt, Rinehart & Winston.

Beck, A. T. (1976). *Cognitive therapy and the emotional disorders*. International Universities Press.

Beck, J. (2005). *Cognitive therapy for challenging problems: What to do when the basic don't work*. Guilford Press.

Bjork, D. W. (1997). *BF Skinner: A life*. American Psychological Association.

Christensen, A., Dimidjian, S., & Martell, C. R. (2015). Integrative behavioral couple therapy. In A. S. Gurman, J. Lebow, & D. K. Snyder (Eds.), *Clinical handbook of couple therapy*. Guilford Press.

Dattilio, F. M. (1999). Pad and pencil technique. *Journal of Family Psychotherapy, 10*(1), 75–80.

Dattilio, F. M. (2010). *Cognitive-behavioral therapy with couples and families: A comprehensive guide for clinicians*. Guilford Press.

Ellis, A. (1962). *Reason and emotion in psychotherapy*. Lyle Stuart.

Epstein, N., & Baucom, D. (2002). *Enhanced cognitive behavioral therapy for couples: A contextual approach*. American Psychological Association.

Falloon, I. R. H. (1988). *Handbook of behavioral family therapy*. Guilford Press.

Forehand, R., Sturgis, E. T., McMahon, R. J., Aguar, D., Green, K., Wells, K. C., & Breiner, J. (1979). Parent behavioral training to modify child noncompliance: Treatment generalization across time and from home to school. *Behavior Modification, 3*(1), 3–25.

Gehart, D. (2012). *Mindfulness and acceptance in couple and family therapy*. Springer Publishing Company.

Gottman, J. M. (1999). *The marriage clinic: A scientifically based marital therapy*. W. W. Norton.

Gottman, J. M. (2002). *The seven principles for making marriage work*. Three Rivers Press.

Heiman, J., & LoPiccolo, J. (1988). *Becoming orgasmic: A sexual and personal growth program for women*. Prentice Hall.

Hertlein, K. M., Weeks, G. R., & Gambescia, N. (2009). *Systemic sex therapy*. Routledge/Taylor & Francis.

Jacobson, N. S., & Christensen, A. (1996). *Integrative couple therapy*. W. W. Norton.

Jacobson, N. S., & Margolin, G. (1979). *Marital therapy: Strategies based on social learning and behavior exchange principles*. Psychology Press.

Kaplan, H. S. (2013). *New sex therapy: Active treatment of sexual dysfunctions*. Routledge.

LoPiccolo, J., & Steger, J. C. (1974). The Sexual Interaction Inventory: A new instrument for assessment of sexual dysfunction. *Archives of sexual behavior, 3*(6), 585–595.

Masters, W. H., & Johnson, V. E. (1966). *Human sexual response*. Little Brown.

Premack, D. (1965). Reinforcement theory. In D. Levine (Ed.), *Nebraska Symposium on Motivation* (Vol. 13, pp. 123–188). University of Nebraska Press.

Schnarch, D. M. (1991). *Constructing the sexual crucible: An integration of sexual and marital therapy*. W. W. Norton.

Stuart, R. B. (2003). *Helping couples change: A social learning approach to marital therapy*. Guilford Press.

Transgenerational Family Therapy

7

LEARNING OBJECTIVES

After reading this chapter, you should be able to:

1. Identify model developers and other key figures associated with transgenerational marriage and family therapy (MFT) models
2. Describe assessment processes in transgenerational MFT models
3. Review the main interventions/techniques of transgenerational MFT models
4. Identify goals of transgenerational MFT models
5. Develop the role of the therapist in in transgenerational MFT models

RELEVANT EXAM DOMAINS

- *Domain 1—The Practice of Systemic Therapy*
  Includes tasks related to incorporating systemic theory and perspectives into practice activities and establishing and maintaining ongoing therapeutic relationships with the client system.
- *Domain 2—Assessing, Hypothesizing, and Diagnosing*
  Includes tasks related to assessing the various dimensions of the client system, forming and reformulating hypotheses, and diagnosing the client and family system in order to guide therapeutic activities.
- *Domain 3—Designing and Conducting Treatment*
  Includes tasks related to developing and implementing interventions with the client system.

INTRODUCTION

Transgenerational approaches offer a historical perspective to current family problems by attending to family relational patterns over multiple generations. Proponents of these approaches believe current family patterns are embedded in unresolved issues in the families of origin. If these problems remain unsettled, they persist and repeat across generations, resulting in both individual/family dysfunction and the inability to form attachments, manage intimacy, deal with power, and resolve conflict. This approach to family therapy is most exemplified by Bowen family systems theory and in the work of Ivan Boszormenyi-Nagy and James Framo.

MODEL DEVELOPERS AND SIGNIFICANT CONTRIBUTORS

MURRAY BOWEN

Murray Bowden is the founder of Bowen family systems, the originator of the genogram, and the founder of the American Family Therapy Academy (AFTA). In 1954 Bowen began working at the National Institute of Mental Health (NIMH), where he initiated a project that hospitalized entire families if a member was schizophrenic. When the NIMH project ended in 1959, Bowen moved to Georgetown University, where he began working with families whose problems were less severe. He discovered that many of the same mechanisms he had observed in psychotic families were in use. This convinced him that all families vary along a continuum from emotional fusion to differentiation. Bowen encouraged the direct descendants of his approach to work on triangles and intergenerational patterns in their own families of origin. This generation of trainees has produced the current leaders of Bowenian therapy, such as Michael Kerr at the Georgetown Family Center and Philip Guerin and Thomas Fogarty at the Center for Family Learning.

BETTY CARTER AND MONICA MCGOLDRICK

Although the core concepts of Bowen's theory have changed little over the decades, strong female voices have been added to the MFT profession. Betty Carter at the Family Institute of Westchester and Monica McGoldrick at the Multicultural Family Institute of New Jersey expanded the lens of Bowen family systems with their focus on life cycle stages and the incorporation of a feminist perspective.

IVAN BOSZORMENYI-NAGY

At the Eastern Pennsylvania Psychiatric Institute (EPPI) in Philadelphia, Pennsylvania, Nagy and colleagues started to see inpatient clients with their families instead of treating them individually. He is best known for developing contextual therapy, a comprehensive model that integrates interpersonal, existential, systemic, and intergenerational dimensions of individual and family life and development.

JAMES FRAMO

James Framo was a theorist who used an object relations approach to intergenerational and family-of-origin therapy. He wrote several books, including *Family-of-Origin Therapy: An Intergenerational Approach* (2013).

MODEL OVERVIEW

BOWEN FAMILY SYSTEMS

Bowen was influenced by events in his life history, especially his difficulties with his family of origin. He believed unless individuals examine and address patterns passed down from previous generations, they are likely to repeat these behaviors in their own families. The possibility of repeating certain behaviors in interpersonal relations is particularly likely if family members, especially between the generations, are characteristically either emotionally overinvolved (i.e., fused) with each other or emotionally cut off (psychologically or physically) from each other. Focusing on the family's emotional system, Bowen articulated the following eight interlocking principles (Bowen, 1966, 1978):

1. *Nuclear family emotional process:* Bowen's focus was on patterns that develop in families to defuse anxiety. A key generator of anxiety in families is the perception of either too much closeness or too great a distance in a relationship. The degree of anxiety in any one family will be determined by the current levels of external stress and the sensitivities to particular themes that have been transmitted down the generations. If family members do not have the capacity to adaptively think through their responses to relationship problems, but rather react anxiously to perceived emotional demands from their loved ones, a state of emotional reactivity ensues.
2. *Differentiation: Differentiation of self* refers to the ability of persons to distinguish themselves from their family of origin at an emotional and intellectual level, as well as to balance the intrapsychic and interpersonal dimensions of the self. The level of differentiation exists on a continuum, with *autonomy* at one end (which signals an ability to think through a situation clearly) and *undifferentiated* on the other (which implies an emotional dependency on one's family members, even if one is living away from them). This relationship is described as being fused but was originally conceptualized as an undifferentiated family ego mass. The greater the degree to which these two systems are fused, or undifferentiated, the more the individual responds to the impulses of their emotional system. When an individual is anxious, the systems are also much more likely to fuse and lose their ability to function separately. The extent to which individuals have differentiated their thinking system from their feeling system determines how able they are to maintain a sense of self in a relationship. The more their thinking can be differentiated from their feelings, the more they will sense a separate "self" in an intimate relationship.
3. *Triangles:* There is inherent conflict in dyadic relationships as each partner reacts to the other's reaction until at some point, someone feels threatened. At that point, a third person or entity is brought into the dyadic struggle to reduce tension, thus creating a triangle. In families in which the differentiation is low and tension high, the emotional reactivity reverberates through many interconnected triangles.
4. *Emotional cutoff:* A central hypothesis of Bowen's theory is that the more people maintain emotional contact with the previous generation, the less reactive they will be in current relationships. Bowen describes emotional cutoff as the way undifferentiated family members manage the intensity of fusion between the generations. A cutoff can be achieved through physical distance or through forms of emotional withdrawal. Bowen distinguishes between "breaking away" in emotional cutoff from the family and "growing away" from the family. "Growing away" is viewed as part of differentiation—adult family members follow independent goals while also recognizing that they are part of their family system. A cutoff is more like an escape; people decide to be completely indifferent to their family of origin. Although immediate pressure might be relieved by cutoff, in intense family relationships, it does not improve patterns of reactivity or the individual's level of differentiation.
5. *Family projection process: Family projection process* refers to the observation that children's level of differentiation generally approximates that of their parents. However, this process often distributes differentiation unevenly among the children. One child may grow up with a high level of differentiation, whereas a brother or sister may grow up with a low level of differentiation. Such variability often occurs when parents attempt to diffuse their emotional conflicts through a particular child. In a sense, the parents project their own emotional conflicts onto a child and attempt to control them.

6. *Multigenerational transmission process:* This concept of Bowen's theory describes how patterns, themes, and positions in a triangle are passed down from generation to generation through the projection of parent to child. The impact is different for each child depending on the degree of triangling they have with their parents.
7. *Sibling position:* With regard to sibling position, Bowen stressed that individuals can develop fixed personality characteristics based on their functional birth order in the family. The more closely a marriage replicates a couples' sibling positions in their family of origin, the better their chance for success.
8. *Societal emotional process:* Societal regression essentially extends triangles outside the immediate family domain. According to Bowen, society also produces emotional forces that tend to diminish intellectual functioning and increase chronic anxiety in family systems. It is assumed that societal influences follow the major concepts of the Bowen family systems theory. Bowen family therapists may lead family members in exploring fears and anxieties about how well the world is functioning.

CONTEXTUAL FAMILY THERAPY

Contextual family therapy is a transgenerational approach that encompasses multiple generations in the family session. By revisiting family-of-origin relationships years later in adulthood, the strategies used in this model are intended to recognize the patterns that lead to repair and enrichment of the present and future relationship (Boszormenyi-Nagy, 1965; Boszormenyi-Nagy & Spark, 1973).

ENTITLEMENT

Entitlement, according to Nagy, is the amount of merit a person accrues for behaving in an ethical manner toward others. Entitlement can be constructive or destructive. Constructive entitlement develops when family members receive a fair return for their generosity in the form of acknowledgment, praise, and recognition. Destructive entitlement, conversely, refers to unfair returns and imbalances in family-of-origin relationships that are revisited in future intimate relationships. For example, if a child is parentified, they may seek justice and retribution years later in new relationships. The child, now an adult, believes they should be taken care of and is justified in behaving in this manner because of the unhealthy blueprint fostered in their family of origin.

LOYALTY

Loyalty is an ethical concept of obligation to another person in a close relationship. Although many times this duty is made explicit, loyalty can also be invisible in some cases when children unconsciously take on commitments and obligations to help their families at the expense of their own freedom and growth. Split loyalty occurs when a person is forced to be more loyal or more disloyal to significant people in their life. For example, this can often be seen in children involved in a messy divorce, where to be loyal to one parent, the child must be disloyal to the other.

PARENTIFICATION

This concept refers to the misuse of parental authority by engaging in asymmetrical relationships between parent and child. It's a type of role reversal that causes an imbalance in the trajectory and evolution of normal parent–child relationships. Common examples include children who are forced to "take care" of their parents, and children who are infantilized to meet some unexpressed need of their mother or father.

REVOLVING SLATE

Describing a multigenerational transmission of injustice and destructive entitlement, this process usually occurs when adults are damaged and have unresolved issues with their family of origin. These adults typically seek their entitlement from their own children in order to try and compensate for what they did not get from their own parents in their family of origin. By doing so, they rob their own child of their own just entitlement. This creates the repetition of the same injustices and distrust experienced by the parents in their families, which is then repeated again in the child's experience of their family.

LEDGER OF MERITS

This concept describes the balance between give and take within a relationship. When this ledger is in balance, the feeling of fairness and equity for each family member is stimulated, thus giving people a sense of trustworthiness in the relationship. The contextual therapy approach allows the therapist to pay attention to the balance of the ledger in the family relationships. An imbalance in the system, created if a person continues to give and does not receive back from the relationship, is the foundation for pain, unfairness, and loss of trust.

FOUR DIMENSIONS OF REALITY

1. Facts—Demographics, cultural background, socioeconomic status, basic historical facts, and so on
2. Individual psychology—The domain of most individual psychotherapies
3. Systemic transactions—The domain covered by traditional family systems theory
4. Relational ethics—The balance of fairness in relationships

FRAMO'S FAMILY-OF-ORIGIN THERAPY

In this transgenerational approach, problems originate from an individual's family of origin and are then repeated later in intimate relationships such as with a spouse or child. When early parent–child relationships are negative (hostile, unstable, etc) or overly helpful/intrusive, the child may view all objects (relationships) as all good or all bad when they are an adult. The adult may then put these unrealistic behaviors on present objects, which can cause conflict.

Change occurs when a person understands the issues that originated in the family of origin and how they are projected onto that individual's current intimate relationships. A corrective experience must occur with the individual's family of origin to help facilitate that change (Framo, 1965, 1981).

ASSESSMENT

BOWEN FAMILY SYSTEMS

GENOGRAM SYMBOLS

Prior to becoming an intervention, the genogram is used as powerful assessment tool in Bowen family systems to track patterns and relationships across the generations. Although there is general agreement on the basic genogram structure and symbols, some variations exist from one author to another. If you understand the following rules, you will be able interpret the most detailed genogram.

In Figure 7.1, the male is noted by a square and the female by a circle. A family is shown by a horizontal line connecting the two. The children are placed below the family line from the oldest to the youngest, left to right. In a standard genogram, there are three different types of children (see Figure 7.2): biological/natural child, adopted child, and foster child. A triangle is used to represent a pregnancy, miscarriage, and abortion. In the case of a miscarriage, a diagonal cross is drawn on top of the triangle to indicate the death of the fetus. The abortion is displayed similar to the miscarriage, but with an additional horizontal line. A stillbirth is displayed by gender; however, the gender symbol appears twice as small, whereas the diagonal cross remains the same size. The child links are joined together for multiple births, such as twins, triplets, quadruplets, and so on. Identical twins (or triplets...) are shown through the addition of a horizontal line between the siblings. For example, in Figure 7.3, the mother had two fraternal twin brothers, two identical twin sisters, and triplets, one of whom died at birth.

FAMILY RELATIONSHIPS

The next component of the genogram is the family relationship, used to describe the union of two individuals (see Exhibit 7.1). Other types of family relationships are divorce, separation, cohabitation, engagement, and so on. Genograms can also illustrate the quality of relationships (see Exhibit 7.2).

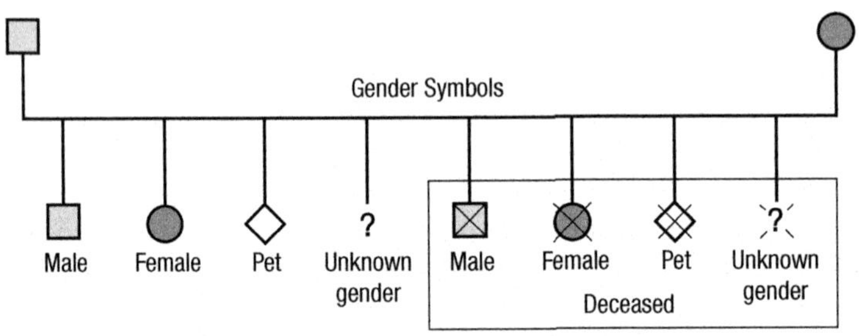

Figure 7.1 Gender Symbols in a Standard Genogram
Source: Adapted from McGoldrick, M., Gerson, R., & Petry, S. S. (2008). ***Genograms: Assessment and intervention***. W. W. Norton.

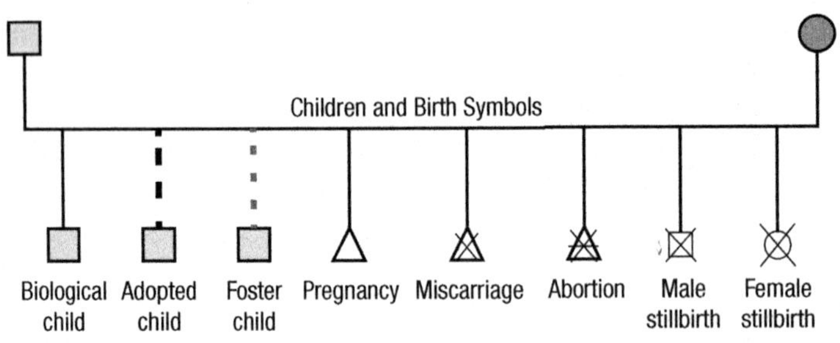

Figure 7.2 Children and Birth Symbols in a Standard Genogram
Source: Adapted from McGoldrick, M., Gerson, R., & Petry, S. S. (2008). ***Genograms: Assessment and intervention***. W. W. Norton.

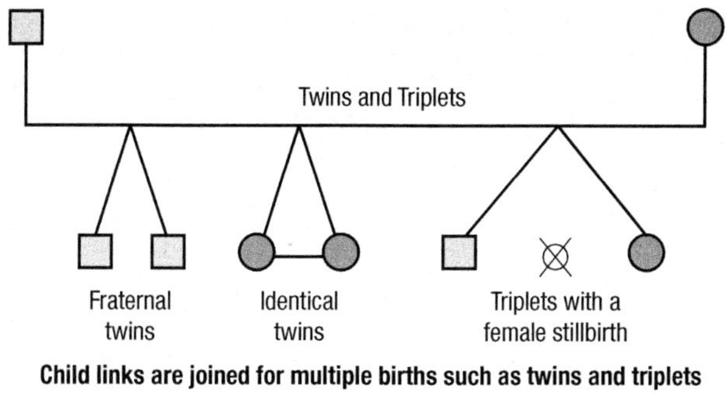

Figure 7.3 Twins and Triplets Illustrated in a Standard Genogram

Source: Adapted from McGoldrick, M., Gerson, R., & Petry, S. S. (2008). ***Genograms: Assessment and intervention***. W. W. Norton.

Exhibit 7.1 Relationships Between Two Individuals in a Standard Genogram

 Marriage	This family relationship represents a married couple. There is no special symbol to distinguish a civil marriage and/or a religious marriage.
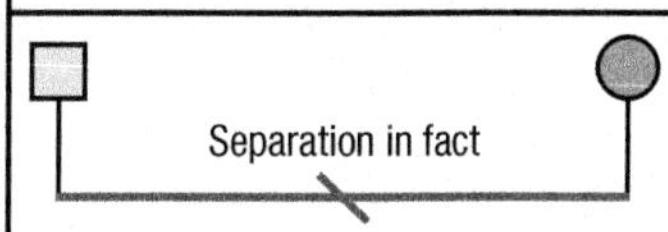 Separation in fact	This is the generic symbol used to describe a married couple no longer living together. A separation is displayed by a single oblique bar.
 Legal separation	The married couple is separated and started legal procedure for an eventual divorce.
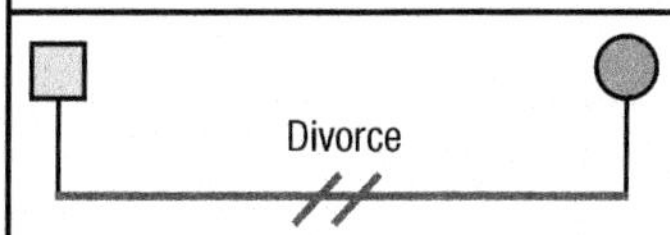 Divorce	The married couple has divorced.
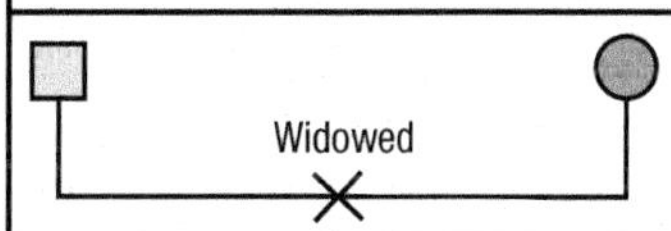 Widowed	One spouse died while married.
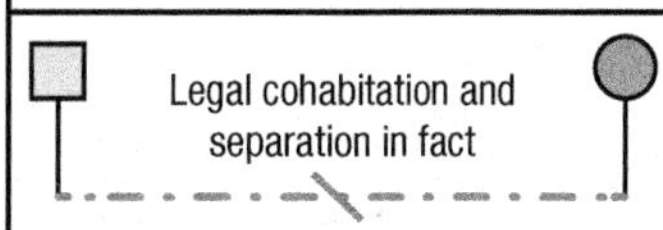 Legal cohabitation and separation in fact	Two individuals no longer live together and are in the process of terminating their cohabitation contract.
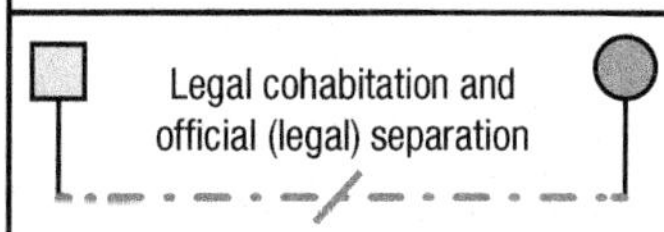 Legal cohabitation and official (legal) separation	The cohabitation contract has been terminated.
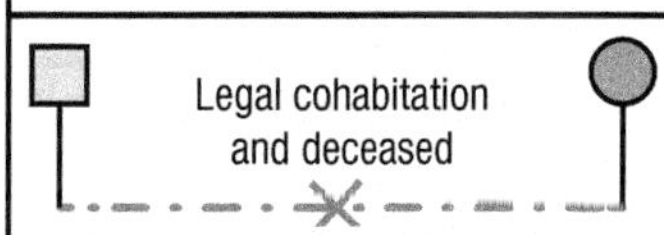 Legal cohabitation and deceased	One of the partners died without being married.
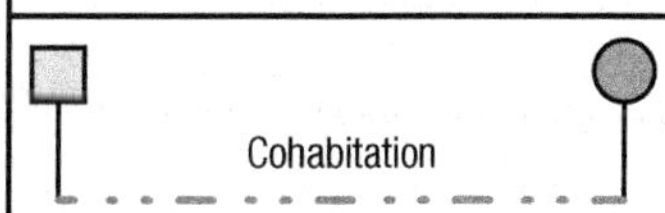 Cohabitation	Although there is no legal definition of *cohabitation*, it generally means to live together as a couple without being married.

(*continued*)

Exhibit 7.1 Relationships Between Two Individuals in a Standard Genogram (***continued***)

Cohabitation and separation	The generic symbol of two individuals no longer living together.
Non-sentimental cohabitation	Two individuals live together but there is no affection toward the other.
Dating/sporadic relationship	The representation of seeing someone or dating.
Rape/force relationship	One individual has abused the other individual, including rape. This type of relationship is mostly used in therapy or when a child is the product of such relationship.

Source: Adapted from McGoldrick, M., Gerson, R., & Petry, S. S. (2008). ***Genograms: Assessment and intervention***. W. W. Norton.

Exhibit 7.2 Relationship Quality Illustrated in a Standard Genogram

Cutoff/estranged	A cutoff relationship in which the two individualshave no contact at all, characterized by extreme disengagement.
Indifferent/apathetic	An apathetic relationship in which one or bothindividuals is indifferent to the other.
Distant/poor	A distant relationship between two individuals. Communication is very limited, usually because of lifestyle differences.
Plain/normal	An ordinary relationship.
Friendship/close	A close relationship (friendship) between two individuals.
Intimacy/very close	An intimate relationship, where communication is open, uncensored, and without secrets.
Hostile/conflictual	Defines a hostile relationship between two individuals. The two individuals have conflicts and argue on major issues.
Violence	A violent relationship between two individuals. The two individuals have conflicts that result in extreme actions such as physical force or excessive power.
Physical abuse	One individual is physically abusing another individual. Any nonaccidental injury to an individual, typically to a child or a woman.
Emotional abuse	One individual is emotionally abusing another individual. Reflects any attitude or behavior that interferes with mental health or social development. This includes yelling, screaming, name-calling, shaming, negative comparisons to others, telling them they are "bad, no good, worthless" or "a mistake."

(*continued*)

Exhibit 7.2 Relationship Quality Illustrated in a Standard Genogram (*continued*)

Sexual abuse 	One individual is sexually abusing another individual. Any sexual act between an adult and child, or a forced sexual act between two adults.
Neglect (abuse) 	Failure to provide for a child's physical needs. This includes lack of supervision, inappropriate housing or shelter, inadequate provision of food, inappropriate clothing for season or weather, abandonment, denial of medical care, and inadequate hygiene.

Source: Adapted from McGoldrick, M., Gerson, R., & Petry, S. S. (2008). *Genograms: Assessment and intervention*. W. W. Norton.

CONTEXTUAL FAMILY THERAPY

During the assessment phase, the contextual therapist's role is to listen to the clients and invite them to think about the issues of fairness and trustworthiness. The therapist should be very direct in asking questions to assess the basic ethical balances and learn the fundamentals of all the relationships, both historical and current, in the family system. The therapist also uses the assessment process to identify the level of trustworthiness reserves among family members.

INTERVENTIONS AND TECHNIQUES

BOWEN FAMILY SYSTEMS

GENOGRAM

In addition to recording historical family data throughout multiple generations, the genogram is used to trace relationship qualities, including conflicts, cutoffs, and triangles. More than just an assessment tool, this process of collecting information is sometimes therapeutic and a powerful intervention all by itself. The most comprehensive guide to working with this tool is Monica McGoldrick's (2016) *Genogram Casebook*.

DETRIANGULATING

The same process of emotional triangulation that families employ to stabilize their conflicts is also used to pull the therapist into their emotional forcefield during therapy. When therapists stay calm and emotionally regulated, however, clients are better able to reduce their own emotional reactivity and begin to think more clearly about their problems (Bowen, 1966, 1978).

PROCESS QUESTIONS

Each family member is asked a series of questions aimed at calming anxiety, reducing excess emotionality, and fostering objective reflection. Process questions are also used to help manage and neutralize triangles, including those between the therapist and members of the family system. Given that process questions decrease anxiety and promote clarity, clients may be able move to a more differentiated position by responding to these therapists' inquiries (Bowen, 1966, 1978).

RELATIONSHIP EXPERIMENTS/GOING HOME AGAIN

The goal of relationship experiments is to help family members become aware of systemic emotional processes and learn to recognize their own role in them. In going home again, the family therapist instructs the individual client to return home in order to get to know their family of origin better. The idea behind this technique is that with this type of information, individuals can differentiate themselves more clearly and practice what they have learned in Bowenian coaching (Bowen, 1966, 1978).

THE "I"-POSITION

An "I"-position is a calm and clear statement of personal opinion. In situations of increased tension, it often has a stabilizing effect if one person is able to detach from the emotionality and adopt an "I"-position. Speaking from a grounded place without the influence of the family of origin is one of the most direct ways to break cycles of emotional reactivity (Bowen, 1966, 1978).

CONTEXTUAL FAMILY THERAPY

MULTIDIRECTED PARTIALITY

Multidirected partiality prevents therapists from siding with one particular family member over another in the therapy room. The specific techniques used with multidirected partiality include (Boszormenyi-Nagy, 1965; Boszormenyi-Nagy & Spark, 1973):

1. *Empathy*—Refers to the therapist's ability to create emotional connectedness with clients' loss, pain, and grief.
2. *Crediting*—The therapist acknowledges unfairness, violations, and imbalance that the client is experiencing, while at the same time crediting the love and trustworthiness that was the intention behind prior misguided actions.
3. *Acknowledgment*—This emphasizes the attempts and contributions that the client has made in the relationship.
4. *Accountability*—This holds clients responsible for their behaviors in the relationship. After emphasizing the feelings, crediting, and acknowledging their efforts, the therapist holds the client as well as other members of the family responsible for each of their actions that caused pain or violations of love and trustworthiness.

REJUNCTION

During the process of rejunction, the contextual therapist helps clients to recreate the balance of fairness in the family system by exploring how each family member is available for the others and how they use each other for their own needs. According to Nagy, by discovering their own and other family members' part in the imbalance of the system, each member of the relational unit gains a sense of inner entitlement, leading to autonomy and growth (Boszormenyi-Nagy, 1965; Kerr, 1981).

ROLE OF THE THERAPIST

BOWEN FAMILY SYSTEMS

The therapist serves as coach and teacher to the client. In the Bowen model, the differentiation of the therapist is crucial. The Bowen family therapist must maintain a calm, non-anxious presence and be differentiated from their family of origin. Objectivity and neutrality are important behavioral characteristics for therapists to display. By acting as a coach, the Bowenian therapist hopes to avoid taking over for clients or becoming embroiled in family triangles. Coaching doesn't mean telling people what to do. Rather, it means preparing clients for future interactions with challenging family members and asking questions designed to help people figure out family emotional processes and their role in them.

CONTEXTUAL FAMILY THERAPY

Through the process of multidirected partiality, the therapist empathizes and gives credit to each family member, even if the credits may not be obvious at the beginning. This stance allows the therapist to open the dialogue among family members, which is based on responsibility, and encourages family members to reinvest in trustworthiness. It is the contextual family therapist's job to encourage clients to talk about their justified relational position in the family as well as listen respectfully to the response of other family members.

FRAMO'S FAMILY-OF-ORIGIN THERAPY

The therapist creates a strong therapeutic alliance with the client from the beginning to help develop trust. The therapist also takes an active and supportive role in educating the client on how previous experiences have influenced one's present relationships.

ORIENTATION IN TIME

Transgenerational family therapists view past relationships as influencing present family dynamics. These theories posit that the emotional experiences of our past dictate how we respond in the here and now. Current intimate relationships become an arena where family members work through unresolved family-of-origin issues, but this process can be easily upset by conflict, tension, and stress. When conflict or tension occurs, other people are triangled into this process to absorb the excess tension. Transgenerational family therapy encompasses the work of several theorist/practitioners who not only routinely see more than two generations in their sessions, but also conceptualize families and their problems in terms of the psychological dynamics that are passed from generation to generation. They see the past as operating in the present and therefore have evolved theories that help them chart a therapeutic course across time.

PROCESS AND GOALS OF THERAPY

BOWEN FAMILY SYSTEMS

The main goal of Bowen family systems is to reduce chronic anxiety by (a) facilitating awareness of how the emotional system functions and (b) increasing levels of differentiation, where the focus is on making changes for the self rather than on trying to change others. Changes such as these occur when therapists help family members become more diverse and less emotionally reactive in their interactions. In Bowen family systems, the chief focus and place where change is emphasized is the individual or couple. The whole family is usually not seen. Instead, individuals are often targeted for treatment, even though the emphasis of this approach is systemic. Remember, you can still be the family therapist with only one member of the system in the room (Bowen, 1966, 1978).

CONTEXTUAL FAMILY THERAPY

The goal of contextual therapy is the restoration of trustworthiness in the relationship. For clients to reach this goal, the therapist must assess the issues of mistrust and trust among the family members. It is important to note that the concept of trust as it is used in contextual family therapy cannot be forced or imposed by a sense of guilt or manipulation among the family members. Trust must be earned through the actions of giving and earning merits. The fulfillment of the individual is seen to include giving as well as receiving. Through the process of exoneration, clients understand the positive intentions and intergenerational loyalty underpinning actions of family members who have hurt them. When clients develop such understanding, they are less likely to replicate the hurtful behavior they have experienced (Boszormenyi-Nagy & Spark, 1973).

FRAMO'S FAMILY-OF-ORIGIN THERAPY

The main goal of this approach is to help individuals come to terms with problems related to their family of origin. There are three stages in Framo's family-of-origin therapy. Specific treatment goals are developed by each partner and may change as the couple goes through the various stages. In the conjoint stage, the focus is on building trust. Information is gathered here regarding the present couple relationship and the family of origin. The therapist educates the couple on object relations theory. In the couple group therapy stage, it is helpful for couples to see others who are struggling with the same kinds of behavior patterns as they are. The family-of-origin stage consists of two, 2-hour sessions that are done individually with the family of origin. By helping the individual understand how introjections from the past affect current relationships with aging parents and siblings, these sessions allow for a corrective experience to occur with the family of origin (Framo, 1965, 1981).

CONCLUSION

Believing that people need both companionship and independence, Murray Bowen contends that human relationships are driven by two counterbalancing life forces: individuality and togetherness.

Bowen family systems theory has a transgenerational outlook that offers eight interlocking concepts to explain the emotional processes taking place in the nuclear and extended families: differentiation of self, triangles, the nuclear family emotional system, the family projection process, emotional cutoff, multigenerational transmission process, sibling position, and societal emotional process. Chronic anxiety is seen as an inevitable part of nature, transmitted from previous generations as families attempt to balance togetherness and differentiation. Therapists must remain calm and neutral in order to prevent being triangled into the family's emotional process. Genograms offer helpful pictorial depictions of the family's relationship system over at least three generations. Believing that one can be a family therapist with only one client present, Bowen's concern was always with the multigenerational family system, even though he usually only met with individuals or couples.

James Framo is best known for his work regarding family-of-origin therapy, which he views as a branch of multigenerational work using a systems approach. These family-of-origin sessions are essential to the therapeutic process for change to occur and be maintained. Within a family-of-origin session, the therapist works toward discovering issues related to the the old family being projected onto the new spouse and family. The goal in a family-of-origin session is to foster a greater sense of self and to provide an opportunity for a healthy, appropriate, corrective parent or sibling experience.

Based in the foundational roots of forgiveness, ethics, fairness, and morality, Ivan Boszormenyi-Nagy's contextual therapy also bridges intergenerational healing, reconciliation, and acknowledgment with the practice of family therapy. Contextual therapists emphasize the ways in which generations are inherently bound to each other, while also considering intrapsychic and interpersonal elements. Adult children bring invisible loyalties extending across generations that influence their sense of relational ethics, or fairness in relationships.

Every relationship has a ledger of indebtedness and entitlements. The ledger is balanced when the relationship is fundamentally built on equity. The ledger includes both legacy, acquired by family dynamics and experiences, and the record of an individual's accumulated merit by contributing to someone else's welfare. For a relationship to become increasingly more trustworthy and healthier, each party must deal with both indebtedness and entitlements.

KEY TERMS

Coaching: Bowen's term for supervising clients in the process of differentiating the self from the family of origin.

Contextual therapy: Boszormenyi-Nagy's model, which includes relational ethics.

Debt: Boszormenyi-Nagy's term for costs accumulated as a result of failing to meet ethical obligations to other family members.

Detriangulation: The process by which individuals remove themselves from the emotional field of two others.

Differentiation of self: Bowen's term for psychological separation of intellect and emotions and the creation of a self independent from others; it is the opposite of fusion.

Differentiation-of-self scale: The scale ranges from 0, or no self, to 100, a perfectly differentiated self.

Displacement story: Developed by Phil Guerin, a follower of Bowen, this is a technique used to help family members get distance from their problems and become more self-reflective. The therapist might discuss another client with similar problems or use films to illustrate an issue.

Emotional cutoff: Bowen's term for flight from an unresolved emotional attachment.

Emotional distance: A concept inherent in nuclear family emotional processes, especially in triangulations. It is exhibited either by a family member distancing themselves from other family members to reduce the intensity of the relationship or by a family member becoming overly connected to the family unit and absorbing too much of the family's anxiety.

Emotional reactivity: The tendency to respond in a knee-jerk emotional fashion rather than calmly and objectively.

Emotional system: Bowen's term for the recursive emotionally driven problematic interaction patterns that occur is families, particularly those containing high levels of anxiety.

Entitlement: Boszormenyi-Nagy's term for the amount of merit a person accrues for behaving in an ethical manner toward others.

Exoneration: In contextual therapy, helping clients understand the positive intentions and intergenerational loyalty underpinning actions of family members who have hurt them. When clients develop such understanding, they are less likely to replicate the hurtful behavior they have experienced.

Family projection process: The mechanism by which parental conflicts are projected onto the children or a spouse in Bowenian theory.

Fusion: A blurring of psychological boundaries between self and others and a contamination of emotional and intellectual functioning; it is the opposite of differentiation.

Genogram: A schematic diagram of the family system, using squares to represent males, circles to indicate females, horizontal lines for marriages, and vertical lines to indicate children.

Interlocking triangles: Murray Bowen's idea that the most stable and basic unit within a family relationship consists of sets of three persons.

Invisible loyalties: Boszormenyi-Nagy's term for unconscious commitments that children take on to help their families.

Ledger: Boszormenyi-Nagy's term for the accumulated accounts of entitlements and debts within family relationships; it reflects the balance of what has been given and what is owed.

Legacy: Boszormenyi-Nagy's term for expectations associated with the parent–child relationships arising from the family's history.

Merit: A leverage that maintains the balance in relationships. When a person invests in the relationship, that person creates merit and trusts that another party will bring their contributions to the relationship to bring it into balance.

Multidirected impartiality: The therapeutic position at the core of Boszormenyi-Nagy's contextual therapy, which involves an openness to communication from all family members, a duty to ensure open communication between family members, an accountability to all family members affected by interventions, and a duty to facilitate solutions that are in the best interests of all affected family members.

Multigenerational transmission process: Bowen's concept for the process, occurring over several generations, in which poorly differentiated persons marry equally immature partners, ultimately resulting in children who suffer from severe psychological problems.

Rejunction: A contextual therapy intervention during which the therapist invites clients to evaluate and realize their capacity to restore balance between their obligation to give and their entitlement to receive in the relationship.

Relational ethics: Boszormenyi-Nagy's term for the idea that within a family, members are responsible for the consequences of their behavior and have a duty to be fair in their relationships by meeting their obligations.

Split loyalty: The phenomenon that occurs when a person can be loyal to one individual at the cost of being disloyal to another person in a deserving relationship.

Triangle: The smallest stable relational system is a triangle; when under stress, dyads involve a third party to form a triangle. Larger systems are composed of a series of interlocking triangles.

Undifferentiated family ego mass: Bowen's early term for emotional "stuck-togetherness" or fusion in the family, especially prominent in schizophrenic families.

KNOWLEDGE CHECK: CHAPTER 7

1. _________________, the ability to distinguish self from other and to manage interpersonal anxiety, is a fundamental a concept in intergenerational therapy.

   A. Self-actualization
   B. Boundary making
   C. Exoneration
   D. Differentiation

2. Bowen's theory contends clients can shape their own relational development and happiness by_________.

   A. Controlling the emotionality of other family members
   B. Removing themselves from family interactions
   C. Controlling emotionality with their own thinking process
   D. Confronting challenging family members

3. A Bowenian therapist who takes an emotionally engaged, yet nonreactive stance to the family system is creating ___________.

   A. The middle ground
   B. A neutral presence
   C. A non-anxious presence
   D. A holding environment

4. The Bowenian principle of __________ contends that simply teaching a mother behavioral parenting strategies for disciplining her son will be ineffective because this plan ignores the problem that she is overinvolved with the boy as result of her husband's emotional distance.

   A. Enmeshment
   B. Multigenerational transmission process
   C. Cutoff
   D. Triangles

5. Bowenian therapists coach individual family members in three areas—increasing differentiation, avoiding triangulation, and ______________, to help them improve their relationships with challenging parents and siblings.

   A. Repression of emotions
   B. Reopening cutoff family relationships
   C. Increasing cutoff when necessary
   D. Increasing emotionality

(*See answers next page.*)

1. D) Differentiation

Differentiation involves a capacity to manage one's own anxieties and to resist reacting to anxiety in others. Bowen theorized that more highly differentiated individuals can mindfully engage the thinking and feelings systems that govern behavior.

2. C) Controlling emotionality with their own thinking process

The ability to be in emotional contact with others yet still autonomous in one's own emotional functioning is the key to happiness and personal fulfillment. Instead of trying to confront, control, or cutoff from other family members, Bowen focused on the controlling of the self.

3. C) A non-anxious presence

A significant skill of a Bowenian therapist is to be "a non-anxious presence" who is a well differentiated person able to work in a calm way with the family system to help members understand patterns of relating and responding to tensions and stresses.

4. D) Triangles

A triangle is a three-person relationship system. It is considered the building block or "molecule" of larger emotional systems because a triangle is the smallest stable relationship system. A two-person system is unstable because it tolerates little tension before involving a third person. A triangle can contain much more tension without involving another person because the tension can shift around three relationships. If the tension is too high for one triangle to contain, it spreads to a series of "interlocking" triangles. Triangles contribute significantly to the development of clinical problems. Getting pushed from an inside to an outside position can trigger a depression or perhaps even a physical illness. Two parents intensely focusing on what is wrong with a child can trigger serious problems in the child.

5. B) Reopening cutoff family relationships

The concept of emotional cutoff describes how undifferentiated people manage their unresolved emotional issues with parents, siblings, and other family members by reducing or totally cutting off emotional contact with them. Emotional contact can be reduced by moving away from family and rarely going home, or it can be reduced by staying in physical contact with family but avoiding sensitive issues. Relationships may look "better" if people use cutoff to manage them, but the problems are dormant, not resolved. Bowen believed cutoff should be avoided if possible and would help family members to increase their level of differentiation and reopen previous cutoff relationships.

6. All of the following are techniques used by a Bowenian therapist *except*:

   A. Process questions
   B. Genograms
   C. Relational experiments
   D. Realigning hierarchies

7. Which of the following is a role that Bowen would assume in therapy?

   A. Antagonist and system pusher
   B. Detective in charge of uncovering mistaken beliefs or irrational ideas
   C. Coach who tries to help family members learn new ways of interacting
   D. Emotional cheerleader

(*See answers next page.*)

6. D) Realigning hierarchies

Process questions, genograms, and relational experiments are all integral parts of Bowen family systems, whereas realigning hierarchies is a technique clearly associated with structural family therapy.

7. C) Coach who tries to help family members learn new ways of interacting

Bowenian therapists "coach" their clients to identify the emotions occurring within their family unit and note when they are taking on the emotions of other family members. They also coach their clients on how to go home and interact with their family of origin in more a differentiated way.

AUDIO PODCAST 7.1
Bowenian Theory Overview
Eli A. Karam
https://bcove.video/3AvkS9s

REFERENCES

Boszormenyi-Nagy, I. (1965). A theory of relationships: Experience and transaction. In I. Boszormenyi-Nagy & J. Framo (Eds.), *Intensive family therapy: Theoretical and practical aspects*. Harper & Row.

Boszormenyi-Nagy, I., & Spark, G. (1973). *Invisible loyalties: Reciprocity in intergenerational family therapy*. Harper & Row.

Bowen, M. (1966). The use of family theory in clinical practice. *Comprehensive Psychiatry, 7*, 345–374. https://doi.org/10.1016/S0010-440X(66)80065-2

Bowen, M. (1978). *Family therapy in clinical practice*. Aronson.

Framo, J. L. (1965). Rationale and techniques of intensive family therapy. In I. Boszormenyi-Nagy & J. L. Framo (Eds.), *Intensive family therapy* (pp. 143–212). Harper & Row.

Framo, J. L. (1981). The integration of marital therapy with sessions with family of origin. In A. S. Gurman & D. P. Kniskern (Eds.), *Handbook of family therapy* (pp. 133–158). Brunner/Mazel.

Framo, J. L. (2013). *Family-of-origin therapy: An intergenerational approach*. Routledge.

Kerr, M. (1981). Family systems theory and therapy. In A. Gurman & D. Kniskern (Eds.), *Handbook of family therapy* (pp. 226–266). Brunner/Mazel.

McGoldrick, M. (2016). *The genogram casebook: A clinical companion to genograms: Assessment and intervention*. W. W. Norton.

McGoldrick, M., Gerson, R., & Petry, S. S. (2008). *Genograms: Assessment and intervention*. W. W. Norton.

Psychodynamic Family Therapy

8

LEARNING OBJECTIVES

After reading this chapter, you should be able to:

1. Identify model developers and other key figures associated with psychodynamic approaches to systemic therapy
2. Describe the assessment process in psychodynamic approaches to systemic therapy
3. Review the main interventions/techniques of psychodynamic approaches to systemic therapy
4. Identify goals of psychodynamic approaches to systemic therapy
5. Develop the role of therapist in psychodynamic approaches to systemic therapy

RELEVANT EXAM DOMAINS

- *Domain 1—The Practice of Systemic Therapy*
  Includes tasks related to incorporating systemic theory and perspectives into practice activities and establishing and maintaining ongoing therapeutic relationships with the client system.
- *Domain 2—Assessing, Hypothesizing, and Diagnosing*
  Includes tasks related to assessing the various dimensions of the client system, forming and reformulating hypotheses, and diagnosing the client and family system in order to guide therapeutic activities.
- *Domain 3—Designing and Conducting Treatment*
  Includes tasks related to developing and implementing interventions with the client system.

INTRODUCTION

As we reviewed in Chapter 3, renegade psychoanalytically trained clinicians were among the first to break away from the establishment of the time, embrace systems thinking, and practice family therapy. Once thought of as off limits for marriage and family therapists, since the mid-1980s there has been a renewed interest in psychodynamics among family therapists. This revival of interest reflected changes in psychoanalysis—from the individualism of Freudian theory to the more relationship-oriented object relations theories and self-psychology—as well as changes in family therapy itself, especially dissatisfaction with the mechanistic elements of the cybernetic model. In this chapter, we highlight the main points of these theories and articulate their relevance to working both within and between a system.

MODEL DEVELOPERS AND SIGNIFICANT CONTRIBUTORS

SIGMUND FREUD

As the founder of psychoanalysis and a number of techniques for treating dysfunctional behaviors (e.g., free association and dream analysis), Freud highlighted the importance of the unconscious mind and sexuality in human behavior. He developed a theory of personality based on psychosexual development and the resolution of power among the id, ego, and superego.

NATHAN ACKERMAN

This family therapy pioneer attempted to integrate psychoanalytic theory and systems theory by viewing family dysfunction as a failure in role complementarity between members and as the product of persistent unresolved conflict (within and between individuals in a family). Ackerman's therapeutic efforts were aimed at disentangling such interlocking pathologies.

HEINZ KOHUT

The founder of self- psychology, Kohut considered narcissism to be the result of a parental lack of empathy during development. As a consequence, the individual does not develop the full capacity to regulate self-esteem. Empathy in general became an important part of Kohut's work, as he came to feel that overly rigid adherence to Freud's ideas often encouraged analysts to impose their own beliefs on the person they were treating. Self-psychology places a high value on empathy, or the ability of the therapist to understand the experience from the perspective of the client.

MELANIE KLEIN

Klein's theory of the unconscious focused on the relationship between the mother and theinfant rather than that between the father and the infant and inspired the central concepts of the Object Relations School within psychoanalysis.

BRITISH MIDDLE SCHOOL (MICHAEL BALINT, RONALD FAIRBAIRN, HARRY GUNTRIP, AND DONALD WINNICOTT)

This collection of individuals is aptly named because they attempted to maintain a balance between classical Freudian psychoanalysts and the followers of Klein. In general, they hold that an infant's primary need is attachment to a caring, nurturing caregiver, in contrast to Freud's idea that the infant's basic struggle is in coming to terms with sexual and aggressive impulses aimed at acquiring gratification from a parent.

JILL AND DAVID SCHARFF

This husband-and-wife team are leading proponents of object relations family therapy, the group analytic approach to understanding the conscious and unconscious patterns of interaction in a family with a view to relieving the burden on the identified client and giving the family greater insight and flexibility in charting its course through life.

MODEL OVERVIEW

REACTION TO FREUD

According to Freud, an individual's personality consists of three dynamically interrelated parts: the id, superego, and ego. Children go through and must resolve tasks associated with psychosexual stages of development. Much of the emphasis in this theory is on the importance of the unconscious and sexuality in human behavior. Treatment focuses on the release of anxiety and repressed memories.

In the 1960s and 1970s, family therapy totally rejected psychoanalytic thinking in favor of systemic thinking. Then in the 1980s a shift occurred with many family therapists taking a renewed interest in the psychodynamics of the individual. This revival of interest reflected changes in psychoanalysis—from the individualism of Freudian theory based on sex and aggression to the more relationship-oriented object relations theories and self-psychology (Scharff & Savage-Scharff, 1987, 1991).

OBJECT RELATIONS

The bridge between traditional psychoanalysis and family systems is object relations theory. It posits that we relate to others on the basis of expectations formed by early experience. The residue of these early relationships leaves internal objects—mental images of self and others built up from experience and expectation. Those internalized objects form the core of the personality—an open system developing and maintaining its identity through connections with others, both present and past (Slipp, 1988).

Object relations theory is a variation of psychoanalytic theory, which places much less emphasis on biologically based drives and more importance on interpersonal relationships (e.g., the intimacy and nurturing of the mother). In object relations theory, objects are usually persons, parts of persons (such as the mother's breast), or symbols of one of these. The primary object is the mother. The child's relation to an object (e.g., the mother's breast) serves as a prototype for future interpersonal relationships. Objects can be both external (a physical person or body part) and internal, comprising emotional images and representations of an external object (e.g., good breast vs. bad breast). The conceptualization of internal objects is linked to Klein's theory of unconscious fantasy, and development from the paranoid-schizoid position to the depressive position (Segal, 2018).

SELF-PSYCHOLOGY

The essence of self-psychology is that every human being longs to be appreciated. To the very young child, parents are not quite separate individuals; they are, in Kohut's term, selfobjects, experienced as part of the self. As a selfobject, the mother transmits her love by touch, tone of voice, and gentle words, as though they are the child's own feelings. If parents are enthusiastically responsive and appreciative, we internalize this acceptance in the form of a self-confident personality. But to the extent that our parents are unresponsive or rejecting, then the self-concept is negatively impacted. The unhappy child, cheated out of loving affirmation, moves through life forever craving the attention they were denied. This is the origin of narcissism. Kohut formulated three specific types of transferences that reflect unmet selfobject needs (Kohut, 2009):

1. *Mirroring*: In this type of transference, others serve as a mirror that reflects back a sense of self-worth and value. Just as people use a mirror to check appearance, mirroring

transference involves use of the affirming and positive responses of others to see positive traits within the self.

2. *Idealizing*: Kohut believed individuals need people who will make them feel calm and comfortable. An example of this can be seen in children who run to a parent for comfort after falling and getting injured. The external other is idealized as somebody who is calm and soothing, when one cannot provide that for themselves.
3. *Twinship/alter ego*: Kohut suggested that people need to feel a sense of likeness with others. For example, children want to be similar to their parents and mimic the behaviors they observe. Over the course of healthy development, a child becomes more able to tolerate differences.

SPLITTING

Fairbairn maintained that because the infant experiences different sets of encounters with a mother—sometimes nurturing, sometimes frustrating—and cannot control the circumstances or leave the relationship, the infant creates a fantasy world to help reconcile the discrepant experiences. In this mediating process, called *splitting* by Fairbairn, within the first year of life the child internalizes an image of the mother into a good object (the satisfying and loving mother) and a bad object (the unavailable and frustrating mother).

To Fairbairn, these internalized split objects become part of one's personality structure: good-object introjects (imprints of parents or other significant figures) remain as pleasing unconscious memories, and bad-object introjects cause intrapsychic distress. Psychological representations of these introjects unconsciously influence future relationships because current experiences are interpreted through the filter of one's inner object world of good–bad images. As a result, the person may grow up with distorted expectations of others, unconsciously forcing intimates into fitting these internal role models (Fairbairn, 1952).

GOOD-ENOUGH MOTHERING

The infant needs a holding environment in order to thrive. This environment doesn't have to be ideal; an average expectable environment that features "good-enough mothering" is sufficient according to Winnicott (1986).

FALSE SELF

Winnicott's *false self* refers to certain types of false personalities that develop as the result of early and repeated environmental failure, with the result that the true self-potential is not realized but hidden. In this manner, adults hide their true needs in order to gain favor from a potential romantic interest, and children learn to suppress authentic feelings from their parents that they fear may lead to rejection (Winnicott, 1986).

SEPARATION–INDIVIDUATION

Margaret Mahler observed young children and described separation–individuation as a process they experience. After an initial period of total merger, the child begins a gradual process of separation from the mother, progressively renouncing symbiotic fusion with her. The result of successful separation and individuation is a well-differentiated self. Failure to achieve individuation undermines the development of a cohesive self and a differentiated identity, resulting in overly intense emotional attachments (Mahler, 1963).

DEFENSE MECHANISMS

A core component of psychoanalytic therapy is uncovering unconscious impulses and defenses against impulses. Mental conflict arises when children learn and mislearn that expressing these impulses directly will lead to punishment. Defense mechanisms are psychological strategies that are unconsciously used to protect a person from anxiety arising from unacceptable thoughts or feelings. They involve some kind of distortion of reality so that the person is able to cope with a situation. The most of common defense mechanisms include (Vaillant, 1992):

1. *Projection:* Attributing one's unacceptable feelings or desires to someone else.
2. *Projective identification:* A process whereby the subject perceives an object as if it contained unwelcome elements of the subject's personality and evokes responses from the object that conform to those perceptions. Unlike projection, projective identification is interactional.
3. *Denial:* Refusing to recognize or acknowledge real facts or experiences that would lead to anxiety.
4. *Repression:* Blocking difficult thoughts from entering into consciousness.
5. *Regression:* Reverting to the behavior or emotions of an earlier developmental stage.
6. *Rationalization:* Justifying a mistake or problematic feeling with seemingly logical reasons or explanations.
7. *Displacement:* Redirecting an emotional reaction from the rightful recipient to another person altogether.
8. *Reaction formation:* Behaving or expressing the opposite of one's true feelings.
9. *Sublimation:* Channeling sexual or unacceptable urges into a productive outlet, such as work or a hobby.
10. *Intellectualization:* Focusing on the intellectual rather than emotional consequences of a situation.
11. *Compartmentalization:* Separating components of one's life into different categories to prevent conflicting emotions.

ASSESSMENT

In psychodynamic family therapy, assessment takes the form of listening. After listening closely to the client, the therapist should assess the unconscious conflict underlying symptoms and the role of defense mechanisms in managing them. The therapist identifies object relations patterns in a client's interpersonal history by highlighting significant selfobjects during both childhood and adulthood.

INTERVENTIONS AND TECHNIQUES

TRANSFERENCE

Transference is understood as the process in which a client in treatment redirects feelings and desires from childhood to a new object—the therapist. This process occurs in individual analysis to help clients work through their feelings by viewing the therapist as a significant other with whom relationships are unresolved. Transference is also used in family therapy in order to explain dominant feelings within a family unit and to understand why emotions are being directed toward certain members of the system (Scharff & Savage-Scharff, 1987, 1991).

FREE ASSOCIATION

Articulated by Freud, free association involves asking a client to spontaneously say what comes to mind on a given topic, allowing unconscious material to arise. The client may describe recent events, memories, feelings, fantasies, bodily sensations, or any other material. Analysts may have clients lay on a couch rather than sit in a chair to encourage a more relaxed and free-flowing thought process to encourage unconscious thoughts to emerge. The analyst listens carefully for unusual connections, idiosyncratic logic, and efforts to edit or hold back. After this process, the analyst may provide interpretations to help promote insight into the client's process.

INTERPRETATION

Interpretation involves bringing unconscious conflicts between family members into conscious awareness. Depending on the therapist focus, they may interpret defense mechanisms, early childhood events, or selfobject conflicts. Timing is important in the delivery of the interpretation. If the client is not ready, the therapist will experience resistance. In most cases, the closer the material is to conscious awareness, the more ready the client is for interpretation. Although interpretation may not completely resolve conflicts, it takes the covert nature out of the discord and allows therapy of the individual or family to progress in a more straightforward way by increasing the insight of the client into how the past is continuing to affect the present (Savage-Scharff & Scharff, 2003).

WORKING THROUGH

In psychodynamic psychotherapy, working through is the process, through which the client recognizes resistances and overcomes them. The client directly confronts the repressed feelings, threatening impulses, and internal conflicts at the root of their difficulties and develops conscious ways to rebound from, resolve, or otherwise deal with these feelings, impulses, and conflicts.

ROLE OF THE THERAPIST

In psychodynamic treatment, the therapist plays the important roles of listener, interpreter, and internalized selfobject. In addition to using transference and countertransference to promote insight into early attachment relationships, psychodynamic therapists use these immediate in-session interactions to promote corrective emotional experiences. Corrective emotional experiences involve using the therapeutic relationship to work through old attachment wounds and relational traumas. When this is done with true empathy and without reactivity on the part of therapist, this can be a truly reparative and restorative experience for the client.

ORIENTATION IN TIME

Psychodynamic approaches are firmly rooted in the past. Individuals and families must be prepared to explore the roots of their difficulties, including early childhood–parent interactions in a long-term, time-intensive and oftentimes expensive treatment.

PROCESS AND GOALS OF THERAPY

The essential aim of psychodynamic therapy is to help clients understand their basic motives and resolve conflicts over expressing those yearnings in a healthy fashion. The goals of treatment, therefore, are to break dysfunctional interactions within the family based on unconscious processes and to resolve individual dysfunction through insight.

CONCLUSIONS

During the 1980s family therapists took a renewed interest in the psychology of the individual. Different from a traditional psychodynamic framework, however, this time a client's internal world was no longer divided into Freud's drive psychology but had become relational and interactional. Object relations theory and self-psychology replaced Freudian drive psychology for many clinicians in offering useful explanations of development of people and their problems. The essential aim of psychoanalytic therapy is to help clients develop insight around their deepest desires and "work through" conflicts over expressing them. Freudians focus on libidinal impulses around sex and aggression, self-psychologists focus on the longing for appreciation, and object relations therapists concentrate on the need for secure attachment. All of these approaches; however, are united in the belief that client systems will function better collectively if their individual members understand and begin to resolve their own personal conflicts.

KEY TERMS

Countertransference: A term in psychoanalysis for the positive or negative wishes, fantasies, and feelings that a therapist unconsciously directs or transfers to a client, stemming from their own unresolved conflicts.

Defense mechanism: A psychological response originating in the unconscious that helps protect a person from anxiety and other negative emotions that accompany stress.

Depressive position: Klein's term for the tendency to react to mother figures in infancy, or significant others in adulthood, as complex individuals who have both good and bad characteristics.

Fixation: Refers to an obsessive drive that may or may not be acted on that involves an object, concept, or person; thought to result from the partial arrest of attachment or mode of behavior during an early stage of development.

Good and bad objects: According to object relations theory, infants, by using the defense mechanism of splitting, come to view the mother figure as two separate people: the good object whom they long for and who satisfies their needs, and the bad object with whom they are angry because they long for her and she frustrates them. By splitting, infants may protect the good object from the threat of annihilation, by directing their intense anger exclusively at the bad object.

Id: A term in psychoanalysis for the part of the personality present at birth and expressed as biological urges that strive continually for gratification. The id is where human instincts reside. It functions according to the pleasure principle, containing the psychic energy (libido) of the person.

Identification: Refers to the act of integrating characteristics of an admired parental figure into one's own personality or identity.

Insight: Refers to an act of self-understanding and increased awareness about one's problems and the factors that are influencing one's behaviors.

Internal objects: Mental images and fantasies of oneself and others, formed by early interactions with caregivers.

Interpretations based on the triangle of conflict: These are interpretations that link the present defense mechanisms with the underlying anxiety felt about an unacceptable impulse or feeling, often involving sex, aggression, or grief.

Interpretations based on the triangle of person: Interpretations that draw parallels between the client and therapist transference relationship, the family-of-origin relationship between client and parent, and the current life relationship between client and partner or significant other.

Introject: Refers to a primitive mental representation of part of a person, for example, "good objects" and "bad objects" are introjects.

Introjection: A primitive form of identification in which one takes in aspects of other people, which then become part of one's self-image.

Need-exciting and need-rejecting objects: According to object relations theory, the bad object is split into a need-exciting object, which is craved by the infant, and a need-rejecting object toward which the infant experiences rage. These two object relations systems are repressed and are distinct from the central conscious self, which is attached with feelings of security and satisfaction to an ideal good object.

Neo-Freudians: Followers of Sigmund Freud who put more emphasis than Freud did on adulthood and defense mechanisms and who challenged Freud's concepts of the instinctual drive, the Oedipus complex, and the motivational primacy of sex and aggression. Leading neo-Freudians include Anna Freud, Harry Stack Sullivan, Karen Horney, and Eric Fromm.

Object relations: These are internalized images of self and others based on early parent–child interactions that determine a person's mode of relationship to other people.

Object relations theory: Psychoanalytic theory derived from Melanie Klein and developed by the British Middle School (Bion, Fairbairn, Guntrip, Winnicott) that emphasizes relationships and attachment, rather than libidinal and aggressive drives, as the key issues of human concern.

Oedipus complex: Refers to a conflict that occurs during the phallic stage (ages 3–5 years) of psychosexual development. According to the theory, during this stage, boys have a sexual desire for or erotic interest in their mothers together with hostile feelings for and fear of castration by their fathers. The complex is resolved when boys identify with their fathers and vicariously possess their mothers through such an identity. In girls this is known as the *Electra complex.*

Pleasure principle: The principle by which the id operates in Sigmund Freud's schema of the personality. The id is dominated by the pleasure principle, seeks immediate gratification of its needs, and avoids any unpleasantness or pain. It is the opposite of the reality principle.

Projection: The act of attributing an aspect of the self, either positive or negative, to another person.

Projective identification: A defense mechanism that operates unconsciously whereby unwanted aspects of the self are attributed to another person and that person is induced to behave in accordance with these projected attitudes and feelings.

Psychosexual stages of development: Sigmund Freud's psychoanalytic theory is based on psychosexual stages of development. Each stage of development is characterized by a particular area of the body thought to provide maximal erotic gratification during that stage. According to Freud, the four stages of psychosexual development are oral, anal, phallic, and genital. There is a latency period between the phallic and genital stage.

Regression: This refers to a return to a less-mature level of functioning in the face of stress.

Resistance: Oppositional behavior that clients or families engage in to oppose or retard the progress of therapy.

Selfobject: Kohut's term for a person the self sees not as a separate individual, but as an extension of the self that affirms well-being and security.

Self-psychology: Heinz Kohut's version of psychoanalysis that emphasizes the need for attachment and appreciation.

Separation–individuation: A process whereby the infant begins, at about 2 months of age, to draw apart from the symbiotic bond with the mother and to develop autonomous functioning.

Splitting: A psychoanalytic term for viewing object representations dichotomously as either all good or all bad. The result is a projection of good and bad qualities onto persons within one's environment. Through splitting, people can control their anxiety and even the objects (i.e., persons) within their environment by making them predictable. However, those who engage in splitting pay a high price because of the misrepresentation of the person in question.

Subconscious: A psychoanalytic concept that includes aspects of the conscious and unconscious mind.

Superego: A psychoanalytic concept for that part of the psyche that contains the values of parents and parental figures. The superego operates according to these moral principles by punishing a person through the conscience when they disobey parental messages and by rewarding the person through the ego ideal when parental teachings are followed.

Transference: This refers to distorted emotional reactions in present relationships that occur because of unresolved, early family relations.

Unconscious: This refers to memories, feelings, and impulses of which a person is unaware.

Working through: A psychoanalytic technique that refers to the client's movement toward insight and understanding in the latter stages of a therapeutic relationship.

KNOWLEDGE CHECK: CHAPTER 8

1. Psychodynamic approaches share the basic practice of ____________.
   - A. Modifying client behavior
   - B. Addressing negative cognitions
   - C. Working through problematic emotions
   - D. Fostering client insight into their personality dynamics

2. Countertransference occurs when a therapist ________.
   - A. Keeps their emotional reactions toward the client in check
   - B. Projects back onto a client in a manner that jeopardizes therapeutic neutrality
   - C. Has insight into their unconscious reactions to their clients
   - D. Draws a parallel with what the client is currently facing to what the therapist has experienced in the past

3. Freud focused his work on the _______area of the consciousness.
   - A. Unconscious
   - B. Conscious
   - C. Preconscious
   - D. Subconscious

4. Object relations theorists focus on how early __________ relationships become the template for all future relationships.
   - A. Sibling
   - B. Sexual
   - C. Caregiver
   - D. Violent

5. Psychoanalytic family therapy aims at personality change and growth through the therapeutic technique of ________.
   - A. Confrontation
   - B. Projection
   - C. Introjection
   - D. Working through

(*See answers next page.*)

1. D) Fostering client insight into their personality dynamics

The pursuit of insight is generally regarded as a defining feature of psychoanalytic psychotherapy, which is often referred to as *insight-oriented therapy*.

2. B) Projects back onto a client in a manner that jeopardizes therapeutic neutrality

Signs of countertransference in therapy can include a variety of behaviors, including excessive self-disclosure on the part of the therapist or an inappropriate interest in irrelevant details from the life of the person in treatment. A therapist who acts on their feelings toward the person being treated or that person's situation or engages in behavior not appropriate to the treatment process may not be effectively managing countertransference.

3. A) Unconscious

According to Freud, the unconscious mind is the primary source of human behavior. The unconscious mind comprises mental processes that are inaccessible to consciousness but that influence judgments, feelings, or behavior. The unconscious mind contains our biologically based instincts for the primitive urges for sex and aggression. Freud argued that our primitive urges often do not reach consciousness because they are unacceptable to our rational, conscious selves. People use a range of defense mechanisms to avoid knowing what their unconscious motives and feelings are.

4. C) Caregiver

In object relations theory, therapists help people identify patterns in their lives that may be impacting their relationships with others. Therapists refer to significant others in a person's life, particularly a person's primary caregiver (mother, father, etc.) as the object in object relations theory.

5. D) Working through

In psychodynamic terms, working through is seen as the process of repeating, elaborating, and amplifying interpretations. It is believed that such working through is critical to the success of therapy.

AUDIO PODCAST 8.1
Psychodynamic Family Therapy Overview
Eli A. Karam
https://bcove.video/3pPaQLy

REFERENCES

Fairbairn, W. (1952). *An object relations therapy of personality*. Basic Books.

Kohut, H. (2009). *The restoration of the self.* University of Chicago Press.

Mahler, M. S. (1963). Thoughts about development and individuation. *The Psychoanalytic Study of the Child, 18*(1), 307–324.

Savage-Scharff, J., & Scharff, D. (2003). Object relations and psychodynamic approaches to couple and family therapy. In T. Sexton, G. Weeks, & M. Robbins (Eds.), *Handbook of family therapy* (pp. 59–82). Brunner-Routledge.

Scharff, D., & Savage-Scharff, J. (1987). *Object relations family therapy*. Aronson.

Scharff, D., & Savage-Scharff, J. (1991). *Object relations couple therapy.* Aronson.

Segal, H. (2018). *Introduction to the work of Melanie Klein*. Routledge.

Slipp, S. (1988). *The technique and practice of object relations family therapy*. Aronson.

Vaillant, G. E. (1992). *Ego mechanisms of defense: A guide for clinicans and researchers*. American Psychiatric Press.

Winnicott, D. W. (1986). The theory of the parent-infant relationship. *Essential papers on object relations*, 233–253.

Postmodernism, Social Constructionism, and the Feminist Critique

9

LEARNING OBJECTIVES

After reading this chapter, you should be able to:

1. Identify model developers and other key figures associated with postmodernism, the feminist critique, and collaborative therapy
2. Describe the aims of the feminist critique
3. Review the main interventions/techniques of feminist family therapy and collaborative therapy
4. Identify goals of feminist family therapy and collaborative therapy
5. Develop the role of therapist in feminist family therapy and collaborative therapy

RELEVANT EXAM DOMAINS

- *Domain 1—The Practice of Systemic Therapy*
  Includes tasks related to incorporating systemic theory and perspectives into practice activities and establishing and maintaining ongoing therapeutic relationships with the client system.
- *Domain 2—Assessing, Hypothesizing, and Diagnosing*
  Includes tasks related to assessing the various dimensions of the client system, forming and reformulating hypotheses, and diagnosing the client and family system in order to guide therapeutic activities.
- *Domain 3—Designing and Conducting Treatment*
  Includes tasks related to developing and implementing interventions with the client system.

INTRODUCTION

The postmodern movement, along with its constructivist epistemology, has significantly impacted the field of family therapy. Unlike classic structural, strategic, and experiential family therapy models, postmodern therapies reject the idea that there is an objective truth observable to all. Instead, they focus on the subjective perceptions of the truth or reality that each client and family system present. Postmodernists contend that multiple views of reality exist, and that absolute truth can never be known. It is important to note the cultural context in which these postmodern trends emerged, as a rapidly changing social and political landscape challenged traditional views of gender and family life.

The feminist critique was the first and perhaps most influential of the challenges to the traditions of family therapy. In taking a stand against mother bashing, feminists challenged the essence of systems thinking by pointing out that concepts like complementarity and circular causality can imply that subjugated women were as much to blame as their oppressors.

MODEL DEVELOPERS AND SIGNIFICANT CONTRIBUTORS

TOM ANDERSEN

Andersen, a Norwegian family therapist dissatisfied with traditional ways of observing family systems behind the mirror, pioneered the reflecting team approach. Parallel to the process of the Houston Galveston team, Andersen began over time to de-emphasize intervention, and substitute instead noninvasive, nonjudgmental reflecting. Andersen's reflecting team model and the collaborative model of Anderson and Goolishian have influenced each other (Andersen, 1987).

HARRY GOOLISHIAN AND HARLENE ANDERSON

Harry Goolishian was involved in the creation of the collaborative therapy model and was soon joined by Harlene Anderson at what is now known as the Houston Galveston Institute. Goolishian and Anderson began to de-emphasize intervention and put more emphasis on building a therapeutic partnership and joining with clients through curious conversation (Anderson, 1997).

KARL TOMM

Tomm classified questions according to the therapist's intent (orienting and influencing) and assumptions (lineal or circular). *Orienting intent* refers to the therapist trying to understand the client's situation, and *influencing intent* refers to the therapist influencing the client's situation. Orienting changes the therapist, whereas influencing changes the client. The circular assumptions orient the therapist to look beyond lineal cause and effect and toward systemic interactions (Tomm, 1987a, 1987b, 1988).

RACHEL HARE-MUSTIN

Rachel Hare-Mustin's feminist critique stressed consciousness-raising, equality in relationships (couple, family, and therapeutic), enhancing women's self-esteem by encouraging experiences outside of oppressive gender roles, altering therapeutic interventions to be less sexist, and working toward broader societal changes (Hare-Mustin, 1978).

THE WOMEN'S PROJECT IN FAMILY THERAPY

Four bright, energetic, and humorous women, Betty Carter, Peggy Papp, Olga Silverstein, and Marianne Walters, joined together with the common goal of de-pathologizing women in family therapy. They aimed to move the focus of the profession of family therapy from a deficit model to one that emphasized the strengths and resources of women (Walters et al., 1991).

MODEL OVERVIEW

POSTMODERNISM/SOCIAL CONSTRUCTIONISM

A profoundly different way of considering reality came from the social constructionism movement. This ideology suggests that reality is co-created through language in an ongoing interactional and relational process. Family therapists became interested in the active process of meaning-making with their clients. Postmodern social construction therapies reject the idea that there is an objective truth observable to all. Instead, they focus on the subjective perceptions of the truth or reality that each client presents. Characteristics of social constructionist models include (Hoffman, 2002):

- Assumptions about the presenting problems are explored.
- The therapist has permission not to be an expert.
- The client is the expert.
- The therapist does not bring preconceived ideas into the session.
- Language is the vehicle used for forming new constructions.
- The focus of attention is cognition instead of behavior.
- Culture shapes beliefs.

Postmodernists believe people's personalities are almost completely shaped by interactions, language, and conversations with others. If conversation results in someone feeling better about their circumstances, then that conversation was "therapeutic." These postmodern therapists take the view that the traditional approach of mainstream family therapy placed too much influence on the therapist as an expert, did not respect the knowledge and resources of the client, and encouraged the therapist to be more concerned about curing the client family than caring for them.

Diversity issues are more likely to be considered in a postmodernist/social constructivist framework. Not looking for the "truth" of the situation, the therapist can learn about differing views offered by different family members, rather than promoting their own socially acquired prejudices.

Postmodern therapists resist the first-order cybernetic position of classic marriage and family therapy (MFT) models such as strategic family therapy. First-order cybernetics is characterized by the therapist's observation of the system from the outside. In this conceptualization, the therapist remains removed from the system because of their expert position. Second-order cybernetics, on the other hand, appreciates and acknowledges the observer as part of the system because the observer is no longer considered neutral and detached.

COLLABORATIVE THERAPY

In collaborative therapy, problems are considered stories that clients have agreed to tell themselves, consistent with the postmodern view that the problems people bring to therapy are primarily social constructions, made up of faulty narratives. Influenced by hermeneutics, the collaborative model contends that language allows us to construct and make sense of what we are experiencing, to help organize and attribute meaning to our stories. The reality we attribute to events, experiences, and people in our lives does not exist in the thing itself but is a socially constructed attribution created within a particular culture and shaped and reshaped by language (Anderson, 2003).

Frustrated by the cybernetic model, the proponents of the collaborative model see traditional family therapy as too focused on doing therapy "on" a client rather than "with" a client. This emphasis on technique and outcome damages the caring quality of the relationship and therefore reduces the space for therapeutic healing. Because the client knows best in this conversational model, the therapist is more likely to be interested in the client's thinking and views on what needs to change and how it needs to change (Anderson, 1997).

FEMINIST FAMILY THERAPY

Feminist therapists have been critical of the traditional practice of family therapy, contending that it has been filled with outdated patriarchal assumptions and grounded on a male-biased perspective of gender roles and gender-defined functions within the family. Feminists assert that our patriarchal society subjugates women and blames them for inadequate mothering. Feminists remind us that patriarchy has negative effects on both women and men. They assert that gender and cultural issues need to be made more intentional in the therapy room (Hare-Mustin, 1978).

Feminist therapy is deliberately political. Its aim is to replace patriarchy with a feminist consciousness. This involves helping clients realize that how they define themselves and relate to others is often distorted by gender-role expectations. A feminist view of family therapy focuses on gender and power in relationships and encourages a personal commitment to challenge gender inequity. They espouse a vision of a future society that values equality between women and men. Examining the power differential in their relationships often helps partners demystify differences between them. Feminist family therapists share a number of roles, each of which is based on a specific value orientation: They make their values and beliefs explicit so that the therapy process is clearly understood, they strive to establish egalitarian roles with clients, they work toward client autonomy and client empowerment, and they emphasize commonalities among women (Feminist Therapy Institute, 1996).

Feminist therapists contend that all therapists have values and that it is important to be clear with clients about these values. This is different, however, from imposing values on clients. An imposition of values is inconsistent with viewing clients as their own best experts. Clients should be encouraged to make their own choices; their choices can be challenged but need to be supported by their therapist.

Current issues of feminist concern surround wage discrepancies, the increased cost of healthcare for women, decreased access to education, and reproductive choice resources for women of color and women of lower socioeconomic status are a few of the significant issues that may be addressed in a feminist therapy session.

ASSESSMENT

Postmodern orientations, including feminist and collaborative family therapy, do not propose a structured assessment process, but focus entirely on the importance of the social context as a determiner of behavior. For example, feminist family therapy assesses how a client system has been impacted by the consequences of traditional socialization practices that primarily disadvantage women, including stereotyped sex roles and the statuses prescribed by society for females by males. Collaborative therapy would take a "not-knowing" approach to assessment by creating an open dialogue of curiosity through which the therapist can create a rich interchange with the client about what brings them to therapy and what they would like to change about their current condition.

INTERVENTIONS AND TECHNIQUES

FEMINIST FAMILY THERAPY AND COLLABORATIVE THERAPY: NOT TECHNIQUE BASED

Given that feminist family therapy serves more as a lens than a specific set of techniques, the approach may be used alone or as a supplement to the therapist's chosen model. Feminist therapy, therefore, highlights systematic oppression based not only on the organizing principle of gender, but also to race, class, and other socially constructed means for perpetuating inequality and oppression. Techniques are typically not addressed in the collaborative therapy model either, which makes it challenging to describe what occurs in session. Both approaches share a philosophy about what the therapeutic relationship ought to entail and what they want to avoid in the relationship. They are in agreement that the therapist's relationship with the client is one of respect and equality.

CONVERSATIONAL QUESTIONS

Conversational questions are similar to the Rogerian style of questioning in which the therapist reflects back to the client what the client is saying, but it goes further in that the conversational therapist will actively collaborate on generating solutions if that is what the client wishes. The key variable appears to be the way in which opinions or ideas are offered, very tentatively and respectfully, almost as a question. This style of therapeutic questioning is in stark contrast to most first wave family therapy models which emphasized a more directive and assertive therapist approach.

USE OF REFLECTING TEAMS

Reflecting teams are made up of a group of therapists who sit behind a one-way mirror to focus on listening to the conversation taking place in the therapy room. When using a reflecting team during a session, the therapist will solicit comments from the professionals behind the mirror, and the family and therapist become the observers as team members have a conversation about the family interaction they have just observed. Without prior knowledge of the family or use of preplanning strategies, and unencumbered by hypotheses meant to understand the family's own construction of reality, the team members spontaneously present their views based on what they observed during that particular session. After the team finishes its reflections, family members have an opportunity to talk about the reflecting team's comments. Shifting between inner and outer dialogue offers two differing perspectives on the same events and stimulates the search for new outlooks. In the process, the family feels heard, validated, and important. Andersen contended that sharing hypotheses about the family from the reflecting team directly helps demystify therapy and leads to the use of a common "public language" rather than the hidden "private language" professionals often use when discussing cases (Andersen, 1991).

PSYCHOEDUCATION

Psychoeducation is a useful tool in feminist therapy, which operates under the assumption that knowledge is empowering.

IDENTIFICATION OF VALUES

A useful intervention is to ask each family member to identify a few people who were influential in their upbringing and describe their relationships. Then ask the client to identify what values this person or relationship taught the client about relationships, about men, and about women. Then ask the client to identify which of these values they would like to keep and which they would like to replace. This intervention both facilitates the identification of values and encourages freedom of choice in feminist therapy.

ROLE OF THE THERAPIST

COLLABORATIVE THERAPY

Deliberately avoiding the expert's interventionist stance of designing therapeutic change as used in the modernist tradition, therapists using this postmodern collaborative approach view themselves as *learners* (the clients are the *knowers*), conducting therapy from a position of "not knowing." This is not to say that the therapist lacks knowledge or is without therapeutic skills, but rather that the therapist maintains respectful listening, stays in sync with the unfolding story, and tries not to begin with any set ideas about what should or should not change.

FEMINIST FAMILY THERAPY

A feminist family therapist is transparent, honors egalitarian relationships, and serves as both a therapist and an activist. It is clear that feminist therapists do not take a neutral stance with respect to gender roles and power in relationships. They advocate for definite change in the social structure, especially in the area of equality; power in relationships; the right to self-determination; freedom to pursue a career outside the home; the right to an education; and social justice for all races, cultures, and sexual orientations. These feminist values may not conform to the values people in other cultures hold. Values, such as equality and self-determination, may not be prized as much in some cultures as honoring one's extended family and putting the welfare of the family before one's personal agenda. Above all, the therapist must be respectful of the client's value system.

ORIENTATION IN TIME

Feminist family therapy and collaborative therapy are both present focused, but pay attention to how clients have been minimized or disenfranchised in the past.

PROCESS AND GOALS OF THERAPY

COLLABORATIVE THERAPY

Collaborative therapy is aimed at "dissolving," as opposed to solving the problem. The problem, created through language, becomes a nonproblem through language, as alternative meanings of the troublesome thoughts or feelings emerge. Change, whether in understanding or behavior, follows naturally from the "therapeutic conversation" as new solutions arise, dissolving the problem. The therapeutic goal is reached when a conversation takes place in which the complaint is no longer a part of the story.

FEMINIST FAMILY THERAPY

The main goal of feminist therapy is to look closely at the power differences between people and examine how they could be contributing to the family system's presenting problem. It is based on the idea that gender shapes everything about us: our worldview, our identity and our well-being in general. The goals of feminist family therapy are to empower the client, enabling that person to potentially address aspects of social transformation; nurture the self and establish a strong self-concept; and restructure and enhance personal beliefs about identity.

CONCLUSION

The postmodern revolution in family therapy challenged everything that came before, including traditional cybernetic thinking. In the postmodern view, there is no absolute truth—instead, reality is socially co-constructed. Postmodern marriage and family therapists value diversity and construct meaning that is culturally determined from our experiences. Ethnicity, culture, gender, sexual orientation, and so forth must be addressed in determining a family's functioning level. Social constructionism figures prominently in the therapies influenced by the postmodern revolution. These therapists reject the customary "therapist as expert" mentality, instead adopting a collaborative approach that supports clients' rights to self-determination. The postmodern, systemic therapist is also committed to engaging families in collaborative dialogues in which language and meaning take precedence over behavioral sequences or family interactive patterns.

The collaborative approach (Harry Goolishian and Harlene Anderson) and the reflecting team (Tom Andersen) are examples of a social constructionist influence on therapy. This collaborative approach pays particular attention to meanings generated between people, as therapists and clients engage in a shared inquiry aimed at dissolving problems by co-creating stories that open up new possibilities. This approach offers no special techniques but rather offers an authentic way of being in the therapy room. The reflecting team technique employs two-way mirrors so that professionals and families can reverse roles and observe one another, offering differing perspectives or tentative speculations on family issues. This second-order cybernetic demystifying of the therapeutic process breaks down professional–client barriers and helps all participants communicate respectfully with a shared language.

The feminist critique in family therapy brought to the surface historical power inequalities between men and women that were traditionally ignored in MFT theory and practice. Feminist family therapy is not attributed to any single developer. Instead, the approach arose from increasing sociopolitical awareness and critiquing of traditional family therapy processes. Some of the primary leaders in applying the feminist critique to therapy include Rachel Hare-Mustin, Marianne Walters, Betty Carter, Peggy Papp, and Olga Silverstein. These women were among the first and most prominent to criticize the field of family therapy for perpetuating the oppression of women within the sexist status quo of traditional therapy approaches. Walters established The Women's Project in MFT to help reform family therapy practice, so as not to perpetuate sexism and oppression of women in therapy.

KEY TERMS

Client's voice: This refers to the client's own unique perspective that comes through with support and reassurance from the therapist.

Collaboration: The process of working together in postmodern therapy with one or more clients in such a way that everyone's ideas are valued and everyone puts forth the same or a similar amount of effort.

Collaborative therapy: A client-centered approach that places the emphasis on collaboration, honesty, respect, and empowerment for both therapist and client. Includes a more egalitarian view of the therapist's role; advocated by critics of what is viewed as authoritarianism in traditional approaches to family therapy.

Constructivism: A relativistic point of view that emphasizes the subjective construction of reality. Implies that what we see in families may be based as much on our preconceptions as on what's actually going on.

Curiosity: An interviewing position of impartiality that is characterized by an openness not only to the validity of each system member's viewpoint, but also an openness to multiple possible constructions of clients' situations as well as a respect for the integrity of the system and its way of operating.

Curious questions: Genuine, open requests for new information meant to elicit the client's true perspective, as opposed to accusations or statements disguised as questions.

Deconstruction: A postmodern approach to exploring meaning that takes apart and examines taken-for-granted categories and assumptions, making newer and sounder constructions of meaning possible.

Dialogue: Genuine back-and-forth conversation between client and therapist in the collaborative model.

Feminism: A movement to help women advance in society and end prejudice toward them.

Feminist theory: An attitude and body of ideas concerning gender hierarchy, socialization, and power and their impact on conducting therapy. Feminists recognize the overriding importance of sexism as a factor in the problems women have in society and how important it is to eliminate sexist practices that are detrimental to women.

Feminist therapy: Based on the idea that women's problems are inseparable from societal problems that socialize women to assume inferior roles. Therapy focuses on issues such as the sharing of power between men and women, acceptance of one's body as is, and non–gender-biased careers.

Galveston Family Institute: The family therapy center started by Harry Goolishian and Harlene Anderson, and where the collaborative therapy model emerged; now known as the Houston Galveston Institute.

Hermeneutics: The art of analyzing literary texts or therapeutic conversations, understood as fundamentally ambiguous, by interpreting levels of meaning.

Historical oppression: The notion that throughout time, certain groups of people have had unfair advantages compared to other groups. Women, people of color, the poor, members of minority religious groups, the disabled, and those who are seen as too different in any way, among others, have been disadvantaged.

Interventive interviewing: A term coined by Karl Tomm to refer to an orientation in which every question the therapist asks in a session is thought of as an intervention.

Languaging: Carol Anderson and Harry Goolishian's term for talking about a problem with a view to exploring new and more useful constructions.

Multiversa: Tom Andersen's term for the multitude of possible ways of thinking about clients' problems and solutions.

Not-knowing approach: Harlene Anderson and Harry Goolishian's term for taking a nonexpert collaborative position in which clients and therapist explore multiple possible co-constructions of the problem and possible solutions. In the not-knowing approach, therapists avoid the use of diagnosesand therapeutic directives because these may limit possibilities for co-constructing new solutions.

Postmodernism: A theory that views knowledge as relative and context dependent and that questions assumptions of objectivity that characterize modern science. In family therapy, it challenges the concept of scientific certainty and is linked to the method of deconstruction.

Problem-determined system: Harlene Anderson and Harry Goolishian's term for a group of people who agree in conversation that a problem exists and whose beliefs about the problem maintain its existence.

Problem-organizing and problem-dissolving systems: Harlene Anderson and Harry Goolishian's term for the therapeutic system that includes the therapist and members of the problem-determined system. This system is organized by a belief that there is a problem and that the problem dissolves through conversation.

Reflecting team: Tom Andersen's technique of having the observing team share its reactions with the family following a session.

Second-order cybernetics: The idea that anyone attempting to observe and change a system is therefore a part of that system. The role of the observer is appreciated and acknowledged rather than disguised; the observer no longer remains neutral and detached.

Social construction: An idea about the way things are or should be that is built more on the shared perceptions of members of a society than on objective reality. This concept maintains there is no objective reality and no universal human nature.

Stuck systems: Systems become stuck when they focus on one or a limited number of possible ways of thinking about problems and solutions and are closed to multiple possibilities.

KNOWLEDGE CHECK: CHAPTER 9

1. Postmodern systemic therapists believe most families _______.
   - A. Lack resilience
   - B. Accurately perceive an objective reality
   - C. Collectively construct a sense of reality
   - D. Need the therapeutic intervention to create clinically significant change

2. __________ theory played a major part in the deconstruction of family therapy's gendered, philosophical roots.
   - A. Structural
   - B. Family life cycle
   - C. Systems
   - D. Feminist

3. The family therapist who joins a family and engages in a dialogue to become part of the system rather than observing from outside is probably a proponent of __________.
   - A. First-order cybernetics
   - B. Second-order cybernetics
   - C. First-order change
   - D. Strategic interventions

4. Feminists disagree with traditional family therapy models because these early approaches______.
   - A. Are supportive of mothers
   - B. Ignore gender and power discrepancies between men and women
   - C. Overemphasize power distinctions between men and women
   - D. Overemphasize feedback loops

5. _______family therapy would be *least likely* to challenge dominant culture as a part of the model.
   - A. Feminist
   - B. Narrative
   - C. Strategic
   - D. Collaborative

(*See answers next page.*)

1. C) Collectively construct a sense of reality

The proponents of postmodern models questioned many of the premises that historically sustained psychotherapeutic practice, and they offered alternative ways of conceptualizing and doing therapy. This movement is not represented by a single school or model, but by the work of many theorists and practitioners who share some philosophical and epistemological common ground. In addition to co-constructing their sense of reality, therapists and clients focus on deconstructing common beliefs and examining their value in an individual's life. The relationship between client and therapist is highly collaborative rather than authoritative. Change comes about primarily through open dialogue.

2. D) Feminist

Feminist theory tended to be most concerned with responding effectively to the extensive gender-related problems that had been ignored, marginalized, or distorted by the lenses of mental health professions that had been dominated by androcentric theories and practices. The feminist critique of the mental health professions focused primarily on four overlapping issues: (a) theories and research that supported biased models of therapy; (b) double standards of mental health that overvalued attributes described as "masculine" and devalued attributes considered "feminine"; (c) diagnostic practices that contributed to labeling clients without regard to contextual, situational contributors to distress; and (d) psychotherapeutic relationships in which an all-powerful therapist defined reality for the client.

3. B) Second-order cybernetics

Cybernetics is the interdisciplinary study of the structure of complex systems, especially communication processes, control mechanisms, and feedback principles. Cybernetics is closely related to systems theory. From a first-order epistemological stance, the therapist perceives reality as something that one can discover through a process of observation without being influenced by this process. Conversely, second-order cybernetics (also known as the *cybernetics of cybernetics* and the *new cybernetics*) is a philosophy of communication and growth that acknowledges the recursive nature of relationships and interpersonal influence. It holds that those who observe systems, such as family therapists, cannot be separated from the systems they observe and are thus constantly helping to shape reality for all members.

4. B) Ignore gender and power discrepancies between men and women

The main goal of feminist therapy is to look closely at the power differences among people and examine how they could be contributing to the client's personal issues. It is based on the idea that gender shapes everything about us: our worldview, family life, and our well-being in general.

5. C) Strategic

Strategic therapy, often associated with its "therapist as expert" mentality and maligned for a patriarchal ideology, would be the least likely of these four options to challenge dominant culture. Feminist, narrative, and collaborative models, on the other hand, would take a postmodern approach to challenging dominant society and deconstructing previously held ideologies around psychotherapy and change.

AUDIO PODCAST 9.1
Postmodernism, Social Constructionism, and the Feminist Critique
Eli A. Karam
https://bcove.video/3CGmiB3

REFERENCES

Andersen, T. (1987). The reflecting team: Dialogue and meta-dialogue in clinical work. *Family Process, 26,* 415–428. https://doi.org/10.1111/j.1545-5300.1987.00415.x

Andersen, T. (1991). *The reflecting team: Dialogues and dialogues about the dialogues.* W. W. Norton.

Anderson, H. (1997). *Conversation, language and possibilities. A postmodern approach to therapy.* Basic Books.

Anderson, H. (2003). Postmodern, social construction therapies. In T. Sexton, G. Weeks, & M. Robbins (Eds.), *Handbook of family therapy* (pp. 125–146). Brunner-Routledge.

Feminist Therapy Institute. (1996). The feminist therapy institute code of ethics. *Women & Therapy, 19,* 79–91. https://doi.org/10.1300/J015v19n01_07

Hare-Mustin, R. T. (1978). A feminist approach to family therapy. *Family Process, 17,* 181–194.

Hoffman, L. (2002). *Family therapy: An intimate history.* W. W. Norton.

Tomm, K. (1987a). Interventive interviewing part I. Strategizing as a fourth guideline for the therapist. *Family Process, 25,* 4–13. https://doi.org/10.1111/j.1545-5300.1987.00003.x

Tomm, K. (1987b). Interventive interviewing part II. Reflexive questioning as a means to enable self-healing. *Family Process, 26,* 167–183. https://doi.org/10.1111/j.1545-5300.1987.00167

Tomm, K. (1988). Interventive interviewing part III. Intending to ask linear, circular, strategic or reflexive questions. *Family Process, 27,* 1–15. https://doi.org/10.1111/j.1545-5300.1988.00001.x

Walters, M., Carter, B., Papp, P., & Silverstein, O. (1991). *The invisible web: Gender patterns in family relationships.* Guilford Press.

Solution-Focused Therapy

10

LEARNING OBJECTIVES

After reading this chapter, you should be able to:

- Identify model developers and other key figures associated with solution-focused therapy (SFT)
- Describe the assessment process in solution-focused therapy
- Review the main interventions/techniques of solution-focused therapy
- Identify goals of solution-focused therapy
- Develop the role of therapist in solution-focused therapy

RELEVANT EXAM DOMAINS

- *Domain 1—The Practice of Systemic Therapy*
  Includes tasks related to incorporating systemic theory and perspectives into practice activities and establishing and maintaining ongoing therapeutic relationships with the client system.
- *Domain 2—Assessing, Hypothesizing, and Diagnosing*
  Includes tasks related to assessing the various dimensions of the client system, forming and reformulating hypotheses, and diagnosing the client and family system in order to guide therapeutic activities.
- *Domain 3—Designing and Conducting Treatment*
  Includes tasks related to developing and implementing interventions with the client system.

INTRODUCTION

Historically, clients see their problems as overwhelming and occurring frequently. Times that are free of problems go unnoticed or are dismissed as trivial. The art of solution-focused therapy (SFT), therefore, becomes a matter of helping clients see that their problems have exceptions, and that these times offer potential solutions they already have in their repertoires that can be used to address current problems. Contending that it isn't necessary to know what causes problems in order to improve the situation, solution focused therapists view their clients as experts in their own lives. SFT assumes that people who come to therapy are capable of finding their own solutions, but that their effectiveness has been constrained by a negative mindset. Drawing their attention to forgotten capabilities helps release clients from preoccupation with their failures and restores them to their more capable selves.

MODEL DEVELOPERS AND SIGNIFICANT CONTRIBUTORS

STEVE DE SHAZER

Steve de Shazer began his therapeutic career by working at the Mental Research Institute (MRI) in the mid-1970s, where he developed a friendship with John Weakland. In the late 1970s, de Shazer and a group of individuals working in Milwaukee established the Brief Family Therapy Center. de Shazer first gained national attention as director of the Brief Family Therapy Center and, with his emphasis in therapy on solutions instead of problems, began to gain recognition as a major theorist in family therapy during the 1980s.

INSOO KIM BERG

Born in Korea, Berg married Steve de Shazer and helped to found both the Solution-Focused Brief Therapy Association and the Brief Family Therapy Center in Milwaukee, where she served as executive director. Berg was usually found in front of the mirror as the leader in the clinical implementation of solution-focused therapy, while her husband focused his work behind the mirror on supervision and consultation.

BILL O'HANLON

After earning a degree from Arizona State University, O'Hanlon went on to be mentored by Milton Erickson in exchange for being Erickson's gardener. Erickson's influence on O'Hanlon was profound and shifted his attention to focusing on solutions in therapy. O'Hanlon was also influenced by the work done at the MRI. O'Hanlon set out to become a major proponent of solution-oriented therapy, which is also referred to as *possibility therapy*. His motivation was to shift the focus of family therapy from problems to solutions (O'Hanlon & Weiner-Davis, 2003).

MICHELE WEINER-DAVIS

As a former student of Steve de Shazer's, Weiner-Davis has helped to evolve solution-focused therapy with her focus on couples. She has written some of the most popular books on solution-oriented family therapy, including *Divorce Busting* (Weiner-Davis, 1992), and set up a Divorce Busting Center in Boulder, Colorado.

MODEL OVERVIEW

SFT, also known as *solution-focused brief therapy (SFBT)*, was developed by the husband-and-wife team of Steve de Shazer and Insoo Kim Berg in collaboration with their colleagues at the Milwaukee Brief Family Therapy Center beginning in the late 1970s as part of the postmodern movement in marriage and family therapy (MFT). SFT is future focused, goal directed, and emphasizes solutions rather than the problems that brought clients to seek therapy.

The overarching belief in this approach is that clients already know what they need to do to solve their problems. The therapist helps them use that knowledge differently. The overall aim of this approach is to help clients start the solution process. SFT's basic rules are (de Shazer, 1982, 1985, 1988, 1991, 1994):

1. If it is not broken, do not fix it.
2. Once you know what works, do more of it.
3. If something does not work, do not do it again. Do something different.

This model is built on the philosophy of social constructionism, which is the belief that knowledge is bound by time and culture. Therapeutic treatment of families or persons must include their social, historical, and cultural contexts. Reality is not an objective entity, but rather a reflection of observation and experience. The social constructionist paradigm emphasizes that meaning is constructed through certain cultural conversations and contexts, and it challenges the notion of objective knowledge or absolute truth.

While de Shazer was heavily influenced by MRI's brevity and focus on feedback loops, SFT departs significantly from MRI both in theory and execution. Solution-focused therapists aid the family in discovering its own creative solutions for becoming "unstuck." In short, although MRI therapists try to get clients to change the behavior that has not worked, solution-focused therapists try to get them to change their cognitions and to open up to the possibility of finding new ways to deal with the problem. The MRI model is problem focused; the Milwaukee model is solution focused. The former urges clients to do things differently, whereas the latter urges them to view things differently.

Families often begin their relationship with family therapists by assuming a defensive posture. Expecting this, solution-focused therapists work toward a collaborative relationship and try to minimize defensiveness by normalizing the family problems as part of the normal developmental processes that all families experience. The following assumptions provide the framework of SFT (de Shazer, 1982, 1985, 1988, 1991, 1994):

1. There are significant advantages in focusing on the positive and on solutions for the future. Focusing on strengths and solution talk increases the likelihood that therapy will be brief.
2. Individuals who come to therapy do have the capacity to act effectively. This capacity, however, is temporarily blocked by negative cognitions.
3. There are exceptions to every problem.
4. Clients tend to present one side of the problem. Solution-focused therapists invite clients to view their problems from a different side.
5. Small change fosters bigger change. Small improvement can boost confidence and reinforce families to help them realize they can make progress.
6. Clients want to change, they have the capacity to change, and they are doing their best to make change happen.
7. As each individual is unique, so too is every solution.

SOLUTION-ORIENTED THERAPY

Bill O'Hanlon's approach to solution-focused therapy, known as *solution-oriented therapy*, is guided by three principles (O'Hanlon & Weiner-Davis, 2003):

1. Acknowledge and validate clients' reality and experience.
2. Guide clients to shift how they view things (perceptions of the problem) and/or do things (patterns that support or create the problem).
3. Tap into clients' resources, expertise, and experiences to look for solutions and consult clients on their preferences for the process and direction of therapy.

ASSESSMENT

SFT takes a strengths-based, nonpathologizing approach to client systems, not using the *Diagnostic and Statistical Manual of Mental Disorders* (5th ed.; *DSM-5;* American Psychiatric Association, 2013) or individual diagnoses in an opening assessment. The solution-focused therapist assumes that the family has made numerous attempts at solving the problem on their own and have been unsuccessful. The therapist, therefore, is very interested in assessing what solutions they have tried and why family members think they did not work.

Solution-focused therapists also assess the different positions of clients in each family system. de Shazer categorizes clients into three groups: visitors, complainants, or customers. Visitors may be there at someone else's suggestion or demand, do not describe a clear complaint, do not expect change, and do not really want to engage in therapy. Complainants are willing to describe the perceived basis for their unhappiness but are not currently willing to work on constructing solutions, perhaps waiting for their partner to change first. Customers, on the other hand, describe their complaints and are prepared to take action to construct a solution. Different family members may occupy differing positions at different times (de Shazer, 1982, 1985, 1988, 1991, 1994).

A team of therapists, collectively known as *consultants*, observe and assess from behind a one-way mirror and transmit messages to the therapist at a designated break time in the session. Thus, the family in treatment can be the beneficiary of multiple inputs (Lipchik, 2002).

INTERVENTIONS AND TECHNIQUES

PRESESSION CHANGE QUESTIONS

The therapist asks the client these presession questions during the initial call for an appointment so as to notice any changes that take place between then and the time of the first session. Often clients report that they have managed to contain the problem, or in some way improve their situation (de Shazer, 1982, 1985, 1988, 1991, 1994). Examples of presession questions follow:

Have there been changes for better or worse since you decided to come to therapy?

Who else noticed this?

MIRACLE QUESTION

The miracle question opens the door to the client's preferred outcomes and possibilities resulting from therapy by asking them to consider what an alternate reality might look like—one in which things are different, better, and problems are resolved.

I'm going to ask you a kind of strange question now. Suppose you go to bed and to sleep tonight as usual and while you are asleep a miracle happens and the problem that brought you here today is solved. But you are asleep and don't know that it has been solved. What will be the first small signs that this miracle has happened and that the problem is solved?

Most clients begin to connect to hope as they describe their solutions in the context of the miracle question. The next step is to invite clients to identify the most recent times when the have experienced some aspect (even the smallest pieces) of their miracle description and invite them to experiment with replicating these in the context of their everyday lives (de Shazer et al., 1986).

SCALING QUESTIONS

These questions are extremely useful in highlighting small increments of change or for plotting what outcome is likely if the direction of change is continued. Scaling questions allow the family therapist to ask family members to give their best estimate of where on a scale of a given variable they might fall (de Shazer, 1982, 1985, 1988, 1991, 1994).

> *Please think of a scale from 0 to 10 with 10 being the best. Zero is how you felt when things were at their worst. Ten is as good as things can be in relation to this problem. Where are you on that scale right now?*
>
> *How long will it take to get to 10?*
>
> *Maybe 10 is too big a goal? Is something lower more realistic? What number will be acceptable for you? How will you recognize when you are one point further up the scale?*
>
> *What else will be different when you are one point further up? Who will notice? How long will it take to get one point up the scale?*

EXCEPTION QUESTIONS

Solution-focused therapists help family members move toward solutions by helping them search for and identify any exceptions to the typical problem cycle or pattern. Looking for moments when someone didn't lie, or didn't create a problem, or was different than before gives everyone an opportunity to understand what made that exception possible, what unique characteristics of that event made it possible for the pattern to be avoided. The premise is that if something happened once in a different way that was more functional for everyone, then maybe it can happen again if the same conditions were recreated (de Shazer, 1982, 1985, 1988, 1991, 1994).

> *What is different about times when the problem is not happening? Or when it is less of a concern?*
>
> *You mentioned earlier that some days are better . . . what is it like at these times?*
>
> *What are you doing differently at these times?*
>
> *What else is better at these times?*

COPING QUESTIONS

These questions are a reminder that all clients are resilient and engage in many proactive coping strategies even in times of overwhelming difficulties. Coping questions, such as *How have you managed to carry on?* or *How have you managed to prevent things from becoming worse?* allow a different way of looking at client's fortitude and determination (de Shazer, 1982, 1985, 1988, 1991, 1994).

COMPLIMENTS

Based on careful observation of positive things the client has already done or said, offering compliments in therapy sessions serves to punctuate and validate what the client is doing that is working. Indirect compliments are often conveyed in the form of appreciatively toned questions. Asking *How did you do that?* invites the client to self-compliment by virtue of answering the question (Berg, 1994).

BRIDGING STATEMENT

The bridging statement is a "bridge" from what has been discussed and the logical next step. It connects the compliments and the behavioral task portion of the message. In other words, the therapist takes the client's words and helps the client make something useful of them (Berg, 1994).

HOMEWORK/TASKS

Homework or *experiments* are suggestions for clients to try, not assignments they are commanded to do. These between-session tasks should be suggestions that flow from where clients *are* to where clients *want to be* (Berg, 1994).

ROLE OF THE THERAPIST

In their role as consultants, solution-focused therapists empower their clients to take charge in finding solutions in their lives. The role is more collegial than directorial. The relationship between the therapist and family becomes less hierarchical and moves closer to a solution-building partnership.

ORIENTATION IN TIME

SFT is a both a here-and-now and future-oriented therapy, with most therapist-driven questions usually focused on the present or on the future. This reflects the basic belief that problems are best solved by focusing on what is already working, and how a client would like their life to be, rather than focusing on the past and the origin of problems. For example, the therapist may ask, *What will you be doing in the next week that would indicate to you that you are continuing to make progress?*

PROCESS AND GOALS OF THERAPY

A foundational belief of this approach is that causal understanding is unnecessary in the creation of adaptive solutions to client problems. SFT is considered a brief therapy, given that it will conclude when the desired client solution is achieved. Goals, central to the monitoring and progress of SFT, should be measurable and easily identifiable. They help to identify specific preferred client behaviors and interactions.

CONCLUSION

SFT is a short-term, goal-focused approach that helps clients change by constructing solutions rather than focusing on problems. In the most basic sense, SFT is a future-oriented vehicle used to formulate, motivate, achieve, and sustain desired behavioral change. Solution-focused practitioners help clients develop their own solutions by first generating a detailed description of how the client's life will be different when the problem is gone, or their situation improved to a degree satisfactory to the client. Therapist and client then carefully search through the client's life experience and behavioral repertoire to discover the necessary resources needed to co-construct a practical and sustainable solution that the client can readily implement. Typically, this process involves identifying and exploring previous "exceptions," or times when the client has successfully coped with similar difficulties and challenges.

SFT has developed a set of techniques for changing problem talk into solution talk. These techniques include exception, miracle, scaling, and coping questions, along with formula first-session tasks and compliments. These techniques are put into practice as soon as possible to keep the work brief and to discourage clients from dwelling on the negative side of their experience. SFT continues to be very popular across various mental health disciplines because the techniques are based on interventive questions and take minimal therapeutic skill to implement effectively. Yet this easy-to-learn formula leads some critics to dismiss it as superficial and a model that will not work with more multiproblem and constrained client systems.

KEY TERMS

Complainant: de Shazer's term for a relationship with a client who describes a complaint but is at present unwilling to work on solving it.

Compliments: Technique used in solution-focused therapy to convey support and encouragement.

Coping questions: Questions asked in solution-focused therapy to help clients realize that they have been managing difficult circumstances.

Customer: de Shazer's term for a client who not only complains about a problem ("complainant") but is motivated to resolve it.

Exception: de Shazer's term for times when clients are temporarily free of their problems. Solution- focused therapists focus on exceptions to help clients build on successful problem-solving skills.

Formula first-session task: In order to focus on strengths in the system and begin the solution-generating process, at the end of the first session, solution-focused therapists routinely ask clients to think about what they do not want to change as a result of therapy.

Miracle question: Refers to asking clients to imagine how things would be if they woke up tomorrow and their problem was solved. Solution-focused therapists use the miracle question to help clients identify goals and potential solutions.

Scaling questions: Solution-focused clients are asked to use a 10-point scale to rate how much they want to resolve their problems, how bad the problem is, how much better the problem is than the last time, and so on. These questions are designed to break change up into small steps.

Visitor: de Shazer's term for a client who does not wish to participate in therapy, does not have a complaint, and does not want to work on anything.

KNOWLEDGE CHECK: CHAPTER 10

1. *If 1 is where you were when you began this therapy and 10 is where you would be if you successfully solved all the issues that brought you here, where are you today?* is an example of a ________________________.

   A. Scaling question
   B. Presuppositional question
   C. Coping question
   D. Miracle question

2. Solution-focused therapy (SFT) is _______________ rather than _______________, contending that the problem is not always related to the solution.

   A. Problem focused; solution focused
   B. Therapist driven; client driven
   C. Individual; collaborative
   D. Exception driven; problem focused

3. Solution-focused therapy (SFT) usually involves clients leaving the first session with ________________________________.

   A. A paradoxical directive from the therapist
   B. Small action steps to take toward solutions
   C. Insight into the cause of their problem
   D. Increased problem-solving skills

4. Solution-focused therapists believe that ________ is inevitable and always possible.

   A. Happiness
   B. Satisfaction
   C. Hope
   D. Change

5. When successfully delivered, the miracle question allows clients to ____________________.

   A. Focus on unrealistic outcomes, rather than reality
   B. Envision the future without the problem
   C. Identify the problem in context
   D. Assess their progress in family therapy

6. As a solution-focused family therapist, the purpose of asking questions about circumstances in which the problem does not occur is designed to ______________________.

   A. Maintain rapport with the family
   B. Change the direction of the interview
   C. Assess the resources and strengths of the family
   D. Contextualize the problem

(*See answers next page.*)

1. A) Scaling question

Scaling questions ask clients to rate their priorities, goals, satisfaction, problems, coping strategies, successes, motivation for change, safety, confidence, treatment progress, and hope on a numerical scale from 1 to 10. These questions have great versatility and can be used to assess the client's perception of almost anything. They are quick, simple, and easy to ask, making them especially useful for busy clinicians struggling with increasing workloads and briefer appointment times. Solution-focused scales are self-anchored rather than normed scales. The client, not the therapist, defines what a 3 or 7 or 10 means. Scaling questions are used to facilitate treatment and are based on clients' perceptions. Clients may more readily take ownership of their treatment goals and progress when asked to rate them on a scale. Scaling questions help direct the treatment toward what clients want and what is most important to them, increasing their motivation and confidence to change and helping to facilitate agreement among client, therapist, and others participating in treatment. Scaling questions can also help defuse intense emotion in a conversation.

2. D) Exception driven; problem focused

SFT is a short-term, goal-focused therapeutic approach, which incorporates positive psychology principles and practices, to help clients change by focusing on exceptions to construct solutions rather than focusing on problems. This model is a positive-emotion-eliciting, future-oriented vehicle used to formulate, motivate, achieve,, and sustain desired behavioral change.

3. B) Small action steps to take toward solutions

A central tenet in SFT, is that only a small change is necessary. Once clients are able to value minimal changes, they are more likely to expect and look forward to even greater changes.

4. D) Change

Although any of those responses could make sense in the stem, "change" is clearly the best response. Contending that change is inevitable, a solution-focused therapist emphasizes that it is only a matter of time before change occurs, employing language that underscores possible solutions.

5. B) Envision the future without the problem

The power of the miracle question appears to be in its ability to break clients out of their stuck patterns, lifting their constraints and imagining what could be. It helps the client piece together a specific and elaborate vision of what their lives would be like in the absence of a problem. Along with setting goals, the purpose of the miracle question is to prepare the client for exceptions to the problem, glimpsing a world in which the problem is no longer present, either temporarily or permanently. The question helps to create a progressive narrative where the client's life is pictured as becoming better rather than worse.

6. C) Assess the resources and strengths of the family

In their search for exceptions, solution-focused proponents insist that there are always times when the problem is less severe or absent for the client. The goal is for the client to understand and repeat what has worked in the past and that helps.

7. Clients who describe their unhappiness but wait for their partner to change first are known as ______ in solution-focused therapy (SFT).

A. Visitors
B. Customers
C. Nonparticipants
D. Complainants

8. Solution-oriented therapy is based on the ideas of all the following *except:*

A. Salvador Minuchin
B. The ideas of brief therapy
C. Steve de Shazer
D. The ideas of the Mental Research Institute (MRI)

9. Talking about the ______________ is one of the most important means of identifying solutions according to solution-based therapies.

A. Past
B. Present
C. Future
D. The unknown

10. Assessing ______________________ is one of the key practices in solution-based therapies.

A. Symptoms
B. Family history
C. Client strengths
D. Client dysfunction

11. Solution-focused goals should have the following qualities *except*:

A. Be meaningful to clients
B. Be interactional
C. Be situational
D. Take large steps

12. According to de Shazer, all of the following are basic tenets of solution-focused interventions *except:*

A. If it isn't broken, don't fix it
B. Small steps can lead to big changes
C. The solution is usually related to the problem
D. No problem happens all of the time; there are always exceptions

(*See answers next page.*)

7. D) Complainants

In a complainant–therapist relationship, the client has a conflict and is suffering from it, but does not see themselves as part of the conflict or the solution. They do not feel the need to change their own behavior, believing someone or something else is to blame for the conflict and should change. The therapist gives acknowledgment and asks about client strengths. The therapist helps the complainant locate exceptions: Thus, the client is invited to think and talk about a preferred future (without the conflict) rather than focusing on the conflict. By working through this process, the solution-focused therapist may convert the client from an unworkable complainant to a willing customer.

8. A) Salvador Minuchin

Minuchin, of course, is the innovator of structural family therapy, a very different approach to working with families than solution-focused therapy (SFT). SFT, however, originated with de Shazer and Berg in Milwaukee, Wisconsin. In the mid-1970s, this group of researcher clinicians began experimenting with the brief therapy approach originated at the MRI in Palo Alto, California. The influence of the MRI model was initially noticeable in the Milwaukee group's attention to problem formulation, goal setting, and the uses of homework assignments. Some influence from the Milan group in the early 1980s can also be discerned in task construction and the brief nature of therapy. By 1980 the Milwaukee group's model of brief therapy had evolved to the point where it was distinctly their own.

9. A) Past

Solution-focused therapy (SFT) traditionally puts emphasis on a person's present and future circumstances and goals rather than past experiences. This holds true except for the times when therapists help their clients find exceptions from their past that may mobilize them to deal with their current issues.

10. C) Client strengths

Instead of focusing on symptoms, pathology, or deficit, solution-focused therapy (SFT) taps into client health, strengths, skills, resources, and coping abilities that would help in reaching future goals. Clients are encouraged to believe that positive changes are always possible and are encouraged to increase the frequency of current useful behaviors.

11. D) Take large steps

Solution-focused therapists focus on getting clients to take small steps toward their goals. By finding exceptions and working in a future and goal-oriented way, clients are able to take small steps in the direction of their goal during each session. When clients take a small step toward their goals they see change occur, which motivates them to create even more of the same change. By enacting a small doable change, clients move toward larger changes down the line.

12. C) The solution is usually related to the problem

According to de Shazer, the solution is not always directly related to the problem. This tenet is the most shocking and it seems to go against all intuition and knowledge we have about problems and solutions. According to the "problem-solving" approach, there should be a logical and coherent relationship between problems and solutions. However, sometimes this logic does not stand up to real life. Solution-focused therapists encourage clients to take a bold step to "do something differently."

AUDIO PODCAST 10.1
Solution-Focused Therapy Overview
Eli A. Karam
https://bcove.video/3PYSAKm

REFERENCES

American Psychiatric Association. (2013). *Diagnostic and statistical manual of mental disorders* (5th ed.).

Berg, I. (1994). *Family based services: A solution-focused approach*. W. W. Norton.

de Shazer, S. (1982). *Patterns of brief family therapy*. W. W. Norton.

de Shazer, S. (1985). *Keys to solutions in brief therapy*. W. W. Norton.

de Shazer, S. (1988). *Clues: Investigating solutions in brief therapy*. W. W. Norton.

de Shazer, S. (1991). *Putting difference to work*. W. W. Norton.

de Shazer, S. (1994). *Words were originally magic*. W. W. Norton.

de Shazer, S., Berg, I., Lipchik, E., Nunnally, E., Molnar, A., Gingerich, W., & Weiner-Davis, M. (1986). Brief therapy, focused solution development. *Family Process*, *25*, 207–222.

Lipchik, E. (2002). *Beyond technique in solution-focused therapy*. Guilford Press.

O'Hanlon, W. H., & Weiner-Davis, M. (2003). *In search of solutions: A new direction in psychotherapy*. W. W. Norton.

Weiner-Davis, M. (1992). *Divorce busting: A revolutionary and rapid program for staying together*. Summit Books.

Narrative Therapy

11

LEARNING OBJECTIVES

After reading this chapter, you should be able to:

1. Identify model developers and other key figures associated with narrative therapy
2. Describe the assessment process in narrative therapy
3. Review the main interventions/techniques of narrative therapy
4. Identify goals of narrative therapy
5. Develop the role of the therapist in narrative therapy

RELEVANT EXAM DOMAINS

- *Domain 1—The Practice of Systemic Therapy*
  Includes tasks related to incorporating systemic theory and perspectives into practice activities and establishing and maintaining ongoing therapeutic relationships with the client system.
- *Domain 2—Assessing, Hypothesizing, and Diagnosing*
  Includes tasks related to assessing the various dimensions of the client system, forming and reformulating hypotheses, and diagnosing the client and family system in order to guide therapeutic activities.
- *Domain 3—Designing and Conducting Treatment*
  Includes tasks related to developing and implementing interventions with the client system.

INTRODUCTION

The stories our clients tell themselves have powerful consequences for therapy. For many postmodern family therapists, making meaning through studying first-order cybernetics (feedback loops, interactive behavioral cycles) has been replaced by making meaning through the use of language and stories. According to narrative therapy, clients frequently construct negative, self-defeating, hopeless narratives about their lives. Narrative therapy contends that to achieve change, people need to learn to consider alternate ways of examining the values, assumptions, and meanings of their lives and see how existing stories dominate their views of themselves and their problems. Successful client systems author new stories, opening themselves to new possibilities in the reshaping of their lives. Narrative therapy involves respectful, nonpathologizing conversations in which clients are the experts in their own lives and are assumed to have the skills and competencies needed to construct more positive stories about themselves. Renewed outlooks lead to new ways of constructing meaning to life experiences and, ultimately, new behaviors.

MODEL DEVELOPERS AND SIGNIFICANT CONTRIBUTORS

MICHAEL WHITE

A therapist from Adelaide, Australia, Michael and his wife, Cheryl White, and their colleagues at the Dulwich Center have influenced narrative therapists throughout the world through training workshops and short publications, as well as through feature presentations given at national marriage and family therapy conferences in the late 1980s and early 1990s. Like other constructivists, he focuses on the effects and influences problems have on individuals and families, with particular attention paid to the way the problem takes over and controls an individual or family. According to Michael White, this reiteration of a story about the self becomes self-limiting and self-perpetuating. Because the way people think about themselves (their story) is so determinative of their options and actions, White's first step is to try to put distance between the person and their problem story. He works at externalizing the problem story through disciplined and detailed use of language.

DAVID EPSTON

Michael White's colleague David Epston collaborated with him on many publications, including their major work *Narrative Means to Therapeutic Ends* (White & Epston, 1990). He was born in Canada but traveled to Auckland, New Zealand, in his late teens, where he studied anthropology and sociology before traveling to Britain to study community work and then social work. Social work led him to becoming a family therapist in the late 1970s, and family therapy led him back to Auckland, where he co-founded his practice, The Family Therapy Centre, during the 1980s. Since White's death, Epston has continued to write, practice, and teach the narrative approach.

MODEL OVERVIEW

In narrative therapy, stories are defined as interpretations of life events and are thought of as being linked, sequentially across time, within a plot. Narrative therapists hold a series of assumptions that steer their approach to their work (White, 1997, 2000, 2005):

1. The problem is the problem; the person is not the problem.
2. Problems are never present 100% of the time.
3. Our understanding of life experiences changes over time.
4. Problems are constructed within cultural contexts.
5. There is no "one" objective truth; there are only multiple "truths."
6. People are the experts in their own lives and have skills/beliefs/values and abilities to help them with problems.
7. The therapist should take up a nonexpert position.
8. The use of therapeutic documentation and ritual is a valuable resource to sustain change.

Culture has a strong influence over the way we understand our lives and which stories are dominant or marginalized. The narrative perspective is that problems grow when supported by larger cultural ideas and beliefs (e.g., racism is supported by ideas of White privilege and power, which perpetuates the social–economic and political domination of non-White ethnic groups). Narrative therapists use deconstruction conversations to decipher the cultural beliefs that assist the problem and help the person view the problem differently.

ASSESSMENT

Believing that people are not their problems, narrative therapists do nothing to further stigmatize clients. Narrative therapy finds no cause or reason to diagnose and/or label a person's lived experience. Although narrative therapy does not have a structured assessment protocol, the early phase of treatment focuses on the following three domains:

1. Know the client apart from the problem.
2. Identify unique outcomes.
3. Map the effects of the problem on the client, as well as how the client has affected the life of the problem.

INTERVENTIONS AND TECHNIQUES

NARRATIVE QUESTIONS

Questions asked within conversations are the main tool of the narrative therapist. They are used to build narratives and scaffold the person or family's challenge to their problems. Narrative questions make direct reference to the person's language. The following are different types of narrative interventive questions:

1. Enabling openings *Can you describe the last time you managed to get free of the problem for a couple of minutes? What was the first thing you noticed in those few minutes? What was the next thing?*
2. Linking openings with preferred experience *Would you like more minutes like these in your life?*
3. Moving from openings to alternative story development *What was each of you thinking/feeling/doing/wishing/imagining during those few minutes?*
4. Broadening the viewpoint *What might your friend have noticed about you if she had met up with you in those few minutes?*
5. Exploring landscapes of action *How did you achieve that? How did your friend help you with that?*
6. Exploring landscapes of consciousness *From those few minutes, what have you learned about what you can manage?*
7. Linking with the exceptions in the past *When are times when you have managed to achieve a similar few minutes in the past?*
8. Linking exceptions from the past with the present *When you think about those times in the past when you have achieved this, how might this alter your view of the problem now?*
9. Linking exceptions from the past with the future *Thinking about this now, what do you expect to do next?*

EXTERNALIZING

To externalize the problem is to refer to the problem as if it existed outside of the client or family. Ask the client, *How long have you had to struggle with this problem pattern?* or *Has the yelling problem been dominating your lives in ways that you all feel is unfair?* or *What would you be doing more of in your family if this problem wasn't trying to run your lives?* Such questions move the family slightly outside the actual problem and help the members consider more independent action. If the problem is external to all of them, then they and the family therapist can work together as a team to overcome it. If certain family members have been identified as embodying the problem, then finding ways to externalize the problem is helpful in freeing them to work against the problem rather than spending their energy defending themselves.

Externalizing the problem does not mean minimizing personal responsibility. This technique should not be used when working with issues of violence and/or sexual abuse. There is a risk that the victim could interpret the externalization process to mean that the perpetrator is not responsible for their actions. Therefore, the therapist could unintentionally reinforce the abuse.

White used externalization in his work with a young boy plagued by encopresis, which was externalized and named "Sneaky Poo." Naming the problem is a part of the externalizing process and helps to further separate the problem from the person. The problem is known as "it" until a suitable name is identified; this is done in close collaboration between the person and the therapist as it is vital that the therapist does not use their own language (Madigan, 2011; Morgan, 2000).

UNIQUE OUTCOMES/SPARKLING MOMENTS

The narrative therapist will look for unique outcomes (aka "sparkling moments"), or times in which the personal story comes out differently. This effort is noticeably difficult for those clients who feel dominated and constrained by their problems. They are more familiar with talking about examples of times when their problem got the best of them versus a time when they were able to minimize the effects of the problem. They assume they have relatively little influence on the problem. But the narrative family therapist can search for examples when the family members stood up to the problem and prevented it from taking undue influence on their lives. The clients may be asked whether their influence on the problem has grown or declined over the past years (Freedman & Combs, 1996).

SCAFFOLDING

Scaffolding questions introduce ideas that are not so different from the person's self-concept that they are immediately dismissed. The questions act as a support of the familiar ideas, while at the same time they provide an opportunity for reassessment of past events and reconnection with skills that might otherwise be overlooked (Freedman & Combs, 1996).

THERAPEUTIC LETTER WRITING

Epston is credited with developing the use of letters and documents in therapeutic work. He wrote letters to people after therapy sessions to summarize the main ideas from the session and as part of the collaboration between himself and the clients. By extending the therapeutic conversation, these letters are used alongside other documentation to summarize knowledge, reiterate goals, and capture progress and change in the therapeutic work. The language used in the letters and documents is selected to reinforce and continue the externalization process and encourage the person or family in their endeavors between sessions and on completion of therapy. Family members can be encouraged to contribute to the change process by replying to the letter, and letter-writing campaigns can follow (Epston, 1994).

RITUALS

Rituals and celebrations, both formal and informal, are used to mark significant points in the therapeutic process. They are used to commemorate the process of moving away from the problem-saturated story toward the preferred future and act as a reinforcing parallel of this process. They are personalized and specific to the person involved. For celebrations, invitations to significant people are issued, an agenda is set, and people are invited to speak about their observations of the progress of the person being celebrated. The therapist might take part or may not even be present (Epston & White, 1992).

ROLE OF THE THERAPIST

The client is the primary "author" of the conversations, but the therapist is the editor—the one who makes the power of language and sociocultural influences explicit. The therapist is influential, not through structuring interventions, but through their use of questions that help the client to tell a new, more adaptive story.

ORIENTATION IN TIME

Narrative therapy focuses on revisiting past patterns and history to re-author the client's story, thereby changing their current perspective, and improving their trajectory heading into the future.

PROCESS AND GOALS OF THERAPY

The process of this postmodern approach explores the strengths and positive aspects of an individual or family system through their narrative. Therefore, the main goal of therapy is to improve the person's perspective internally (toward themself) and externally (toward the world and others). The client will reconstruct a personal story using unique outcomes, focusing on the positive aspects of a previous story in order to achieve a desired outcome. This process is based on the premise that clients can continually and actively re-author their own lives.

CONCLUSION

Narrative therapists help clients gain access to preferred story lines in order to replace the outdated, negative, self-defeating narratives they tell about themselves. Deconstructing constraining, restrictive ways of thinking and replacing them with multiple possibilities helps reduce the power of dominating, problem-saturated stories. The therapeutic process calls for attending to and overcoming oppressive self-narratives as well as negative societal narratives. To narrative therapists, the client is not the problem; the problem is the problem. Thus, therapeutic conversations typically begin by externalizing the problem. In some cases, the problem is personified, further identifying it as an outside force. Helping families reclaim their lives from the problem, narrative therapy takes the form of questions asked, often of a deconstructing kind, as the therapist helps clients achieve "thick" descriptions of an alternate story line about their future. Unique outcomes are searched for as possible entryways to developing alternate stories. As clients gain a history of the problem-saturated stories that have dominated their lives, they begin to develop a sense of other options involving more open-ended and feasible stories. Change calls for creating alternative narratives; the process is facilitated by various means for "thickening" or enriching the new story line and connecting to it in future options. With the therapist serving as story line editor, clients are helped to create and internalize new dominant stories, draw new assumptions about themselves, and open themselves up to future possibilities by re-authoring their lives.

KEY TERMS

Alternative story: This is a life story that does not support the dominant story and indicates new possibilities for future life.

Bringing-it-back practices: Practices that involve clients allowing others who are trapped by similar oppressive narratives to benefit from their new knowledge and skills.

Deconstruction: This is the act of interpreting the beliefs, ideas, and experiences of the person and others that underpin the story of the problem.

Dominant cultural discourse: These are cultural norms that can have a controlling effect on one's story of oneself.

Dominant story: These are fixed beliefs about the person that affect their past, present and future understanding of themselves.

Externalization: Refers to Michael White's technique of personifying problems as external to persons.

Externalizing conversations: The use of questions to develop the externalization of the problem and establish its personality, for example, "*What does anxiety take away from your friendships?*"

Landscape-of-action questions: These are questions about unique outcomes that inquire about sequences of behavior and interaction, such as "*What happened next?*"

Landscape-of-consciousness questions: These are questions about unique outcomes that inquire about meaning, intentions, beliefs and values, such as "*What does that say about you as a person?*"

Narrative: A story that usually involves characters and a plot. Most people have dominant and subjugated personal narratives, with the former having greater influence on their lives than the latter.

Outsider witness groups: Significant members of clients' social networks who are invited to witness new self-narratives.

Positioning: In narrative therapy, this occurs when a collaborative co-authoring consultative position is adopted.

Problem-saturated stories: These are the usual pessimistic and blaming accounts that clients bring to therapy, which are seen as helping keep them stuck.

Re-authoring/re-storying conversations: The process of helping clients develop new and liberating self-narratives that promote problem resolution.

Relative influence questions: These are questions designed to explore the extent to which the problem has dominated the client versus how much the client has been able to control it.

Scaffolding: An incremental process of moving a person from a story that is known and familiar to one that is unfamiliar.

Subjugated narratives: These are the infinite number of alternatives to the dominant narrative, some of which entail worldviews, which open possibilities for resolving presenting problems.

Therapeutic certificates: In narrative therapy, clients may be issued certificates to indicate that they have resolved their problems and they may use these certificates to substantiate their new self-narratives.

Therapeutic letters: In narrative therapy, therapists may send clients letters that consolidate new self-narratives by, for example, referring to unique outcomes mentioned in therapy and the implications of these for the clients' self-narratives.

Thin description: Description that excludes other more positive or adaptive meanings.

Thickening the story: Refers to expanding and engaging with the balanced details and content of a person's life and the lives of those around them, which reinforces the alternative story.

Unique outcome or sparkling moments: Michael White's term for times when clients acted free of their problems, even if they were unaware of doing so. Narrative therapists identify unique outcomes to help clients challenge negative views of themselves.

KNOWLEDGE CHECK: CHAPTER 11

1. By __________, the therapist helps clients create more balanced descriptions of the events of their lives to enable clients to build more accurate and appreciative descriptions of themselves and others.

   A. Enacting preferred narratives
   B. Meeting the person
   C. Thickening the plot
   D. Editing errors

2. When a narrative therapist wants to externalize the problem, such as anxiety, from the person, they might ask a question such as __________.

   A. What is it like for you to be an anxious person?
   B. How has anxiety impacted your life?
   C. In what ways are you anxious?
   D. How often are you anxious?

3. In narrative therapy, couples who are childless by choice and couples involved in polyamorous relationships are examples of _______.

   A. Unique outcomes
   B. Alternative discourses
   C. Dominant discourses
   D. Nontraditional outcomes

4. Unlike the cybernetic metaphor, which focuses on self-defeating patterns of _________, the narrative metaphor focuses on self-defeating _________.

   A. Culture(s); emotion(s)
   B. Cognition(s); behavior(s)
   C. Emotion(s); cognition(s)
   D. Behavior(s); cognition(s)

5. All of the following are phases of narrative therapy *except*:

   A. Meeting the person apart from the problem
   B. Listening
   C. Connecting the person with problem
   D. Enacting preferred narratives

6. From a narrative perspective, ______________ are not the problem; problems are the problem.

   A. Families
   B. Symptoms
   C. Cultures
   D. People

(*See answers next page.*)

1. C) Thickening the plot

While all four options might look like possibilities for this stem, C is the best choice. Change comes from "thickening the plot" by finding new subplots and alternative plots. This consists of helping clients consider new possibilities about their lives and the way they relate to others. It also hopefully gives them a wider array of choices in dealing with the situations they bring to therapy.

2. B) How has anxiety impacted your life?

Narrative therapy views problems as separate from the client and uses the technique of externalization to distinguish this separation. Externalization is achieved by a discursive shift through which problems are referred to as nouns, and thus, as separate objectified entities. The client chooses a name for the problem through collaborative conversations with the therapist. Through externalizing conversations, the many contexts and discourses that have reinforced a problem's definitive stature are removed, allowing the problem to stand independently. This also creates space that allows for the collaborative investigation of the problem and its effects, so that the client can experience life without the problem's complete dominance.

3. B) Alternative discourses

A discourse is a system of words, actions, rules, and beliefs that share common values. Think of a discourse as a worldview in action. Particular discourses sustain particular worldviews. The dominant discourses in society powerfully influence what gets "storied" and how it gets storied. Discourses tend to be invisible, that is, they are taken for granted as part of the fabric of "reality." In narrative therapy, therapists seek to identify the discourses that support problematic stories in client's lives. Narrative therapists locate problems in discourses, rather than in the client's mind. When therapist and client make this perceptual shift collaboratively, they can more easily oppose, undermine, or alter the influence of those discourses, making robust, viable unproblematic life stories more possible. Room for alternative discourses, or nontraditional ways of living, is created and honored in this collaborative narrative deconstructing process.

4. D) Behavior(s); cognition(s)

Remember the cybernetic metaphor of the black box—the idea that because the mind is so complex, it is better to study people's input and output (behavior, communication) than to speculate about what goes on in their minds. While this may have worked for strategic family therapists, the concept no longer fit in the postmodern world of narrative therapy. Within narrative therapy, there is a strong emphasis on separating the person from the problem, thus modifying maladaptive thoughts and cognitions to focus on the person's own resources of self-help. The therapist only helps the client to co-author a new narrative about themselves free of self-defeating thoughts.

5. C) Connecting the person with problem

Obviously, this answer is the exact opposite of what a narrative therapist would seek to accomplish. Narrative therapy views problems as separate from the person and uses the technique of externalization to distinguish this separation, and meet people away from their problems.

6. D) People

The problem is the problem; the person is not the problem. This idea ran counter to almost everything that had been taught to systemic therapists up to that point. White and Epston believed that people's realities resulted from their interactions with other people and the world around them. Problems result when people subscribe to negative, self-defeating views of the world based on their past and present interactions. They further believed that people have within themselves all the tools they need to rewrite, or re-story their lives in more positive ways that allow them to live happy, productive lives.

7. A common goal of narrative therapy is to increase a client's sense of ________, the sense that they influence the direction of their lives.

A. Efficacy
B. Family
C. Agency
D. Insight

8. __________ help clients to further "unpack" their stories to see how they have been constructed, identifying the influence of dominant and local discourses. These typically target problematic beliefs, practices, feelings, and attitudes.

A. Constructive questions
B. Externalizing questions
C. Conventional questions
D. Deconstructive questions

9. Narrative therapists might ask questions designed to ________.

A. Stump the client
B. Assess the function the symptom
C. Clarify the family's power over the problem
D. Ignore the problem and go for the solution

10. According to narrative therapy, clients who bring pessimistic and blaming accounts into therapy, week after week, are stuck in __________.

A. An unowned story
B. A problem-saturated story
C. Projective identification
D. A dead-end story

11. All of the following are considered communication theorists and first generation, nonpostmodern family therapists *except*:

A. Jay Haley
B. Virginia Satir
C. Michael White
D. Don Jackson

12. In narrative therapy, letters are used for each of the following purposes *except*:

A. To solidify preferred narratives
B. To emphasize client agency
C. To consolidate gains in therapy
D. To scrutinize the problem story

(*See answers next page.*)

7. C) Agency

In narrative therapy, *personal agency* refers to clients recognizing that their behavior may be maintaining the problem as well as overcoming or helping to overcome the problem. Personal agency encompasses any reference to qualities in the client or others in the family system, celebrating their strengths.

8. D) Deconstructive questions

Dominant stories may subjugate a person's life story. Subjugating stories can involve gender, race, class, age, sexual orientation, and/or religion. Deconstructive questioning takes a stand against certain practices of power in society.

9. C) Clarify the family's power over the problem

A narrative therapist would never try to stump or confuse the client (A) or jump right into the solution (D) as might be recommended in solution-focused therapy. Assessing the function of the symptom (B) is what a strategic family therapist would do, whereas a narrative therapist continually tries to separate the client from the problem.

10. B) A problem-saturated story

Oftentimes, client stories are dominated by distorted, unhelpful, disempowering assumptions and meaning-making. In narrative therapy, these are called *problem-saturated stories*. Narrative therapists strive to work collaboratively with clients to help them make sense of their experiences and revise their life stories to be more empowering, thereby challenging unhelpful interpretations and assumptions, and changing narrow, self-defeating views of self, others, and the world.

11. C) Michael White

Michael White was a postmodern thinker who prioritized client agency, seeing clients as the experts and authors of their own life stories. The other three options (Jackson, Haley, and Satir) were all associated with the Mental Research Institute (MRI) at one point in their careers and take an expert stance.

12. D) To scrutinize the problem story

Never used to scrutinize a story or further link a client to a problem, letters as narrative typically record and summarize the session and provide an opportunity to document, support, and retell the client their own emerging and preferred story. In the process, these letters also increase agency and solidify therapeutic gains.

AUDIO PODCAST 11.1
Narrative Therapy Overview
Eli A. Karam
https://bcove.video/3CGmBfb

REFERENCES

Epston, D. (1994). Extending the conversation. *Family Therapy Networker, 18*(6), 31–37.

Epston, D., & White, M. (1992). *Experience, contradiction, narrative and imagination: Selected papers of David Epston and Michael White, 1989–1991*. Dulwich Centre Publications.

Freedman, J., & Combs, G. (1996). *Narrative therapy: The social construction of preferred realities*. W. W. Norton.

Madigan, S. (2011). *Narrative therapy*. American Psychological Association.

Morgan, A. (2000). *What is narrative therapy?* Dulwich Centre Publications.

White, M. (1997). *Narrative therapists' lives*. Dulwich Centre Publications.

White, M. (2000). *Reflections on narrative practice: Essays and interviews*. Dulwich Centre Publications.

White, M. (2005). *Narrative practice and exotic lives: Resurrecting diversity in everyday life*. Dulwich Centre Publications.

White, M., & Epston, D. (1990). *Narrative means to therapeutic ends*. W. W. Norton.

PART III

Assessing, Hypothesizing, and Diagnosing (Domain 2)

Domains of Systemic Assessment

12

LEARNING OBJECTIVES

After reading this chapter, you should be able to:

1. Outline the domains of systemic assessment in marriage and family therapy (MFT)
2. Identify standardized assessment instruments used in MFT
3. Organize process and structure of an initial family assessment
4. Categorize stages and tasks associated with the family life cycle in MFT

RELEVANT EXAM DOMAINS

- *Domain 2—Assessing, Hypothesizing, and Diagnosing*
  Includes tasks related to assessing the various dimensions of the client system, forming and reformulating hypotheses, and diagnosing the client and family system in order to guide therapeutic activities.

INTRODUCTION

Systemic assessment depends on several factors, including the format of therapy (individual, couple, or family), the therapist's theoretical orientation, the nature of the client's presenting problem(s), and the stage of therapy. In general, however, the primary goals are to initially identify client needs and to determine the best interventions for addressing those needs. In this chapter, the initial tasks of assessment are summarized, general guidelines for conducting a comprehensive systemic assessment are presented, and methods of assessment are described.

INITIAL CONTACT

The initial contact with a new client is often a phone call during which the client indicates why they are seeking therapy either for themselves alone, with a partner, or for the entire family. Regardless of who calls, it is essential during this first contact to obtain certain information and establish a professional, welcoming atmosphere. Essential information to be gathered includes the name and phone number of the caller, the referral source, history of previous therapy, and any potential safety or legal issues driving the referral. A concise statement of the problem to be addressed is also helpful, even if it is modified or changed later after including other system members' perspectives. When the conversation results in setting up an appointment, the information obtained from the initial contact/intake call can be used to develop one or more working hypotheses about the client system and the presenting problem that will help the therapist organize their first impressions and cultivate questions to ask during the initial interview.

WHOM TO INCLUDE IN THE FAMILY EVALUATION

Based on the initial phone call, the question arises as to whom to include in the initial family assessment. Therapists should consider the following issues when determining attendance

- Who the family wants to attend therapy sessions and why,
- Who is involved with the presenting problem,
- The potential benefits of having family members attend if the problem is primarily an individual one, and
- The likelihood that the presence of one or more family members will constrain the therapy process.

As long as there are no contraindicators regarding these list factors that would constrain the opening assessment, most therapists would agree that it is important to include all members of the family in the evaluation sessions. This usually means all members of a nuclear family—the mother, father, and children. In addition to nuclear family members, significant others must be included if they are directly connected to the presenting issue that brings the family system to therapy. It is easier to include all family members for assessment at the beginning rather than waiting until later in the course of treatment to invite them to join. This allows a marriage and family therapist to obtain a clearer picture of family process and communication patterns.

JOINING

The first step in helping a family during the initial session(s) is for therapists to establish a sense of trust between themselves and the members of the family. This stage is referred to as *joining*. It is essentially the formation of a therapeutic alliance with the family and is a crucial component of family therapy that requires therapists to meet, greet, and form a bond with family members in a rapid, but relaxed and authentic way. Therapists must make the family comfortable through social exchange with each member. Joining can be done in many ways, such as through empathy, being friendly, or sharing common stories with the family. Joining the family allows the counselor to understand the family's rules, boundaries, structure and hierarchy, and stress.

THE PRESENTING PROBLEM

The therapist must explore the presenting problem from multiple perspectives by having each client describe it in terms of its affective, cognitive, and behavioral effects and how other people view it. It is also important to understand the point of view of different family members within the system, both from those in session as well as other family members or friends. Obtain details about each problem, who it affects, and how each person is affected, including information about its frequency, duration, precipitating events, and consequences. Evaluate the degree to which each problem is affecting the client by, for example, having the client rate its severity on a 10-point scale. Assess the degree to which the client believes each problem is changeable. Ask about previous attempted solutions to determine what methods the client system has tried in the past to resolve each presenting problem.

The therapist views a client's issues in the context of what is going on in the larger system (i.e., home, work, school, friendship network) and looks for any patterns or feedback loops that maintain the presenting problem or homeostasis. A therapist can assess these patterns using a series of questions, first by identifying the emergence of the problem and then tracing each person's emotional and/or behavioral responses to others until "normalcy" or homeostasis is achieved again.

In addition to understanding the history of the presenting problem, marriage and family therapists obtain other background information such as the following:

- Highest or current level of education achieved
- Relevant family history
- Recent life changes
- Health situation and medications
- History of mental disorders and/or substance abuse
- History of previous therapy
- History of childhood abuse
- History of trauma

ASSESSMENT TECHNIQUES

OBSERVATION

Families, like individuals, have unique personalities. They come into therapy and display these personalities in both a verbal (content) and nonverbal (process) manner. In contrast to individual therapy, one of the hallmarks of family therapy is the ability to assess the family's structure and interactional patterns around the presenting problem through observation. These techniques range from informal observations made during interviews to more formal strategies involving observation during enactments, role-plays, structured family or couple tasks, or experiential family play. Therapists may ask themselves the following questions to assess system-wide dynamics and family functioning:

- How far do members sit from each other and who sits next to whom?
- How do family members communicate?
- What repetitive patterns or cycles do you notice?
- What subsystems are operative in this family?
- What do you notice about family boundaries?
- Who carries the power in the family?
- How well are the family members differentiated from each other?
- What part of the family life cycle is the family experiencing and are their adjustment methods stage appropriate?

HIGHLIGHT INDIVIDUAL AND FAMILY STRENGTHS

Identifying strengths, both for each individual and the family system, is another part of an opening family assessment. The therapist must be able to connect to the strengths, which are the flip side of the presenting problem, while still remaining aware of the problem. If you approach the assessment from a place of health and strength, you will always find a wide range of abilities with even the most constrained of client systems, especially if you consider looking into the past as well as the present and future. When assessing individual strengths and resources in a system, the therapist can begin by reviewing both abilities and personal qualities. Naming their abilities can increase clients' sense of hope and confidence in their ability to cope with what has brought them to therapy. Identifying positive personal qualities may also give clients or therapists creative ideas about how to solve a current problem.

IDENTIFY PHYSICAL OR COMMUNITY SUPPORTS

When assessing for other resources both within and outside of the family system, the marriage and family therapist should look for physical, emotional, and community supports. Physical support includes people who may help with running errands, picking up the children, or doing tasks around the house. Emotional support may take the form of people who listen and help resolve relational problems. Community support includes resources and acceptance provided by any collective and is almost always there in some form for a person who may be feeling marginalized because of culture, sexual orientation, language, religion, or another factor. These communities are critical for coping with the stress of marginalization. Simply identifying and recognizing these various forms of support can immediately increase a client's sense of hope and reduce feelings of loneliness.

TAP INTO SPIRITUAL RESOURCES

Marriage and family therapists are becoming more aware of how clients' spiritual resources can be used to address their problems. For this reason, therapists should become familiar with the major religious traditions, but also a broader sense of spirituality that cannot be captured within the confines of organized religion. Spirituality can be defined as how a person conceptualizes their relationship to the universe, life, or God (or however the person constructs that which is larger than the self). Given that almost everyone has some form of belief in how the universe operates, asking about spirituality should be a part of every new systemic assessment.

STANDARDIZED ASSESSMENTS

Even though good family measures are available, therapists frequently do not use standardized or formal family assessments in their practices. Evaluations conducted at the beginning of treatment can provide a rich source of information about the family and can be used to develop initial hypotheses about problem areas, causes of problems, and potential areas of strength. Assessment also ensures that a broad range of routine information is collected to make certain that important areas are not overlooked. Self-report measures are easy to collect in a clinical setting and can be administered in repeated sessions to document changes within the family. Thus, these measures can be a convenient gauge of changes in outcomes that help to determine whether the therapy is working. By using a battery of self-report methods, a substantial amount of information can be ascertained with minimal clinician time. In addition, because most clients and family members initially view the presenting problem as residing within an individual, completing family assessment instruments begins to redefine the problem as a system-wide issue.

More than 1,000 instruments are available to family therapists to assess families and couples, covering areas as diverse as intimacy, power, parenthood, and adjustment (Grotevant & Carlson, 1987). A few of the more popular standardized assessments are mentioned here.

THE FAMILY ASSESSMENT DEVICE (THE MCMASTER MODEL)

This assessment covers family problem-solving, communication, family roles, emotional responsiveness, emotional connection, and behavioral control strategies. The model enables therapists trained in its use to target interventions at whatever dimension the "problem" is located. The model has been widely used in research (Epstein et al., 1983).

FAMILY ASSESSMENT MEASURE—III (FAM III)

FAM III measures task accomplishment, role performance, communication, affective expression, involvement, control, values, and norms. It provides measures of these dimensions at three levels: whole family system, various dyadic relationships, and individual functioning (Skinner et al., 1995).

FAMILY ADAPTABILITY AND COHESION SCALE (THE CIRCUMPLEX MODEL)

This assessment covers family cohesion (closeness/distance), flexibility (rigid/chaotic), and communication. There is a wealth of research based on this model, which grew out of structural family therapy ideas. It has an observational scale used by therapists (Olson, 2000).

THE BEAVERS SYSTEMS MODEL

This model covers family competence and family style. This measure was one of the earliest attempts to demonstrate that there was a connection between individual difficulties and family difficulties (Beavers et al., 1985).

MARITAL SATISFACTION INVENTORY—REVISED

This instrument contains 150 items and measures affective communication, role orientation, problem-solving, communication aggression, family history of distress, time together, dissatisfaction with children, disagreement about finances, conflict over child rearing, sexual dissatisfaction, global distress. It was developed and normed in the United States (Snyder, 1997).

ADOPTION CHALLENGES

Despite the utility of an increasing number of couple and family therapy measurement devices, therapists are reticent to use them. One reason for this lack of adoption is that they are proprietary and often have a cost associated with their use that therapists are unwilling to pay. Others contend that using assessment instruments removes family therapists from the fluidity and flexibility of asking conversational assessment questions. In addition, many practitioners lack adequate training in use of family assessment instruments Those family therapists who do employ measuring devices in their practices most often use individually focused assessment instruments, such as the Minnesota Multiphasic Personality Inventory-2 (MMPI-2) and the Myers–Briggs Type Indicator.

GRAPHIC TECHNIQUES

Graphic assessment techniques that capture family dynamics and patterns (both current and historical) include the genogram, family map, eco-map, social network map and grid, and timeline.

GENOGRAM

Resembling a family tree that captures relationships over three or more generations, a genogram includes information on the name, age, and gender of each family member; significant family events (e.g., birth, deaths, divorces); and family structure, roles, and relationships. Symbols are used to indicate individual family members and their relationships, for example, a square is drawn for a male, a circle for a female, a square within a square for a male-identified patient, a circle within a circle for a female-identified patient, a solid connecting line for a married partner, a dotted connecting line for unmarried partners in a committed relationship, and a solid connecting line with two forward slash marks for divorced partners. Genograms track relational patterns and help families see the patterns that may not be helpful to the family's overall functioning. They can also be used to shift the family's focus from a problem within one individual family member, to seeing the interactional, transgenerational nature of the issue (McGoldrick, 2008). (See Chapter 7 for a more detailed description.)

FAMILY MAP

Adapted from structural family therapy, a family map describes a visual representation of a family's organizational structure. It depicts family members around the presenting problem while illustrating the family's coalitions and boundaries.

ECO-MAP

An eco-map is used to depict the strength and nature of the relationships between an individual or family and people, institutions, and agencies in the social environment (e.g., extended family, friends, work, school, church, welfare agencies). It can be particularly useful in disenfranchised families to get a detailed picture of their social and family relationships and/or to map areas of isolation or disconnection that may need to be addressed.

SOCIAL NETWORK MAP AND GRID

With its many links, a social network is complex, just like the nature of human relationships. The social network map and grid are used together to help family members identify their sources of social support (e.g., friends, work/school, agencies/service providers) and the quality and quantity of support they receive from each source. This method helps in figuring out which individuals hold what level of influence over another individual or group.

TIMELINE

A timeline depicts the chronological sequence of important individual or family life events and is useful for providing a context for understanding current problems.

FAMILY LIFE CYCLE STAGE

When thinking about families as cohesive units, therapists prefer to think about the family moving through time together rather than as individuals on their own. Therefore, as part of the assessment process, the therapist explores how the family fits into what is referred to as the *family life cycle*. This model proposes that families tend to share similar developmental stages. It is important to recognize that different families might have different challenges in these stages and indeed not every family will pass through all the stages. For instance, adoptive families might skip the early childhood stage. So the model is not prescriptive nor is it universal, but it provides a guide to the therapist about the types of typical challenges the family might be facing. The model also suggests that families need to adapt as they move from one stage to another. A typical example would be how parenting needs to adapt for young children as opposed to teens. If there are unexpected vertical stressors on the family, then the family will need to have greater resources to overcome them. At this point, many families will present to therapists. Examples of a vertical stressor include illness, unemployment, or external social pressure such as institutional racism.

Although some families continually struggle with problems throughout their lives, others experience difficulties only during specific transitions in the life cycle. A family is subject to inner pressure from developmental changes in its own members and to external pressure from demands to accommodate to the significant social institutions and other outside forces (Carter & McGoldrick, 1988).

The family life cycle suggests that transitions between stages might lead to family problems related to (a) an inability to cope adequately with the tasks of the current family stage, (b) the need to move on to a new family stage, or (c) the stress of unexpected life events (Table 12.1).

Table 12.1 The Family Life Cycle

Family Life Cycle Stage	Processes of Transition	Changes Required
Leaving home: single young adults	Accept emotional and financial responsibility for self	Differentiate self from family of origin Develop intimate peer relationships Establish work and independence
Joining of families through cohabiting/ marriage	Commit to new relationships	Form a new family system Realignrelationships with family and friends
Families with young children	Adjust from a dyad to triads and larger systems	Make space for children in the relationship Create a co-parenting team to raise children Realign with family and friends
Families with adolescents	Increase flexibility to allow for growing independence and reviewing aging family members	Shift to allow children to develop outside relationships Adjust to midlife issues: career, etc Care for older generations
Launching children	Accept changes in the family system	Renegotiate the intimate partnership (empty nest) Develop adult relationships with children Deal with issues of the older generation Reevaluate life goals, work, and relationships
Families in later life	Accept changes in generational roles (from caring to being cared for)	Maintain relationships during the physical challenge of growing older Support the middle generation Conduct a life review Embrace grandparenthood Find function and direction in a world that values youth Cope with loss and issue of mortality

Source: Adapted from Carter, B. E., & McGoldrick, M. E. (1988). *The changing family life cycle: A framework for famlly therapy*. Gardner Press.

SAFETY ISSUES

Another essential aspect of assessment is evaluating the client system for issues of safety that require immediate action. (Additional information on assessing and responding to safety issues is provided in Chapters 15 and 16.)

SUICIDE RISK

Suicide risk is evaluated by asking the client about their intent to commit suicide, administering a suicide screening test, and assessing whether the client displays factors that have been linked to an increased risk. Major depressive disorder, borderline personality disorder, excessive use of drugs or alcohol, family history of suicide, and recent bereavement are all associated with an elevated risk of suicide.

RISK FOR VIOLENCE

Risk for violence to others is assessed by asking the client about any history of violent behavior and current intentions about harming others. Having a concrete plan, access to lethal means, a history of loss of control, and chronic anger are all associated with an increased risk for violence.

INTIMATE PARTNER VIOLENCE

Given that victims of abuse may be reluctant to report abuse in the presence of their partner, a good strategy is to interview each partner alone. Assess for intimate partner violence (IPV) by asking the client to describe how they handle conflict with their partner and whether their arguments ever involve physical fights. Identification also requires recognizing the signs of abuse like unexplained physical injuries, evasiveness when describing injuries, and submissive behavior in the presence of the abuser.

CHILD AND ELDER/DEPENDENT ADULT ABUSE

The assessment of child or elder/dependent adult abuse usually results from disclosure by the victim, perpetrator, or therapist's recognition of the indicators of abuse. For example, child abuse should be suspected when a child has unexplained bruises or other injuries, provides unconvincing answers to questions about these injuries, or seems afraid of their parent when the child's parent is present.

CULTURAL AND CONTEXTUAL FACTORS

Culturally competent therapists take client cultural histories into account before undertaking assessments and forming clinical judgments. They assume there is no single theory applicable to all families but instead urge the adoption of a pluralistic outlook that calls for multiple perspectives that are sensitive to particular cultures. In addition to learning more about specific cultures, therapists should gain greater awareness of their own values, assumptions, and beliefs that arise from their own cultural heritage (Lee, 1999).

Family therapists must try to distinguish between a client family's patterns that are universal (common to a wide variety of families), culture specific (common to a group, such as African Americans or Cuban Americans or perhaps lesbian families), or idiosyncratic (unique to this particular family) in their assessment of family functioning. Family therapists also must keep in mind that while gaining awareness of differences that might be attributable to ethnicity or racial characteristics of a specific group is typically helpful, there is also a risk in assuming uniformity among families sharing a common cultural background (McGoldrick & Giordano, 1996).

A therapist must always be aware that cultural differences between the therapist and client may lead to misunderstandings. For instance, a therapist should be cautious when interpreting nonverbal behaviors because those behaviors may have different meanings in different cultures. For example, direct eye contact is considered disrespectful in some cultures.

The consideration of cultural factors can provide useful information about a client's functioning as well as the client's comfort with therapy. Other factors that a therapist should assess when working with clients from culturally diverse backgrounds include acculturation, racial/ethnic identity, and cultural mistrust (Ivey & Ivey, 2007).

ACCULTURATION

Acculturation refers to the extent to which an individual from one cultural group has adopted the beliefs, attitudes, values, and other characteristics of another cultural group. It is a complex process that may increase the risk for depression and lead to conflicts between family members who have integrated in the mainstream culture to varying degrees. Moving from your country of origin to another country can be more difficult for immigrants who move to a city in another country that shares very few similarities with their home city.

RACIAL/ETHNIC IDENTITY

Racial/ethnic identity refers to a sense of group or collective identity based on a person's perception that they share a common racial or ethnic heritage with a particular group. A client's racial/ethnic identity may have à substantial impact on assessment and treatment.

CULTURAL MISTRUST

Members of an ethnic/racial minority group may have difficulty trusting a Caucasian therapist from the majority because of past experiences with prejudice and discrimination. Consequently, mistrust in therapy may reflect an adaptive psychological response to oppression and should not be automatically interpreted in a negative manner by the therapist. The best strategy is to discuss the meaning of the mistrust with the client. However, when a client has a high degree of cultural mistrust, it may be difficult to form a strong therapeutic alliance and referral to another therapist may be indicated. When a client's cultural background appears to be relevant to their presenting problems, useful strategies to make cultural issues explicit are (a) demonstrating curiosity in the client's culture, (b) defining the client's problems within the context of their cultural background and values, and (c) identifying and challenging stereotypic attitudes and behaviors and discussing how cultural differences might impact the therapy (Sue et al., 1996).

SPECIAL POPULATIONS

AFRICAN AMERICAN CLIENTS

Discussion of a presenting problem should be framed in a context that recognizes the totality of life experiences faced by African American clients. Equality is sought in the therapist–client relationship, and therapists are less distant and more disclosing. Emphasis is placed on the importance of clients' changing their environment—not only for the good of clients themselves, but also for the greater good of their communities. Focus on alternatives to problem behaviors that underscore personal rituals, cultural traditions, and spiritual well-being. Therapy is a process that involves gaining power in the forms of knowledge, spiritual insight, and community health.

ASIAN AMERICAN CLIENTS

Incorporate cultural knowledge and maintain flexible attitudes as a therapist. Given the importance of providing services in the native language, use co-therapist teams in which one member is Asian and bilingual (if necessary). Visit client homes to improve family involvement in treatment, if given permission. Explore client coping mechanisms that draw on cultural strengths. Be open to acupuncture or other traditional practices for detoxification and healing.

LATINO CLIENTS

The therapist should recognize aspects of Latino culture that can be assets in treatment—strength, perseverance, flexibility, and an ability to survive. Therapists should explain the concept of confidentiality regardless of the mode of therapy because many Latinos, especially undocumented workers or recent immigrants, are fearful of deportation. Latino clients may benefit from use of a community approach that involves social clubs, religious resources, and family support systems.

NATIVE AMERICAN CLIENTS

Give the client ample time to adjust to the setting at the beginning of each session. Pay attention to the stories, experiences, dreams, and rituals of the client and their relevance to the client. Accept extended periods of silence during sessions by giving time for the client to process information. Greet the client with a gentle (rather than firm) handshake and show respect to cultural rituals of welcome. Offer suggestions instead of directions (preferably more than one, to allow for client choice).

CONCLUSION

Through systemic assessment, therapists gain information that helps them formulate hypotheses and respond appropriately to the families with whom they are working. For example, therapists gain insight into a family's structure (i.e., roles, boundaries), culture (i.e., social position, cultural heritage), and development (stage of life). They also uncover what family members expect from therapy, how problems are maintained, and what treatment might be best.

KEY TERMS

Acculturation: The modification of the culture of a group or individual as a result of contact with a different culture.

Assessment: The administration of formal or informal tests or evaluation instrument(s) along with behavioral observations.

Biopsychosocial approach: An approach that considers the necessary relationship between a person's health and their mental and social conditions (mind and body connection).

Case conceptualization: Also known as *case formulation*; this refers to a way to tailor interventions to specific client needs. Case conceptualization includes making sense out of complex clinical data by analyzing case information, formulating hypotheses, and making treatment decisions.

Cisgender: A term used to describe a person whose gender identity aligns with the sex assigned to them at birth.

Cultural competence: This refers to a set of congruent policies, behaviors, and attitudes that collaboratively work together in a system and allows that system to work successfully in cross-cultural conditions.

Culture: A learned set of values, beliefs, customs, norms, and perceptions shared by a group of people that provide a general design for living and a pattern for interpreting life.

Eco-map: A graphic representation of the social systems that make up a person's life, such as friends, family, work, worship, and other community and societal links with which the individual is involved. Like a sociogram or a genogram, an eco-map depicts visually where and with whom a person is connected and can provide a more holistic view of a client.

Enneagram: A nine-factor personality system that is measured through a specific test. The nine factors are orderliness, helpfulness, image focus, hypersensitivity, detachment, caution, adventurousness, strength, and calmness.

Ethnicity: Refers to common ancestry through which individuals have evolved shared values and customs.

Ethnocentrism: When people use their own culture as a standard of reference for measuring all other cultures and thus view themselves as superior.

Family life cycle: A sociological term used to describe the various developmental stages within a family over time.

Family of origin: This refers to the family into which a person is born or adopted.

Family of procreation: Refers to the family a couple creates through marriage.

Gender: A social construct used to classify a person as a man, woman, or some other identity.

Gender expression: External appearance of one's gender identity, usually expressed through behavior, clothing, haircut or voice, and may or may not conform to socially defined behaviors and characteristics typically associated with being either masculine or feminine.

Gender identity: One's innermost concept of self as male, female, a blend of both or neither—how individuals perceive themselves and what they call themselves. One's gender identity can be the same or different from their sex assigned at birth.

Genogram: Murray Bowen's visual diagram of a person's family tree over at least three generations depicted in geometric figures, lines, and words. It is used to trace reoccurring patterns within a family.

Intersex: Adjective used describe the experience of naturally (that is, without any medical intervention) developing primary or secondary sex characteristics that do not fit neatly into society's definitions of male or female.

LGBTQIA+: Acronym that stands for lesbian, gay, bisexual, trans, queer/questioning, intersex, asexual. The + symbol stands for all other sexualities, sexes, and genders that are not included in these few letters.

Nodal events: Those family transitions that require adaptation, such as entering and leaving the family, birth, parenthood, children leaving home, retirement, and death.

Patriarchal: Relating to or characteristic of a culture in which men are the most powerful members.

Psychosocial assessment: A report that contains a practitioner's assessment of a client in terms of psychosocial factors and functioning, including motivation for treatment, cognitive ability, social and family relationships, marital status, vocational/educational functioning, drug and alcohol use, and health factors.

Race: A group of people united or classified together on the basis of common history, nationality, or geographic distribution.

Sex: A medically constructed categorization, sex is often assigned based on the appearance of the genitalia, either in ultrasound or at birth.

Sexual orientation: Sexual orientation is the label for one's primary sexual attraction, although it often refers to sexual, romantic, and emotional feelings. Usually it indicates the gender to which a person is attracted and may also imply the gender of the person expressing the attraction. It may be constant throughout one's life, or it can be fluid and flexible, although the breadth and depth of that change varies with each person.

Transgender/Trans: An umbrella term for people whose gender identity differs from the sex they were assigned at birth. The term *transgender* is not indicative of gender expression, sexual orientation, hormonal makeup, physical anatomy, or how one is perceived in daily life.

Transtheoretical model of change: A way to conceptualize different levels of readiness for change: precontemplation, contemplation, preparation, action, and maintenance. Assessing a client's readiness for change according to these levels informs decisions regarding treatment and interventions.

Worldview: An individual's perception of the world based on personal experiences as well as the socialization processes of the person in interaction with members of their reference group.

KNOWLEDGE CHECK: CHAPTER 12

1. Formal written assessments have been standardized to help therapists obtain a more ______________ assessment of client functioning.

   A. Subjective
   B. Objective
   C. Inclusive
   D. Systemic

2. Before making a systemic diagnosis, a marriage and family therapist should consider __________ factors that include age, ethnicity, and family dynamics.

   A. Global
   B. Relational
   C. Contextual
   D. Intrapsychic

3. ______________________ is a collaborative process of working with clients and other professionals to develop a comprehensive plan of care that considers resources and services necessary to successful treatment outcomes.

   A. Case management
   B. Safety planning
   C. Collateral care
   D. Case documentation

4. From a family-life-cycle perspective, symptoms in a member of the system represent __________.

   A. Intrapsychic distress
   B. Interpersonal distress
   C. A person having problems mastering the developmental tasks at that stage in the cycle
   D. Homeostasis

5. _______________ are typically *not* part of a clinical treatment plan.

   A. Therapeutic tasks
   B. Client goals
   C. Interventions
   D. Therapist perspectives

(*See answers next page.*)

1. B) Objective
Formal assessments are objective and involve the use of tools such as tests, questionnaires, checklists and rating scales. In informal assessment, the interview/evaluation usually lacks such structure or organization, and is subjective in nature.

2. C) Contextual
Family systems theory originated to account for individuals in the context of their family and how the process of interaction between family members impacted the individual members. Family as a dynamic system is influenced by a variety of contextual factors such as social, religious, economic, and political situations and crises.

3. A) Case management
Although case management is a concept more commonly associated with social work than marriage and family therapy, it is distinct from the practice of traditional psychotherapy. It helps empower and increase autonomy in clients by connecting them to community resources.

4. C) A person having problems mastering the developmental tasks at that stage in the cycle
Transitioning successfully from one stage of development to the next in the family life cycle requires the accomplishment of certain developmental tasks. Members of a family system who fail to accomplish these tasks often become "stuck" and unable to move forward. This impasse frequently leads to heightened stress reactions and crippled channels of communication.

5. D) Therapist perspectives
A treatment plan is simple but specific. Although treatment plans vary, a treatment plan generally contains the following fields: client demographic information, diagnostic summary, presenting problem, diagnosis, treatment goals, measurable objectives, interventions, and signatures. Therapist perspectives or opinions, however, are not a part of treatment plans.

6. During an opening family session, the father is constantly complaining about everyone else. The mother is trying to calm him down and give compliments, while the teenage son sits in the corner on his phone, seeming unbothered by this whole interaction transpiring around him. The therapist is trying to assess why each member in the system is intent on playing a certain role in family. In this interaction, blaming, placating, and distracting are ___________.

   A. Examples of psychodynamic defense mechanisms
   B. Roles Whitaker would say the family is using to win the Battle for Structure
   C. Positions articulated by Satir that family members use to hide their true emotions
   D. Typical reactions that a structural family therapist would see in an inverted hierarchy

7. When working with a couple presenting with sexual dysfunction, the first thing to consider during the assessment process is to ___________.

   A. Gain an understanding of the clients' past sexual history
   B. Rule out any medical basis for the dysfunction by making a referral to a medical doctor
   C. Perform an evaluation with each member of the couple individually
   D. Evaluate the clients for previous for sexual trauma

8. Tina and Adrian bring their 14-year-old daughter, Sandy, to see a therapist because they are concerned about her "sneaky" behavior around food. The initial assessment indicates that the daughter has all the symptoms of bulimia, but Sandy indicates that her parents are distant, have never dealt with past problems in their marriage, and detour their problems onto her. The therapist's unit of treatment should be ___________.

   A. The parents, to strengthen their relationship
   B. The daughter alone
   C. The entire family
   D. The mother alone

9. Rebecca comes to see a therapist for individual treatment because she "wants to work on herself" instead of always worrying about others. She tells the therapist that she and her husband are also currently in couple therapy together with another therapist, but she has recently discovered that her husband has had an affair. How should the individual therapist best proceed?

   A. Obtain a release to speak to the couple therapist to coordinate treatment before starting with Rebecca
   B. Begin therapy with Rebecca immediately
   C. Tell Rebecca that it is not ethical to see two therapists at the same time
   D. Begin therapy with Rebecca and obtain a release to speak to the couple therapist

(*See answers next page.*)

6. C) Positions articulated by Satir that family members use to hide their true emotions

Virginia Satir defined five communication styles—blaming, placating, computing, distracting, and congruent communication—to assess how family members react to stress and threats to their self-esteem.

7. B) Rule out any medical basis for the dysfunction by making a referral to a medical doctor

This question is asking what the therapist should first consider in assessing a couple with a presenting problem around sex. It is always important for a therapist to refer a client for a medical evaluation to rule out medical reasons for any physical symptoms reported by clients. After ruling out a biological basis for the sexual dysfunction, the therapist should gather information included in answers A, C, and D.

8. C) The entire family

One of the best ways to determine the unit of treatment is to see who is in the room with you. Since the whole family is here right now, and one of the presenting complaints is that the family's complete focus is on the daughter, it is safe to say that the entire family should be the unit of treatment. Seeing the daughter (B), the mother (D), or the parents (A) alone would not help the family address the multiple issues that the system members report.

9. D) Begin therapy with Rebecca and obtain a release to speak to the couple therapist

It would be unethical for the therapist to begin individual treatment with Rebecca if she were working with another individual therapist on the same issues. Since Rebecca is working with another therapist on couples' issues, it is appropriate for this therapist to start seeing her individually. It would also be clinically appropriate to get a release to speak to her couple therapist about coordinating treatment. Thus, B and C are out, and D is correct.

10. Jason and Jill come to couple therapy because Jill has never achieved an orgasm with her husband. The marriage and family therapist's initial response is to ___________.

A. Normalize the situation by saying that many women are unable to achieve orgasm
B. Assess what Jill and Jason have done previously to address this problem
C. Send them to a sex therapist since this is outside of a licensed marriage and family therapist's scope of practice
D. Refer them to a physician to rule out a possible medical issue

11. A 75-year-old client, Harold, is experiencing impairments in memory and cognition. This decline is very sudden, and both Harold and his family are very concerned about this development. What should the therapist do?

A. Refer Harold for a medical evaluation
B. Refer Harold for psychological testing
C. Use behavioral techniques focused on increasing memory and recall
D. Diagnose Harold with a neurocognitive disorder

12. Mike and Molly bring their 13-year-old twins, James and John, to family therapy. The parents are concerned with how disrespectful James is to Molly. Whenever she tries to discipline him, he engages in profanity and threatens physical violence. The therapist asks Molly to report something from the week, and notices that the husband rolls his eyes in disdain and looks away dismissively as she begins to speak. When the therapist calls attention to the husband's response, James immediately lashes out at his mother. A structural family therapist would assess this interaction as an example of _______.

A. Conflict-detouring
B. Reciprocal inhibition
C. Equifinality
D. Fusion

13. In regard to mental status information on an opening assessment, a therapist __________.

A. Should indicate the client's mental status
B. Should indicate client's mental status if the client has obvious deficiencies
C. Could choose whether or not to include the client's mental status
D. Does not need to include the client's mental status

14. When taking an assessment, a therapist should NOT include ________.

A. A client's limitation
B. A client's strengths
C. A client's diagnosis of self
D. A client's chief complaint

15. In the assessment phase of family therapy, a genogram is used to __________.

A. Examine family relationship patterns over several generations
B. Identify biological contributions to maladaptive behavior
C. Explore interactions between a family and its environment
D. Evaluate the progress and outcome of therapy

(*See answers next page.*)

10. B) Assess what Jill and Jason have done previously to address this problem
The therapist would first want to determine what the couple has done in the past to help define what the problem is and how best to proceed. A referral to a physician may be appropriate (D), but not before determining what this couple has done in the past. Jill may have already discussed the issue with her physician, so further exploration is needed. Although it may be important for this couple to know that many women experience anorgasmia, this (A) would not be your initial response. Sex therapy may be an appropriate referral in the future (C) but treating this couple would be within your scope of practice if the problem is related to a relational issue.

11. A) Refer Harold for a medical evaluation
Before assigning a diagnosis, the therapist must refer Harold for a physical examination to rule out an underlying medical condition or the effects of a substance. In addition, a medical professional can determine whether Harold should receive medication. In neurocognitive disorders, the cognitive deficits usually have a progressive course, and the individual denies or is unaware of the impairments.

12. A) Conflict-detouring
Conflict-detouring occurs when conflict from one subsystem is detoured to another subsystem. This is often what is occurring in situations in which there is a family scapegoat. This is the only structural term listed among the four responses.

13. A) Should indicate the client's mental status
Assessments should contain specific information about a client, always indicating the client's mental status. Mental status explains cognitive and behavioral functioning. It is based on the clinician's observations and the client's subjective descriptions.

14. C) A client's diagnosis of self
When compiling an assessment, it is important that the therapist include the client's input on strengths/limitation and the presenting problem, but not a self-diagnosis.

15. A) Examine family relationship patterns over several generations
A genogram is a schematic diagram of a family's relationships and usually includes at least three generations. The primary purpose of a genogram is to assess for transgenerational behavior patterns that recur in the family. The genogram focuses on relationships, not biological contributions (B) or therapy progress (D). To examine interactions with a family and its environment, use an eco-map (C).

AUDIO PODCAST 12.1
Systemic Assessment
Eli A. Karam
https://bcove.video/3ARezPb

REFERENCES

Beavers, W. R., Hampson, R. B., & Hulgus, Y. F. (1985). Commentary: The Beavers systems approach to family assessment. *Family Process, 24*(3), 398–405. https://doi.org/10.1111/j.1545-5300.1985.00398.x

Carter, B. E., & McGoldrick, M. E. (1988). *The changing family life cycle: A framework for family therapy*. Gardner Press.

Epstein, N. B., Baldwin, L. M., & Bishop, D. S. (1983). The McMaster family assessment device. *Journal of Marital and Family Therapy, 9*(2), 171–180.

Grotevant, H. D., & Carlson, C. I. (1987). Family interaction coding systems: A descriptive review. *Family Process, 26*(1), 49–74. https://doi.org/10.1111/j.1545-5300.1987.00049.x

Ivey, A., & Ivey, M. (2007). *Intentional interviewing and counseling: Facilitating client development in multicultural society*. Brooks/Cole.

Lee, W. M. L. (1999). *An introduction to multicultural counseling*. Accelerated Development.

McGoldrick, M., & Giordano, J. (1996). Overview: Ethnicity and family therapy. In M. McGoldrick, J. Giordano, & J. K. Pearce (Eds.), *Ethnicity & family therapy* (pp. 1–27). Guilford Press.

McGoldrick, M., Gerson, R., & Petry, S. S. (2008). *Genograms: Assessment and intervention.* W. W. Norton.

Olson, D. H. (2000). Circumplex model of marital and family systems. *Journal of Family Therapy, 22*(2), 144–167.

Skinner, H., Steinhauer, P. D., & Santa-Barbara, J. (1995). *Family Assessment Measure III (FAM III)*. Multi-Health Systems Inc.

Snyder, D. K. (1997). *Marital satisfaction inventory, revised (MSI-R).* Western Psychological Services.

Sue, D. W., Ivey, A. E., & Pedersen, P. B. (1996). *A theory of multicultural counseling and therapy*. Brooks/Cole.

Diagnosing With the *DSM-5*

13

LEARNING OBJECTIVES

After reading this chapter, you should be able to:

1. **Identify major changes in the way disorders are classified in the most recent edition of the *Diagnostic and Statistical Manual of Mental Disorders* (5th ed.; *DSM–5*; American Psychiatric Association, 2013) compared with its predecessor, the *Diagnostic and Statistical Manual of Mental Disorders* (4th ed., text rev.; *DSM-IV-TR*; American Psychiatric Association, 2000)**
2. **Describe the relationship between the *DSM-5* and the *ICD-10* (World Health Organization, 2004)**
3. **Demonstrate understanding of the *DSM-5* diagnostic model**
4. **Review common diagnoses relevant to marriage and family therapy practice**

RELEVANT EXAM DOMAINS

- *Domain 2—Assessing, Hypothesizing, and Diagnosing*
  Includes tasks related to assessing the various dimensions of the client system, forming and reformulating hypotheses, and diagnosing the client and family system in order to guide therapeutic activities.

INTRODUCTION

The release of the fifth edition of the *DSM-5* in May 2013 by the American Psychiatric Association (APA) was an anticipated event in the mental health world. The *DSM-5* covers all categories of mental health disorders for both adults and children. It contains descriptions, symptoms, and other criteria necessary for diagnosing mental health disorders. Although many elements from the previous version of the diagnostic manual (*DSM-IV-TR*; APA, 2000) remained intact, there were significant changes in this new version (Regier et al., 2013). Most prominent, the latest manual deleted the previous multiaxial system of generating a psychiatric diagnosis. Used in conjunction with structured clinical interview and mental status evaluations conducted at the onset of treatment, knowledge of the *DSM-5* is essential to make an accurate diagnosis. Just as with medical conditions, many insurance carriers require a specific diagnosis to approve payment for treatment of mental health conditions. Therefore, in addition to being used for psychiatric diagnosis and treatment recommendations, marriage and family therapists also use the *DSM* in order to get paid!

MAKING A DIAGNOSIS

THE *DIAGNOSTIC AND STATISTICAL MANUAL OF MENTAL DISORDERS*

As indicated, the *DSM* is the handbook used by healthcare professionals in the United States and much of the world as the authoritative guide to the diagnosis of mental disorders. The *DSM* contains descriptions, symptoms, and other criteria necessary for diagnosing mental disorders. It provides a common language for clinicians to use to communicate about their patients and establishes consistent and reliable diagnoses that can be used in the research of mental disorders. It also provides a common language for researchers to use to study the criteria for potential future revisions and to aid in the development of medications and other interventions.

The *DSM* is updated and modified on a regular basis, with text revisions of the manual being published in between editions. Although the *DSM-5* contains more than 400 different categorical classifications of disorders, it does not predict treatment outcomes nor does it provide insight into the etiology of the mental disorders. The book contains 20 chapters, each containing grouping of similar disorders or spectrum of disorders. Chapters roughly follow developmental patterns, with the disorders of childhood coming before disorders seen in older adults (APA, 2013).

ICD-10 VS. *DSM-5*

The *ICD-10* is the 10th revision of a classification tool used for medical diagnoses compiled by the World Health Organization (WHO). Formally known as the *International Statistical Classification of Diseases and Related Health Problems* (typically abbreviated to simply *ICD*), this medical classification list contains codes for diseases, signs and symptoms, abnormal findings, complaints, social circumstances, and external causes of injury or diseases.

It may appear that the *DSM-5* is redundant and unnecessary in light of the *ICD-10* coding system. However, the *DSM-5* gives mental health professionals the criteria and definitions needed to classify diseases through a common language, whereas *ICD-10* assigns a code that is used for reimbursement in claims processing. It is also important to note that the *DSM-5* is strictly intended for *mental disorders.* Although the *ICD-10* includes those same conditions, it contains conditions and diseases related to the entire human physiology and does *not* cover mental disorders in the same depth as the *DSM-5* does. This is one of the most important differences between *ICD-10* and *DSM-5*.

The important practical difference between these two volumes is that therapists use the *DSM-5* codes for diagnostic and treatment purposes, whereas *ICD-10* codes are used for reimbursement: *DSM-5* codes are not strictly reimbursable by insurance payers, therapists must submit *ICD-10* codes on insurance claims or the claims will be rejected (WHO, 2004).

MENTAL STATUS EXAMINATION

The Mental Status Examination (MSE) is often used to determine a *DSM-5* diagnosis and may be considered the psychological equivalent of a physical examination. In psychiatric evaluations it is especially important to evaluate, quantitatively and qualitatively, a range of mental functions and behaviors at a specific point in time. The MSE provides important information for diagnosis and assessment of the disorder's course and response to treatment. Observations noted throughout the interview become part of the MSE, which begins when the clinician first meets the client. Information is gathered about the client's behaviors, thinking, and mood.

CONTEXTUAL FACTORS

Before making a diagnosis, therapists should consider contextual factors, such as age, ethnicity, family dynamics, language, religion, economic issues, sexual orientation, trauma history, addictions, and cognitive ability. Taking such issues into consideration improves the accuracy of diagnosis (APA, 2013).

MEDICAL EXCLUSIONS

When making a diagnosis, therapists should consult the *DSM-5*, as each diagnosis requires that a certain number of criteria be met. Medical causes should always be ruled out first in order to make an accurate diagnosis. Depending on the diagnosis reached, the therapist may also elect to send the client on for a medication evaluation from a psychiatrist. Diagnoses with symptoms that typically warrant referrals to collateral psychiatric services include depression, anxiety, mania, psychosis, and alcohol and substance abuse (APA, 2013).

MEDICAL NECESSITY

Most third-party payers require that therapists document that the diagnosable condition meets the criteria of medical necessity and that there is significant impairment in functioning. Impairment manifests itself in client daily activities, social relationships, mental health, physical health, work and school, and family life.

ANXIETY DISORDERS

Anxiety is a normal reaction to stress and can be beneficial in some situations. It can alert us to dangers and help us prepare and pay attention. Anxiety disorders differ from normal feelings of nervousness or anxiousness and involve excessive fear or anxiety. Anxiety disorders are the most common mental disorders and affect nearly 30% of adults at some point in their lives. Fear is an emotional response to an immediate threat and is more associated with a fight-or-flight reaction—either staying to fight or leaving to escape danger. Anxiety disorders can cause people to try to avoid situations that trigger or worsen their symptoms. Job performance, school, work and personal relationships can be affected. In general, for a person to be diagnosed with an anxiety disorder, the fear must prevent normal functioning, must be out of proportion to the situation or age inappropriate.

GENERALIZED ANXIETY DISORDER

Generalized anxiety disorder (GAD) involves persistent and excessive worry that interferes with daily activities. This ongoing worry and tension may be accompanied by physical symptoms, such as restlessness, feeling on edge or easily fatigued, difficulty concentrating, muscle tension, or problems sleeping. Often the worries focus on everyday things such as job responsibilities, family health or minor matters such as chores, car repairs, or appointments (APA, 2013).

PANIC DISORDER

The core symptom of panic disorder is recurrent panic attacks, which involve an overwhelming combination of physical and psychological distress (APA, 2010). Generally, if a person has four or more panic attacks and constantly worries about having another, the person is classified as having panic disorder. For at least one month after the panic attack, a person with panic disorder has persistent concern or worry about additional panic attacks or their consequences and/or a significant change in behavior related to trying to avoid the panic attacks. Symptoms of a panic attack may include pounding heart, nausea, dizziness, chills, chest pain, and other symptoms of physical distress. Panic disorder can be upsetting and disabling. An attack can last from a few minutes to an hour or sometimes longer. Because the symptoms are so severe, many people who experience a panic attack may believe they are having a heart attack or another life-threatening illness. They may go to a hospital emergency department. Panic attacks may be expected, such as in response to a feared object, or unexpected, apparently occurring for no reason. The mean age for onset of panic disorder is 20–24 years. Panic attacks may occur with other mental disorders such as depression or posttraumatic stress disorder (PTSD; APA, 2013).

SPECIFIC PHOBIA

A specific phobia involves excessive and persistent fear of a specific object, situation, or activity that is generally not harmful. Patients know their fear is excessive, but they cannot overcome it. These fears cause such distress that some people go to extreme lengths to avoid what they fear. Examples are fear of public speaking, fear of flying, or fear of spiders (APA, 2013).

AGORAPHOBIA

Agoraphobia is the fear of being in situations where escape may be difficult or embarrassing, or help might not be available in the event of panic symptoms. The fear is out of proportion to the actual situation and lasts generally 6 months or more and causes problems in functioning. A person with agoraphobia may experience this fear in enclosed places, while being in a crowd of people, or outside of the familiar surroundings of home. The individual actively avoids the situation, requires a companion, or endures the situation with intense fear or anxiety. Untreated agoraphobia can become so serious that a person may be unable to leave the house. A person can only be diagnosed with agoraphobia if the fear is intensely upsetting, or if it significantly interferes with normal daily activities (APA, 2013).

SOCIAL ANXIETY DISORDER

A person with social anxiety disorder has significant anxiety and discomfort about being embarrassed, humiliated, rejected, or looked down on in social interactions. People with this disorder will try to avoid the situation or endure it with great anxiety. Common examples are extreme fear of public speaking, meeting new people, or eating/drinking in public. The fear or anxiety causes problems with daily functioning and lasts at least 6 months (APA, 2013).

SEPARATION ANXIETY DISORDER

A person with separation anxiety disorder is excessively fearful or anxious about separation from those with whom the person is attached. The feeling goes beyond what is appropriate for the person's age, persists (at least 4 weeks in children and 6 months in adults), and causes problems functioning. A person with separation anxiety disorder may be persistently worried about losing the person closest to them, may be reluctant or refuse to go out or sleep away from home or without that person, or may experience nightmares about separation. Physical symptoms of distress often develop in childhood, but symptoms can carry though adulthood (APA, 2013).

MEDICATIONS

Each of the antianxiety medications listed belongs to a class of drugs known as *benzodiazepines*. Benzodiazepines are the most commonly prescribed class of drugs used to treat anxiety disorders:

- Valium (diazepam)
- Xanax (alprazolam)
- Ativan (lorazepam)
- Klonopin (clonazepam)

DEPRESSIVE DISORDERS

MAJOR DEPRESSIVE DISORDER

Major depressive disorder (MDD) is a common and serious medical illness that negatively affects how people feel, think, and act. It can lead to a variety of emotional and physical problems and can decrease the ability to function at work and at home. Depression symptoms can vary from mild to severe and can include:

- Feeling sad or having a depressed mood
- Loss of interest or pleasure in activities once enjoyed
- Changes in appetite—weight loss or gain unrelated to dieting
- Trouble sleeping or sleeping too much
- Loss of energy or increased fatigue
- Increase in purposeless physical activity (e.g., inability to sit still, pacing, handwringing) or slowed movements or speech (these actions must be severe enough to be observable by others)
- Feeling worthless or guilty
- Difficulty thinking, concentrating, or making decisions
- Thoughts of death or suicide

Symptoms must last at least 2 weeks and must represent a change in previous level of functioning for a diagnosis of depression. Also, medical conditions can mimic symptoms of depression, so it is important to rule out general medical causes (APA, 2013).

In the *Diagnostic and Statistical Manual of Mental Disorders* (4th ed.; *DSM-IV*; APA, 1994), clinicians were advised to refrain from diagnosing major depression in individuals within the first 2 months following the death of a loved one in what has been referred to as the *bereavement exclusion*. By advising clinicians not to diagnose depression in recently bereaved individuals, the *DSM-IV* bereavement exclusion suggested that grief somehow protected someone from major depression. As part of the ongoing study of major depression, the bereavement exclusion has been removed from *DSM-5* (APA, 2013). Although the grieving process is natural and unique to each individual and shares some of the same features of depression, such as intense sadness and withdrawal from customary activities, grief and depression are also different in important aspects:

- In grief, painful feelings come in waves, often intermixed with positive memories of the deceased; in depression, mood and ideation are almost constantly negative
- In grief, self-esteem is usually preserved; in MDD, corrosive feelings of worthlessness and self-loathing are common
- Although many believe that some form of depression is a normal consequence of bereavement, MDD should not be diagnosed in the context of bereavement because diagnosis would incorrectly label a normal process as a disorder

PREMENSTRUAL DYSPHORIC DISORDER

Premenstrual dysphoric disorder (PMDD) was added to the *DSM-5* in 2013. A woman with PMDD has severe symptoms of depression, irritability, and tension about a week before menstruation begins. Common symptoms include

- Mood swings
- Irritability or anger
- Depressed mood
- Marked anxiety or tension
- Decreased interest in usual activities
- Difficulty concentrating
- Lack of energy or easy fatigue
- Changes in appetite with specific food cravings
- Trouble sleeping or sleeping too much
- A sense of being overwhelmed or out of control
- Breast tenderness or swelling
- Joint or muscle pain
- A sensation of "bloating," or weight gain

These symptoms begin a week to 10 days before the start of menstruation and improve or stop around the onset of menses. The symptoms lead to significant distress and problems with regular functioning or social interactions.

For a diagnosis of PMDD, symptoms must have occurred in most of the menstrual cycles during the past year and must have an adverse effect on work or social functioning. It is estimated that between 1.8% and 5.8% of menstruating women are affected by PMDD each year. Premenstrual syndrome (PMS) is similar to PMDD in that symptoms occur 7–10 days before a woman's period begins. However, PMS involves fewer and less severe symptoms than PMDD (APA, 2013).

DISRUPTIVE MOOD DYSREGULATION DISORDER

Disruptive mood dysregulation disorder is a condition that occurs in children and youth ages 6 to 18 years. It involves chronic and severe irritability resulting in severe and frequent temper outbursts. These outbursts can be verbal or can involve behavior such as physical aggression toward people or property. These outbursts are significantly out of proportion to the situation and are not consistent with the child's developmental age. They must occur frequently (three or more times per week on average) and typically in response to frustration. In between the outbursts, the child's mood is persistently irritable or angry most of the day, nearly every day. This mood is noticeable by others, such as parents, teachers, and peers.

In order for a diagnosis of disruptive mood dysregulation disorder to be made, symptoms must be present for at least 1 year in at least two settings (such as at home, at school, with peers) and the condition must begin before age 10. Disruptive mood dysregulation disorder is much more common in males than females. It may occur along with other disorders, including major depressive, attention deficit hyperactivity, anxiety, and conduct disorders.

Disruptive mood dysregulation disorder can have a significant impact on the child's ability to function and a significant impact on the family. Chronic, severe irritability and temper outbursts can disrupt family life, make it difficult for the child/youth to make or keep friendships, and cause difficulties at school (APA, 2013).

PERSISTENT DEPRESSIVE DISORDER

A person with persistent depressive disorder (PDD: previously referred to as *dysthymic disorder*) has a depressed mood for most of the day, more days than not, for at least 2 years. In children and adolescents, the mood can be irritable or depressed, and must continue for at least 1 year. Other symptoms that happen much of the time include poor appetite, eating or sleeping too much, lethargy, and difficulty concentrating. PDD often begins in childhood, adolescence, or early adulthood and affects an estimated 0.5% of adults in the United States every year. The symptoms cause significant distress or difficulty in work, social activities, or other important areas of functioning. Although the impact of PDD on work, relationships, and daily life can vary widely, its effects can be as great as or greater than those of MDD. A major depressive episode may precede the onset of PDD but may also arise during (and be superimposed on) a previous diagnosis of PDD. Older people who have PDD find it difficult to care for themselves. They feel isolated and may also have medical illnesses. People who have PDD may have periods of normal mood that can last up to 2 months. Family members and friends may not even know that their loved one is depressed. Even though this type of depression is mild, it may be difficult for a person to function at home, school, or work (APA, 2013).

PERIPARTUM DEPRESSION

Peripartum depression refers to depression occurring during pregnancy or after childbirth. The use of the term *peripartum* recognizes that depression associated with having a baby often begins during pregnancy, which carries risks for the mother and child. An estimated one in seven women experiences peripartum depression. Mothers with perinatal depression experience feelings of extreme sadness, anxiety, difficulty concentrating, and fatigue that may make it difficult for them to carry out daily tasks, including caring for themselves or others. A woman experiencing peripartum depression usually has several of these symptoms, and the symptoms and their severity may change. These symptoms may cause new mothers to feel isolated, guilty, or ashamed. To be diagnosed with peripartum depression, symptoms must begin during pregnancy or within 4 weeks following delivery (APA, 2013).

SEASONAL AFFECTIVE DISORDER

Seasonal affective disorder (SAD) is a form of depression also known as *seasonal depression* or *winter depression*. In the *DSM-5* (APA, 2013), this disorder is identified as a type of depression: Major Depressive Disorder with Seasonal Pattern.

People with SAD experience mood changes and symptoms similar to depression. The symptoms usually occur during the fall and winter months, when there is less sunlight, and usually improve with the arrival of spring. The most difficult months for people with SAD in the United States tend to be January and February. Although it is much less common, some people experience SAD in the summer.

SAD is more than just "winter blues." The symptoms can be distressing and overwhelming and can interfere with daily functioning. However, it can be treated. About 5% of adults in the United States experience SAD and it typically lasts about 40% of the year. It is more common among women than men. SAD has been linked to a biochemical imbalance in the brain prompted by shorter daylight hours and less sunlight in winter. As seasons change, people experience a shift in their biological internal clock or circadian rhythm that can cause them to be out of step with their daily schedule. SAD is more common in people living far from the equator, where there are fewer daylight hours in the winter.

Common symptoms of SAD include fatigue, even with too much sleep, and weight gain associated with overeating and carbohydrate cravings. SAD symptoms can vary from mild to severe and can include many symptoms similar to those of major depression (APA, 2013).

MEDICATIONS

Each of the antidepressants listed here are in a class of drugs known as selective serotonin reuptake inhibitors (SSRIs). These are the most commonly prescribed antidepressants:

- Prozac (fluoxetine)
- Celexa (citalopram)
- Zoloft (sertraline)
- Lexapro (escitalopram)
- Paxil (paroxetine)
- Luvox (fluvoxamine)

BIPOLAR AND RELATED DISORDERS

Bipolar disorder is a brain disorder that causes changes in a person's mood, energy, and ability to function. People with bipolar disorder experience intense emotional states that typically occur during distinct periods of days to weeks, called *mood episodes*. These mood episodes are categorized as manic/hypomanic (abnormally happy or irritable mood) or depressive (sad mood). People with bipolar disorder generally have periods of neutral mood as well. When treated, people with bipolar disorder can lead full and productive lives.

People without bipolar disorder experience mood fluctuations as well. However, these mood changes typically last hours rather than days. Also, these changes are not usually accompanied by the extreme degree of behavior change or difficulty with daily routines and social interactions that people with bipolar disorder demonstrate during mood episodes. Bipolar disorder can disrupt a person's relationships with loved ones and cause difficulty in working or going to school. Bipolar disorder is a category that includes three different diagnoses: bipolar I, bipolar II, and cyclothymic disorder (APA, 2013).

BIPOLAR I

Bipolar I disorder is diagnosed when a person experiences a manic episode. During a manic episode, people with bipolar I disorder experience an extreme increase in energy and may feel on top of the world or uncomfortably irritable. Some people with bipolar I disorder also experience depressive or hypomanic episodes, and most people with bipolar I disorder also have periods of neutral mood (APA, 2013).

BIPOLAR II

A diagnosis of bipolar II disorder requires someone to have at least one major depressive episode and at least one hypomanic episode. People return to their usual functioning between episodes. People with bipolar II disorder often first seek treatment as a result of their first depressive episode, because hypomanic episodes often feel pleasurable and can even increase performance at work or school. People with bipolar II disorder frequently have other mental illnesses, such as an anxiety disorder or substance use disorder, the latter of which can exacerbate symptoms of depression or hypomania (APA, 2013).

CYCLOTHYMIC DISORDER

Cyclothymic disorder is a milder form of bipolar disorder involving many "mood swings," with hypomania and depressive symptoms that occur frequently. People with cyclothymia experience emotional ups and downs but with less severe symptoms than exhibited in bipolar I or bipolar II disorder. Cyclothymic disorder symptoms include the following:

- For at least 2 years, the individual experiences many periods of hypomanic and depressive symptoms, but the symptoms do not meet the criteria for hypomanic or depressive episode.
- During the 2-year period, the symptoms (mood swings) have lasted for at least half the time and have never stopped longer than 2 months (APA, 2013).

MEDICATIONS

Each of the medications listed belongs to a class of drugs known as *mood stabilizers*, which are used to treat bipolar disorder.

- Lithium
- Depakote (divalproex sodium)
- Lamictal (lamotragine)
- Abilify (aripiprazole)

NEURODEVELOPMENTAL DISORDERS

ATTENTION DEFICIT HYPERACTIVITY DISORDER

Attention deficit hyperactivity disorder (ADHD) is characterized by (a) a difficulty in focusing one's attention on a single task and (b) a tendency toward hyperactivity and impulsive behaviors (although some individuals are either predominantly inattentive or predominantly hyperactive-impulsive). The definition of ADHD has been updated in the fifth edition of the *DSM* to more accurately characterize the experience of adults. This revision is based on nearly two decades of research showing that ADHD, although a disorder that begins in childhood, can continue through adulthood for some people. Previous editions of the *DSM* did not provide appropriate guidance to clinicians in diagnosing adults with the condition. By adapting criteria for adults, *DSM-5* aims to ensure that children with ADHD can continue to get care throughout their lives if needed (APA, 2013).

ADHD is characterized by a pattern of behavior, present in multiple settings (e.g., school and home), that can result in performance issues in social, educational, or work settings. As in the *DSM-IV* (APA, 1994) symptoms are divided into two categories—inattention or hyperactivity and impulsivity— that include behaviors like failure to pay close attention to details; difficulty organizing tasks and activities; and excessive talking, fidgeting, or an inability to remain seated in appropriate situations. Children must have at least six symptoms from either (or both) the inattention group of criteria and the hyperactivity and impulsivity criteria, whereas older adolescents and adults (over age 17) must present with five. Although the criteria have not changed from the *DSM-IV* (1994), examples have been included to illustrate the types of behavior children, older adolescents, and adults with ADHD might exhibit. The descriptions help clinicians better identify typical ADHD symptoms at each stage of patients' lives. Using the *DSM-5* (APA, 2013), several of the individual's ADHD symptoms must be present prior to age 12 years, compared to 7 years as the age of onset in the *DSM-IV*.

MEDICATIONS

Each of the stimulant medications listed belongs to a class of drugs known as *amphetamines*, which are used to treat ADHD.

- Ritalin/Concerta (methylphenidate)
- Adderall (amphetamine)
- Dexedrine (dextroamphetamine)

AUTISM SPECTRUM DISORDER

The three main characteristics of autism are: (a) impaired social development, (b) diminished communication skills, and (c) restrictive/repetitive behavior. The disorder is highly variable and is now described in terms of a spectrum rather than a set of discrete categories. One of the most important changes in the *DSM-5* (APA, 2013) involves changes in the diagnosis of autism spectrum disorder (ASD). *DSM-5* combines four independent diagnoses—autistic disorder, Asperger syndrome, pervasive developmental disorder-not otherwise specified (PDD-NOS), and childhood disintegrative disorder—into the singular diagnosis of autism spectrum disorder. The rationale for this change is that these disorders have the same essential symptoms, but at varying degrees of severity. The revised diagnosis represents a new, more accurate, and medically and scientifically useful way of diagnosing individuals with autism-related disorders.

People with ASD tend to have communication deficits, such as responding inappropriately in conversations, misreading nonverbal interactions, or having difficulty building friendships appropriate to their age. In addition, people with ASD may be overly dependent on routines, highly sensitive to changes in their environment, or intensely focused on inappropriate items. Again, the symptoms of people with ASD will fall on a continuum, with some individuals showing mild symptoms and others having much more severe symptoms. This spectrum allows clinicians to account for variations in symptoms and behaviors from person to person. Under the *DSM-5* (APA, 2013) criteria, individuals with ASD must show symptoms from early childhood, even if those symptoms are not recognized until later. These criteria changes encourage earlier diagnosis of ASD but also allow people whose symptoms may not be fully recognized until social demands reveal these communication deficits.

Although there is no medication that can cure ASD, some medications can help treat certain symptoms and behaviors. The FDA has approved the use of some antipsychotic drugs, such as risperidone and aripiprazole, for treating irritability associated with ASD in children.

INTELLECTUAL DISABILITY

As a DSM-5 diagnostic term, intellectual disability (intellectual developmental disorder) replaces mental retardation, which is used in previous editions of the manual. The disorder is considered chronic and often co-occurs with other mental conditions like depression, ADHD, and ASD (APA, 2013). Intellectual disability involves impairments of general mental abilities that impact adaptive functioning in three domains, or areas. These domains determine how well an individual copes with everyday tasks:

- The conceptual domain includes skills in language, reading, writing, math, reasoning, knowledge, and memory.
- The social domain refers to empathy, social judgment, interpersonal communication skills, the ability to make and retain friendships, and similar capacities.

- The practical domain centers on self-management in areas such as personal care, job responsibilities, money management, recreation, and organizing school and work tasks. Although intellectual disability does not have a specific age requirement, an individual's symptoms must begin during the developmental period and are diagnosed based on the severity of deficits in adaptive functioning.

SOCIAL COMMUNICATION DISORDER

The new diagnosis of social (pragmatic) communication disorder (SCD) in the *DSM-5* (APA, 2013) more accurately recognizes individuals who have significant problems using verbal and nonverbal communication for social purposes, which lead to impairments in their ability to communicate effectively, participate socially, maintain social relationships, or otherwise perform academically or occupationally. Previous editions of the *DSM* did not provide an appropriate diagnosis for people with such symptoms, which led to inconsistent treatment across clinics and treatment centers. For these individuals, SCD brings social and communication deficits out of the shadows of a "not otherwise specified" label to help them get the services and treatment they need.

SCD is characterized by a persistent difficulty with verbal and nonverbal communication that cannot be explained by low cognitive ability. Symptoms include difficulty in the acquisition and use of spoken and written language as well as problems with inappropriate responses in conversation. The disorder limits effective communication, social relationships, academic achievement, or occupational performance. Symptoms must be present in early childhood even if they are not recognized until later when speech, language, or communication demands exceed abilities.

SPECIFIC LEARNING DISORDER

Specific learning disorder is diagnosed through a clinical review of the individual's developmental, medical, educational, and family history, reports of test scores and teacher observations, and response to academic interventions. The diagnosis requires persistent difficulties in reading, writing, arithmetic, or mathematical reasoning skills during formal years of schooling. Symptoms may include inaccurate or slow and effortful reading, poor written expression that lacks clarity, difficulties remembering number facts, or inaccurate mathematical reasoning. Current academic skills must be well below the average range of scores in culturally and linguistically appropriate tests of reading, writing, or mathematics. The individual's difficulties must not be better explained by developmental, neurological, sensory (vision or hearing), or motor disorders and must significantly interfere with academic achievement, occupational performance, or activities of daily living. Because of the changes in the *DSM-5* (APA, 2013), clinicians will be able to make this diagnosis by identifying whether patients are unable to perform academically at a level appropriate to their intelligence and age.

NEUROCOGNITIVE DISORDERS

MILD NEUROCOGNITIVE DISORDER

The diagnosis of mild neurocognitive disorder in the *DSM-5* (APA, 2013) provides an opportunity for early detection and treatment of cognitive decline before patients' deficits become more pronounced and progress to major neurocognitive disorder (dementia) or other debilitating conditions. Its inclusion in the manual helps clinicians develop effective treatment plans as well as encourages researchers to evaluate diagnostic criteria and potential therapies. Mild neurocognitive disorder goes beyond normal issues of aging. It describes a level of cognitive decline that requires compensatory strategies and accommodations to help maintain independence and perform activities of daily living. To be diagnosed with this disorder, there must be changes that impact cognitive functioning. These symptoms are usually observed by the individual, a close relative, or other knowledgeable informant, such as a friend, colleague, or clinician, or they are detected through objective testing. There is substantial clinical need to recognize individuals who need care for cognitive issues that go beyond normal aging. The impact of these problems is noticeable, but clinicians have lacked a reliable diagnosis by which to assess symptoms or understand the most appropriate treatment or services.

OBSESSIVE-COMPULSIVE AND RELATED DISORDERS

The *DSM-5* (APA, 2013) includes a new chapter on obsessive-compulsive and related disorders to reflect the increasing evidence of these disorders' relatedness to one another and their distinction from other anxiety disorders, as well as to help clinicians better identify and treat individuals suffering from these disorders. Disorders grouped in this new chapter have features in common such as an obsessive preoccupation and repetitive behaviors. The disorders included in this new chapter have enough similarities to group them together in the same diagnostic classification but enough important differences to exist as distinct disorders. Disorders in this chapter include obsessive-compulsive disorder, body dysmorphic disorder, and trichotillomania (hair-pulling disorder), as well as two new disorders: hoarding disorder and excoriation (skin-picking) disorder.

HOARDING DISORDER

This disorder is characterized by persistent difficulty discarding or parting with possessions, regardless of the value others may attribute to these possessions. The behavior usually has harmful effects—emotional, physical, social, financial, and even legal—for the person suffering from the disorder and family members. For individuals who hoard, the quantity of their collected items sets them apart from people with normal collecting behaviors. They accumulate a large number of possessions that often fill up or clutter active living areas of the home or workplace to the extent that their intended use is no longer possible. Symptoms of the disorder cause clinically significant distress or impairment in social, occupational, or other important areas of functioning, including maintaining an environment for self and/or others. Although some people who hoard may not be particularly distressed by their behavior, their behavior can be distressing to other people, such as family members or landlords. Hoarding disorder is included in the *DSM-5* (APA, 2013) because research shows that it is a distinct disorder with distinct treatments. This is particularly important as studies show that the prevalence of hoarding disorder is estimated at approximately 2%–5% of the population. These behaviors can often be quite severe and even life-threatening. Beyond the mental impact of the disorder, the accumulation of clutter can create a public health issue by completely filling people's homes and creating fall and fire hazards.

EXCORIATION (SKIN-PICKING) DISORDER

Excoriation (skin-picking) disorder is characterized by recurrent skin picking resulting in skin lesions. Individuals with excoriation disorder must have made repeated attempts to decrease or stop the skin picking, which must cause clinically significant distress or impairment in social, occupational, or other important areas of functioning. The symptoms must not be better explained by symptoms of another mental disorder. This disorder is included in the *DSM-5* (APA, 2013) because of substantial scientific literature on excoriation's prevalence, diagnostic validators, and treatment. Studies show that the prevalence of excoriation is estimated at approximately 2%–4% of the population. Resulting problems may include medical issues such as infections, skin lesions, scarring, and physical disfigurement.

GENDER DYSPHORIA

The term *transgender* refers to a person whose sex assigned at birth (i.e., the sex assigned by a physician at birth, usually based on external genitalia) does not match their gender identity (i.e., one's psychological sense of their gender). Some people who are transgender will experience *gender dysphoria*, which refers to psychological distress that results from an incongruence between one's sex assigned at birth and one's gender identity. Although gender dysphoria often begins in childhood, some people may not experience it until after puberty or much later.

People who are transgender may pursue multiple domains of gender affirmation, including social affirmation (e.g., changing one's name and pronouns), legal affirmation (e.g., changing gender markers on one's government-issued documents), medical affirmation (e.g., pubertal suppression or gender-affirming hormones), and/or surgical affirmation (e.g., vaginoplasty, facial feminization surgery, breast augmentation, masculine chest reconstruction, etc.). Of note, not all people who are transgender will desire all domains of gender affirmation, as these are highly personal and individual decisions.

It is important to note that gender identity is different from gender expression. Whereas *gender identity* refers to one's psychological sense of their gender, *gender expression* refers to the way in which one presents to the world in a gendered way. Gender identity is also different from sexual orientation. *Sexual orientation* refers to the types of people toward whom one is sexually attracted. People who are transgender have the same diversity of sexual orientations as people who are cisgender (people whose sex assigned at birth matches their gender identity).

People whose gender at birth is contrary to the one they identify with will be diagnosed with gender dysphoria in the *DSM-5* (APA, 2013). This diagnosis is a revision of *DSM-IV*'s (APA, 1994) criteria for gender identity disorder and is intended to better characterize the experiences of affected children, adolescents, and adults. The *DSM* not only determines how mental disorders are defined and diagnosed, it also impacts how people see themselves and how we see each other. Although diagnostic terms facilitate clinical care and access to insurance coverage that supports mental health, these terms can also have a stigmatizing effect. The *DSM-5* aims to avoid stigma and ensure clinical care for individuals who see and feel themselves to be a different gender than their assigned gender. It replaces the diagnostic name *gender identity disorder* with *gender dysphoria*, as well as makes other important clarifications in the criteria. It is important to note that gender nonconformity is not in itself a mental disorder. The critical element of gender dysphoria is the presence of clinically significant distress associated with the condition. For a person to be diagnosed with gender dysphoria, there must be a marked difference between the individual's expressed/experienced gender and the gender others would assign that person, and it must continue for at least 6 months. In children, the desire to be of the other gender must be present and verbalized. This condition causes clinically significant distress or impairment in social, occupational, or other important areas of functioning. Gender dysphoria is manifested in a variety of ways, including strong desires to be treated as a person of the other gender or to be rid of one's sex characteristics, or a strong conviction that one has feelings and reactions typical of the other gender.

SCHIZOPHRENIA SPECTRUM AND OTHER PSYCHOTIC DISORDERS

SCHIZOPHRENIA

Schizophrenia is characterized by delusions, hallucinations, disorganized speech and behavior, and other symptoms that cause social or occupational dysfunction. For a diagnosis, symptoms must have been present for 6 months and include at least 1 month of active symptoms. The *DSM-5* (APA, 2013) raises the symptom threshold, requiring that an individual exhibit at least two of the specified symptoms. Additionally, the diagnostic criteria no longer identify subtypes. Subtypes had been defined by the predominant symptom at the time of evaluation. But these were not helpful to clinicians because patients' symptoms often changed from one subtype to another and presented overlapping subtype symptoms, which blurred distinctions among the five subtypes and decreased their validity. Some of the subtypes are now specifiers, which help provide further detail in diagnosis. For example, catatonia (marked by motor immobility and stupor) is used as a specifier for schizophrenia and other psychotic conditions such as schizoaffective disorder. This specifier can also be used in other types of disorders, such as bipolar disorders and major depressive disorder.

MEDICATIONS

Each of the medications listed belongs to a class of drugs known as *antipsychotics*, which are used to treat schizophrenia.

- Haldol (haloperidol)
- Thorazine (chlorpromazine)
- Seroquel (quitiapine)
- Risperdal (risperidone)
- Zyprexa (olanzapine)

TRAUMA- AND STRESSOR-RELATED DISORDERS

POSTTRAUMATIC STRESS DISORDER

Posttraumatic stress disorder (PTSD) is included in a new chapter in *DSM-5* (APA, 2013) on trauma- and stressor-related disorders. This move from the *DSM-IV* (APA, 1994), which addressed PTSD as an anxiety disorder, is among several changes approved for this condition, which is increasingly at the center of public as well as professional discussion. The diagnostic criteria for the manual's next edition identify the trigger to PTSD as exposure to actual or threatened death, serious injury, or sexual violation. The exposure must result from one or more of the following scenarios, in which the individual

- Directly experiences the traumatic event,
- Witnesses the traumatic event in person,
- Learns that the traumatic event occurred to a close family member or close friend (with the actual or threatened death being either violent or accidental), and/or
- Experiences first-hand repeated or extreme exposure to aversive details of the traumatic event (not through media, pictures, television, or movies unless work-related).

The disturbance, regardless of its trigger, causes clinically significant distress or impairment in the individual's social interactions, capacity to work, or other important areas of functioning. It is not the physiological result of another medical condition, medication, drugs or alcohol (APA, 2017).

MEDICATIONS

Several medications are recommended to treat PTSD symptoms. Originally designed to treat depression, these medications can reduce PTSD symptoms.

- Sertraline (Zoloft)
- Paroxetine (Paxil)
- Fluoxetine (Prozac)
- Venlafaxine (Effexor)

ADJUSTMENT DISORDERS

This *DSM-5* (APA, 2013) category of diagnosis is for people who are responding to either negative stressors (e.g., divorce) or positive stressors (e.g., marriage). Appropriate modifiers, such as *with depressed mood* or *with anxiety*, must accompany the diagnosis. Impairment of persons who fall under this category should have occurred within 3 months of the stressor(s). The diagnosis itself, which is considered among the mildest in the *DSM* classification system, is time limited and must have changed after 6 months.

FEEDING AND EATING DISORDERS

BINGE-EATING DISORDER

Binge-eating disorder was approved for inclusion in *DSM-5* (APA, 2013) as its own category of eating disorder. In the *DSM-IV* (1994), binge-eating disorder was not recognized as a disorder but rather described in Appendix B: Criteria Sets and Axes Provided for Further Study and was diagnosable using only the catch-all category of *eating disorder not otherwise specified. Binge-eating disorder* is defined as recurring episodes of eating significantly more food in a short period of time than most people would eat under similar circumstances, with episodes marked by feelings of lack of control. Someone with binge-eating disorder may eat too quickly, even when they are not hungry. The person may have feelings of guilt, embarrassment, or disgust and may binge eat alone to hide the behavior. This disorder is associated with marked distress and occurs, on average, at least once a week over 3 months. This change is intended to increase awareness of the substantial differences between binge-eating disorder and the common phenomenon of overeating. Although overeating is a challenge for many Americans, recurrent binge eating is much less common, far more severe, and is associated with significant physical and psychological problems.

ANOREXIA NERVOSA

Anorexia nervosa, which primarily affects adolescent girls and young women, is characterized by distorted body image and excessive dieting that leads to severe weight loss combined with a pathological fear of becoming fat. The criteria have several minor but important changes. Criterion A focuses on behaviors, like restricting calorie intake, and no longer includes the word *refusal* in terms of weight maintenance as that implies intention on the part of the patient and can be difficult to assess. The *DSM-IV* (APA, 1994) Criterion D requiring amenorrhea, or the absence of at least three menstrual cycles, has been deleted. This criterion cannot be applied to males, premenarchal females, females taking oral contraceptives, and postmenopausal females. In some cases, individuals exhibit all other symptoms and signs of anorexia nervosa but still report some menstrual activity (APA, 2013).

BULIMIA NERVOSA

Bulimia nervosa is characterized by frequent episodes of binge eating followed by inappropriate behaviors, such as self-induced vomiting, to avoid weight gain. The *DSM-5* (APA, 2013) criteria reduce the frequency of binge eating and compensatory behaviors that people with bulimia nervosa must exhibit, to once a week from twice weekly as specified in the *DSM-IV* (APA, 1994).

DISRUPTIVE, IMPULSE-CONTROL, AND CONDUCT DISORDERS

CONDUCT DISORDER

Conduct disorder is characterized by behavior that violates either the rights of others or major societal norms. These symptoms must be present for at least 3 months with one symptom having been present in the past 6 months. To be diagnosed with conduct disorder, the symptoms must cause significant impairment in social, academic, or occupational functioning. The disorder is typically diagnosed prior to adulthood. In the *DSM-5* (APA, 2013), the criteria for conduct disorder are largely unchanged from *DSM-IV* (APA, 1994), but the limited prosocial specifier is new to *DSM-5*. The specifier applies to those individuals with a more serious pattern of behavior characterized by a callous and unemotional interpersonal style across multiple settings and relationships. The specifier goes beyond the presence of negative behavior and reflects an individual's typical patterns in emotional and interpersonal functioning. People with conduct disorder who show this specifier display limited empathy and little concern for the feelings, wishes, and well-being of others. Individuals with conduct disorder who meet criteria for the specifier have a relatively more severe form of the disorder and a different treatment response. Thus the specifier allows clinicians to more accurately identify and diagnose individuals who need more intensive and individualized treatment. The specifier attempts to avoid stigmatizing language and focuses on a limited display of prosocial emotions such as empathy and guilt.

SOMATIC SYMPTOM DISORDER

Somatic symptom disorder (SSD) is characterized by somatic symptoms that are either very distressing or result in significant disruption of functioning, as well as excessive and disproportionate thoughts, feelings, and behaviors regarding those symptoms. To be diagnosed with SSD, the individual must be persistently symptomatic (typically at least for 6 months; APA, 2013). Several important changes have been made from previous editions of the *DSM*. The *DSM-IV* (APA, 1994) disorders of somatization disorder, hypochondriasis, pain disorder, and undifferentiated somatoform disorder have been removed, and many, but not all, of the individuals diagnosed with one of these disorders could now be diagnosed with SSD. The *DSM-IV* diagnosis of somatization disorder required a specific number of complaints from among four symptom groups. The SSD criteria no longer have such a requirement; however, somatic symptoms must be significantly distressing or disruptive to daily life and must be accompanied by excessive thoughts, feelings, or behaviors (APA Division of Research, 2013).

SLEEP–WAKE DISORDERS

Disturbed sleep, whether because of quality, timing, or duration, can have many adverse health consequences. The most obvious concerns are fatigue and cognitive focus, but mood can be greatly affected, too. A sleep disorder is not only a risk factor for subsequent development of certain mental conditions, but a potential warning sign for serious mental or medical issues. For example, sleep disturbances can signal the presence of medical and neurological problems such as congestive heart failure, osteoarthritis, and Parkinson's disease. Sleep disorders range from insomnia disorder to narcolepsy and breathing-related disorders to restless legs syndrome. They are diagnosed through comprehensive assessment, which may entail a detailed patient history, physical exam, questionnaires and sleep diaries, and clinical testing. They often are addressed in similarly comprehensive ways involving behavioral, pharmacologic, and other treatments in combination with medical care (APA, 2013).

CHANGES TO SLEEP–WAKE DISORDERS

A primary goal of the changes to the *DSM-5* (APA, 2013) sleep–wake disorders is to increase the clinical utility of definitions and diagnostic criteria, especially for general medical or mental health clinicians, and to clarify when referral is appropriate to a sleep specialist. To that end, some conditions that were separate in the *DSM-IV* (APA, 1994) now are grouped together to help facilitate diagnosis. Others have been divided based on greater understanding of the pathology triggering certain disorders or their underlying neurobiological and genetic factors. To help capture the dynamic relationship between sleep–wake disorders and certain mental or medical conditions, a greater emphasis is placed on how they can interact and impact each other. These disorders have been shown to be mutually exacerbating. The *DSM-5* underscores the need for independent clinical attention of a sleep disorder regardless of mental or other medical problems that may be present. Two previous diagnoses—sleep disorder related to another mental disorder and sleep disorder related to another medical condition—have been eliminated and greater specificity of co-existing conditions has been provided for each of the 10 sleep–wake disorders defined. The *DSM-5* also replaces primary insomnia with the diagnosis of insomnia disorder, a switch made to avoid the Sleep-Wake Disorders primary/secondary designation when this disorder co-occurs with other conditions and to reflect changes made throughout the classification (APA, 2013).

PARAPHILIC DISORDERS

Most people with atypical sexual interests do not have a mental disorder. To be diagnosed with a paraphilic disorder, the *DSM-5* (APA, 2013) requires that people with these interests

- Feel personal distress about their interest, not merely distress resulting from society's disapproval
- Have a sexual desire or behavior that involves another person's psychological distress, injury, or death, or a desire for sexual behaviors involving unwilling persons or persons unable to give legal consent

To further define the line between an atypical sexual interest and a disorder, the names of these disorders help to differentiate between the behavior itself, and the disorder stemming from that behavior (i.e., Sexual Masochism in the *DSM-IV* [APA, 1994] was renamed Sexual Masochism Disorder in the *DSM-5* [APA, 2013]). It is a subtle but crucial difference that makes it possible for an individual to engage in consensual atypical sexual behavior without inappropriately being labeled with pathology. With this revision, the *DSM-5* clearly distinguishes between atypical sexual interests and mental disorders involving these desires or behaviors. The chapter on paraphilic disorders includes eight conditions: exhibitionistic disorder, fetishistic disorder, frotteuristic disorder, pedophilic disorder, sexual masochism disorder, sexual sadism disorder, transvestic disorder, and voyeuristic disorder.

PERSONALITY DISORDERS

Personality disorders are associated with ways of thinking and feeling about oneself and others that significantly and adversely affect how an individual functions in many aspects of life. These disorders fall within 10 distinct types: paranoid personality disorder, schizoid personality disorder, schizotypal personality disorder, antisocial personality disorder, borderline personality disorder, histrionic personality, narcissistic personality disorder, avoidant personality disorder, dependent personality disorder, and obsessive-compulsive personality disorder (APA, 2013).

CLUSTER A

PARANOID PERSONALITY DISORDER

This personality disorder is marked by a pattern of being suspicious of others and seeing them as mean or spiteful. People with paranoid personality disorder often assume people will harm or deceive them and do not confide in others or become close to them.

SCHIZOID PERSONALITY DISORDER

This personality disorder is marked by being detached from social relationships and expressing little emotion. A person with schizoid personality disorder typically does not seek close relationships, chooses to be alone, and seems not to care about praise or criticism from others.

SCHIZOTYPAL PERSONALITY DISORDER

This personality disorder is marked by a pattern of being very uncomfortable in close relationships, having distorted thinking, and exhibiting eccentric behavior. A person with schizotypal personality disorder may have odd beliefs or odd or peculiar behavior or speech or may have excessive social anxiety.

CLUSTER B

ANTISOCIAL PERSONALITY DISORDER

This personality disorder is marked by a pattern of disregarding or violating the rights of others. A person with antisocial personality disorder may not conform to social norms, may repeatedly lie or deceive others, or may act impulsively.

BORDERLINE PERSONALITY DISORDER

This personality disorder is marked by a pattern of instability in personal relationships, intense emotions, poor self-image, and impulsivity. A person with borderline personality disorder may go to great lengths to avoid being abandoned; make repeated suicide attempts; display inappropriate, intense anger; or have ongoing feelings of emptiness.

HISTRIONIC PERSONALITY DISORDER

This personality disorder is marked by a pattern of excessive emotion and attention seeking. People with histrionic personality disorder may be uncomfortable when they are not the center of attention, may use physical appearance to draw attention to themselves, or have rapidly shifting or exaggerated emotions.

NARCISSISTIC PERSONALITY DISORDER

This personality disorder is marked by an extreme need for admiration and lack of empathy for others. A person with narcissistic personality disorder may have a grandiose sense of self-importance, a sense of entitlement, take advantage of others, or lack empathy.

CLUSTER C

OBSESSIVE-COMPULSIVE PERSONALITY DISORDER

This personality disorder is marked by a pattern of preoccupation with orderliness, perfection, and control. A person with obsessive-compulsive personality disorder may be overly focused on details or schedules, may work excessively not allowing time for leisure or friends, or may be inflexible in their morality and values. (*This is NOT the same as obsessive-compulsive disorder.*)

AVOIDANT PERSONALITY DISORDER

This personality disorder is marked by a pattern of extreme shyness, feelings of inadequacy, and extreme sensitivity to criticism. People with avoidant personality disorder may be unwilling to get involved with people unless they are certain of being liked, may be preoccupied with being criticized or rejected, or may view themselves as not being good enough or socially inept.

DEPENDENT PERSONALITY DISORDER

This personality disorder is marked by a pattern of needing to be taken care of as well as submissive and clingy behavior. People with dependent personality disorder may have difficulty making daily decisions without reassurance from others or may feel uncomfortable or helpless when alone because of fear of inability to take care of themselves.

SUBSTANCE-RELATED AND ADDICTIVE DISORDERS

SUBSTANCE USE DISORDER

Substance use disorder (SUD) is a complex condition in which there is uncontrolled use of a substance despite harmful consequences. People with SUD have an intense focus on using a certain substance(s), such as alcohol, tobacco, or illicit drugs, to the point where the person's ability to function in day-to-day life becomes impaired. People keep using the substance even when they know it is causing or will cause problems. The most severe SUDs are sometimes called *addictions*. Substance use disorder in the *DSM-5* (APA, 2013) combines the *DSM-IV* (APA, 1994) categories of substance abuse and substance dependence into a single disorder measured on a continuum from mild to severe. Each specific substance is addressed as a separate use disorder (e.g., alcohol use disorder, stimulant use disorder, etc.), but nearly all substances are diagnosed based on the same overarching criteria. In this overarching disorder, the criteria have not only been combined, but strengthened. People can develop an addiction to:

- Alcohol
- Marijuana
- Phencyclidine (PCP), lysergic acid diethylamide (LSD), and other hallucinogens
- Inhalants, such as paint thinners and glue
- Opioid pain killers, such as codeine and oxycodone, heroin
- Sedatives, hypnotics, and anxiolytics (medicines for anxiety such as tranquilizers)
- Cocaine, methamphetamine, and other stimulants
- Tobacco

In addition to substances, people can also develop an addiction to behaviors, such as gambling and internet gaming.

INTERNET GAMING DISORDER

The internet is now an integral, even inescapable part of many people's daily lives; they turn to it to send messages, read news, conduct business, and much more. But recent scientific reports have begun to focus on the preoccupation some people develop with certain aspects of the internet, particularly online games. The "gamers" play compulsively, to the exclusion of other interests, and their persistent and recurrent online activity results in clinically significant impairment or distress. People with this condition endanger their academic or job functioning because of the amount of time they spend playing. They experience symptoms of withdrawal when kept from gaming. Much of this literature stems from evidence gathered from Asian countries and centers on young males. The studies suggest that when these individuals are engrossed in internet games, certain pathways in their brains are triggered in the same direct and intense way that a drug addict's brain is affected by a particular substance. The gaming prompts a neurological response that influences feelings of pleasure and reward, and the result, in the extreme, is manifested as addictive behavior (APA, 2013).

THE *DSM-5-TR*

Changes will appear in the *Diagnostic and Statistical Manual of Mental Disorders, Fifth Edition, Text Revision (DSM-5-TR)*, to be released by American Psychiatric Association Publishing in late 2022. This edition features the most current text updates based on scientific literature with contributions from more than 200 subject matter experts. The revised version includes a new diagnosis (prolonged grief disorder), clarifies modifications to the criteria sets for more than 70 disorders, includes *International Classification of Diseases, Tenth Revision, Clinical Modification (ICD-10-CM*; WHO, 2004) symptom codes for suicidal behavior and nonsuicidal self-injury, and updates descriptive text for most disorders based on an extensive review of the literature. In addition, *DSM-5-TR* (APA, 2022) includes a comprehensive review of the impact of racism and discrimination on the diagnosis and manifestations of mental disorders. The manual will help clinicians and researchers define and classify mental disorders, which can improve diagnoses, treatment and research.

Note: The DSM-5-TR *is scheduled to published in 2022, shortly after the release of the book you are currently reading. The changes made in this new edition, however, will not be used on an AMFTRB Exam for quite some time. The exam you take will use information from the* DSM-5 *(APA, 2013) as has been reviewed in this chapter.*

CONCLUSION

As we continue our review of the MFT profession, it is important to reflect on mental health assessments and how family therapists fit into the larger culture of mental health treatment. Today, traditional mental health treatment approaches use a medical model that involves diagnosing a problem using the fifth edition of *the Diagnostic and Statistical Manual of Mental Disorders* (APA, 2013). This approach is accepted among healthcare providers, insurance companies, and many community agencies. Although the MFT profession has remained unique in its relational/contextual views of mental health problems and their corresponding solutions, family therapists generally practice in environments in which it is necessary to assess mental status and provide an accurate *DSM-5* diagnosis.

KEY TERMS

Agoraphobia: An exaggerated and irrational fear of being in an unfamiliar place or of leaving one's home.

Amphetamines: A class of stimulant drugs that temporarily energize, increase mental alertness, produce a sense of euphoria, ward off sleep, and reduce fatigue. Amphetamines are addictive and can cause anxiety, restlessness, headaches, rapid heartbeat, and difficulty breathing.

Anorexia nervosa: An eating disorder that primarily affects young women that involves an avoidance of food and severe weight loss based on a distorted self-perception of being fat or overweight. Physical harm, such as malnutrition or even death, results from untreated anorexia.

Antisocial personality disorder: A disorder characterized by irresponsible behavior, low tolerance for frustration, frequent conflicts, lack of remorse or acknowledged responsibility for one's actions, and a low level of socialization. Someone with this disorder is sometimes referred to as a *psychopath* or *sociopath*.

Anxiety disorders: Disorders characterized by a chronic state of tension, uneasiness, worry, and fear that is reoccurring and has no known source or cause. Anxiety disorders take on a number of forms, and generalized anxiety (characterized by at least 6 months of persistent and excessive anxiety or worry), social anxiety (characterized by emotional discomfort or apprehension over social situations that require interaction with others), and panic disorder (characterized by intense and unexpected fear that something bad will happen, usually accompanied by physical symptoms such as heart palpitations, sweating, or dizziness) are among the most common.

Aptitude test: A type of ability test; a standardized measurement device used to assess the readiness of someone to learn and become proficient in a given area in the future. The Armed Services Vocational Aptitude Battery (ASVAB), the General Aptitude Test Battery (GATB), and the Miller Analogies Test (MAT) are examples of aptitude tests.

Attention deficit hyperactivity disorder: A common childhood disorder that may also be diagnosed in adults that includes specific symptoms of inattention (i.e., trouble focusing), hyperactivity, and impulsivity. In addition to displaying these three major symptoms, a child or adult must meet the following criteria to be diagnosed with ADHD: (a) display several symptoms before the age of 1 year; (b) display symptoms in more than one setting, such as at school, at home, with friends, or during other activities; (c) show clear evidence that the symptoms interfere with functioning at school, at work, or in social situations; and (d) have symptoms that are not explained by another condition, such as mood or anxiety disorders. ADHD is often treated and managed through medication and behavior therapy. Subtypes of this disorder include *predominately inattentive type, predominately hyperactive–impulsive type*, and the *combined type*.

Autism: A developmental disorder that begins before 30 months of age. Major characteristics include a lack of responsiveness to people, severe language impairment, and strong resistance to change in routine or the environment.

Benzodiazepines: A group of prescription drugs that are widely used in the treatment of anxiety and insomnia; they include diazepam (Valium), chlordiazepoxide (Librium), and triazolam (Halcion). Benzodiazepines can be addictive. They often are used as street drugs to treat the adverse effects of cocaine, heroin, and alcohol.

Bipolar disorder: An affective disorder in which the patient experiences alternating periods of depression and mania.

Borderline personality disorder: A disorder characterized by impulsive, unpredictable, and often self-destructive behaviors; intense mood swings; chronic boredom; manipulation of others for short-term gain; uncontrollable anger; and maladaptive patterns of relating toothers.

Bulimia: An eating disorder characterized by periods of binge eating followed by purging.

Comorbidity: This refers to the simultaneous presence of two conditions in a client, such as anxiety and substance abuse.

Compulsion: An irresistible, persistent impulse to perform a repetitive behavior (usually the result of an obsession), for example, washing one's hands every few minutes.

Compulsive disorder: A disorder that involves repetitive behaviors, often performed in a ritualistic manner.

Conduct disorder: A disorder in which children or adolescents exhibit a number of behavioral and emotional symptoms, some of which include aggression to people and animals, such as bullying or cruelty; deliberate destruction of property, deceitfulness, lying, or stealing; and serious violations of rules, such as staying out all night or truancy from school.

Cyclothymic disorder: This is the term for a mild case of bipolar disorder.

Delusion: A false, strongly held belief despite a lack of support for it; the two most common forms are those of grandeur and persecution.

Dementia: The deterioration of intellectual functions, such as memory loss or impairment. The onset is often due to medical conditions such as stroke, head trauma, or Parkinson's disease. Alzheimer's disease is an example of dementia that progresses slowly.

Developmental disability: A disability that is the result of a disease, genetic disorder, or impaired growth pattern that occurs before adulthood; may continue indefinitely and require specific and lifelong care; examples include intellectual disability, cerebral palsy, and Down syndrome.

Diagnosis: An interpretation, derived from the use of assessment information, of a person's condition (e.g., level of functioning). The *Diagnostic and Statistical Manual of Mental Disorders (DSM)* and *International Classification of Diseases (ICD)* are often used in making a diagnosis because of the criteria they have established in regard to classifying and labeling physical and emotional categories of diseases and disorders.

Diagnostic test: A test that is used to help in the diagnosis of a client.

Differential diagnosis: The process of distinguishing a disease or condition when coexisting diagnoses, such as addiction and another mental disorder, occur simultaneously.

Dissociative disorders: Disorders that involve an alteration in consciousness, such as memory loss or alternate personality states, that is not organic or psychotic in nature. The *DSM-5* classifies dissociative identity disorder (formerly known as *multiple personality disorder*), dissociative fugue, dissociative amnesia, and depersonalization disorder in this category.

Dysgraphia: A learning disability, specifically a difficulty in writing or the inability to write.

Dyslexia: A learning disability marked by an impairment in recognizing and comprehending written words that often results in reversing letters and difficulty reading.

Egosyntonic: A disorder that involves an integral part of the self, such as personality disorder.

Excoriation: This refers to picking at one's skin.

Factitious disorders: Feigned illnesses or disabilities; people with these disorders are usually resistant to treatment.

Fugue: A relatively long period of amnesia during which a person takes flight by leaving the immediate environment; described in *DSM-5* as a dissociative fugue.

Gender identity disorder: A sexual and gender identity disorder in the *DSM-5* that is characterized by a strong and persistent cross-gender identification coupled with a discomfort about one's own assigned sex.

Hallucinations: Imagined perceptions of an object, sound, or phenomenon that is not present in reality that are often symptoms of severe disorders such as schizophrenia.

Hallucinogen: A substance, such as lysergic acid diethylamide (LSD), mescaline, phencyclidine hydrochloride (PCP), or peyote, that when ingested induces hallucinations. The user may experience panic, confusion, suspicion, anxiety, or loss of control. Delayed effects, or flashbacks, can occur in some cases, even after use has ceased.

Hypochondriasis: A somatoform disorder characterized by a preoccupation with the idea of having a serious illness.

Hypomania: A disorder with similar symptoms to mania but most likely associated with cheerful or pleasurable feelings; persons with this disorder may not be able to make rational decisions because of their heightened state.

Medical model: The characteristics of medical practice that involve diagnosing illness and symptoms as a first step toward treatment planning; often criticized in family therapy as an over-reliance on the labeling of symptoms in a way that depersonalizes a client.

Mental status examination: A structured interview process that provides a controlled interpersonal setting in which to observe and elicit the symptoms and signs of possible mental disorders, as well as cognitive and perceptual functioning or deficits and levels of judgment and insight.

Mood disorders: Disorders, classified in the *DSM-5* as bipolar or depressive in nature, that have an emotional base and cause clinically significant distress in people's lives, including impairing their ability to fulfill important life roles.

Narcolepsy: A sleep disorder characterized by irresistible attacks of sleep.

Narcotics: A group of depressant drugs, such as heroin, methadone, codeine, morphine, and opium, that relieve pain and anxiety but are addictive and may have major side effects (e.g., drowsiness, nausea, vomiting); an overdose can produce shallow breathing, clammy skin, convulsions, coma, and possible death.

Objective test: A test that yields scores that are independent of any opinion or judgment of the scorer. An objective test is usually multiple choice in nature. Examples include the Minnesota Multiphasic Personality Inventory–2 (MMPI-2) and the Myers–Briggs Type Indicator (MBTI).

Obsessive-compulsive personality disorder: A disorder, listed under the broader category of anxiety disorders in the *DSM-5*, characterized by perfectionist behavior, an insistence on having others do things a certain way, a preoccupation with trivial matters and rules, an inability to make decisions or prioritize, and a limited ability to express warmth or tenderness.

Oppositional defiant disorder: A disorder in children characterized by an ongoing pattern of uncooperative, defiant, and hostile behavior toward authority figures. This behavior seriously interferes with the child's day-to-day functioning. Symptoms of ODD may include frequent temper tantrums, excessive arguing with adults, active defiance and refusal to comply with adult requests and rules, deliberate attempts to annoy or upset people, the blaming of others for one's mistakes or misbehavior, hateful talk when upset, and revenge seeking.

Personality disorders: Longstanding, deeply ingrained, maladaptive behaviors that take many forms (e.g., antisocial, avoidance, borderline, dependent, paranoid, obsessive-compulsive, narcissistic); highly resistant to treatment because clients' perceptions of their personality disorders typically are egosyntonic (i.e., the disorder is an integral part of the self), and thus they may be less likely to believe that their problems are changeable.

Pervasive development disorders: Neurological conditions that are first diagnosed in infancy, childhood, and adolescence but are manifested later; includes autistic disorder, Asperger's disorder, Rett's disorder, and childhood disintegrative disorder.

Phobia: An irrational, exaggerated, and/or unrealistic fear of a specific object or situation.

Posttraumatic stress disorder: A disorder following a trauma (e.g., an accident, rape, combat) with symptoms of increased arousal and avoidance of stimuli associated with the trauma; other symptoms include reexperiencing of the trauma through flashbacks, sleep disturbance, nightmares, anxiety, and intrusive thoughts of the incident.

Psychopathology: The study of disorders and dysfunctional behavior.

Psychopharmacology: The study of the effects of drugs in the treatment of disorders.

Retardation: A term used to describe significantly lower than average intellectual ability or significantly slower than average psychomotor reaction. Intellectual retardation is classified as mild (IQ level 50–55 to 70), moderate (IQ level 35–40 to 50–55), severe (IQ level 20–25 to 35–40), and profound (IQ level below 20–25).

Schizophrenia: A mental disorder characterized by a loss of contact with reality, withdrawal from others, and a loss of interest in external activities. In addition, there is a breakdown of personal habits and an inability to deal with daily events. Delusions, hallucinations, and thought abnormalities are also usually present.

Semi-structured clinical interview: An interview that addresses the same issues as a structured interview but provides more flexibility in sequence, wording, and interpretation.

Sexual dysfunctions: A category under sexual and gender identity disorders in the *DSM-5* that involves problems in the expression of one's sexuality that are usually straightforward and respond well to behavioral interventions.

Sleep disorders: A *DSM-5* category of disorders, including insomnia, hypersomnia, narcolepsy, nightmares, night terror, and sleepwalking, that can be either primary (not caused by other medical conditions) or secondary (related to other specific disorders) in nature. There are multiple factors involved in these disorders, for example, emotions, environment, and lifestyle.

Structured clinical interview: Consists of a list of relevant behaviors, symptoms, and events to be addressed during the interview with questions asked in an ordered sequence; guidelines for conducting the interview and procedures for recording and analyzing the data are provided.

Somatoform disorders: Mental disorders that take the form of physical illnesses, such as conversion reaction, hypochondriasis, and body dysmorphic disorder in the *DSM-5*.

Substance-related and addictive disorders: A category in the *DSM-5* that includes psychological and behavioral disorders associated with substance abuse (e.g., abuse of alcohol, amphetamines, caffeine, cannabis, cocaine, hallucinogens, inhalants, nicotine, opiates, phencyclidine hydrochloric, sedatives, polysubstances) as well as induced disorders resulting from the abuse.

Trichotillomania: Refers to the compulsion to pull out one's hair.

Upcoding: When a therapist assigns a more serious diagnosis than is warranted to obtain more authorized sessions from a managed care company.

KNOWLEDGE CHECK: CHAPTER 13

1. Ricky, 17 years old, comes to therapy with his mother, Barbara, because he keeps getting in trouble at school. The problem started when he was 15 and he was caught defacing school property. Since then, he has been suspended twice for theft, and most recently for bullying and starting fights with classmates. What would the best *DSM-5* diagnosis for Ricky be?

   A. Conduct disorder
   B. Antisocial personality disorder
   C. Adult antisocial behavior
   D. Oppositional defiant disorder

2. Karen has entered therapy reporting overwhelming headaches, and she's convinced that these symptoms mean that she has brain cancer. This incessant worry about her health has made it difficult for Karen to obtain employment or maintain friendships. Multiple medical exams from specialists have ruled out a physical cause for her symptoms, but she is convinced there is a biological basis for these headaches. The most likely *DSM-5* diagnosis for Karen is ____________.

   A. Somatoform disorder
   B. Conversion disorder
   C. Pain disorder
   D. Somatic symptom disorder

3. During your first session with Donald, you notice that his speech is accelerated and hard to follow. He exhibits grandiosity when talking about his life and contends he doesn't need sleep in order to perform. Donald also reports that he's been feeling invincible because of these symptoms for the last couple of weeks. What is Donald's most likely *DSM-5* diagnosis?

   A. Caffeine intoxication
   B. Bipolar I disorder
   C. Panic disorder
   D. Hyperactive II disorder

4. During her first therapy session, Denise complains of chronic fatigue and overwhelming anxiety. Although this client reports a history of anxiety and depression, she says nothing has ever been as intense as what she is currently experiencing. She can think of nothing that led to this change in her physical health and mental state. What would the therapist's first priority be?

   A. Recognizing that the fatigue and anxiety are symptoms of Denise's mental state, design a treatment plan around an anxiety disorder
   B. Include in the treatment plan the use of behavioral techniques to alleviate Denise's anxiety
   C. Refer Denise to a colleague for psychological assessment
   D. Refer Denise to a physician to rule out a physiological cause because her symptoms might be due to a medical condition

(*See answers next page.*)

1. A) Conduct disorder

Ricky meets the criteria for conduct disorder, which includes a pattern of behavior that violates the rights of others or animals. Ricky would need to have more pervasive traits of exploitation, aggression, violation of others' rights and lack of remorse for a diagnosis of Antisocial personality disorder (B). Also, he does not have the requisite minimum of 3 years of Conduct Disorder symptoms dating from before age 15. Adult antisocial behavior (C) would apply for isolated incidents of aggression or assaultive behavior, and Ricky is not yet an adult. A diagnosis of oppositional defiant disorder (D) could work here if Ricky had not previously violated the rights of others.

2. D) Somatic symptom disorder

The most likely diagnosis for Karen is somatic symptom disorder, which is characterized by the presence of one or more somatic symptoms accompanied by excessive thoughts, feelings, or behaviors related to the symptoms. Somatoform disorder (A) is a DSM-IV-TR (APA, 2000) diagnosis and is not included in the DSM-5 (APA, 2013): The DSM-IV-TR category of somatoform disorders has been replaced with somatic symptom and related disorders in the DSM-5. A diagnosis of conversion disorder (B) requires the presence of symptoms that involve a disturbance in voluntary motor or sensory functioning and doesn't fit here.

3. B) Bipolar I disorder

The nature and duration of Donald's symptoms are consistent with a diagnosis of Bipolar I disorder. Caffeine intoxication (A) involves the development of characteristic symptoms after recent consumption of caffeine, but the vignette doesn't mention that Donald has consumed caffeine. Although caffeine intoxication and bipolar I disorder share some symptoms, Donald's symptoms and their duration are more consistent with bipolar I disorder. Donald's symptoms are not characteristic of a panic attack (C), and hyperactive II disorder (D) is not a real disorder.

4. D) Refer Denise to a physician for ato rule out a physiological rule-outcause because her symptoms might be due to a medical condition

Referral for a medical exam is always a first step when physical factors may underlie a client's symptoms. Because the client's symptoms might be due to a medical condition, before developing a treatment plan or determining whether psychological testing is needed, the therapist would want to refer Denise to a physician for a medical evaluation.

5. Tim was referred to you by his cardiologist who could find no medical explanation for Tim's symptoms. Tim reports that he has experienced unexpected cardiac episodes that involved chest pain and feeling unable to breathe and that these events s make him feel like he's going to die. What additional information would help confirm a diagnosis of panic disorder?

   A. Onset of psychotic symptoms immediately after a panic attack
   B. Panic attacks triggered by a fear of scrutiny by others
   C. Persistent worry about having another panic attack
   D. Mood symptoms when thinking about panic attacks

6. Maria comes to therapy as an adjunct to participating in a 12-step program. Even though she attends Alcoholics Anonymous several times a week, Maria reports rarely being able to abstain from alcohol for more than a few days at a time. The therapist should be concerned that Maria is going through alcohol withdrawal, which traditionally requires medically supervised detoxification, if she has experienced which of the following?

   A. Dysphoric mood, vivid dreams, insomnia, and increased appetite
   B. Hand tremor, insomnia, hallucinations, and seizures
   C. Poor coordination, nystagmus, impaired memory, and mood lability
   D. Dysphoric mood, restlessness, insomnia, and fever

7. Trina was both physically and sexually abused as a child. Her childhood was so traumatic that she currently has large gaps in her memory. She can remember some of her childhood friends, the schools she went to, and some toys she had, but she has absolutely no recall of family vacations or spending any time with siblings or grandparents. The most likely *DSM-5* diagnosis is which of the following?

   A. Dissociative amnesia
   B. Posttraumatic stress disorder (PTSD)
   C. Dissociative identity disorder
   D. Histrionic personality disorder

8. Cliff has entered therapy due to anxiety stemming from parts of his new job. His new boss is requiring all employees at his level to make regular presentations in front of their peers and prospective new clients. Cliff hates public speaking and fears that his colleagues will judge him harshly and he will appear foolish to them and the clients. He is actually considering quitting this company, where he has worked for the past 12 years, because of this new requirement. Cliff experiences panic-like symptoms whenever he has to speak in front of a group. What is the most likely *DSM-5* diagnosis for Cliff?

   A. Social anxiety disorder
   B. Panic disorder
   C. Specific phobia
   D. Generalized anxiety disorder

(See answers next page.)

5. C) Persistent worry about having another panic attack

Persistent worry about having additional attacks is characteristic of panic disorder. Panic attacks do not involve mood symptoms (D) or trigger psychotic symptoms (A), and anxiety related to a fear of scrutiny by others is characteristic of social anxiety disorder (B).

6. B) Hand tremor, insomnia, hallucinations, and seizures

A diagnosis of alcohol withdrawal is assigned when cessation of or reduction in heavy, prolonged alcohol use results in at least two characteristic symptoms. These symptoms are associated with alcohol withdrawal. Option A points to stimulant withdrawal, option C is associated with alcohol intoxication, and option D is consistent with opioid withdrawal.

7. A) Posttraumatic stress disorder (PTSD)

According to the DSM-5 (APA, 2013), the essential feature of dissociative amnesia is an inability to recall important personal information that is usually of a traumatic or stressful nature and is too extensive to be explained by normal forgetfulness. Dissociative amnesia has been associated with childhood trauma.

8. A) Social anxiety disorder

Cliff's symptoms meet the diagnostic criteria for social anxiety disorder, which is diagnosed when the individual experiences marked fear or anxiety of fear of scrutiny by others in one or more social situations that are out of proportion to the actual threat posed by the situation. The diagnosis is not panic disorder (B) because that is characterized by sudden, unexpected panic attacks. Cliff's panic only occurs when speaking in front of groups and, therefore, is not unexpected or "out of the blue." Specific phobia (C) is characterized by marked fear or anxiety about a specific object or situation, whereas the fear or anxiety associated with social anxiety disorder relates to a fear of scrutiny by others. Generalized anxiety disorder is a not a fit in this scenario because it involves excessive anxiety and worry about multiple events or activities and the anxiety and worry are not necessarily due to a fear of scrutiny by others.

9. Never feeling quite comfortable with her body or appearance for as long as she can remember, 24-year-old Madison recalls having problems related to her eating behaviors for about the last 14 months. During that time period, she lost over 35 pounds and appears gaunt and emaciated to her friends and family, who have requested that she get help immediately for this problem. Her symptoms include repeated attempts to control her weight through food restriction, use of laxatives, and over-the-counter appetite suppressants. She fears being fat, and reports to the therapist that these behaviors are her safeguards against obesity. What is the most likely *DSM-5* diagnosis for Madison?

   A. Bulimia nervosa
   B. Major depressive disorder
   C. Anorexia nervosa
   D. Adjustment disorder

10. Luther was advised to reach out to a marriage and family therapist by several of his friends after the unexpected death of his wife after a car wreck several months ago. Even though he feels a little better over the last few days, Luther reports extended periods of uncontrollable crying, sleeplessness, eating very little, and wanting to be alone even though he has many friends offering to visit and spend time with him. The therapist is more likely to assign a *DSM-5* diagnosis of uncomplicated bereavement to Luther than a diagnosis of major depressive disorder if ___________.

   A. Luther's feeling of loss is accompanied by bouts of anxiety, a sense of emptiness, and intrusive thoughts about his wife and their relationship
   B. Luther's symptoms have dissipated in intensity over time and occur primarily when he thinks about his wife and their relationship
   C. Luther has had persistent symptoms for less than 2 months
   D. Luther's wife died less than 6 months ago and he considers his reaction to her death to be normal

11. Jake, a pre-med student, presents to therapy with extreme anxiety. He has been fearful and tense in anticipation of the Medical College Admission Test (MCAT) next week. Although Jake has a great grade point average, he has historically suffered from test anxiety and often cannot even complete the MCAT review because his heart rate shoots up and he feels like he is about to faint when he attempts to study. What should the therapist do first?

   A. Refer Jake for a medical evaluation
   B. Call a doctor to and recommend anti-anxiety medication
   C. Treat Jake's test anxiety and have a doctor prescribe an anti-anxiety medication
   D. Advise that Jake take anti-anxiety medication before the MCAT so that he is more in control of his test anxiety

12. Which *DSM-5* disorder is *least* likely to include a psychotic episode?

   A. Schizotypal
   B. Bipolar II
   C. Schizophrenia
   D. Major depression

(*See answers next page.*)

9. C) Anorexia nervosa

Madison's most significant symptom, in terms of making an accurate diagnosis, is her significant weight loss. Individuals with bulimia (A) usually have engaged in a purging behavior and do not experience significant weight loss. Individuals with major depressive disorder (B) do not engage in compensatory behaviors for the purpose of staying thin. Adjustment disorder (D) does not fit at all for Madison's symptoms as described in the vignette, and thus should be easily ruled out.

10. B) Luther's symptoms have dissipated in intensity over time and occur primarily when he thinks about his wife and their relationship

Uncomplicated bereavement is not a mental disorder but is included in the *DSM-5* with Other Conditions That May Be a Focus of Clinical Attention. It involves a feeling of emptiness or loss that tends to decrease in intensity over days to weeks and is associated with thoughts or reminders of the deceased. Option A would more likely associated with major depressive disorder, and options C and D would not work because the *DSM-5* does not specify a particular duration of symptoms and does not specify a particular interval of time since the death as a requirement for a diagnosis of uncomplicated bereavement.

11. A) Refer Jake for a medical evaluation

Given that the question asks what the therapist should do first, referring Jake for a medical evaluation is the best action. He is having physical symptoms (feeling faint, perception of increased heart rate) as well as behavioral and emotional responses to what appear to be anxiety-arousing situations. These symptoms, however, could have a medical basis. In addition, a medical professional would be qualified to determine whether this person should take medication. Options B, C, and D should be eliminated because these choices suggest either that the therapist decides Jake needs this medication (a marriage and family therapist cannot determine this) or that the therapist would ask the physician to give Jake a prescription without actually first seeing the client.

12. A) Schizotypal

Although clients with schizotypal personality disorder present with odd speech or behavior, they do not usually experience psychotic symptoms. Options B, C, and D however, are all disorders that might exhibit psychotic symptoms.

13. During your first session with Clayton, he reports that he "is not here for himself." Clayton is worried about his wife, Holly, who has suddenly become passive and very lethargic. She is sleeping more than usual and has virtually has no sex drive or desire to be intimate with her husband. Your first intervention in this clinical situation should be ________.

A. To ask Clayton to bring Holly to the next therapy session
B. To call Holly and suggest that she come for individual treatment
C. To continue treating Clayton and attempt to identify and address his role in his wife's symptoms
D. To suggest that Clayton tell his wife to have a physical examination

14. Thirteen-year-old Micah has had difficulty focusing and staying on task in the last few months as part of his transition to junior high. Based on the initial evaluation of Micah and corroborating input from his teachers and parents, the therapist believes the nature and number of his symptoms suggest a *DSM-5* diagnosis of attention deficit hyperactivity disorder (ADHD), predominantly inattentive presentation. Before assigning the diagnosis, the therapist will want to confirm that some symptoms were present before Micah was _____ years of age and that he exhibits them in at least _____ settings.

A. 12; 2
B. 7; 2
C. 6; 3
D. 10; 3

15. Timmy's parents are concerned that at 3 years of age their son doesn't speak and, according to his dad, appears to be "in his own world." Timmy shows no interest in the other children at daycare, and usually sits in a corner by himself and rocks back and forth repetitively. These symptoms are indicative of which disorder?

A. Autism spectrum disorder
B. Childhood schizophrenia
C. Intellectual disability
D. Social pragmatic communication disorder

(*See answers next page.*)

13. D) To suggest that Clayton tell his wife to have a physical examination
More than one of these interventions may be appropriate at some time but the question asks what you should do first. Ruling out physiological factors and biological causes underlying Holly's symptoms is an important first step.

14. A) 12; 2
For a diagnosis of ADHD, the *DSM-5* requires that several inattentive or hyperactive-impulsive symptoms were present prior to age 12 and that symptoms are present in at least two settings.

15. A) Autism spectrum disorder
Some of the symptoms an autistic child might exhibit are little or no verbal communication, lack of social interaction, repetitive stereotyped manipulation of materials, and/or repetitive motor mannerism such as flapping fingers or rocking. Childhood schizophrenia (B) is not a real diagnosis in *DSM-5*. Intellectual disability (C) diagnosis would not include repetitive behaviors. Social pragmatic communication disorder (D) is diagnosed if a child's cognitive and language abilities are intact but their social communication (eye contact, inference, timing of speech, ability to take turns in conversation, and nonverbal cuing) is not normative compared to peers.

REFERENCES

American Psychiatric Association. (1994). *Diagnostic and statistical manual of mental disorders.* (4th ed.).

American Psychiatric Association. (2000). *Diagnostic and statistical manual of mental disorders.* ((4th ed., text rev.) ed.).

American Psychiatric Association. (2010). *Guideline for the treatment of patients with panic disorders.* APA.

American Psychiatric Association. (2013). *Diagnostic and statistical manual of mental disorders.* (5th ed.).

American Psychiatric Association. (2017). *Clinical practice guideline for the treatment of post-traumatic stress disorder (PTSD) in adults.* APA.

American Psychiatric Association. (2022). *Diagnostic and statistical manual of mental disorders.* ((5th ed., text rev.) ed.).

American Psychiatric Association Division of Research. (2013). Highlights of changes from *DSM-IV* to *DSM-5*: Somatic symptom and related disorders. *Focus, 11*(4), 525–527.

Regier, D. A., Kuhl, E. A., & Kupfer, D. J. (2013). The *DSM-5*: Classification and criteria changes. *World Psychiatry, 12*(2), 92–98.

World Health Organization. (2004). *ICD-10: International statistical classification of diseases and related health problems.* ((10th rev., 2nd ed.) ed.).

PART IV

Evaluating Ongoing Progress and Terminating Treatment (Domain 4)

Evaluating Progress and Terminating Treatment

14

LEARNING OBJECTIVES

After reading this chapter, you should be able to:

1. Identify brief practical ways to measure client change in marriage and family therapy (MFT)
2. Describe nonstandardized and standardized forms of client feedback
3. Explain the importance of progress monitoring
4. Outline the categories and proper procedures for the termination phase of therapy

RELEVANT EXAM DOMAINS

- *Domain 4—Evaluating Ongoing Process and Terminating Treatment*
  Includes tasks related to continuously evaluating the therapeutic process and incorporating feedback into the course of treatment, as well as planning for termination.

INTRODUCTION

Although the specific goals of MFT often vary for each client system, the underlying assumption exists that the process will be helpful to in making changes in their lives. But how do you know that your client is progressing as expected? Routinely monitoring client progress during therapy, by using standardized and nonstandardized measures, is an important part of evidence-based practice in systemic therapy. In order to receive reimbursement, many insurance companies now require client evaluations of their progress in addition to therapist descriptions. These third-party payers have shifted from having providers complete treatment plans, to having clients complete progress checklists to assess whether therapy is warranted and effective. In addition to focusing on tasks related to continuously evaluating the therapeutic process and incorporating feedback into the course of treatment, this chapter discusses the process of termination. Termination occurs when therapeutic goals are reached or when the client system is no longer interested in continuing services. Evaluating the progress toward goal achievement and working through resistance are often included in the termination phase, which also helps clients to anticipate and resolve future problems and locate additional resources if needed.

THE VALUE OF CLIENT FEEDBACK

Eliciting feedback can help therapists evaluate client progress throughout the therapy process. Specifically, collecting feedback from the client may lead to understanding clients' subjective experiences, cultivating a healthy alliance, and supporting clients' abilities to choose their goals and how to meet them. One way to offer clients the chance to give feedback and reflect on their experience is to have them fill out informal evaluations or ask them for verbal feedback. Some research has indicated, however, that therapists think they check in with clients in this informal way far more frequently and consistently than they actually do. Indeed, numerous studies have found that therapists, despite their confidence that they accurately appraise the strength of the alliance and client progress, are poor at gauging these elements when using clinical judgment alone.

In practice, therapists typically evaluate these important factors informally, but this is an area in which therapists—and clients—can benefit from a more formal type of feedback. The term *formal* in this case refers to using validated tools to elicit client feedback about their perception of both the therapeutic alliance and outcome. The idea of using a form to obtain client feedback may create resistance among some therapists, but it is important to remember that these feedback measures are more than just assessment devices. Rather, they are primarily dialogue tools between therapist and clients used to stimulate important discussion about the therapeutic process and treatment progress. Through this dialogue, the therapist and client work collaboratively to make adjustments and customize the therapy being delivered.

Any good treatment plan, in addition to highlighting goals and proposed interventions, specifies methods that will be used to monitor therapy progress. These methods may include client self-reports, therapist observations, and feedback instruments that are administered at the beginning of therapy to obtain baseline data, as well as throughout treatment to measure change.

Monitoring the progress of treatment through feedback at regular intervals provides the information needed to (a) inform the therapist, client, and third parties about the client's improvement; (b) help the therapist determine whether the treatment plan should be modified; and (c) help the therapist and client determine when it is appropriate to terminate therapy. In addition, this routine evaluation might address the quality of the expanded therapeutic alliance, the client system's motivation and satisfaction, and other relevant factors. Each phase of treatment should include methods of evaluating progress that are relevant to the treatment objectives for that phase (Hannan et al., 2005; Miller et al., 2006).

NONSTANDARDIZED INFORMAL FEEDBACK

Nonstandardized informal feedback is derived from the verbal or written descriptions of change created by either the client or the therapist. There are several easy ways to gather information for this type of helpful feedback. Therapists should simply ask clients to assess their progress since the last meeting, paying special attention to changes in specific symptoms or advances toward goals. To operationalize growth between sessions, the therapist may guide clients to rate their own change using solution-focused scaling questions. In addition to using a scale, therapists can explore both the clients' and their own assessment of progress in a narrative style. These data should be documented and included in the client's file or clinical record. The advantages to this type of progress feedback are that it can be done at every session, it organically flows into the conversational style and structure of the therapy session, and it is completely free for the therapist to administer. Nonstandardized feedback, however, may not work as well with younger clients, those with severe pathology, or those lower functioning clients who are unable to accurately recall events between sessions. With certain couples or families, data should be collected on paper to get assessments that are not influenced by the comments of other members. Although some research suggests that clients' assessment of their level of functioning is useful, such informal self-reports are generally considered less reliable and valid than more standardized feedback measures.

STANDARDIZED FORMAL FEEDBACK

Standardized feedback measures are generally considered more accurate than nonstandardized measures. These evaluations involve pen-and-paper or electronic questionnaires that are completed by clients and/or significant others. They have been tested for reliability and validity and allow therapists to more carefully track changes and compare a single client with a group norm, which is most meaningful when the client is similar to a comparable group. The common problem with these evaluations is that many are proprietary and must be purchased. Some require a fee for each administration of the instrument, which can quickly become expensive for therapists with limited financial or professional development resources. Integrating this type of feedback requires more therapist and client time, and many will be reluctant to engage without first seeing how it would be beneficial to the therapy. Not all measures are adapted to be used with diverse populations or available in the client's primary language.

Although this type of standardized formal feedback can be extremely beneficial, neither therapists nor their clients will use these measures on a regular basis if they are too long or burdensome to complete. Therefore, these instruments should be brief and not get in the way of the real "work" in therapy. Brief measures are assessment instruments that require fewer than 10 minutes to complete. Two of the more common brief measures are the Outcome Questionnaire (OQ) and the Symptom Check List (SCL; Lambert, 2015). Embodying a "buy it to sell it" mentality, therapists should convey the clinical utility of the feedback instrument to improve treatment outcomes if they expect their clients to take 5–10 minutes outside of session to compete the form.

PROGRESS MONITORING

Progress monitoring refers to the routine collection of client feedback in psychotherapy services that is used to track client progress, identify at-risk clients, and facilitate adjustment of therapy to prevent premature dropout or negative outcome. Progress monitoring involves repeated assessment of client progress during therapy, typically conducted from the client's perspective at every session or every other session. A key aspect of progress monitoring involves continuous feedback to the therapist on the client's status, which facilitates the assessment of treatment progress and may suggest changes to the course of treatment, if necessary. Research indicates that progress monitoring is related to positive client outcomes, increases in treatment efficiency, decreases in negative outcomes, and increases in trainee improvement when used in clinical supervision (Shimokawa et al., 2010). Further, growing evidence suggests that progress monitoring can help to increase treatment efficacy with diverse populations and in diverse contexts (Sparks, 2015).

Although progress feedback systems have been extensively tested in individual psychotherapy, development of scientifically sound and viable feedback systems for couple and family therapy is still in its early stages (Pinsof et al., 2009). Despite the demonstrated positive impact of using feedback monitoring tools and clinicians' generally positive attitudes toward the usefulness of gathering progress data and providing feedback to their clients, only a small minority of practitioners are currently using them at least once per month or even on a less regular basis.

THE THERAPEUTIC ALLIANCE

Tracking the relationship between therapist and client is essential for feedback and to monitor change over the course of treatment. In MFT, the expanded therapeutic alliance offers the opportunity for a corrective relationship experience and is a necessary (but not sufficient) condition for therapeutic change. A growing body of empirical evidence demonstrates that the therapeutic alliance is the best predictor of psychotherapy outcome in individual therapy, and a similar line of clinical research shows this is true for MFT as well (Norcross, 2010). The working alliance consists of three parts: tasks, goals, and bond. Tasks, the structure of therapy, are what the therapist and client agree need to be done to reach the client's goals. Goals are what the client hopes to gain from therapy, based on their presenting concerns. The bond forms from trust and the feeling component that exists between client and therapist. The functions of a therapeutic alliance include instilling hope in the family and creating an environment of safety. As opposed to the linear, one-on-one focus of individual therapy, a marriage and family therapist must form an alliance with several people at once, who often have quite different motivations and agendas for therapy. If not balanced among different members of the system, a split alliance may occur. If the participant has come involuntarily, as with many adolescents and most court-mandated clients, the situation is even more complicated. By rolling with the resistance, the therapist must work to develop a connection with each person, with the various subsystems, and with the family on a whole.

FEEDBACK-INFORMED TREATMENT

Feedback-informed treatment (FIT), a form of progress monitoring, is an evidence-based practice in which therapists gather real-time input from clients using standardized measures to identify what is and is not working in therapy and then make adjustments to better meet client's needs (Duncan & Reese, 2015). FIT aims to incorporate the client's perspective into the therapeutic relationship. The two measures used at every session are the Session Rating Scale (SRS) and the Outcome Rating Scale (ORS; Miller et al., 2003).

The SRS is a four-item measure of the therapeutic alliance that the therapist administers at the end of each session. Ultra-brief by design, it takes only a few minutes to complete. The first three items of the SRS correspond directly with the domains of the alliance—task, goals, and bonds—previously mentioned. The fourth item simply asks how the client felt about the session overall. The four items of the SRS are as follows:

- Relationship (degree to which the client felt heard, understood and respected)
- The goals and topics (degree to which the client was able to focus on what they wanted to in session)
- The approach or method (how the client felt about the therapist's approach)
- Overall (degree to which the overall session felt right and on track for the client)

Each of the items is ranked on a 10-point visual-analog scale. Clients are asked to reflect on the session, complete the brief form, and then discuss their feedback with the therapist.

The ORS is another ultra-brief four-item tool for measuring the client's perspective of change or improvement (or lack of improvement) in relation to the initial score at intake. The therapist administers the ORS at the beginning of each session. Again, it usually only requires about a minute of session time to complete. The first three items are based on three domains of the much longer Outcome Questionnaire-45, while the last item refers to the client's general sense of well-being. The four items of the ORS are as follows:

- Individual (personal well-being)
- Interpersonal (family, close relationships)
- Social (work, school, friendships)
- Overall (general sense of well-being)

Both the SRS and ORS have good reliability and validity for such brief measures and, unlike longer measures geared toward research, they are designed to be used in everyday practice.

TERMINATION

Addressing the termination of treatment is an important phase of the therapeutic process. For termination to be handled properly, discussions between the therapist and client system should occur in advance and be addressed in a thoughtful and sensitive manner. It is best that clients do not feel that they have been abandoned. If continued treatment is needed, the therapist must make an effort to assist the client in obtaining ongoing services to ensure that these needs are adequately addressed. Proper documentation of the termination of the therapeutic relationship with the client provides support for the therapist's effort to meet the clients' needs as treatment ends. This documentation, in the form of a current treatment plan, should indicate the criteria for determining the readiness for termination and the strategies that will be used during the final phase of therapy to help ensure that the client system maintains the changes they have made. The primary factor to consider when determining readiness for termination is the achievement of therapy goals: Ideally, the termination process begins when the therapist and client agree that goals have been accomplished. However, in some situations, termination may be appropriate when all goals have not been fully achieved but the client has acquired the skills needed to deal with any remaining problems. The termination process should be a gradual one that allows the therapist and client to resolve disagreements about the appropriateness of termination, review the gains the client has made in therapy, and address any feelings of loss or abandonment. Certain circumstances may support a delay of the termination. For instance, it is not recommended that a therapist end treatment when a client system is in crisis at the time termination is being considered. Marriage and family therapists have the responsibility to see that clinical services are not withheld when a client is in crisis. Postponing termination is preferred, if possible, until steps are in place to handle the crisis (see Chapter 15).

Although it is always best when planned, there are many valid reasons described in the following list as to why the therapist–client relationship may end the therapy prematurely. Some of those reasons include:

- Client has needs that are beyond the therapist's scope of competence. For example, the client requires a different level of treatment (e.g., inpatient) or more specialized treatment (e.g., trauma or substance abuse) than the therapist has training for.
- Therapist is unable or unwilling, for appropriate reasons, to continue to provide care, that is, the therapist is retiring/closing practice or on medical leave.
- Conflict of interest is identified after treatment begins.
- Client fails to make adequate progress toward treatment goals or fails to comply with treatment recommendations.
- Client fails to engage in therapy due to no-shows, or cancellations.

In addition to these reasons, terminations can fall into the following categories.

FORCED TERMINATION

A forced termination is an ending of the therapy relationship before the work of therapy or goals have been fully accomplished. This process may happen in many clinics or settings that employ therapists-in-training who are rotated in and out of service in a way that may be disjointing to their clients. These clients may feel anger toward the therapist, perceiving the end of the relationship as abandonment. It is most likely to occur if the therapist does not mention termination until very close to the intended end date. Other reactions from clients might include sadness at losing a relationship on which they have come to depend, or indifference at the end of the relationship. These emotions are oftentimes easier or more comfortable to express that anger or separation anxiety. The manner in which other significant relationships in the client's past have ended will very likely impact their reaction to the end of this therapeutic relationship. Although unresolved issues surrounding past relationships can be played out in a parallel process during the termination process, the therapist is in a restorative position to provide the client with a healthy end to a productive relationship that they can look back on positively and feel comfortable with.

Therapists may also experience many emotions in a forced termination, including guilt and loss. Premature endings may leave therapists feeling as though they are abandoning their clients just as good progress is finally being made and can lead to a sense of feeling responsible for whatever might happen to the client as a result of the end of the relationship. Other therapists may struggle with a sense of omnipotence, or the feeling that they are the only one who can understand or help the client system. On the other hand, it is normal to feel a sense of impotence, or the feeling that the relationship was not at all helpful to the client and that the client will be helped more effectively by a different therapist. When working with a client for only a short period of time, it can be difficult to see whether any progress was made, especially if the client is not communicating any improvements to the therapist. In such cases, it is important for the therapist to become more comfortable with the feeling of "not knowing" in this process.

CLIENT-INITIATED TERMINATION

A client system may initiate termination when therapeutic goals have been accomplished or when they decide that problematic areas have been reduced or eliminated. If the therapist agrees that goals have been met and the timing for ending treatment is appropriate, termination can be a rewarding, gratifying experience for all involved. In other cases, clients may initiate termination if they do not feel comfortable with the therapist or do not feel that they are ready to fully engage in the therapy process. In such cases, therapists often feel a sense of insecurity in their ability to effectively connect with the clients, discomfort about being unsuccessful, or possibly relief at being rid of a relationship or client system that they were challenged by. In this case, it is very important for therapists to process with a supervisor their own feelings about the end of the relationship and how it might affect future interactions with other client systems.

THERAPIST-INITIATED TERMINATION

Therapist-initiated termination may occur when the clinician determines that the client has made progress toward achieving goals, notices a reduction in or elimination of the presenting problem, or feels that the client has gained enough insight and skill to deal with future recurring symptoms. This type of termination is also an ethical duty if the therapist realizes they are unable to adequately help the client system. If this is the case, it is the therapist's responsibility to make appropriate referrals and to obtain the professional training that would enable them to work with similar clients effectively in the future.

TIPS FOR TERMINATION

Therapists should assess a client system's ongoing treatment needs prior to initiating termination. Termination should be discussed early so all parties can have a number of sessions during which to discuss ending therapy. Ideally, this should be done at least two to three sessions prior to the final meeting, providing the therapist an opportunity to ask clients to talk about relationships that have ended in their past, how they have ended, and how that might affect the end of this therapeutic relationship. If there is the option of spacing out the last few sessions, it may help to gradually transition the client system away from therapy and foster in them a sense of confidence in their ability to handle things in their family apart from the therapist's intervention.

Conduct the final session face-to-face, if possible. Avoid ending with a text, in an email, or with a voicemail message. Highlight the progress that the client system has made during treatment. Very often, clients will forget the advances they have made, or neglect to give themselves credit for their accomplishments. Asking clients what they learned and what they found helpful about their sessions can instill confidence and provide them with a positive perspective on the therapy process. Review the tools and operationalized skills that clients have acquired through the therapy process. These tools will be critical in helping clients be self-sufficient in handling the problems that had originally brought them to therapy. Finally, strategies for preventing and dealing with relapse should be incorporated into the final phase of treatment and may include such techniques as enhancing coping skills and self-efficacy, identifying sources of support and ways for making positive lifestyle changes, and identifying specific strategies to use to respond to and manage a relapse. Remember to document discussions about termination in progress notes.

Allow clients to talk about their feelings surrounding termination. They will likely have many emotions to work through and time should be spent acknowledging and processing them. Conversely, therapists should also be aware of their own feelings surrounding the termination process. It is normal to feel many emotions when ending a therapeutic relationship with client system.

If continued treatment is needed, provide referrals to at least three qualified mental health professionals, with addresses and phone numbers. If possible, and with the client system's consent, assist in the transition to other healthcare providers.

THE TERMINATION LETTER

Formalize the termination with a personalized termination letter (not a form letter). This is a good practice for therapists to follow once treatment has ended, regardless of the reason, that documents and formally ends the therapeutic relationship. This letter provides clarity to the client and helps avoid any implication that the therapist has an ongoing responsibility. The termination letter should be in the form of a business letter and includes:

- Client's name
- Date treatment began
- Effective date of termination
- The reason(s) for the termination (e.g., treatment goals have been met, client's needs are beyond the scope of social's workers practice or area of expertise, non-compliance with treatment recommendations, therapist is retiring/closing practice)
- Treatment summary, including whether you feel further treatment is recommended
- If continued treatment is needed, three referrals to mental health professionals with contact information
- Retain a copy of the letter for the client's file
- Do not mention confidential therapeutic treatment information in the letter

CONCLUSION

The marriage and family therapists' duty of care requires maintaining an appropriate awareness of therapeutic progress and suggesting the appropriate changes to the treatment plan. Regardless of the precision of the initial treatment plan, neither therapist nor client system can possibly know what the precise outcome of treatment will be. A good practice is to inform new clients that treatment plans are subject to an ongoing process of review and that such reviews are intended to ensure their input into, and agreement with, the treatment plan. Measures for monitoring client progress can be nonstandardized or standardized. Nonstandardized measures are informal techniques that involve asking the client about their progress, whereas standardized measures are commercially available checklists, questionnaires, and inventories that have standardized administration and scoring procedures and evidence of reliability. Finally, the process of termination is the last part of the therapeutic cycle. Termination works best when clients are prepared for it and when both the therapist and family agree to it. If conducted properly, termination can help clients reflect on what they have accomplished, and motivate members of the system to continue new adaptive behaviors.

KEY TERMS

Client-directed outcomes: Treatment outcomes that fit with the client's goals, rather than being set by the therapist alone.

Resistant client: A client who is unwilling to change or is opposed to change. Such an individual may actively seek counseling but does not wish to go through the pain that change demands. Instead, the client clings to the certainty of present behavior, even when such action is counterproductive and dysfunctional. Resistance can be displayed in many ways, such as through (a) noncompliance (e.g., not following through with homework assignments, showing up late for appointments, missing appointments altogether), (b) avoidance (e.g., displaying in-session extremes expressed as outbursts against the counselor, debating, attempting to derail or detour conversation with such terms as "I don't know" or by changing the subject, manipulating the session by waiting until the end of the session to bring up important information), and (c) ambivalence (e.g., having mixed feelings about the proposed change, e.g., smoking cessation).

Stages of change: This refers to the five positions clients take as they consider making changes: precontemplation, contemplation, preparation, action, and maintenance.

Termination: This refers to the mutual, ending of services between a client system and therapist, traditionally at the conclusion of a course of treatment that is aimed at the amelioration or cessation of the diagnosed problem.

Therapeutic alliance: The relationship between the client system and therapist based on the tasks, goals, and bonds of therapy. The positive nature of the client–therapist relationship that may account for 30% of positive outcomes as measured by client feedback.

Treatment plan: A plan that explains why the client is receiving services and what is going to take place in counseling. It lists measurable and desired outcomes of treatment and is sometimes called a *plan of care, service plan, habitation plan, residential plan,* or *case management plan,* depending on the type of services provided and the agency providing those services.

KNOWLEDGE CHECK: CHAPTER 14

1. The Outcome Rating Scale (ORS) is an ultra-brief questionnaire that is designed to be used ________.

   A. At every session
   B. Monthly
   C. At the start and termination of therapy
   D. Whenever the client chooses

2. Marriage and family therapists should do all of the following except ____________ when customizing therapeutic fit with different client systems.

   A. Figure out what worked best in your personal therapy and apply it to your clients
   B. Solicit client feedback
   C. Learn a wide range of theories and techniques
   D. Incorporate client values and preferences

3. The disadvantage of using standardized evaluations as opposed to more informal methods in ongoing treatment monitoring is that __________.

   A. They are considered more reliable and valid
   B. The therapist is better able to make cross-client comparisons
   C. The therapist is better able to make comparisons across time
   D. They are easily adapted for diverse clients

4. Two general options for measuring therapeutic progress are _________.

   A. Quasi-experimental and experimental measures
   B. Linear and circular measures
   C. Nonstandardized and standardized measures
   D. Client self report and therapist opinion

5. Client progress is best measured by assessing client satisfaction and ________.

   A. The impact of theory
   B. The impact of techniques
   C. Clinical outcomes
   D. Therapist experience

6. A behavioral therapist measures client progress by using _____________ that refers back to _____________ behaviors.

   A. Measurable objectives; baseline
   B. Milestones; measurable
   C. Measurable objectives; historical
   D. Evidence-based data; objective

(*See answers next page.*)

1. **A) At every session**

The ORS assesses personal or symptomatic distress, family interactions, and larger social relationships. It is critical that the ORS is used at every session, as it ensures that client's voice remains central in directing the therapy. Also, the ORS is used in each and every session to monitor benefit, so therapist and client can regroup if therapy is not helping. This introduction of the ORS builds a feedback culture in the first session and sets the client up for success.

2. **A) Figure out what worked best in your personal therapy and apply it to your clients**

All of the other options (B, C, and D) prioritize either client choice or therapist flexibility, whereas response A prioritizes the therapist's worldview, which may or may not be a good fit for the client system they are working with.

3. **D) They are easily adapted for diverse clients**

Therapists using standardized evaluations may sometimes receive negative feedback from diverse client systems because the evaluation is not culturally sensitive or presents a barrier to receiving help—the reason they sought out therapy in the first place. Therapists with diverse client systems should assess fit, address any such potential barriers, and involve clients in the process before selecting a particular type of standardized assessment.

4. **C) Nonstandardized and standardized measures**

For many years the most common approach used to measure progress was the nonstandardized, written treatment plan, which includes clear goals and objectives identified by the client. These goals and objectives are discussed throughout the course of therapy to determine progress and completion of treatment. More recently, various standardizing outcome scales and checklists have been developed to track therapy progress, effectiveness, and outcomes in an even more quantitative and concrete manner. These measures range from brief (e.g., 1–2 minutes) rating scales completed by a client every session to much more comprehensive and lengthy measures incorporating both client and therapist perspectives, which can take 20 minutes or more to complete at various intervals throughout treatment.

5. **C) Clinical outcomes**

Tracking clinical outcomes helps to determine whether or not treatment is effective and measuring results aids both the client and clinician through the treatment process, regardless of whether you use self-reporting or performance-based measures. By setting goals with new clients, they can track their own progress on these desired outcomes over time, giving them the motivation to continue treatment and celebrate successes along the way.

6. **A) Measurable objectives/baseline**

Although all options in this question deserve consideration, this response is the most correct. Although the choices in options B, C, and D complete the sentence, option A does a better job, and uses the language most frequently associated with behavioral therapy and associated treatment plans. The other options are not necessarily incorrect; however, option A is simply a better answer.

7. A cognitive behavioral therapist has been working with a family for eight sessions. In the middle stage of treatment, the father brings up the issue of termination. Which of the following statements is indicative of how a cognitive behavioral therapy-oriented family therapist should respond?

   A. "How do each of you feel about ending therapy?"
   B. "You are the clients, but as your family therapist, I feel as though this is a premature decision."
   C. "What do you as a family and what do you as individuals think about termination?"
   D. "We are coming close to the end of therapy. What do you all think about it?"

8. The Jones family comes to therapy with the presenting problem of poor communication. They have two teenagers, Tom and Sarah, whom the therapist sees for a short period time—four sessions. After a few of these sibling sessions, the parents then reports better communication. Even though there have only been two sessions in which all members of the system are present, the parents report they no longer need therapy because everyone is talking with each other outside of the therapy sessions and is able to solve problems without the therapist's help. The therapist should ________________.

   A. See the couple together to work on marital issues
   B. Continue to see the two teens together to improve their relationship because they seem to be benefitting from this therapy
   C. Challenge the family's "flight into health" and discourage the family from trying to be their own therapist by encouraging them to save significant issues for family sessions
   D. Begin the termination process since the Jones family has accomplished their goals

9. A family is seeing the therapist for issues relating to their daughter's refusal to complete homework. As a structural family therapist, the therapist would know that the family is making progress when ________________.

   A. The family begins talking about terminating the therapy
   B. The parents, serving as the family's executive system, are exerting more control over the girl's behavior
   C. The transference has turned from negative to positive
   D. The daughter becomes more differentiated from her mother

10. Dan, a 63-year-old widower, has been attending therapy for the past 6 months for help with depression and grief/loss issues after the death of his wife. During the past few sessions, he tells the therapist he has been feeling much better and that the therapy has served its purpose. The therapist has increased the length of time between sessions, as part of preparation for termination. Dan comes for the next session despondent over the sudden death of his dog, Fred. Which of the following would be best for the therapist to do?

    A. Increase the frequency of sessions to facilitate the grief and loss process
    B. Ask Dan how therapy can be most helpful in dealing with the loss of Fred
    C. Continue with the longer length of time between sessions to encourage Dan's s independence in dealing with life stressors
    D. Increase the frequency of sessions due to the client's history of depression and loss

(*See answers next page.*)

7. C) "What do you as a family and what do you as individuals think about termination?"

From a cognitive behavioral therapy (CBT) frame, you needed to select the answer that suggests a thinking, rather than an emotional, affective approach to therapy, ruling out option A. The therapist would be interested in exploring and addressing with the family group and with each individual the reasons, rational and irrational, underlying their cognitive beliefs that therapy should end now. Rather than giving their own opinion (B), a cognitive behavioral therapist would be more likely to elicit and examine the clients' thoughts about termination as this reinforces the skills they are learning in therapy. Response D is incorrect because it includes the assumption that the therapist agrees with the family that it is almost time to end therapy.

8. D) Begin the termination process since the Jones family has accomplished their goals

Although this therapy was brief and there were only two, full-family therapy sessions, the question addresses what should occur when the presenting problem has been resolved. The presenting problem was poor communication, and the family now reports good communication; therefore, they have achieved their therapeutic goal. The therapist should begin the termination process.

9. B) The parents, serving as the family's executive system, are exerting more control over the girl's behavior

This is an excellent indicator of therapeutic progress from a structural perspective, whereas option A does not necessarily give evidence that the family is making progress. It could be that they may be feeling uncomfortable with the process instead. Option C refers to a psychodynamic perspective and turning the transference from "negative to positive" is not necessarily an indicator of therapeutic progress. Option D is referring to progress from a Bowenian perspective.

10. B) Ask Dan how therapy can be most helpful in dealing with the loss of Fred

Involving Dan in the decision to modify the treatment plan is the best first step. It empowers the client to make decisions about his own care and creates an opportunity for the therapist to assess the situation. Making a treatment decision (options A, C, and D) without involving Dan could send a message that either he is not competent to deal with loss without the therapist's help or it ignores his progress.

11. Michelle, a Bowenian therapist, is considering termination with her client Justine. What indicator of treatment would be most important in making this decision?

A. Justine's ability to speak for herself

B. Changes in Justine's family system

C. The symptoms that brought Justine into therapy have been alleviated

D. Justine is better able to separate thinking from feeling in her interactions with her family of origin

12. According to Prochaska and DiClemente's stages of change (transtheoretical) model, David, a client in the __________ stage has made a tentative plan with his therapist to stop his problematic procrastinating behavior. He is willing to take actions that will alter this behavior in the next 30 days before he starts his graduate program.

A. Action

B. Contemplative

C. Preparation

D. Goal attainment

13. After attending 27 sessions over the course of the past year, Marina leaves a message on your voicemail saying she is ending therapy without offering any other details or context. Even though she has made some progress on the issues that originally brought her to therapy, there has been no previous discussion of termination between you and she. What should you do?

A. Call Marina immediately

B. Call Marina and insist that she return for at least one wrap-up, termination session

C. Allow Marina to leave without further discussion because she is the one who should make the decision

D. Contact Marina to make sure she is not in crisis and is comfortable with her decision

14. Jan, a client you have been seeing for 6 months, misses three appointments in a row even though she keeps rescheduling and pays the missed-session fee. You should ____________________.

A. Terminate the therapeutic relationship

B. Refer the client to another therapist

C. Consult with colleagues

D. Bring the issue up directly with Jan

15. The Brown family comes to see a family therapist who uses solution-focused therapy (SFT). How would the therapist best evaluate the family's progress during the course of the therapy?

A. Through assessing how much of the problem area remains a focus of the Brown family's presentation

B. By asking the miracle question

C. By the lack of problems that the Brown family brings into sessions

D. By the Brown family exhibiting their own ability to deal with stressors, develop their own solutions, and move toward goals without the therapist's input

(*See answers next page.*)

11. D) Justine is better able to separate thinking from feeling in her interactions with her family of origin
This is the definition of *differentiation of self*, which is a primary goal of Bowenian therapy. Option A does involve taking the "I" position, which is roughly the same as speaking for oneself. However, upon reading all the choices, D is clearly the better choice.

12. C) Preparation
Prochaska and DiClemente's model distinguishes among five stages of change: precontemplation, contemplation, preparation, action, and maintenance. A client in the preparation stage is planning to take action in the near future, a time period usually defined as in the next month.

13. D) Contact Marina to make sure she is not in crisis and is comfortable with her decision
This is a general question without information about what occurred in the last session and not much other context on what is going on with Marina. You needed to choose the best answer even without this information. This is the best answer of the options given. It is most respectful of Marina, her self-determination, and the therapeutic relationship. Although it is true that clients should make their own decisions about when to end therapy (C), clients frequently leave when they are in crisis and feeling hopeless; therefore, you have an ethical obligation to do what is in their best interests, which includes making sure there is not a crisis.

14. D) Bring the issue up directly with Jan
Jan's reasons for missing therapy could range from practical reasons, such as previous commitments, to therapeutically important reasons, such as resistance. Before deciding on the direction of therapy, a therapist would attempt to determine directly from Jan the reasons why she has missed therapy.

15. D) By the Brown family exhibiting their own ability to deal with stressors, develop their own solutions, and move toward goals without the therapist's input
SFT is aimed at bringing clients' "exceptions" into their awareness and helps them to repeat the successful things they do when the problem is not there or less severe. This focus on the client's own abilities and solutions helps the client move toward the preferred future they have identified. Asking the miracle question (B) will give the therapist an idea of what change will look like, but option D is a much more complete response. Families may have fewer problems, but the goal of SFT is to help the family handle problems more effectively, rather than the unrealistic goal of no longer having problems (C).

AUDIO PODCAST 14.1
Monitoring Progress and Outcomes
Eli A. Karam
https://bcove.video/3e0ubXD

REFERENCES

Duncan, B. L., & Reese, R. J. (2015). The Partners for Change Outcome Management System (PCOMS): Revisiting the client's frame of reference. *Psychotherapy*, *52*(4), 391–401. https://doi.org/10.1037/pst0000026

Hannan, C., Lambert, M. J., Harmon, C., Nielsen, S. L., Smart, D. W., Shimokawa, K., & Sutton, W. (2005). A lab test and algorithms for identifying clients at risk for treatment failure. *Journal of Clinical Psychology: In Session*, *61*, 155–163. https://doi.org/10.1002/jclp.20108

Lambert, M. J. (2015). Progress feedback and the OQ-system: The past and the future. *Psychotherapy*, *52*(4), 381. https://doi.org/10.1037/pst0000027

Miller, S. D., Duncan, B. L., Brown, J., Sorrell, R., & Chalk, M. B. (2006). Using formal client feedback to improve retention and outcome: Making ongoing, real-time assessment feasible. *Journal of Brief Therapy*, *5*, 5–22.

Miller, S. D., Duncan, B. L., Brown, J., Sparks, J., & Claud, D. (2003). The Outcome Rating Scale: A preliminary study of the reliability, validity, and feasibility of a brief visual analogue measure. *Journal of Brief Therapy*, *2*, 91–100

Norcross, J. (2010). The therapeutic relationship. In B. Duncan, S. Miller, B. Wampold, & M. Hubble (Eds.), *The heart and soul of change: Delivering what works* (2nd ed.). American Psychological Association.

Pinsof, W. M., Zinbarg, R. E., Lebow, J. L., Knobloch-Fedders, L., Durbin, E., Chambers, A., Latta, T., Karam, E., Goldsmith, J., & Friedman, G. (2009). Laying the foundation for progress research in family, couple, and individual therapy: The development and psychometric features of the initial systemic therapy inventory of change. *Psychotherapy Research*, *19*(2), 143–156. https://doi.org/10.1080/10503300802669973

Shimokawa, K., Lambert, M. J., & Smart, D. W. (2010). Enhancing treatment outcome of patients at risk of treatment failure: Meta-analytic and mega-analytic review of a psychotherapy quality assurance system. *Journal of Consulting and Clinical Psychology*, *78*, 298–311. 10.1037/a0019247

Sparks, J. (2015). The Norway couple project: Lessons learned. *Journal of Marital and Family Therapy*, *41*(4), 481–494. https://doi.org/10.1111/jmft.12099

PART V

Managing Crisis Situations in Marriage and Family Therapy (Domain 5)

15

Common Marriage and Family Therapy Crisis Situations and Appropriate Therapist Responses

LEARNING OBJECTIVES

After reading this chapter, you should be able to:

1. Distinguish between crisis intervention and traditional therapy
2. Describe the types, phases, and balancing factors of a mental health crisis
3. Recognize signs, symptoms, and contributing factors of a mental health crisis
4. Identify ethical and legal concerns related to the care of clients experiencing a mental health crisis or emergency

RELEVANT EXAM DOMAINS

- *Domain 5 Managing Crisis Situations*
  Includes tasks related to assessing and managing emergency situations, and intervening when clinically indicated and/or legally mandated.

INTRODUCTION

A crisis situation is, by definition, both a short-term and overwhelming event. As a result, crisis situations require assessment and treatment methods that differ in a number of ways from methods used in traditional therapy. For example, crisis interventions are ordinarily characterized by a "here-and-now" orientation, a time-limited course of intervention (typically one to six sessions), a view of the client's behavior as an understandable reaction to stress, and the assumption that an active directive role is needed by therapists and others trained in crisis intervention methods. Included in this chapter are an overview of crisis intervention, a brief review of legal and ethical issues relevant to crisis situations, and a discussion of specific crisis situations (i.e., situations involving suicidal clients, dangerous clients, clients who have been the victims of abuse).

TYPES OF CRISES

Crisis intervention provides opportunities for clients to learn new coping skills while identifying, mobilizing, and enhancing those they already possess. The following are characteristics of crisis events:

- The event precipitating the crisis is perceived as threatening.
- There is an apparent inability to modify or reduce the impact of stressful events.
- There is increased fear, tension, and/or confusion.
- There is a high level of subjective discomfort.
- A state of disequilibrium is followed by rapid transition to an active state of crisis.

Crises can be categorized as maturational, situational, or adventitious. Individuals may simultaneously experience more than one type in a given situation.

MATURATIONAL CRISES

Maturational or developmental crises may occur at any transitional period in the normal process of biopsychosocial growth and development. The periods of transition into successive stages of life require cognitive and behavioral changes, and a crisis can develop at any stage of transition when the person is unable to envision being in a new role, lacks adequate resources or communication skills, or others in the social system refuse to see the person in a different role. Examples of maturational crises include marriage, having a baby, retirement, or sending a child off to college. These are all normal life events, but they can cause stress (Kanel, 2019).

SITUATIONAL CRISES

Situational crises often revolve around grief and loss, usually the loss of an established support or role. They arise suddenly and unexpectedly from an external source and are events or circumstances that threaten the physical, social, and psychological integrity of individuals. These events may originate in the physical body as a result of disease or injury or in social or emotional situations (Kanel, 2019). Such events may include:

- Unexpected job loss
- Change in financial status
- Academic failure
- Divorce
- Mental illness
- Birth of a child with a disability
- Diagnosis of chronic or terminal illness
- Serious injury
- Death of a child
- Loss of a spouse

ADVENTITIOUS CRISES

Adventitious crises have been called *events of disaster* (Kanel, 2019). They are rare, unexpected happenings that are not part of everyday life and may result from:

- Natural disasters, such as floods, fires, and earthquakes
- Global pandemics, such as influenza and COVID-19
- National disasters, such as airplane crashes, riots, and wars
- Interpersonal disasters, such as assault and rape
- Acts of terrorism

A defining feature of a crisis is that it is time-limited and ordinarily lasts for no more than 6–8 weeks. However, without appropriate resolution, a crisis may produce lasting cognitive, affective, and behavioral problems.

CRISIS INTERVENTION GOALS

The goals of a crisis intervention depend on the nature of the crisis and the client's reaction to it but generally include the following:

1. Relieve the client's current symptoms.
2. Help the client identify and gain some understanding of the factors that led to the crisis state.
3. Restore the client to their precrisis level of functioning.
4. Help the client develop adaptive coping strategies that can be used in the current and future situations.
5. Help the client connect current stresses with earlier life experiences.

ROBERTS' SEVEN-STAGE MODEL OF CRISIS INTERVENTION (ROBERTS, 2000)

1. Plan and conduct a thorough biopsychosocial and crisis assessment. This also includes assessing suicidal and homicidal risk, need for medical attention, drug and alcohol use, and negative coping strategies. Assessing resilience and protective factors as well as family and other support networks is helpful.
2. Make contact and establish rapport. By conveying respect and acceptance, the responder develops a solid therapeutic relationship with the client. Displaying a nonjudgmental attitude and neutrality are important in crisis work.
3. Examine and define the dimensions of the problem or crisis. Identifying any issues and challenges the client may have faced, especially the precipitant to the crisis, provides valuable insight into the presenting problem.
4. Encourage an exploration of feelings and emotions. This can be achieved by actively listening to the client and responding with encouraging statements. Reflection and paraphrasing can also help this process.
5. Explore past positive coping strategies and alternatives. Viewing the individual as a resourceful and resilient person with an array of potential resources and alternatives can help this process. Crisis workers should be creative and flexible in resolving crisis situations.
6. Implement the action plan. At this stage, identify supportive individuals and contact referral sources. The client should be able to implement some coping strategies.
7. Establish a follow-up plan. It is important to follow up with clients after the initial intervention to determine the client's status and ensure that the crisis has been resolved.

CHILD ABUSE AND NEGLECT

RISK FACTORS

Research has revealed many risk factors or attributes associated with child maltreatment. These risk factors may potentially contribute to child abuse and neglect.

PARENT OR CAREGIVER RISK FACTORS

1. Individual characteristics: An individual's risk factors may include mental health issues, adverse response to stress, and trauma history.
2. Substance abuse: Studies have shown that between one third and two thirds of child maltreatment cases involve substance use to some degree.
3. Teen parents: Studies of physical abuse, in particular, tell us that higher rates of child abuse occur when parents are in their teenage years.
4. Additional factors contributing to the risk factors listed include lower socioeconomic status, lack of social support, and high stress levels.

CHILD RISK FACTORS

1. The child's age, health—physical, mental, and emotional—and social development may increase susceptibility to abuse and neglect. Given their size, early development status, and need for constant care, infants and young children are more vulnerable to certain types of maltreatment, including abusive head trauma and physical or medical neglect.
2. Childhood trauma
3. Child aggression, behavior problems, and attention deficits

PARENTING METHODS AND HOUSEHOLD RISK FACTORS

1. The attitudes of the parents, family structure, and approach to raising the child(ren) are all potential risks for abuse and neglect.
2. Domestic violence is a frequent contributor to child maltreatment. In 30%–60% of families in which spousal abuse in involved, mistreatment of the child also occurs.

COMMUNITY AND ENVIRONMENTAL RISK FACTORS

1. The child's neighborhood conditions, such as low socioeconomic status, presence of violence in the vicinity, and social attitudes, can place the child at greater risk for maltreatment.
2. Poverty can add to the probability of abuse and neglect. If this condition is added to other risk factors, including depression, substance abuse, and social isolation, the chances of maltreatment increase.

Child abuse is not limited to one race/ethnic group, gender or age group, or social or economic status. Additional risk factors include a history of abuse or neglect as a child, physical or mental illness, family crisis or stress, unemployment, family isolation, and inadequate parenting skills.

An abused child may exhibit signs of guilt, shame, or confusion. If the abuse involves a parent, relative, or family friend, it is likely the child will be afraid to tell anyone about the maltreatment and will develop a noticeable fear or discomfort when around parents, adult caregivers, or family friends. It is vital to be on the alert for such red flags.

INDICATORS OF CHILD MALTREATMENT

Indicators of physical abuse do not, in and of themselves, prove that a child has been abused. Keep in mind that injuries occur accidentally when children play. Physical abuse should be considered when the explanation does not fit the pattern or frequency of injury. When physical abuse has occurred, indicators can be behavioral as well as physical. Physical indicators of physical abuse include:

- Unexplained injuries
- Unbelievable or inconsistent explanations of injuries
- Multiple bruises in various stages of healing
- Bruises located on faces, ears, necks, buttocks, backs, chests, thighs, back of legs, and genitalia
- Bruises that resemble objects such as a hand, fist, belt buckle, or rope
- Injuries that are inconsistent with a child's age/developmental level
- Burns

Behavioral indicators of physical abuse include:

- Fear of going home
- Extreme apprehensiveness or vigilance
- Pronounced aggression or passivity
- Flinching easily or avoiding touch
- Abusive behavior or talk during play
- Unable to recall how injuries occurred
- Account of injuries is inconsistent with the nature of the injuries
- Fear of parent or caregiver

Physical indicators of sexual abuse or exploitation include:

- Seep disturbances
- Bedwetting
- Pain or irritation in genital/anal area
- Difficulty walking or sitting
- Difficultly urinating
- Pregnancy
- Positive testing for sexually transmitted disease or HIV
- Excessive or injurious masturbation

Behavioral indicators of sexual abuse or exploitation include:

- Sexual promiscuity
- Developmentally age-inappropriate sexual play and/or drawings
- Cruelty to others
- Anxiety
- Withdrawn aspect

Identifying serious physical neglect in children may seem more difficult than identifying other forms of abuse because neglect usually involves the absence of a certain behavior, rather than its presence. Physical indicators of serious physical neglect include:

- Lack of adequate medical and dental care
- Often hungry
- Lack of shelter
- Child's weight is significantly lower than what is normal for his/her age and gender
- Developmental delays
- Persistent (untreated) conditions (e.g., head lice, diaper rash)
- Exposure to hazards (e.g., illegal drugs, rodent/insect infestation, and mold)
- Clothing that is dirty, inappropriate for the weather, too small, or too large

Behavioral indicators of serious physical neglect include:

- Not registered in school
- Inadequate or inappropriate supervision
- Poor impulse control
- Frequently fatigued
- Parentified behaviors (when children are forced to take on the role and responsibilities of a parent)

ASSESSMENT

The primary goals of assessment are to find out whether child maltreatment has occurred and, if so, determine the type (physical abuse, sexual abuse, and neglect), frequency, and severity of the maltreatment and the current level of threat to the child's safety. Interview the child and parents/caregivers separately when feasible. The initial identification of child maltreatment often relies on the therapist's familiarity with its risk factors and indicators. Although some of these may be apparent through observation, others require the use of more formal methods of assessment such as structured interviews and psychological tests. During the assessment, it is important for a marriage and family therapist to maintain a neutral attitude and avoid the use of words, gestures, and facial expressions that convey disapproval or shock. Use open-ended exploratory questions to avoid misinterpretations or accusations.

The initial screening ordinarily begins with observation of the child and the child's parents/caregivers and asking general questions that, when appropriate, are followed by more specific questions. When speaking to parents, ask general questions about the child's safety at home and school and about any behavior changes and problems. Questions for children should be aimed at daily life at home, questionable injuries, and inappropriate touching. These questions are most useful when they are general, concrete, and nonleading, and provide opportunities for spontaneous disclosure.

Whenever a family therapist has reasonable suspicion that reportable child abuse has occurred, the therapist is mandated to make a report to the appropriate authorities. Although not required by law, telling the family that a report is being made is often therapeutically advisable unless the therapist believes it would put the child at a greater immediate risk.

INTERVENTION

Treatment for child maltreatment often involves a multidisciplinary approach that begins with crisis intervention and, once the initial crisis has stabilized, providing therapy and other services to the child, the child's parents/caregivers, and the entire family. The primary goals of crisis intervention are: (a) meeting reporting requirements, (b) obtaining medical treatment for the child, and (c) taking actions to reduce the threat of danger to the child (Barnett & Johnson, 2008).

Interventions for children include individual and group therapy. Individual therapy gives children the individual attention they often need so they can work through abuse issues. Play therapy is primarily beneficial for preschool and school-aged children who are unable to verbalize their feelings and have behavioral problems. Group therapy has been found to reduce feelings of isolation with sexually abused children. In addition to mobilizing support systems, therapists may teach parents appropriate use of time-outs and help the family develop other parenting techniques and coping strategies. Additional interventions will depend on the situation, including the type of maltreatment and the therapist's role within the multidisciplinary team of the child welfare system. Other interventions should be aimed at increasing self-esteem and impulse control, reducing depression and anxiety, and modifying parental behaviors and family interactions that underlie the maltreatment. Intervention with parents is most effective when supplemented with parent education programs, support groups, and other interventions and services.

ABUSE AND NEGLECT OF ELDER AND DEPENDENT CLIENTS

RISK FACTORS

Victims of elder or dependent adult abuse often do not report the abuse due to fear of retaliation or a desire to protect their caregiver. Risk factors for elder abuse include the following:

VICTIM RISK FACTORS

- Reduced functional capacity
- Poor health
- Cognitive impairment
- Physical disability
- Mental illness

PERPETRATOR RISK FACTORS

- Mental illness
- Substance abuse
- A history of violence
- Financial dependence on the victim
- Inability to cope with stress related to caregiving

ENVIRONMENTAL RISK FACTORS

- Shared living arrangements
- Social isolation

INDICATORS OF ELDER ABUSE

PHYSICAL ABUSE

- Appears to have physical injuries that have not been cared for properly, are in various stages of healing, and/or are incompatible with explanations given for them.
- Exhibits signs of physical restraint (e.g., rope burns on wrists or ankles).
- Evidence of inadequate or inappropriate medication has been found (e.g., oversedation).
- Displays fear, withdrawal, depression, confusion, agitation, and/or other behavioral signs.
- Reports being hit, slapped, kicked, or mistreated.

SEXUAL ABUSE

- Complains of abdominal pain, unexplained vaginal or anal pain or bleeding, or recurrent genital infections.
- Exhibits unexplained changes in behavior (e.g., aggression, withdrawal).
- Reports being sexually assaulted.

FINANCIAL ABUSE

- There is unusual activity in bank account.
- Will has been changed to benefit the caretaker.
- Has signed documents they cannot understand.
- Caregiver is overly concerned with the elder's money.
- Reports loss or theft of money, jewelry, and so on.

NEGLECT

- Displays signs of dehydration or malnutrition (e.g., sunken eyes, weight loss).
- Has untreated health problems.
- Wears inappropriate clothing.
- Exhibits poor personal hygiene.
- Lives in unsanitary or unsafe conditions.
- Reports being neglected or mistreated.

ASSESSMENT

The primary goals of assessment are to determine the type, frequency, and severity of the elder abuse and the current level of threat to the adult's safety. When conducting an assessment for elder/dependent adult abuse, it is important to describe the purpose of the assessment to the adult, normalize the process as much as possible, and provide information about limits on confidentiality, noting that family therapists are legally required to make a report to the appropriate authorities whenever they have reasonable suspicion that elder or dependent adult abuse has occurred. Given that elder/dependent adults may be hesitant to talk about their abuse, it is recommended that screening questions begin with general, less sensitive inquiries about the adult's life. These questions are then followed, as appropriate, with abuse-related questions.

INTERVENTION

The primary goals of crisis intervention with elder abuse are to (a) meet reporting requirements, (b) procure medical treatment for the abuse victim if needed, and (c) take actions to reduce the threat of danger to the victim. The treatment of victims of elder or dependent adult abuse involves a multidisciplinary approach that begins with crisis stabilization. Treatment typically includes a combination of therapy and supportive, rehabilitative, and preventive services for the elder/dependent adult and the caregiver system. Individual therapy for the elder/dependent adult focuses on providing psychoeducation about abuse and its prevention. Therapists help the client explore alternative living arrangements, collaborate on safety planning, and mobilize support systems (e.g., other family members, self-help groups, day care). In addition, family therapy may be useful for mediating conflicts and resolving family dynamics that contribute to the abuse.

INTIMATE PARTNER VIOLENCE

Intimate partner violence (IPV) is a well-recognized mental health issue that affects people from all ethnic and socioeconomic backgrounds. Although women are most often the target of domestic violence, men may also be victims. IPV occurs in both same-sex and heterosexual relationships. Under current law, therapists generally are not required to report IPV. It is assumed that clients would not be forthcoming about their abuse, either as victims or perpetrators, if they knew the situation would be reported. Therapists working with clients experiencing IPV need to make difficult decisions regarding how to intervene in such cases if reporting is not done. The therapist's goal is to protect victims from any further harm, including protecting any children the couple may have at home. In many states, therapists are required to report a situation of child abuse if children are known to have witnessed domestic violence because they may be psychologically damaged.

SITUATION VIOLENCE VS. INTIMATE TERRORISM

It is important to be able to distinguish between situational couple violence and intimate terrorism. Situational violence occurs when conflicts turn violent and physical force is used without a need to control. Both partners, men and women alike, can engage in this form of violence in response to situations that escalate as a result of rising tension or emotions. Their inability to communicate verbally or resolve conflict through nonviolent means can lead partners to be physically aggressive. The violence may be minor and occur as an isolated incident that never happens again, or it may be the way a couple gets used to dealing with conflict on an ongoing basis.

Although situational violence can potentially be as harmful and life-threatening as intimate terrorism, the latter accounts for most serious injury and death. The difference is not about the type of assault that may occur, but the absence of an overriding power and control dynamic. Motives in situational couple violence vary and might be associated with expressions of extreme anger and frustration or attempts to get one's partner to listen. Although control might be the motive in a particular situation, it typically does not involve the chronic pattern of coercive control that characterizes intimate terrorism.

RISK FACTORS

Risks for IPV are associated with several characteristics, many of which are exhibited by both survivors and perpetrators. For example, survivors and perpetrators often have low self-esteem, accept gender-role stereotypes, have severe reactions to stress, are socially isolated and emotionally dependent on their partner, and were physically and/or sexually abused in childhood or witnessed violence in their family of origin.

INDICATORS

The survivor may have symptoms of post-traumatic stress disorder (PTSD), chronic anxiety, and depression. The survivor may report suicidal ideation or have made previous attempts. In addition to obvious injuries at various stages of healing, a survivor will have a history of frequent emergency room visits for injuries with questionable explanations. If interviewed conjointly, the survivor may look to their partner before answering questions and exhibit anxiety or fear during the interview process. The male perpetrator may attempt to control the situation by speaking for his partner, being extremely overprotective and condescending during the interview.

ASSESSMENT

The goals of assessment are to determine whether IPV has occurred, the category of violence (situational or intimate terrorism), its frequency/severity, risk of future violence, and the client system's current safety needs. If there are children in the house, determine whether they are being abused or are at risk for abuse. The assessment of IPV involves considering risk factors and indicators; asking direct questions about abuse; and integrating information from a number of sources, including medical and legal records. Survivors of IPV are not likely to volunteer information about abuse but may acknowledge that it has occurred when asked about it. If a therapist suspects IPV, it is important to ask a woman questions in a private setting. Normalize screening questions by stating that it is your policy to ask questions about inappropriate interactions, and discuss how any sensitive information that the woman reveals will be handled. Direct questions about IPV include the following:

- *Have you been physically, emotionally, or sexually injured by your partner?*
- *Has your partner threatened to harm you or your children?*
- *Have you or your partner ever used physical force during an argument or conflict?*
- *Do you ever feel frightened by what your partner says or does?*

If the response to an initial question suggests that abuse has occurred, be sure to follow up with questions to clarify the frequency, severity, and other characteristics of the abuse.

Many violent relationships follow a common pattern or cycle. The entire cycle may happen in 1 day or it may take weeks or months to complete. It is different for every relationship and not all relationships follow the cycle. It is necessary to assess the cycle of violence (Walker, 2006).

PHASE 1: TENSION BUILDING

This phase may last for days to years and involves an escalation of tension with verbal abuse and minor physical abuse. During this phase, the woman attempts to placate her partner to avoid a serious incident of abuse.

PHASE 2: ACUTE BATTERING INCIDENT

An increasing escalation of tension leads to a severe violent incident that may last up to several hours. Women often seek help during or immediately after this phase.

PHASE 3: LOVING CONTRITION

This is a period of calm that follows the acute battering incident. During this phase, the man becomes apologetic and loving and promises to change.

INTERVENTION

The failure to recognize domestic violence can have disastrous consequences for both the family and the therapist. It may be unsafe to bring individuals together for family therapy or conjoint sessions in cases involving family violence or high conflict. The therapist is responsible for determining when there is a potential for physical or emotional danger. If the abuser has completed a course of treatment, there may be a possibility of doing therapy with the couple, depending on the assessment provided by the treatment facility. In situations involving domestic violence, there are both ethical and legal issues to consider. In cases in which there are conflicts between ethical and legal dimensions of practice, it is especially important for couple therapists to seek consultation.

The primary goals of crisis intervention for survivors of IPV are building safety and alleviating emotional and psychological symptoms that may interfere with treatment. Therapists help survivors achieve these goals by (Yassen & Harvey, 1998):

- Ensuring the woman receives a medical evaluation and treatment if necessary
- Developing a safety plan and providing information on local domestic violence shelters and crisis hotlines
- Educating about abuse myths, types of abuse, and the cycle of violence
- Providing information about legal alternatives

Group psychotherapy and support groups are useful for reducing feelings of isolation, normalizing the woman's experience, and providing opportunities for support and information sharing.

The use of conjoint therapy is controversial because it may increase the risk for violence, provide the perpetrator with opportunities to justify his behavior, and foster a sense of blame in the survivor. Consequently, it is considered acceptable only when certain conditions are met, for example, when there is a low to moderate level of aggression in the relationship and both partners acknowledge that violence is a problem, express a desire to work toward achieving a nonviolent relationship, and freely choose conjoint therapy. In contrast, conjoint therapy is contraindicated when risk factors for lethality are present. These factors include the following:

- The survivor fears being seriously injured by the perpetrator.
- The survivor and/or perpetrator have a history of uncontrolled continuous use of alcohol or other substance.
- The perpetrator is obsessed with his partner and has negative reactions to her autonomy.
- The perpetrator has a history of violence in current or past relationships that resulted in injury requiring medical attention, has used a weapon against his partner or threatened to kill his partner, has engaged in sadistic violence or other bizarre forms of violence, or has been convicted of a violent crime or violated a restraining order.

Stith, McCollum, and Rosen (2011) developed a treatment model, Domestic Violence Focused Couples Therapy. Concrete steps taken in the model include having the partners sign a no-violence contract and commit to a time-out plan for high-risk situations. They propose using solution-focused brief therapy to find solutions for couples if violence has occurred and now both have a desire to work on the relationship together. The underlying assumption is that individuals who take responsibility for the violence they have inflicted and realize that the violence is a choice, can end the pattern of violence. Sessions are structured very carefully due to the history of violence. The therapist teaches safety planning and mindfulness for self-soothing during argumentative periods.

SUICIDE AND SELF-HARM

RISK FACTORS

When assessing risk of suicide, consider the following risk factors:

- Gender (males are four times more likely to commit suicide than females)
- Race (Whites, Native Americans, and Alaska Natives have the highest suicide rates, whereas Hispanics, African Americans, Asians, and Pacific Islanders have the lowest rates)
- Older adults (White men over the age of 85 have the highest risk factor)
- History of mental illness
- Substance abuse
- Prior suicide attempt
- Family history of suicide
- Family violence, including physical or sexual abuse
- Firearms/lethal means available and easy to access
- Hopelessness
- Age (older people and adolescents are at greater risk)
- Depression (a history of a mood disorder (e.g., depression, bipolar disorder) increases suicide risk)
- Impulsivity (a history of impulsive or aggressive behavior heightens the probability of suicide)
- Helplessness (feeling that one is unable to change the current situation increases risk)
- Serious and recent losses
- Lack of social support

PROTECTIVE FACTORS

Protective factors associated with a decreased risk for suicide include (Greene et al., 2000):

- Good coping and problem-solving skills
- A sense of responsibility toward family, ability to garner social support
- Moral/religious values that discourage suicide, fear of suicide
- Motivation to seek help and access to mental health services
- A strong therapeutic alliance

INDICATORS

In addition to these general risk factors, there are several warning signs of suicide that may manifest in a client's behavior prior to a suicide attempt:

- Talking about suicide
- Writing about suicide
- Neglecting self; decreased focus on hygiene and appearance
- Worsening mood; becoming more depressed and hopeless
- Sudden loss; sudden personal crisis or relational loss
- Sudden change in mood; dramatic elevation in mood
- Suicide planning; formulating a plan for suicide
- Becoming distant and withdrawn from relationships
- Preparing by giving away belongings, buying a weapon, saving pills
- Offering vague thanks or good-byes to friends, family members, or counselor

ASSESSMENT

The primary goal of assessment is to estimate client's immediate and future risk for suicide. Assessment for suicide risk involves considering risk and protective factors and integrating information obtained from a variety of sources, including a clinical interview, a mental status exam, the client's family members, the client's physician, and other healthcare providers. There are no formulas for combining risk and protective factors to accurately predict the probability that a particular person will attempt or commit suicide; but, in general, the greater the number of risk factors and fewer the number of protective factors, the higher the level of risk. Also, certain risk factors carry more weight than others: For example, the presence of a concrete, detailed, and lethal suicide plan and the means to carry out that plan suggest a high risk even when no other risk factors are present (Capuzzi, 2004).

Carefully assess a suicidal client's specific ideations related to suicide, any plans, level of intent to carry out the plan, and access to various means for self-harm. Do not forget to inquire about recent losses, previous suicide attempts, and significant models for suicide (e.g., family members, friends, admired celebrities). Provide clients with a clear picture of the limits to confidentiality during the informed-consent process (Granello, 2010).

INTERVENTION

The primary goals in working with suicidal clients are to ensure the client's safety by eliminating or reducing access to common methods of suicide and to establish a strong therapeutic alliance by developing trust and rapport. The secondary goal is to reduce future suicide risk by addressing mania, depression, and other conditions and risk factors (Granello & Granello, 2007).

Safety planning, paramount to working with this population, can mean a variety of different concepts and interventions depending on the clinical setting. Fundamentally, safety planning is the process of creating a set of strategies designed to use the support and protective factors in a client's life. Specifically, safety plans are best designed to provide options and actions steps for care before a client becomes acutely suicidal.

Interventions for clients at risk for suicide can be categorized in terms of three types: hospitalization, outpatient crisis intervention, and outpatient psychotherapy. The choice of an intervention depends on the client's level of risk, the client's preferences, and the potential benefits of each approach.

HOSPITALIZATION

Hospitalization is appropriate for a client who has just attempted suicide or is at imminent risk for suicide as indicated by the presence of a specific suicide plan with access to lethal means in conjunction with other risk factors mentioned previously. The initial step should be to encourage voluntary hospitalization, but an involuntary hold should be initiated if the client refuses to enter a treatment facility voluntarily.

OUTPATIENT CRISIS INTERVENTION

Outpatient crisis intervention is appropriate when the client is at moderate risk for suicide as evidenced by suicidal intent with a lack of access to lethal means, fair or good judgment and problem-solving skills, the presence of adequate social support, and a willingness to comply with treatment recommendations. It includes making appropriate referrals (e.g., to a support group or a psychiatrist for a medication evaluation) and addresses the following issues: reducing social isolation (e.g., by having a client who lives alone move in temporarily with a friend or relative), removing lethal means of suicide, encouraging the client to express anger in alternative ways, relieving anxiety and sleep problems (e.g., by referring to a physician for medication or providing relaxation training), and focusing on the client's ambivalence about suicide and persuading the client to postpone a decision about suicide until after the crisis has ended.

OUTPATIENT PSYCHOTHERAPY

Outpatient psychotherapy is an appropriate follow-up to hospitalization and crisis intervention or as the intervention for clients who are at low risk for suicide as evidenced by suicidal ideation with an absence of a specific suicide plan, generally good judgment and problem-solving skills, the presence of adequate social support, and willingness to talk about problems and comply with treatment. Several therapies have been identified as beneficial for suicidal clients, including cognitive behavioral therapy (CBT) and dialectical behavior therapy (DBT).

When working with high-risk clients, seriously consider consultation with colleagues with demonstrated expertise in this area. When you identify a client as at risk for suicide, be sure to tailor the treatment plan to the client's level of risk. Consider more frequent appointments or inpatient admission when this is appropriate. When obtaining a safety plan from suicidal clients where they guarantee not to harm themselves before seeking help from you or another provider, recognize that these plans may not prevent a suicide or protect you from legal repercussions. Be familiar with policies and practices related to both voluntary and involuntary psychiatric admission in your area. Make sure suicidal clients know exactly how to contact you or an appropriate colleague, answering service, or emergency room. Clearly document in the client's record the client's mental status, your ongoing risk assessments, and a rationale for diagnostic and treatment plan decisions. Be particularly cautious about referring, transferring, or terminating therapy with a client who has been or is currently suicidal. Take extra care to ensure that this transition goes smoothly, and that the client does not feel abandoned in the process.

HARM TO OTHERS

Legal and ethical issues that may be of concern when working with a client who poses a danger to others include the need to maintain the client's confidentiality versus the duty to warn/ protect the client's intended victim(s), to contact the police, and the need to involuntarily hospitalize the client. Information about these issues is provided in Chapter 16 Ethical and Legal Principles.

RISK FACTORS

- The single-best predictor of future violence is a past history of violence, with commitment of a serious violent act at an early age and/or commitment of multiple violent acts being associated with the greatest risk
- Lower socioeconomic status
- Low intelligence
- History of being abused as a child or witnessing domestic violence
- Father with a criminal arrest history
- Psychiatric diagnosis: substance use disorder, antisocial personality disorder, borderline personality disorder, schizophrenia, manic phase of bipolar disorder
- Lack of social support
- High level of stress
- Access to weapons
- Victim specificity and availability
- Noncompliance with treatment

Low risk is suggested when the client has few risk factors, does not have a history of impulsive behaviors, and does not have a specific plan or means to carry out a plan. Moderate risk is suggested when the client has multiple risk factors, expresses low to moderate intent to carry out a plan or does not have the means to carry out a plan, exhibits only minimal cognitive or emotional impairment, and has some protective factors (e.g., adequate social support, willingness to develop a safety plan). High risk is suggested when the client has a concrete plan and access to lethal means to carry out that plan, has multiple risk factors (e.g., impulsivity, significant mental health problems, limited social support), and is unwilling or unable to form a therapeutic alliance.

ASSESSMENT

The primary assessment goals are to determine the likelihood that the client will commit a violent act in the near future and identify the factors that are contributing to the client's dangerous behaviors and intent. The assessment of a client who may be a danger to others requires a comprehensive approach that involves obtaining information on multiple factors from multiple sources. Factors that should be addressed in the assessment include the client's history of violent behavior, access to weapons and potential victims, and other risk factors. Sources of information include the client, family members, medical and mental health records, and police and court documents. Note that any threat of harm against others should always be taken seriously.

Initial screening questions should be general and less sensitive in nature. For example:

- *What types of things make you mad?*
- *What do you do when you get mad?*

- *What is the closest you've come to being violent?*
- *Do you own any firearms or weapons?*

If an elevated risk for violence is suggested by the client's answers to the initial questions, a history of violent behavior, or a stated intent to harm someone, then more detailed questions are asked to obtain information about past incidents of violence and current intent.

INTERVENTION

The initial intervention goals are to build rapport with the client and reduce the client's risk for future violence by bringing violent, aggressive behavior under control. The nature of additional goals depends on several factors, including the setting (inpatient or outpatient), the client's characteristics, and the underlying causes of the client's behavior. The appropriate intervention for a dangerous client is determined by the level of risk and the causes of the dangerous behavior.

HOSPITALIZATION

Voluntary hospitalization of a client who is a danger to others is usually an option before initiating an involuntary hold. However, involuntary hospitalization must be considered when the danger the client poses is imminent and is caused by a mental disorder or chronic alcoholism and the client has refused or is unable to comply with the recommendation to enter a psychiatric hospital voluntarily. In certain circumstances, if an individual is putting themselves or others in danger due to their mental health or substance use symptoms, friends, family, and professionals may be able to initiate a process of having the individual evaluated and/or placed in treatment against their will. This extreme measure, which involves temporarily taking away a person's freedom, is known as a *72-hour mental health evaluat*ion (aka *mental health hold, M1 hold*, or *72-hour hold*). A law enforcement officer or mental health professional can hold a person for evaluation and treatment if the person appears, in the moment, to be an imminent danger to themselves or others. Evaluation and treatment are done in a hospital or mental health facility. The hold is designed to allow this person to be evaluated for mental health needs, which could include voluntary treatment or further involuntary treatment. The law requires that the patient is cared for in the least restrictive environment and encourages voluntary treatment. The individual must be released within 72 hours unless: a mental health professional recommends they need further treatment, the court orders ongoing involuntary treatment, or the person volunteers to go into treatment. When the criteria for hospitalization are not met, it may be necessary to consider alternatives such as referral to a substance abuse treatment program or involvement of the criminal justice system.

OUTPATIENT MANAGEMENT

Outpatient management is indicated when the client is sincere in the desire to change and the risk for violence is low. Intervention strategies may include teaching communication, problem-solving, stress management, and anger management skills. Treatment attempts to foster the development of empathy for potential victims in the client and increase the client's understanding of the consequences of violence. In addition to developing a safety plan that includes reducing environmental triggers and eliminating access to firearms, the client agrees to a no-violence contract. Therapy approaches that have been found to be effective include the following:

- CBT for violent and aggressive behaviors posits that these behaviors are embedded in thought patterns that can be controlled and replaced with prosocial thinking. Strategies include training in cognitive self-control, anger management, social perspective-taking, social problem-solving, and relapse prevention.

- Couple and family therapies are often useful because most violence occurs within families. These interventions include educating family members about the early warning signs of violent behavior and the family dynamics that contribute to violence, training in interventions for high-risk situations (e.g., using time-outs and impulse-delay tactics), and training in communication and problem-solving skills.
- Group therapy is often less threatening to clients than individual therapy and provides group members with opportunities to see that others also struggle with violence and aggression, see how others have successfully dealt with situations that normally trigger violence, and learn to resolve conflicts with other group members in a supportive environment.

PROTECTION FROM VIOLENT CLIENTS

When faced with a potentially violent client, it is important to remain calm, encourage communication by asking open-ended questions, and attempt to determine the intensity of the client's feelings and lethality of their intent (Sue & Sue, 2008). Methods of safeguarding oneself from violent clients range from the less to the more intrusive. Less intrusive methods for reducing a client's agitation and aggression include speaking softly and moving slowly, maintaining adequate physical distance from the client, sitting near the door and leaving the door open, expressing sympathetic concern for the client's well-being, setting limits on behavior, and suggesting alternatives to violence. More intrusive actions may be necessary when these methods fail and include leaving the room and calling for help. Note that calling the police for help is acceptable only when the client's condition permits a violation of confidentiality or the client gives permission for doing so.

CONCLUSION

Crisis intervention is a short-term, acute intervention designed to mitigate the stress reactions associated with a specific incident. The goals of crisis intervention are to stabilize, reduce symptoms, and return to adaptive functioning. Crisis intervention is not a replacement for therapy. Like psychotherapy, crisis intervention involves assessment, planning, and treatment, but the scope is generally much more specific. Although psychotherapy focuses on a broad range of information and client history, crisis assessment and treatment focus on the client's immediate situation, including factors such as safety and immediate needs.

KEY TERMS

ABC-X family crisis model: Reuben Hill's model used to explain whether or not a stressful event would result in a crisis in some families but not in others. It includes the stressor (A), the family's crisis-meeting resources (B), the family's definition of the stressor (C), and the crisis (X).

Abuse: To insult, hurt, injure, rape and/or molest another person. Such behaviors may include, but are not limited to physical abuse, emotional abuse, financial abuse, spiritual abuse, and/or verbal abuse.

Abuser/abusive partner/batterer: Refers to a person who engages in a pattern of coercive, exploitative, and violent tactics against an intimate partner in order to establish and maintain power, control, and dominance over the partner.

Advocacy: Refers to support that domestic violence programs offer to individual survivors. The support can include a 24-hour crisis hotline, crisis intervention, shelter, food, clothing, transportation, legal and medical assistance, accompaniment to court and other services, information and referrals, assistance with rent and utilities, support groups, therapy groups for abusers, and childcare and other programs for children.

Anger management class: An older term used to refer to what are now called *batterer's intervention programs*; the name has been changed to reflect current understanding that abuse is not only about anger, but about control issues with many different causes.

Battering: Refers to all behaviors that harm, gain, or maintain power and control over another person. These behaviors include physical, emotional, psychological, and sexual abuse, as well as sexual exploitation and threats, or any other act that curtails an individual's personal power and/or creates an atmosphere of fear and intimidation.

Best practices: Activities or programs that are in keeping with the best available evidence regarding what is effective.

Child abuse: Maltreatment or neglect of a child, including nonaccidental physical injuries, sexual abuse/exploitation, severe or general neglect, unjustifiable mental suffering/emotional abuse, and willful cruelty or unjustifiable punishment of a child.

Coercion: Occurs when one person forces or attempts to force another to think or act in a different way. Examples include, but are not limited to threatening to report the victim to Child and Family Services or the police, forcing a victim to drop charges against the batterer, and/or forcing a victim to participate in or commit illegal activities.

Contagion: A phenomenon whereby susceptible persons are influenced toward suicidal behavior through knowledge of another person's suicidal acts.

Crisis: A situation or circumstance, usually of recent origin, that breaks down the individual's or the family's usual pattern of functioning and cannot be resolved with usual coping behaviors.

Crisis counseling: Brief counseling focused on minimizing stress, providing emotional support, and improving immediate coping strategies. Like psychotherapy, crisis counseling involves assessment, planning, and treatment, but the scope of service is much more specific.

Crisis hotline: A phone number people can call to get immediate emergency crisis counseling.

Crisis intervention: Refers to immediate, short-term treatment for a person in crisis or extreme distress.

Domestic violence: Physical, emotional, or sexual abuse of persons in a domestic relationship, including partners, children, and older persons. Domestic violence that occurs between two people in a close relationship is known as *intimate partner violence*.

Domestic violence shelter: Refers to a secure facility that provides safety and protection from abuse, advocacy services, and resources to create a nonviolent life.

Double ABC-X family crisis model: This model explores the full effect of stress on families rather than just focusing on a single stressor.

Economic/financial abuse: Occurs when a batterer uses finances to establish and maintain power and control over a victim. Examples include but are not limited to controlling a partner's finances, taking the victim's money without permission, giving the victim an allowance, prohibiting/limiting a victim's access to bank accounts or credit card, denying the victim the right to work, and/or sabotaging a victim's credit.

Elder abuse: Physical abuse (including sexual), financial abuse, neglect, abandonment, isolation, abduction, and/or treatment that causes physical harm or pain or mental suffering, and the withholding of things or services by a care custodian of an older person.

Emotional/psychological abuse: Refers to a batterer's use of emotions, self-esteem, and/or a person's mental state to establish and maintain power and control over a victim. Examples include but are not limited to putting the victim down or making the victim feel bad about themselves, calling the victim names, playing mind games, making the victim think they are crazy, making the victim feel guilty and/or humiliating the victim.

Family preservation services: Coordinated and time-limited crisis intervention services aimed at preventing removal of a child to out-of-home care, while also ensuring the child's and family's safety.

Flashback: Refers to the vivid reoccurrence of a traumatic event in the mind.

Guardian ad litem: Refers to a person appointed by the court to represent the best interests of a child in legal proceedings.

Imminent risk: A situation in which a person's current risk status is believed to indicate actions that could lead to harm of self or someone else.

Intimate partner: Refers to current or former spouses (husband/wife/domestic partner), boyfriends, and girlfriends of any sexual orientation.

Intimate partner violence: A form of domestic violence that occurs between two people in a close relationship.

Means: The instrument or object whereby a self-destructive act is carried out (i.e., firearm, poison, medication).

Means restriction: Techniques, policies, and procedures designed to reduce access or availability to means and methods of deliberate self-harm.

Multidisciplinary team: A group established among agencies and professionals within the child protection system to discuss cases of child abuse and neglect and make decisions during various stages of the case.

Physical abuse: When an abuser uses their body or other objects to cause harm or injury to establish and maintain power and control over a victim. Examples include, but are not limited to hitting, kicking, biting, pushing, scratching, slapping, strangling, beating, using a weapon against another person, punching, throwing, burning, poisoning, stabbing, and shooting.

Postvention: A strategy or approach that is implemented after a crisis or traumatic event has occurred.

Prevention: A strategy or approach that reduces the likelihood of risk of onset or delays the onset of adverse health problems or reduces the harm resulting from conditions or behaviors.

Protection order: Common term used to refer to the existence of an emergency, criminal protective order, and/or civil/family law restraining order. Depending on the legal process, these orders can be temporary or permanent. This order can mandate the abuser not contact, harass, or come within a certain distance of the petitioner and/or other persons named in the order.

Protective factors: Factors that make it less likely that individuals will develop a disorder; may encompass biological, psychological, or social factors in the individual, family, and environment.

Restrained party/person: In a protection order, this refers to the person who is ordered not to have contact or harass the protected party.

Risk assessment: Refers to the process of quantifying the probability of an individual harming self or others.

Risk factors: Those factors that make it more likely that individuals will develop a disorder; these may encompass biological, psychological, or social factors in the individual, family, and environment.

Safe housing: Emergency, transitional or permanent shelter/housing that is confidentially located.

Safety plan: A written list of healthy coping responses, developed in collaboration with a client, for the client to engage in when noticing the early signs of suicidal ideation. With this list, a client can learn to respond to stressors in new ways that reduce the risk of suicide; for example, calling friends, listening to music, exercising, or calling a crisis support line.

Screening: Administration of an assessment tool to identify persons in need of more in-depth evaluation or treatment.

Screening tools: Instruments and techniques (questionnaires, check lists, self-assessment forms) used to evaluate individuals for increased risk of certain health problems.

Secondary trauma/vicarious trauma*:* This refers to negative impact on individuals who provide crisis and/or ongoing support to victims of trauma and/or stark misfortune.

Self-harm: Refers to the various methods by which individuals injure themselves, such as self-cutting, self-battering, taking overdoses, or exhibiting deliberate recklessness.

Sexual abuse: Any nonconsenting or sexually exploitative behavior (verbal or physical) committed without consent may constitute sexual abuse; previous consent does not imply current consent.

Sexual assault: Refers to any unwanted sexual contact or activity forced on one person by another.

Sexual exploitation: A sexual act, interaction, or relationship that occurs when one individual is in the care or under the authority of another. Sexual exploitation involves the abuse of trust and/or power in a relationship in order to engage in a sexual interaction or relationship. Positions of authority, care, or guardianship include but are not limited to parents, teachers, therapists, attorneys, mentors, counselors, and advocates.

Social support: Assistance that may include companionship, emotional backing, cognitive guidance, material aid. and special services.

SOAP notes: A four-section progress or psychotherapy note in which each letter of the acronym represents a section of the note: *S* (subjective) contains the information given to the practitioner by the client during the session, *O* (objective) contains the factual information observed directly by the practitioner, *A* (assessment) contains the practitioner's impression of the client, and *P* (plan) contains the plan for treatment and the practitioner's prognosis for the client.

Stalking: Occurs when one person pursues, follows, or harasses another person against their wishes. Examples include, but are not limited to repeated, unwanted phone calls, following a victim, sending unwanted gifts, destroying or vandalizing a victim's property, repeated threats and/or tracking a victim's online activity. This can include cyberstalking (via computers and the Global Positioning System).

Suicide: Death from injury, poisoning, or suffocation for which there is evidence that a self-inflicted act led to the person's death.

Suicide attempt: A potentially self-injurious behavior with a nonfatal outcome, for which there is evidence that the person intended to kill themselves. A suicide attempt may or may not result in injuries.

Suicidal behavior: A spectrum of activities related to thoughts and behaviors that include suicidal thinking, suicide attempts, and completed suicide.

Suicide survivors: Family members, significant others, or acquaintances who have experienced the loss of a loved one due to suicide; sometimes this term is also used to mean survivors of suicide attempts.

Suicidal ideation: Refers to thoughts associated with killing oneself.

Suicide warning signs: These are indications that an individual is at risk for suicide.

Wrap-around services: Family preservation services geared to meet the total needs of the family through the use of community resources, concrete services, and therapy.

KNOWLEDGE CHECK: CHAPTER 15

1. Components of a ________ include having a specific plan about who to call and what to do if a crisis begins to arise, as well as calming strategies such as journaling and exercising.
   - A. Suicide plan
   - B. Assessment plan
   - C. Safety plan
   - D. Treatment plan

2. When assessing certain risk factors, therapists should be aware of all of the following reportable types of child abuse *except*:
   - A. Sexual abuse
   - B. Physical abuse
   - C. Chronic conflict
   - D. Neglect

3. The therapist should ________ if any crisis issues were identified during the initial assessment.
   - A. Report them to the insurance agency
   - B. Discontinue therapy immediately
   - C. Address the crisis issues in the initial client goals
   - D. Make an appropriate referral

4. Therapists working with potentially dangerous clients are recommended to do all the following *except*:
   - A. Inform client of confidentiality limits
   - B. Record steps taken to protect client and others, if necessary
   - C. Seek consultation
   - D. Make a referral

5. Using minimal client information in progress notes is *not* recommended when ________.
   - A. Interviewing a child
   - B. Documenting a crisis situation
   - C. Meeting with a court ordered client system
   - D. A client has an affair

(*See answers next page.*)

1. C) Safety plan
A suicide safety plan is a written set of instructions created as a contingency plan should a client begin to experience thoughts of self-harm. It provides clients with a specific and prioritized set of coping strategies that can be used in the event of a suicidal crisis, or should suicidal thoughts emerge. Clinicians unfamiliar with safety planning should note that it differs from a no-suicide contract. Empirical evidence that no-suicide contracts prevent suicidal behavior is poor, whereas emerging evidence indicates that developing a safety plan is an evidence-based intervention for reducing suicide risk.

2. C) Chronic conflict
At the federal level, the Child Abuse Prevention and Treatment Act (CAPTA) has defined child abuse and neglect as "any recent act or failure to act on the part of a parent or caregiver that results in death, serious physical or emotional harm, sexual abuse, or exploitation, or an act or failure to act that presents an imminent risk of serious harm" (Clay et al., 2019, p. 3).

3. C) Address the crisis issues in the initial client goals
If a therapist discovers a crisis situation in an opening assessment, they must build it into the goals of treatment with the client. Depending on the nature of crisis and client's reaction, goals include (a) relieve current symptoms, (b) help identify and gain understanding of factors that led to the crisis, (c) use remedial measures/resources to restore precrisis level of functioning, and (d) help develop adaptive coping strategies for current and future situations.

4. D) Make a referral
Responses to threatening or potentially dangerous situations vary but should include careful consideration of clinical factors and options A, B, and C. Therapists must always put the needs of their clients first. Even though a referral may be in order eventually if the therapist cannot stabilize the dangerous situation, this would not be considered among the first recommendations.

5. B) Documenting a crisis situation
Any time a crisis occurs, it must be documented completely in the client's record. The documentation should include the type of crisis intervention that was used, how long the intervention took to implement from beginning to end, and the "reasons" why the intervention was used. Also, clearly identify with the client and outline in the notes what the plan is for follow up. In addition, the therapist should be clear about who the client should contact (and how) should the client feel the need outside of the session.

6. Devonte, a 15-year-old with a history of defiant behavior, has been referred to you for individual therapy by a juvenile detention facility. Although you view Devonte as a sensitive kid without the right parental guidance, he also has a history of alcohol use, school truancy, and is working below grade level. During the previous session, Devonte says, "I hate this kid, Lex. He's a made fun of me because I don't have a dad, and I'm going mess him up the next time I see him after school." What should you do?

   A. Remind Devonte of the legal limits of confidentiality and of your legal obligations
   B. Immediately contact the police and try to locate Lex
   C. Send Devonte back to the detention facility
   D. Warn Lex of the danger he is in and inform law enforcement officials

7. In your eighth session with Doug, he informs you that his house in now in foreclosure after being out of work for the past year. His ex-wife has given up on him, and he reports that his three teenage daughters no longer want to spend time with him. He can longer make payments for sessions. He feels ashamed of himself and tells you that you should not waste any more time on him. He thanks you for all your help and says that he does not plan to return for any more sessions. In this case, how would you *best* proceed?

   A. Consider the client's suicidality when choosing your next intervention
   B. Refer him to a psychiatrist to evaluate and monitor his depression
   C. Reduce your fee and persuade the client to come back for another session
   D. Link him to financial assistance to alleviate the immediate crisis

8. Which of the following interventions is considered *least* appropriate for treating violent clients?

   A. Reviewing the client's history
   B. Examining cognitive distortions
   C. Teaching anger management skills
   D. Encouraging the client to vent feelings

9. A clinically depressed female client comes to a session expressing suicidal ideation. The therapist conducts a thorough suicide assessment and collaborates with the client on a safety plan. As part of the plan, the client agrees that she will stay at a friend's house for the moment. That night, the client commits suicide while at the friend's house. The therapist ________________.

   A. Acted illegally and unethically by not calling the police or an emergency team
   B. Acted unethically only
   C. Acted illegally only
   D. Acted neither illegally nor unethically

10. All of the following indicate a high risk for suicide *except*:

   A. Expressed plan
   B. Depression
   C. Recent loss
   D. Previous attempt

(*See answers next page.*)

6. A) Remind Devonte of the legal limits of confidentiality and of your legal obligations

This question is difficult because it lacks the information needed to fully understand the situation and level of danger. For instance, what does Devonte mean by the words "mess him up?" Having this information would help you determine whether the other boy is in serious danger of being harmed by your client. Whether or not this situation invokes your duty to protect, however, it would be appropriate for you to inform (or remind) Devonte about the legal limits to confidentiality and your related obligations. In addition, you should attempt to clarify what the client means by the words "mess him up."

7. A) Consider the client's suicidality when choosing your next intervention

There are several red flags that indicate possible suicidality in this case (multiple losses, feeling ashamed and worthless, sudden withdrawal from therapy, poor support system, etc.). Thus, it is most important to take into consideration Doug's possible suicide risk as you decide the next steps of intervention. Although options B, C, and D are all valid, the client's possible suicide risk is the immediate concern here.

8. D) Encouraging the client to vent feelings

Even though venting allows for catharsis, a violent individual may not be able to regulate their emotions, resulting in further escalation of feelings, rather than de-escalation. A violent client may also believe that the therapist agrees with their violent actions by allowing the venting.

9. D) Acted neither illegally nor unethically

A therapist is not mandated to call a psychiatric emergency team or the police, but a therapist should do whatever is necessary to prevent the threatened danger, including breaking the client's confidence if that seems necessary to protect the client. The therapist in this scenario, by completing an assessment and safety plan, exercised good judgment and operated both ethically and legally.

10. B) Depression

The question asked to choose the answer that is *not* associated with a high risk for suicide. Options A, B, and D are all associated with a high risk for suicide.

11. Seven-year-old Reina is brought to therapy by her mother, Stephanie. Stephanie reports that her daughter's behavior has recently changed both at home and at school. During the initial interview, the therapist learns that Reina has been sexually abused at her babysitter's house. What is the most appropriate course of action in this situation?

    A. Obtain the mother's consent to make a report, make a report to the authorities, and refer the girl for a medical evaluation
    B. Inform the mother of your duty to report, make a report to the authorities, and refer the girl for a medical evaluation
    C. Inform the mother of your duty to report the abuse, make a report to the authorities, and contact the babysitter
    D. Urge the mother to file a report, make a report to the authorities if she is unwilling to do so, and notify the babysitter

12. Malena, a 29-year-old woman with a history of violence in her marriage, comes into session heavily bruised around the facial area. It is generally accepted that the *first* intervention in this situation should be which of the following?

    A. Provide referrals for a safe environment
    B. Contact an adult protective agency
    C. Help her develop a safety plan
    D. Educate Malena about the battering cycle of violence

13. At an initial family therapy session, the father in the family system clearly arrives intoxicated. How should you best handle this situation?

    A. Take a family history, including alcohol use in the families of origin
    B. Have the father sit in the waiting room and see the rest of the family
    C. Call and report child abuse
    D. Tell the father that you will not work with him while he is under the influence of alcohol and end the session

14. A 21-year-old client has been arrested multiple times for assault and other violent behaviors. He is entering therapy now hoping to avoid a longer jail sentence after his latest transgression. He is at highest risk for future violence against others if he ________________.

    A. Has average intelligence, a history of deliberate self-harm, and depressive illness
    B. Has low intelligence, flat affect, and a history of depressive illness
    C. Has average intelligence, a history of alcohol use, and is socially isolated
    D. Has low intelligence, a history of alcohol use, and exhibits poor impulse control

15. Based on your knowledge of suicide assessment, you would predict that a client would be at the highest risk for suicide if ________________.

    A. He is between the ages of 17 and 27
    B. He has expressed a desire to kill himself
    C. He has a personality disorder
    D. His depressive symptoms have recently worsened

(*See answers next page.*)

11. B) Inform the mother of your duty to report, make a report to the authorities, and refer the girl for a medical evaluation

In this situation, the therapist is legally required to make a child abuse report to the authorities. Informing the mother of your legal duty to do so and referring the girl for a medical evaluation would also be appropriate actions. You do not need the mother's consent to file a report and contacting the babysitter would not be appropriate.

12. C) Help her develop a safety plan

Developing a safety plan is a concrete way of helping the client protect herself. Option A is included in safety planning and option D is something a therapist would do to help someone like Malena; however, it would not be the first intervention because it does not provide her with a means of protecting herself.

13. D) Tell the father that you will not work with him while he is under the influence of alcohol and end the session

A session with an intoxicated client will be unproductive and a session excluding him could be detrimental to the family and the clinical process. Not proceeding with the day's session is the best course of action. Taking a family history and proceeding with therapy is not recommended while a client is intoxicated (A). Having the father sit in the waiting room while the rest of the family has a session risks alienating the substance abuser because he might feel shamed or excluded from the therapeutic process (B). There is no mandated reporting required in this situation and there is no reasonable suspicion of further abuse on the information presented (C).

14. D) Has low intelligence, a history of alcohol use, and exhibits poor impulse control

The best predictor of future violent behavior is previous violence against persons or property. Other predictors include male gender, drug or alcohol use, low intelligence, specific threats, having a weapon available, poor impulse control, extreme or labile affect, anger and irritability, and an absence of depressive illness.

15. B) He has expressed a desire to kill himself

This question makes the responder generalize, but one answer is more likely than the others. An expressed threat to commit suicide is associated with a very high risk for completed suicide. Although options A, B, and C represent high-risk groups, any individual who has made a suicide threat would be at higher risk.

AUDIO PODCAST 15.1
Suicidality
Eli A. Karam
https://bcove.video/3KEKnKx

AUDIO PODCAST 15.2
Intimate Partner Violence
Eli A. Karam
https://bcove.video/3Knx7tr

AUDIO PODCAST 15.3
Child and Elder Abuse
Eli A. Karam
https://bcove.video/3CASOEo

AUDIO PODCAST 15.4
Duty to Warn and Protect
Eli A. Karam
https://bcove.video/3KnqZ4s

REFERENCES

Barnett, J. E., & Johnson, W. B. (2008). *Ethics desk reference for psychologists*. American Psychological Association.

Capuzzi, D. (Ed.). (2004). *Suicide across the life span*. American Counseling Association.

Clay, A. L., Okoniewski, K. C., & Haskett, M. E. (2019). Child Abuse Prevention and Treatment Act (CAPTA). In S. Hupp & J. Jewell (Eds.), *The encyclopedia of child and adolescent development* (pp. 1–10). Wiley.

Granello, D. H. (2010). The process of suicide risk assessment: Twelve core principles. *Journal of Counseling & Development*, *88*, 363–370. https://doi.org/10.1002/j.1556-6678.2010.tb00034.x

Granello, D. H., & Granello, P. F. (2007). *Suicide: An essential guide for helping professionals and educators*. Allyn & Bacon.

Greene, G. J., Lee, M., Trask, R., & Rheinscheld, J. (2000). How to work with clients' strengths in crisis intervention. In A. R. Roberts (Ed.), *Crisis intervention handbook: Assessment, treatment and research* (pp. 31–55). Oxford University Press.

Kanel, K. (2019). *A guide to crisis intervention*. Cengage Learning.

Roberts, A. (Ed.). (2000). *Crisis intervention handbook: Assessment, treatment and research*. Oxford University Press.

Stith, S. M., McCollum, E. E., & Rosen, K. H. (2011). *Couples therapy for domestic violence: Finding safe solutions*. American Psychological Association.

Sue, D. W., & Sue, D. (2008). *Counseling the culturally diverse: Theory and practice (5th ed.)*. Wiley.

Walker, M. U. (2006). The cycle of violence. *Journal of Human Rights, 5*(1), 81–105. https://doi.org/10.1080/14754830500485890

Yassen, J., & Harvey, M. R. (1998). Crisis assessment and interventions with victims of violence. In P. M. Kleespies (Ed.), *Emergencies in mental health practice* (pp. 117–143). Guilford Press.

PART VI

Maintaining Ethical/ Legal/Professional Standards (Domain 6)

Ethical and Legal Principles

16

LEARNING OBJECTIVES

After reading this chapter, you should be able to:

1. Identify major areas related to the ethical practice of marriage and family therapy (MFT)
2. Predict mistakes that lead to ethical boundary violations
3. Review the purpose of ethical codes and steps in ethical decision-making
4. Practice proper use of technology in MFT practice

RELEVANT EXAM DOMAINS

- *Domain 6—Maintaining Ethical, Legal, and Professional Standards*
  Includes tasks related to ongoing adherence to legal and ethical codes and treatment agreements, maintaining competency in the field, and professionalism.

INTRODUCTION

In this chapter, we focus on how ethics and legal issues affect the practice and profession of marriage and family therapy (MFT). Professional ethics is not so much about following a personal code as following the accepted code of the profession. The most widely accepted ethical code for the MFT profession is the one developed by the American Association for Marriage and Family Therapy (AAMFT; 2015). Family therapists must consider multiple factors when making ethical decisions: the ethical implications of the decision, any legal implications of the decision, and any clinical implications of the decision. Professional ethics also has to do with balancing the needs of competing groups and individuals. As a marriage and family therapist, you treat both individuals and family systems.

PURPOSE OF ETHICAL CODES

A code of ethics is a written statement established and distributed by a discipline or profession that expresses how those in the profession should and should not conduct themselves. To guide ethical practice, all mental health associations, like the AAMFT, develop professional codes of ethics. Ethical codes express the dominant morality of the field, articulate values of the profession, and define the standards that both the professionals and users of the professionals' services can expect in any professional interaction. In addition to guiding the conduct of professionals, ethical codes serve as a basis for sanctions. Sanctions may vary from censure to fines, revocation of licensure or certification, denial of privileges, or supervision of future work. Legal ramifications may also occur if laws were broken (Barnett, 2019).

A therapist must weigh three factors when making ethical decisions: the ethical implications of the decision, any legal implications of the decision, and any clinical implications of the decision (Barnett, 2019).

STEPS TO ETHICAL DECISION-MAKING

1. Be aware of potential ethical issues.
2. Define the ethical problem.
3. Gather information from all relevant sources.
4. Define the ethical principles or values that influence your thinking about the problem.
5. Formulate and weigh all possible alternatives.
6. Choose the best ethical alternative and implement the decision.
7. Monitor your decision and the outcome of your decision; reevaluate if necessary.

CONSENT FOR TREATMENT

Informed consent is a legal and ethical term defined as the consent of a client to a proposed psychotherapy, or for participation in a research project or clinical study. For the consent to be informed the client must first achieve a clear understanding of the relevant facts, risks, and benefits, and available alternatives involved. Informed consent requires legal documentation. The concept of informed consent originated with the recognition that individuals have rights: to freedom, autonomy, and human dignity. Clients (whether in inpatient or outpatient treatment) possess these rights and cannot be denied their rights due to mental health status or condition.

Informed consent for treatment should be distinguished from simple consent for treatment. In the latter, a client simply agrees to accept treatment for themselves or for a minor child. To be effective, consent must be provided knowingly and voluntarily. In other words, the client must be at least generally informed about the treatment and understand that they have a right to decline the treatment. In addition, the client must possess the legal capacity to provide consent. For example, a minor (with certain exceptions) lacks the legal capacity to provide consent to their own treatment. Alternately, an intoxicated person may lack the capacity to provide effective consent due to impaired mental condition.

By addressing informed consent at the start of therapy, the client is provided with an opportunity to determine whether they agree with the therapist's assessment and related treatment recommendations. However, issues of informed consent are not confined just to the first session. They may also arise during the course of treatment. At the beginning of treatment, the client and therapist have had limited opportunity to establish a therapeutic relationship. Consequently, initial treatment plans are crafted with the understanding that therapist and client alike are expected to engage in a process of regular review of the therapy. This process of review is founded upon the premise that changes in treatment plans should occur when therapeutic progress is not occurring.

It is easy for therapists and families alike to overlook the relevance of informed consent to the treatment of children and adolescents. Although minors under the age of 12 lack the legal capacity to provide legal consent to their treatment, they certainly can, and should, provide input to their therapist regarding their treatment. Clinicians who treat children are often witnesses to the fact that children feel powerless and/or helpless in the face of traumatic events, such as the divorce of their parents, a change in the composition of their family, or the physical relocation of their family. In these and other circumstances, children are often particularly grateful for the opportunity to express their opinions about the direction of the therapy. Therefore, therapists who work with children have an opportunity to acknowledge the child's need to understand and participate in their own treatment plan.

CONFIDENTIALITY

Confidentiality is the ethical obligation of therapists to keep communications between themselves and their clients strictly private. Confidentiality has unique significance in the practice of MFT, as the challenges around confidentiality increase significantly when therapists work with multiple people in one room. Some of these ethical challenges involve conceptualizing the client(s) served, providing informed consent, and handling relational matters in an individual context. Adding an online component makes a challenging situation even more complicated in cases of couples and family therapy, as confidentiality tends to be less reliable in online therapy than in face-to-face therapeutic encounters. Hackers, online viruses, and other problems that can occur during online exchanges pose threats to confidentiality.

NO SECRETS POLICY

Therapists should explain, negotiate, and set the parameters of services at the very beginning of therapy. This includes getting all parties to agree to limits to confidentiality within the client system and putting this in writing. Therapists need to inform their clients from the beginning of the professional relationship of the limits of confidentiality. When conducting couple or family therapy, this disclosure should also involve explaining a "no secrets" policy, both verbally and in writing, including why such a policy is necessary. The main reason for this policy is to clearly inform the participants that the therapist's primary obligation is to appropriately and effectively treat the couple or the family unit. The client needs to know that this policy is designed to prevent a conflict from arising between an individual participant and the entire unit being treated. Therapists should emphasize that they reserve the right to use their best clinical judgment as to what is necessary to share with members of the client system so that effective treatment can occur (Hecker, 2010).

AUDIO/VIDEO RECORDINGS

Confidentiality must also be maintained in the use of audiotapes or videotapes. When the therapist wishes to audiotape or videotape a session, the therapist must obtain written permission from all participants prior to the session. The consent statement should state how the tape will be used. If the tape is to be used only by the therapist's supervisor, then this fact should be stated. However, if the tape is to be used for instructional purposes in the classroom or at conferences, then its intended use should be made clear.

HEALTH INSURANCE PORTABILITY AND ACCOUNTABILITY ACT

If a family therapist's practice falls under the Health Insurance Portability and Accountability Act (HIPAA) as a "covered entity" (meaning it meets the criteria for HIPAA), the therapist must also give clients a Notice of Privacy Practices and document that the client received it. Covered entities are businesses that transmit any transactions electronically, such as for insurance reimbursement; they have a responsibility to keep clients' protected health information (PHI) confidential. The Notice of Privacy Practices informs clients that their protected health information may be released for treatment, payment, or healthcare operations. However, when state law is more stringent than HIPAA regulations, as is the case with most laws regarding mental health practitioners' clients, then state law is followed. In addition to privacy regulations, HIPAA regulations also address security of electronic protected health information (ePHI) with important safeguards (Hecker & Edwards, 2014; Hudgins et al., 2013).

MANDATED REPORTING

The duty to report, also called *mandated reporting*, refers to a therapist's obligation to report child abuse, older abuse, or abuse of other dependents to the proper authorities. Therapists are expected to help protect those who cannot protect themselves from abuse or neglect. This is an exception to the ethical obligation to keep communications with clients confidential. Therapists should make this exception explicit in the informed consent at the beginning of treatment (see also Chapter 15).

Therapists should review the laws of the state in which they practice to determine under what circumstances the duty to report is triggered. The website for the state professional licensing agency is a good place to find the statutes and regulations that govern therapists. Most states have legislated the duty to report, in which case the therapist has both a legal and an ethical duty to report abuse or neglect. Some states may require the therapist to report suspected abuse within a certain amount of time, such as 24 or 48 hours. Failure to report may result in criminal culpability and/or civil liability, especially if an injury results from the therapist's inaction. Some states require the report to be made to the police, others to social services, an abuse hotline, or some other entity. No one can perform the reporting on the therapist's behalf. When multiple healthcare providers develop a suspicion of abuse or neglect, each of them must make their own report.

DUTY TO WARN/DUTY TO PROTECT

The *duty to warn* refers to the obligation of the therapist to protect third parties from physical harm (and sometimes property damage) from the therapist's own clients. Most states have legislated the duty to warn, which means the therapist has a legal, as well as an ethical duty, to warn an intended victim. A related duty is the duty to protect one's own clients from serious self-harm. Therapists must continually assess their clients' risk for suicide, including their level of suicidal ideation and whether they have an actual intent and ability to follow through. When a therapist believes that a client has become a danger to themselves, they have a duty to protect the client by reporting the risk. The duty to protect a client from serious self-harm could also extend to clients who are not suicidal, but whose actions could potentially be lethal. Nonsuicidal self-injury, such as cutting, and highly risky behaviors, such as adolescent heavy drinking or reckless driving, may trigger the duty to protect.

The Tarasoff case involves both the duty to warn and the duty to protect. While in psychotherapy, Prosenjit Poddar threatened to kill Tatiana Tarasoff. Tarasoff was a fellow student in Poddar's square-dancing class. Although Tarasoff was not mentioned by name, the therapist knew her identity. Tarasoff was not informed of this threat against her life. Two months later, Poddar murdered Tarasoff. The Tarasoff family filed suit, and the court ruled that, when a therapist determines or pursuant to the standards of the profession determine, that his patient presents a serious danger of violence to another, he incurs an obligation to use reasonable care to protect the intended victim against such danger (Stone, 1976). Either by law and/or ethical duty, therapists also have a duty to protect when the following three criteria are met:

1. The therapist has established there is likelihood that the client will cause harm to themselves or to someone else.
2. A therapeutic relationship exists between the therapist and client.
3. There is an identifiable victim(s).

PRIVILEGE

In addition to the ethical obligation to maintain client confidentiality, the therapist is expected to uphold the legal obligation of client privilege. Privilege is a legal right that gives the client the right to prevent the therapist from disclosing confidential information. The therapist–client privilege "belongs" to the client. Only the client can establish the privilege and take the necessary steps to assert or waive it. The therapist, therefore, must take direction from the client.

What the client tells a therapist during a therapy session may or may not be privileged, depending on whether the client intended the communications to be confidential. If the client came to a therapist voluntarily to seek help for a mental or relational problem, and has established a long-term therapeutic relationship, then the sessions are solely for the client's private benefit and are almost certainly intended to be confidential. However, people sometimes contact therapists in conjunction with some particular legal problem, for example, they are involved in a divorce or custody dispute, or they are being mandated to therapy by a judge. In these cases, the client probably expects some of the details of the therapy to be disclosed in later legal proceedings, in which case there is no evidentiary privilege.

Even if a session is privileged originally, the privilege does not apply in the following situations:

- In child abuse cases
- In cases in which the client's mental health is itself a direct legal issue; examples include child custody cases, civil commitment hearings, hearings concerning a defendant's competency to stand trial, and civil cases in which the plaintiff seeks damages for emotional injury
- If the client sues the therapist for malpractice, or the therapist seeks a restraining order against a former client
- If the client is using the session in furtherance of an ongoing or future crime or fraud; discussions of past crimes or wrongdoing are privileged, but not discussions of plans for future crimes or violence
- In duty-to-warn cases; the famous 1976 case of *Tarasoff v. Regents of University of California* established that when a therapist determines that a patient presents a serious threat of violence toward another person, the therapist must take reasonable steps to protect that person, including warning the victim and notifying the police

If lawyers need information from a session, they will try to get it. If the subject of the session is important to some court case, it is probably not privileged. If it is merely tangential information a lawyer wants in order to harass a witness by bringing up their psychological history, then it is probably privileged. Remember that only the lawyers and the client must worry about whether to assert the privilege, and it is the judge who will decide whether the therapist does or does not have to testify. Making these decisions is not the responsibility of the therapist.

If the client whose communications are at issue goes around telling people the substance of what they told the therapist in session, then the privilege is waived forever. On the other hand, if the client tells others about their mental health in general, without revealing what was said at the session, the privilege remains intact.

There is a difference between confidential information and privileged information. The fact that information should be kept confidential because it is in the best interest of the client is legally irrelevant. Lawyers operate under fixed rules of evidence and pretrial procedures that are created and enforced by lawyers and judges who probably know nothing about the therapist–patient relationship and don't care about the ethical guidelines of the AAMFT. In general, the lawyers fight among themselves over privilege issues, but there are four common situations in which a therapist gets dragged into the fight.

If a therapist gets a request from a lawyer for information about a client, the therapist is under no obligation to provide it. Refuse the request unless the lawyer has a court order or a waiver signed by the client. If the lawyer claims to have either of these documents, demand a copy for the file (Youngren & Harris, 2008).

A second common scenario is that a therapist receives a subpoena requesting confidential information, followed by a telephone call from an attorney asking to pick up the material. Handle this request exactly like an informal request—by refusing to comply unless the lawyer has a court order or a waiver signed by the client. A subpoena is *not* a court order; even if it contains a facsimile of the clerk's signature, it is just a fancy request by an attorney.

During a deposition, a lawyer may ask about confidential client information. No judge is present at a deposition to rule on whether the information is legally privileged. What should the therapist do? If one of the lawyers present is the lawyer for the client, the therapist should ask this lawyer whether they should answer the question. If the lawyer says no, don't answer. The lawyers will not get mad at you; they will go fight it out between themselves down at the courthouse. If neither lawyer represents the client, then assert the privilege on the client's behalf, unless either lawyer can produce a court order or a signed waiver.

If in a courtroom with a judge present, and a lawyer asks about confidential or sensitive information, what should the therapist do? If one of the lawyers present is the lawyer for the client, then it is the lawyer's job to object and assert the privilege. If that lawyer does nothing, answer the question. If the lawyer for the opposing side objects, the judge will either "sustain" the objection (don't answer) or "overrule" the objection (then the therapist must answer). If neither lawyer represents the client, then the therapist should assert the privilege on the client's behalf. The therapist can then directly ask the judge whether they should answer the question.

FEES

Prior to the start of therapy, therapists should disclose the fee to be charged for services. Policies regarding fees may be presented in the informed-consent form or a separate fee agreement, which the client acknowledges and signs. The disclosure should include the provider's standard fee, how fees may be raised, information regarding insurance billing, policies on fees for cancellation/missed sessions, and acceptable forms of payment (AAMFT, 2015).

In addition to covering disclosures in writing, make sure to discuss each policy with the client verbally, especially policies regarding charges for missed and canceled sessions. If the therapist forgets to disclose such policies to the client at the outset of treatment, it is recommended not to charge the client for a missed or canceled session.

If there are items that need to be billed outside of therapy sessions, the therapist should consider including those items and the associated fees in the client's fee agreement. If the therapist intends to charge a client for any professional service not fully described in the fee agreement, such as writing a report or appearing at a deposition, it should be discussed with the client in advance. The client should agree to the fee and this should be documented in the record before being charged for the service.

Many therapists are contracted providers for insurance plans. Those who are not contracted providers typically produce a "superbill" so the client can seek reimbursement from the insurance plan directly. Policies regarding insurance billing should be clearly stated in the fee agreement or informed- consent form. This may include information about the therapist's contracted fee schedule, billing procedures, and the client's co-payment. The fee agreement may also specify that the client is responsible for paying for the service rendered, regardless of whether or not the insurance plan actually reimburses for the service.

BARTERING

Bartering is defined as the exchange of goods and services. As it pertains to therapy, more specifically, bartering is the acceptance of services, goods, or other nonmonetary payments from clients in return for psychological or therapeutic services. Bartering for goods, especially if full market valued can be assessed, is often viewed as less complicated than bartering for services, which create dual-relationship situations. Although bartering for services is not prohibited by law or ethical standards, it is not generally encouraged. Therapists should exercise good judgment when faced with a situation in which clients are requesting to barter for therapy services. Consider whether the barter could potentially lead to exploitation of the client or impairment of the therapist's judgment. Seeking clinical and legal consultations in these situations is highly advisable.

RECOVERING FEES

Occasionally, a client, for one reason or another, fails to pay the agreed upon fees for therapy services. As a service provider, the therapist is able to collect unpaid balances from clients, if done so in a diligent manner. Therapists should ask themselves the following questions before trying to collect from a client:

- Which collection route do you want to take?
- What is the possibility of a client retaliating by filing a claim or complaint against you?
- Is it worth pursuing the debt?

It is generally recommended that the therapist attempt to settle the matter with the client before taking legal action. Consider contacting the client to discuss feasible financial arrangements that work for both parties.

If all attempts fail, the available options to collect the money include referring the claim to a collection agency, taking the client to small-claims court, or agreeing to mediation. It is important that the therapist provide the client with reasonable notice of the intention to take legal action. For example, the therapist should send a certified letter to the client informing them of the outstanding balance and the deadline in which the client has to either contact the therapist to discuss financial arrangements or to send payment. If the client fails to respond, the client's claim will be forwarded to collections.

RAISING FEES

Periodically, therapists desire to raise their fees for current clients who are continuing in therapy. Although this practice is acceptable if reasonable notice is given, it is recommended that clients be informed about the policy about raising fees in writing at the outset of treatment. This can reduce the likelihood of clients feeling exploited when they are given notice of the fee increase.

PAYMENT FOR REFERRALS

It is unlawful and unethical for therapists to offer or accept payment for referrals, whether in the form of money or otherwise. A conflict of interest or exploitation of this nature could harm a client. The federal Anti-Kickback Statute prohibits individuals and entities from offering anything of value, whether cash or otherwise, in exchange for any federal healthcare program business. Federal healthcare programs include Medicare, Medicaid, Tricare, Department of Labor health programs, and more. In other words, a therapist cannot refer a client covered by a federal healthcare program, like Medicare, to another therapist's practice in exchange for money or monetary gifts. The purpose of the Stark law is to prevent the referral of a client for a designated health service to another entity in which the healthcare provider (or provider's close relative) has a financial interest. The Stark Law, unlike the Anti-Kickback Statute, flatly prohibits a broad range of financial relationships, and does not require proof of an intent to induce referrals. Note that the Stark law is a strict liability statute, which means that the provider's intent is not taken into consideration when determining violations of the law. Any violations of the Stark law can result in civil fines and program removals (as opposed to the Anti-Kickback Statute, which can result in criminal penalties).

BOUNDARY CROSSINGS AND VIOLATIONS

Boundaries constitute the agreed-upon rules and expectations that articulate the parameters of the therapy relationship. Some boundaries about the therapy include concerns with time and place of sessions, fees, and confidentiality. Other boundaries regulate the nature of the contact between therapists and clients, including therapist self-disclosure, physical contact, giving and receiving gifts, and contact outside of the normal therapy session. Boundary violations, always unethical, occur when therapists cross the line of decency and violate or exploit their clients. Boundary crossing, on the other hand, may not be harmful to clients and involve topics such as therapist self-disclosure, home visits, non-sexual touch, and bartering. Different cultures have different expectations, customs, and values and therefore will judge the appropriateness of boundary crossings differently. More communally oriented cultures, such as Latinos, African Americans or Native Americans, are more likely to expect boundary crossings, and frown upon the rigid implementation of boundaries in therapy (Hecker, 2010).

DUAL RELATIONSHIPS

In psychotherapy, *dual relationship* refers to any situation in which multiple roles exist between a therapist and a client (Hecker, 2010). Examples of dual relationships are when the client is also a student, friend, family member, or employee of the therapist. Harmful boundary violations typically occur when therapists are engaged in exploitative dual relationships, such as sexual contact with current or former clients. Exploitative business relationships also constitute boundary violations.

There are multiple types or categories of dual relationships. A social dual relationship exists when the therapist and client are also friends. Having a client as a Facebook "friend" on a personal, rather than strictly professional basis, may also constitute social dual relationships. A business dual relationship exists when therapist and client are also business partners or have an employer–employee relationship. Examples of communal dual relationships occur when therapist and client live in the same small community, belong to the same place of religious worship, or the therapist shops in a store that is owned by the client. A sexual dual relationship exists when the therapist and client are also involved in a physically intimate relationship; these relationships are always unethical and often illegal.

Avoidable dual relationships occur in large cities or metropolitan areas where there are many therapists. Unavoidable multiple relationships, on the other hand, often cannot be avoided in rural areas. Unexpected multiple relationships occur when a therapist is not initially aware that the client they have been working with is also a friend, colleague, co-worker, or even an ex-spouse of another client. Similarly, unexpected dual relationships take place when, unbeknownst to the therapist, the client joins the same church, book club, or gym as the therapist.

In order to act in an ethical manner, it is recommended that therapists consult with well-informed peers, consultants, and supervisors before entering into complex dual relationships, Separate knowledge of law and ethics from integrity, decency, and care for the client system. A therapist should discuss with clients the potential benefits as well as potential pitfalls and likely risks that may arise due to dual relationships. They should also create office policies that include the risks and benefits of dual relationships.

GIFTS

Client gifts can either be appropriate or inappropriate depending on their type, monetary value, timing, content, frequency, intent of the giver, and their effect on the giver, receiver, or anyone else who may be affected by the gift-giving. Even small gifts can be inappropriate if, for example, they include inappropriate (i.e., romantic) themes. At times, especially in child therapy, therapists may be given gifts by the clients' parents or other family members.

Many therapists agree that rejecting appropriate gifts of small monetary value but of highly symbolic and relational value can be deleterious to the therapeutic alliance, leaving clients feeling rejected or humiliated. These feelings, an experience that many clients are already familiar with, may serve to shut clients down just as they are opening up in the therapy. Therefore, refusing a gift without attempting to understand the client's subjective intent for giving the gift is, at the minimum, a lost clinical opportunity.

Inhabitants of many rural or ethnic settings often readily embrace gift-giving as a common expression of connection and gratitude. Gift-giving in therapy must always be considered within its cultural context. Regardless of the therapist's clinical or ethical stance on the subject of gifts, the therapist must be aware that turning down a small gift may mean disrespect to an individual client or family system originating from a culture that stresses hospitality, reciprocity, and the importance of gift-giving rituals. The wise therapist will learn about each client's culture and gift-giving traditions, if possible, from the clients themselves.

Each gift must be evaluated within the context that it is given. The nature of the therapeutic relationship, the setting, the client's culture, history, and presenting problem are some of the factors that determine the appropriateness of the gift. Besides gifts offered during the holidays and at termination, accepting a symbolic gift (book, card, poem, piece of handmade art) that has special meaning to a client is common and usually acceptable.

SEXUAL CONTACT BETWEEN THERAPIST AND CLIENT SYSTEM

Ethical therapy never includes sexual contact between a therapist and a client. It also never includes inappropriate sexual suggestions, or any other kind of sexual behavior between a therapist and a client. Sexual contact of any kind between a therapist and a client is unethical and illegal. In fact, therapists can be prosecuted both civilly and criminally for engaging in sexual relations with their clients. It is always the responsibility of the therapist to ensure that sexual contact with a client, whether consensual or not, does not occur.

Under the previous AAMFT *Code of Ethics* (2001), a therapist could enter into a sexual relationship with a client's *family member* without fear of repercussions if 2 years have passed since the end of therapy. However, a therapist who engages in a sexual relationship with the former client or their partner is always at some level of risk because if someone says they have suffered emotionally as the result of a romantic relationship with a former therapist, the blame falls on the therapist as it is their responsibility to look out for the well-being of their former client. Gone from the latest AAMFT *Code of Ethics* (2015) is the "2-year rule." The new rule shifts the previous discouragement of sex with former clients into a clear prohibition and extends its reach to include all known members of the client's family system, not just client partners.

COPING WITH SEXUAL FEELINGS FROM A CLIENT

A good first step when a client expresses sexual interest in the therapist is to acknowledge the person's feelings. Validate their courage and vulnerability around bringing their feelings up or having them named. Explain that although the intimacy that often develops within the therapeutic relationship is powerful, it is best described as a kind of contextual positive regard that is specific to the power-differential relationship. Sexualizing this kind of positive regard is detrimental to the client's work in therapy. Make it very clear, through use of both words and body language that a sexual relationship is outside the bounds of the therapeutic relationship. Make every effort not to shame or reject the client. If appropriate, look for therapeutic ways in which the issue of sexuality can be addressed and explored. When sexual feelings are unspoken or unconfirmed, use professional judgment to determine what would best serve the client—either the therapist naming the feelings or waiting for the client to do so. A therapist in this situation should always seek the support of supervision.

COPING WITH THERAPIST SEXUAL FEELINGS FOR A CLIENT

First, it may help if the therapist explores why they may be sexually attracted to a particular client. Is there something about the client that meets one of the therapist's needs? Although it may be a natural need, it is one that must be met elsewhere. The therapist should immediately talk to a colleague who can help them sort out what they are experiencing and take appropriate steps to keep the therapeutic relationship ethical. The therapist should also seek therapy. Working with a counselor can help the therapist resolve these feelings and uncover any issues they may be struggling to deal with effectively. If, after completing these steps, the therapist is still unable to resolve the sexual feelings toward the client, the therapist should terminate the treatment relationship and refer the client to another therapist.

BOUNDARIES AND SOCIAL MEDIA

Therapists who engage in social media face a number of challenges related to privacy and self-disclosure. A client may request that the therapist "connect" with them on a social media platform. In such circumstances, there are important questions to consider, such as:

- Is the client hoping to develop a personal friendship with the therapist? If so, how should the therapist respond?
- Will the client's perception of the therapist change after viewing the therapist's personal profile? How will the therapeutic relationship be impacted?
- Does the therapist's personal profile include information that may potentially embarrass them if seen by a client?
- Will any of the information (including photographs) that is posted online by the therapist potentially embarrass or harm the therapist's professional reputation?

Any client is free to embark on an online search for their therapist. If a therapist elects to grant open access to private thoughts and feelings and information about personal habits, likes and dislikes, and so on, it should not come as a surprise when one of the therapist's clients discovers the information and reacts to it. A therapist must not only consider what is or what is not appropriate to disclose. It is also important to consider what clients might do with this personal information once they have it. Although a client may simply be curious about the therapist, it would be naive to think that in every instance, the client's motivation is entirely benign. There are also safety issues to consider. An angry client may act out against a therapist whom they blame for some disappointment, such as the loss of a relationship or for a negative outcome in a legal matter, and so forth. A related question, conversely, is whether a therapist should ever attempt to access a client's personal information through social media.

The information learned by a therapist in this manner might help the therapist to better understand the client.

RECORD KEEPING

IMPORTANCE OF KEEPING GOOD RECORDS

Good clinical record keeping adds documentation, so therapists do not need to rely on memory to recall details of their clients' lives and the treatment provided. Not keeping any records, conversely, is unethical, below the standard of care, and illegal in many states. In ethical and legal disputes, it is often not the therapist's word against the client's, but the client's word against the psychotherapy records. In fact, many ethical and licensure boards make the decision of whether to pursue a case against a therapist based on experts who develop their opinion from reading the clients' complaints and the therapists' records, but not necessarily interviewing the therapists directly. Also, if the treating therapist becomes disabled, dies, or cannot continue to provide care for other reasons, accurate and complete clinical records help the new therapist to provide continuity of care for the client system.

RECORD STORAGE

Therapists should store hard-copy records in a safe, locked place that is reasonably protected from theft, intrusion, fire, earthquake, water damage, and unauthorized access. Electronic records, conversely, should be protected by use of proper encryption, including password, virus protection, firewall, and access log. Therapists are encouraged to regularly back up records and store this data off site in a secure location.

CONTENTS OF THE CLINICAL FILE

At the beginning of treatment, present clients with therapist-specific office policies and informed-consent forms. Make sure that the records in the clinical file include the following:

- Signed statement of office policies and agreement for treatment
- Signed fee agreement
- Clients' demographic information, which includes how to reach them in emergencies
- Treatment plan (signed by therapist)
- HIPAA forms (if applicable)
- Signed consent to release information
- Copies of test data, medical or educational reports, and any other relevant collateral data
- Termination summary that includes information on who initiated the termination and for what reason and what was or was not achieved; if necessary, add follow-up information and referrals

Enter clinically relevant and meaningful information in the clinical records. Detail clinically meaningful contacts, including important phone calls and important or clinically significant collateral contacts. Include in records the date and type of services provided, fees, charges, payments, balances, and copies of third-party billing. Because no records are immune from disclosure, be careful not to include clinically superfluous or unnecessary details in documentation that can cause undue harm or confusion for clients if they are disclosed or become public.

ESSENTIAL COMPONENTS OF THE TREATMENT PLAN

Treatment plans usually include the presenting problem, diagnosis, goals of treatment, interventions or means to achieve these goals, and the theoretical or evidence-based rationale for your interventions. Update the treatment plan and report on progress, or lack thereof, throughout the duration of therapy as necessary.

RESIST CLONING

Progress notes should reflect therapist competence, thoughtfulness, and knowledge of clinically, ethically and legally relevant decision-making ability. Never repeat the same verbiage on notes (known as *cloning* or *cut and paste*) in consecutive sessions. This lazy practice results in the progress not being specific enough or not accurately reflecting the dynamics and content of the session. In case of audit by a third-party payer, this may also result in reimbursement problems with Medicare and other insurance companies. If a therapist is investigated by a licensing board or the AAMFT, repeating exactly the same notes session after session reflects poorly on clinical competency and sincerity.

RECORD RETENTION

Retain records as long as it is legally mandated or, when applicable, take into consideration institutional requirements, professional organizations' guidelines, professional codes of ethics, or other relevant mandates. Generally, there are no legal requirements to maintain any records beyond the required time. However, therapists must take into consideration the context of therapy and the potential need for records in the future, as well as the potential risk of maintaining outdated or obsolete records for long periods of time.

RETAINING RECORDS AFTER DEATH OF THE THERAPIST

Do not destroy the clinical record after the death of the therapist, even if trying to protect client privacy. Records are kept for the benefit of both the therapist and the client. Remember that clients have specified rights to access (inspect, copy, amend/addend) their records under state law and under HIPAA (for covered providers). Concerns about privacy of the client (and therefore, destruction of the records) are secondary in importance to the maintenance of the records so that the client can continue to be treated by the next therapist, who might need treatment records for continuity of care. Many states have laws that require records to be kept for a prescribed period of time. The time frame is usually different for adults and minors. Some of these laws may address how the requirement to keep records is affected by the death of the practitioner. State law may also specify what happens to the records upon the death of the therapist and what actions the estate of the therapist or others must take to announce the death of the therapist. State law may specify the location and manner of access to the records. Other states may have no law that covers the time frame for the maintenance of treatment records, other than laws that establish therapist–client privilege and the duty of confidentiality.

LOST OR STOLEN RECORDS

Therapists who find themselves with lost or stolen records are rightly afraid of liability, both civilly (lawsuit) and administratively (licensing board/disciplinary action), and usually want to minimize their liability. Depending on the length and content of the records, however, some unintended disclosures can be seriously invasive and cause significant harm or embarrassment to the client.

Sometimes therapists who find themselves in this situation may be reluctant to promptly tell the client because they are hopeful that the records will be found, returned, or recovered. If records are missing because of a theft or other crime, for example, the therapist should promptly file a police report. Although misplaced or lost records may be found or returned, therapists must carefully evaluate the pros and cons of delaying disclosure and must be certain that they act in good faith.

Generally, the therapist is better off telling the clients about the missing records promptly rather than suppressing that information for a period of time. If prompt notice is given, the therapist will not later be found to have intentionally obscured the information in an act of collusion by a licensing board or other governing body. Delaying disclosure, therefore, may increase the liability for the therapist. Prompt and full disclosure is easy when the therapist has not acted negligently with respect to the destruction, theft, or disappearance of the records. If the loss, however, is the result of a therapist's negligence (taking the records home or leaving records out in an unsecured area), or the negligence of the employer (who allowed the records to be taken home and who had no written policy regarding this issue), the therapist and employer may not be fully transparent. In order to minimize this potential risk, think twice before taking records from the place where they regularly are kept.

When records are lost, stolen, or destroyed, the therapist may consider ethical reconstruction of the records for treatment purposes. The ability to reconstruct the records depends on the complexity of the case and the length of time that the client system has been in treatment. Records from former providers can usually be obtained again. Dates of treatment might be retrievable from an appointment book or other records. If records are reconstructed, the date of the reconstruction should be apparent and the reason for the reconstruction should be provided. Remember, the therapist might not be at fault in many cases. For instance, an office or home can be burglarized even though reasonable safeguards have been put in place. A natural disaster, fire, or accident of some kind, not the fault of the therapist or agency, might have caused damage or destruction. Because of the varying circumstances that occur and the different degrees of possible liability, therapists should consult with an attorney and their malpractice insurance provider to help them navigate through this difficult situation.

DISTINCTIONS BETWEEN PSYCHOTHERAPY NOTES AND PROGRESS NOTES

Psychotherapy notes, also called *private notes*, are notes taken by a therapist during a session with a client system that usually include therapist observations and any thoughts or feelings about a client's unique situation. These notes are kept separate from medical records and billing information, and providers are not permitted to share psychotherapy notes without a client's authorization. The client does not have the right to access these notes. Unlike progress notes, psychotherapy notes are private and are do not include:

- Medication details or records
- Test results
- Summary of diagnosis or treatment plan
- Summary of symptoms and prognosis
- Summary of progress

Psychotherapy notes receive special protection under the HIPAA Privacy Rule because they contain sensitive information and because they are a therapist's personal notes. They do not contain information related to a client's medical records, treatment, or healthcare operations and therefore do not need to be shared with clients. These types of notes are meant to help the therapist do their job to the best of their ability. Because psychotherapy notes are not mandatory and are only meant to help a therapist treat a client, there is no required format or structure to follow. Therefore, therapists can construct their psychotherapy notes however they wish, even deciding to scribble the notes down in shorthand that may be illegible to others.

Unlike psychotherapy notes, progress notes are meant to be shared with other healthcare professionals involved in coordinating care for a client. Progress notes inform members of the treatment system about client progress and communicate treatment plans, medical history, and other vital information. Without accurate and up-to-date progress notes, healthcare professionals would waste time and increase the risk of making a mistake when working with clients. Progress notes should be easy to access, clearly written, and consistent in format to help minimize confusion or misunderstanding. Progress notes are also essential documents needed for billing and reimbursement. If using a checklist in the progress note, make sure to add some narrative that reflects more precisely what was covered in the session to the notes of most or all sessions. SOAP (an acronym for subjective, objective, assessment, and plan) and DAP (an acronym for data, assessment, and plan) can be helpful options in structuring and formatting progress notes.

In addition to thorough documentation of crisis situations (see Chapter 15), give special attention in the progress notes to:

- Gifts from clients, therapists, or from third party to therapists
- Bartering arrangements
- Extensive use of touch or self-disclosure
- Recording or videotaping of sessions
- Out-of-office experiences (i.e., home visits, attending weddings or funerals, accompanying a client to a collateral appointment, or any clinically meaningful or incidental/chance encounters)

RELEASE OF CHILD RECORDS

If a therapist practices in a state that does not provide any right of confidentiality to minors, the therapist needs only to obtain parental consent to release the records. If the minor client's parents are married, separated, or divorced with joint custody, only one parent's consent is necessary to release records. If the client's parents are separated or divorced with only one parent having sole custody, only the custodial parent may determine when and to whom the records are released (i.e., records may not be released to the noncustodial parent without the custodial parent's consent).

Although the law designates that minors hold privilege, except in special circumstances, the parents of a nonemancipated minor in treatment have the right to waive the privilege for the minor client. The confusion over this issue stems from the fact that the law refers to clients with guardians or conservators as not holding the privilege. Most courts have interpreted this to mean that minors do NOT hold the privilege or do not have the right to waive the privilege. Parents are, therefore, recognized as having the right to waive the privilege for the minor client, even though the minor legally has the privilege.

THE PRIVACY RULE AND RELEASE OF PSYCHOTHERAPY NOTES

The Privacy Rule distinguishes between mental health information in a mental health professional's private note and that contained in the medical record. It does not provide a right of access to psychotherapy notes, which the Privacy Rule defines as notes recorded by a healthcare provider who is a mental health professional documenting or analyzing the contents of a conversation during a private therapy session or a group, joint, or family therapy session and that are separate from the rest of the client's medical record. Psychotherapy notes are primarily intended for personal use by the treating professional and generally are not disclosed for other purposes. Thus, the Privacy Rule includes an exception to an individual's right of access for psychotherapy notes. However, parents generally are the personal representatives of their minor child and, as such, are able to receive a copy of their child's mental health information contained in the medical record, including information about diagnosis, symptoms, treatment plans, and so on. Although the Privacy Rule does not provide a right for a client or personal representative to access psychotherapy notes regarding the client, HIPAA generally gives providers discretion to disclose the individual's own protected health information (including psychotherapy notes) directly to the individual or the individual's personal representative.

If a therapist needs to share their psychotherapy notes, they must first obtain authorization from the client. The following circumstances, however, do not require authorization and, in some cases, a therapist may be required to disclose their notes:

- To use the notes for treatment
- To defend themselves in court
- To prevent a serious threat to public health or safety
- For the lawful activities of a medical examiner or coroner

RETIREMENT/CLOSING PRACTICE

If a therapist decides to either close their practice or retire, it is paramount to notify clients and to terminate the therapeutic relationship in an ethically appropriate manner. Although there is no standardized process to follow when terminating with a client, therapists are required to act in a manner that is consistent with the applicable standards of care. Therapists are expected to manage the termination process with the degree of skill, knowledge, and care that would be exercised by other members of the profession when practicing under similar circumstances. The AAMFT *Code of Ethics* (2015) encourages therapists to maintain practices that provide undisrupted care and to use sound clinical judgment when terminating therapeutic relationships.

Neither the law nor the AAMFT *Code of Ethics* (2015) dictates the amount of advance notice a therapist is required to provide. Therapists must use their best judgment to determine reasonable notice. This will depend on factors such as the therapist's theoretical orientation and client population. Depending on how long the practice will remain open, it may not be appropriate to establish a therapeutic relationship with a new client without knowing whether you will have the time to assess the client adequately, formulate an effective treatment plan, and help them achieve their treatment goals.

Second, it is helpful to provide clients with meaningful referrals based on their therapeutic needs. Neither the law nor the AAMFT *Code of Ethics* (2015) specifies the number of referrals that a provider is required to offer a client upon termination. However, best practices include providing the client with three referrals to other suitable mental healthcare providers or, if the client uses insurance, referring the client back to their health plan provider. Third, it is necessary to provide clients with appropriate contact information so that they know whom to contact if they need to request a copy of their clinical record in the future.

Even a well-planned strategy can be met with unforeseen circumstances. Although not required by law, having a professional will (a document used by care providers to outline how to handle the closing of a practice in the event of unforeseen circumstances) may give the therapist peace of mind if the therapist becomes unable to fulfill their professional obligations.

TECHNOLOGY AND ONLINE THERAPY

SCOPE OF COMPETENCE

Therapists have a primary ethical responsibility to provide professional services only within the scope of their competence based on their education, training, and supervised experience. Therefore, family therapists should routinely assess both their professional and technical competence when providing online services. Acquiring competence may require pursuing additional educational experiences and training, including but not limited to, a review of the relevant literature and continuing education specific to the delivery of services using telehealth technologies (AAMFT, 2017; Association of Marriage and Family Therapy Regulatory Boards [AMFTRB], 2016; Blumer et al., 2015).

INFORMED CONSENT AND CONFIDENTIALITY

Although it may be more challenging to obtain and document informed consent in situations in which clients are not in the same physical location, therapists should develop and share the policies and procedures that will explain the process of online therapy to their clients. Therapists engaging in online practice take reasonable steps to verify the identity and age of each client.

Therapists should discuss both potential confidentiality and security issues when telehealth technologies are used. Family therapists both understand and inform their clients of the limits to confidentiality and risks of the possible access or disclosure of confidential data and information that may occur during service delivery, including the risks of access to electronic communications (e.g., telephone, email) between the therapist and client. Along this line, be cognizant and make clients aware of some of the inherent risks a given telecommunication technology may pose regarding the failure or unreliability of the equipment (hardware, software, etc.; AAMFT, 2017; AMFTRB, 2016; Blumer et al., 2015).

CRISIS SITUATIONS

Although therapists trained to handle emergency or crisis situations in traditional in-person, face-to-face therapy are generally familiar with the resources available in the local community, this may not be the case when delivering online therapy. At the onset of telehealth services, therefore, family therapists must make a reasonable effort to identify and learn how to access relevant and appropriate emergency resources in the client's local area, such as emergency response contacts. They should prepare a plan to address any lack of appropriate resources, particularly those necessary in an emergency, and other relevant factors that may impact the efficacy and safety of online therapy. As part of emergency planning, therapists should provide clients with clear written instructions as to what to do in an emergency.

TERMINATION AND REFERRAL ISSUES

Family therapists recognize that in some cases, online therapy is not the most appropriate treatment option. Prior to committing to the ongoing provision of online services, therapists engaging in online practice assess whether online services are appropriate to client needs. Be mindful of potential termination strategies, discharge plans, and referral sources when telehealth services are no longer necessary or desirable for a particular client system. For example, if a client regularly experiences crises and their level of need indicates that intensive in-person services may be more appropriate, therapists should take reasonable steps to refer a client to a local mental health resource capable of handling the client's issues.

PRACTICING WITHIN THE PROPER JURISDICTION

With the rapid advances made in telehealth technology, the intentional or unintentional delivery of therapeutic services across state lines and jurisdictions is becoming more of a reality for therapists. Such scenarios may range from the therapist or client being temporarily out-of-state during an online session to the therapist offering their services across jurisdictional borders so as to take advantage of this emerging technology. Because of this unprecedented growth in online therapy, family therapists strive to keep abreast of developments and changes in the licensure and other interjurisdictional practice requirements that may be pertinent to their delivery of online therapy (AAMFT, 2017; AMFTRB, 2016; Blumer et al., 2015).

SUBPOENAS AND TESTIMONY

A subpoena or summons is an order to appear in court or at a deposition, or an order to produce documents, such as the contents of the clinical record. Depending on the jurisdiction, subpoenas may be issued by a judge, by the clerk of the court, or even by an attorney in private practice. Subpoenas may be issued by an attorney representing the therapist's client or by an attorney opposing the therapist's client. A subpoena may be issued in a civil proceeding such as a lawsuit or a divorce or custody dispute, in a criminal proceeding, or in an administrative proceeding.

It is important to understand the distinction between the role and scope of testimony offered by a treating therapist who testifies as a witness and the role of a retained expert. Avoiding opinion or speculation, a treating therapist witness testifies only about things that actually occurred in the therapy. A therapist called to testify as a treating witness will read from the clinical record. A retained expert witness, on the other hand, is hired by a party, or retained by the court, to formulate an opinion based on an objective and forensic analysis of the facts. A retained expert has specialized knowledge of a particular subject matter and relies on that expertise to render an opinion that directly relates to the legal issues at hand. The retained expert relies on information contained in healthcare records, legal documents, other collateral information, and interviews that may involve the patient or other interested parties. Because their roles, scope of testimony, and the type of information relied on are different, serving in the capacity as both a treating therapist witness and a retained expert could give rise to an ethical conflict of interest and dual role.

ADVERTISING

Advertising can educate the public about services available to them and who is available to provide those services. All advertisements by therapists must be true and accurate pertaining to credentials, experience, education and scope of competence. Therapists do not use any professional identification (such as a business card, office sign, letterhead, Internet, or telephone or association directory listing) if it includes a statement or claim that is false or misleading (AAMFT, 2015).

RESEARCH

Therapists respect the dignity and protect the welfare of research participants (AAMFT, 2015). The Belmont Report identifies basic ethical principles to follow when conducting research that involves human subjects. It also sets forth guidelines to ensure these principles are followed throughout the research process:

1. Respect for persons: We recognize the personal dignity and autonomy of individuals, and we should provide special protection of those persons with diminished autonomy.
2. Beneficence: We have an obligation to protect persons from harm by maximizing anticipated benefits and minimizing possible risks of harm.
3. Justice: The benefits and burdens of research should be distributed fairly.

ETHICAL COMPLAINTS

Malpractice claims are legal actions taken against a therapist for acts that are believed to fall below the appropriate standard of care and cause injury to a client or clients. Consumers can file an ethical complaint with a therapist's national professional organization, the state licensing board, or state attorney general. Depending on their veracity, not all complaints result in formal investigations or disciplinary proceedings. If an AAMFT clinical member violates the AAMFT *Code of Ethics* (2015), a consumer may file a complaint with the AAMFT. The AAMFT has a specific decision tree that is followed for every ethical complaint filed. The process for filing, investigating, and resolving complaints of unethical conduct is described on the AAMFT website (www.aamft.org). Therapists accused are considered innocent by the Ethics Committee until proven guilty, except as otherwise provided, and are entitled to due process. If an AAMFT member resigns in anticipation of, or during the course of, an ethics investigation, the Ethics Committee will complete its investigation. Any publication of action taken by the AAMFT will include the fact that the member attempted to resign during the investigation.

CONCLUSION

All therapists have legal and ethical responsibilities to maintain high levels of professional competence. The ethical code of professional organizations like the AAMFT defines standards of conduct for members of the profession, offers guidance in identifying clinical situations in which the therapist must make ethical decisions, and offers principles on which to base those decisions. Balancing the rights and well-being of individuals with the family as a whole is one of the most challenging aspects of ethical practice in MFT. Difficult ethical questions confronted in individual therapy become even more complicated when a number of family members are seen together because in some instances an intervention that serves one member of the system's best interests could burden another family member or even be countertherapeutic. Ethical practice demands that all family therapists avoid becoming advocates of any one family member, believing that all system members contribute to the problems of the whole family.

KEY TERMS

Abandonment: A practitioner's unilateral discontinuation of needed services to a client without reasonable notice. Also refers to discontinuation without provision for or referral to adequate treatment.

Abuse: Nonaccidental infliction of physical harm, continual psychological damage, or denial of emotional needs (neglect).

Affidavit: A voluntary statement of facts or a voluntary declaration in writing that an individual affirms or swears to be true before an official authorized to administer an oath.

Appropriate standard of care: How most professionals would treat a case under similar circumstances.

Aspirational ethics: Ethical values and principles that greatly exceed minimal, prescribed ethical values and principles, which are referred to as *mandatory ethics*.

Assent: The process of consulting with and informing a client regarding their preferences about actions to be taken by the practitioner. This process fulfills the practitioner's ethical obligations to the client with regard to informed consent.

Asynchronous: Communication that is not synchronized or that occurs simultaneously.

Autonomy: The ethical value and principle of taking responsibility for one's own behavior and self-direction; freedom to choose without interfering with others' freedom. In psychotherapy, it refers to the right of clients to determine their own thoughts, actions, and futures, and to regulate their own behavior.

Bartering: The practice of accepting goods, services, or other nonmonetary remuneration from clients in return for clinical services.

Beneficence: The ethical value and principle that guides actions consistent with contributing to the well-being of others. This value implies doing good for others.

Boundary violations: Exploitive or harmful practices in psychotherapy that occur when therapists cross standards of professional behavior for their own sexual, emotional, or financial gain.

Capacity: Refers to the ability to make a rational decision or give informed consent.

Certification: A voluntary means of identifying oneself as a trained and qualified specialist that usually requires meeting national standards of expertise beyond those required for state licensure.

Confidentiality: The ethical obligation of therapists to keep communications with clients strictly private, and not privy to any outside parties.

Conflict of interest: Conflict between loyalties or duties to a client possibly resulting from inhabiting multiple roles with a single client. Arises when a therapist has competing interests that interfere with faithfully exercising their professional judgment and skill in working with clients. Also can arise when the supervisor has competing interests that may interfere with the supervisor's duty to faithfully exercise professional judgment in working with the supervisee.

Custody: Refers to the rights and responsibilities of parents with regard to their children. Legal custody involves the right and responsibility of the parent to make decisions about the child's life, whereas physical custody is the right and responsibility of the parent to reside with the child and provide for the child's immediate well-being (clothes, shelter, food).

Dual relationship: A relationship between a therapist and a client that is not built on mutuality and may be unethical because the counselor assumes a second role with the client in addition to that of treating clinician. Whenever possible, dual relationships should be avoided. The reason for this is that even if a dual relationship seems harmless, a conflict of interest frequently exists, and a professional counselor's judgment may be negatively affected because of a loss of objectivity. Also, clients may be placed in situations in which they cannot be assertive and take care of themselves.

Duty to protect: Refers to the responsibility of the therapist to inform the intended victim(s) if a client threatens to harm a person or group of persons.

Duty to report: Refers to the duty to report abuse or suspected abuse of children, the older, and in some states, the disabled, in a timely manner. Typically, practitioners are expected to meet this duty although different jurisdictions specify other professionals who are also required to meet it. Also called *mandatory reporting*.

Duty to warn: A duty or legal responsibility, based on the special relationship of a practitioner and client to inform an endangered party or parties when it is believed that a client poses a serious danger to them. This creates an exception to the rule of confidentiality and is often referred to as the *Tarasoff duty*.

Electronic communication: Using web-based platforms, cell phones, email, texting, online social networking, video, or other digital methods and technology to send and receive messages, or to post information so that it can be retrieved by others or used at a later time.

Emancipation: Refers to the process by which a minor achieves legal adult status.

Encryption: A mathematical process that converts text, video, or audio streams into a scrambled, unreadable format when transmitted over the internet.

Fidelity: The ethical virtue and principle that directs individuals to keep commitments or promises.

Guardian: Person appointed by a court to protect the interests of and make decisions for a person who is incapable of making their own decisions.

Guardian ad litem: Literally means *guardian for the litigation*; refers to a legal representative, usually an attorney, appointed by a judge to represent the interests of an individual who is a minor or is legally incompetent.

Ethics: The study of what constitutes good and bad human conduct, including related actions and values.

HIPAA compliant: HIPAA (the Health Insurance Portability and Accountability Act) sets the standard for protecting sensitive patient data. Any company that deals with protected health information (PHI) must ensure that all the required physical, network, and process security measures are in place and followed. This includes covered entities (CE), anyone who provides treatment, payment, and operations in healthcare, and business associates (BA), anyone with access to patient information and provides support in treatment, payment, or operations. Subcontractors, or business associates of business associates, must also be in compliance.

Holder of privilege: The individual who is legally empowered to waive or assert a legal privilege against disclosure. Because privilege is the prerogative of the holder, it is important that therapists recognize that the holder of client–therapist privilege is the client.

Incompetence: Refers to the incapacity to perform the function of the therapist role because of insufficient training or experience, unwillingness, or inflexibility.

Informed consent: A document that informs clients about their rights and what to expect during therapeutic treatment.

Institutional review board: A human subjects committee that services an entire institution. Such committees are federally mandated for any organization whose research is federally funded and must include a diverse membership, including a community representative.

Justice: The ethical virtue and principle that fosters fairness and equity and provides equal treatment to all individuals.

Law: A rule that defines the minimum standards society will tolerate that is enforced by the government.

Liability insurance: Refers to a contract in which a client can be compensated for the harm that results from a therapist's negligence in return for premium payments by a therapist.

Licensing board: A government agency empowered to regulate both the issuance of professional licenses as well as the conduct of professionals having such a license.

Licensure: This term refers to a state statute that prohibits the practice of a profession without a license from the state.

Malfeasance: Commission of an unlawful or improper act.

Malpractice: Dereliction of professional duty that causes injury to a client.

Managed care: Provision of healthcare services, including psychotherapy, through medical insurance managed or overseen by a managed care organization that serves as a mediator between insurance carriers and healthcare professionals.

Mandatory reporting law: A law requiring certain professionals to report abuse and neglect to a designated government agency. Such laws take precedence over laws protecting confidentiality, and thus therapists are required to report credible evidence of child abuse.

Maneuverability: Refers to the ability to intervene effectively.

Multiple relationship: Refers to the circumstance of having a professional relationship with a client as well as a personal, business, or intimate type of relationship.

Neglect: Refers to failure to provide necessary food, care, clothing, supervision, emotional support or medical attention for a child, the disabled, and the elder.

Negligence: Refers to an act that directly causes damage to a client. It is the omission or commission of an act that a reasonable therapist would or would not do under given circumstances, and a form of carelessness that constitutes a departure from the standard of care expected of mental health professionals.

No-fault divorce: Refers to grounds for divorce based on relationship incompatibilities and irreconcilable differences, instead of the wrongdoing of a partner. Advocates the avoidance of fault finding to reduce prolonged litigation and the bitterness of divorce.

Nonmaleficence: The ethical value and principle requiring that individuals refrain from any action that might cause harm to another.

Portability: The ability of therapists licensed in one state to move to another state and have their licensing credentials accepted.

Privilege: Refers to the legal right to privacy owned by the client, typically regulated by state statute.

Professional codes of ethics: Written codes of conduct set by professional organizations stating acceptable and unacceptable behaviors and standards for the discipline.

Professional disclosure statement: A written statement that introduces clients to the therapist's qualifications, the nature of the therapeutic process, and other important issues entailed in marital and family therapy.

Progress notes: Notes written by a therapist that document a client's progress, provide a record of events and interventions taken, and that may serve as a means of communication among professionals working with the same client. Usually either problem oriented, focused on progress made in addressing the problem, or goal-oriented, focused on progress made in reaching the treatment goal.

Protected health information: Any information related to the client's condition or health status kept private by law.

Reasonable care: Refers to the level of care that a reasonable person would provide in executing professional services.

Scope of competence: Refers to the range of professional activities of an individual practitioner determined by one's education, training and experience.

Scope of practice: Refers to the services that a qualified professional is deemed competent to perform and permitted to provide within the scope of their professional license.

Secret policies: A written or verbal agreement with marital or family therapy clients indicating how information will be handled in therapy with respect to information shared individually with the therapist (separate from the other member of the couple or the other members of the family).

Social media/social networking: Refers to web-based communication tools that enable people to interact with each other by both sharing and consuming information.

Sole custody: Refers to the right to make decisions and to have physical custody of a child. Being a sole custodian does not mean having sole responsibility. Sole custodians usually receive child support.

Subpoena: A legal document requiring the recipient to appear at a legal proceeding and/or to provide specific information or documents. Disregarding it may result in being held "in contempt of court" and subject to a punishment.

Subpoena duces tecum: A legal document that requires the recipient to appear at a deposition or in court at a specified time, place, and date with a specific set of records that are specifically requested in the subpoena.

Synchronous: Refers to communication that occurs simultaneously in real time.

Tarasoff doctrine: The legal duty, based on the *Tarasoff v. Regents of the University of California* ruling that indicates mental health practitioners must warn and protect identifiable victims of the danger posed to them by a client of the mental health practitioner if such a danger is reasonably foreseeable and imminent.

Telesupervision: Refers to the practice of supervision by a licensed (teletherapy) supervisor through synchronous or asynchronous two-way electronic communication, including but not limited to telephone, videoconferencing, email, text, instant messaging, and social media, for the purposes of developing trainee marital and family therapists, evaluating supervisee performance, ensuring rigorous legal and ethical standards within the bounds of licensure, and as a means for improving the profession of marital and family therapy.

Teletherapy/Technology-assisted services: Refers to the scope of marriage and family therapy practice of diagnosis, evaluation, consultation, intervention, and treatment of behavioral, social, and interpersonal disorders through synchronous or asynchronous two-way electronic communication, including but not limited to telephone, videoconferencing, email, text, instant messaging, and social media.

Therapeutic contract: A client–therapist agreement that usually outlines intended treatment, payment terms, and exceptions to confidentiality. This becomes effective when the agreement is signed or an understanding is reached, usually during the first session.

Umbrella rule: Legal concept permitting all professionals employed in a mental health agency to have some access to confidential client information while imposing confidentiality obligations on all such access. It is the basis on which secretaries and administrators of such agencies can work with files irrespective of whether they are trained practitioners.

Veracity: Refers to an ethical principle regarding truthfulness and integrity.

Verification: Refer to measures taken to verify both therapist and client identities online.

Virtual relationship: A relationship in which people are not physically present but communicate using online, texting, or other electronic communication devices.

KNOWLEDGE CHECK: CHAPTER 16

1. A __________is unlikely to face any kind of punishment brought about by a violation of the American Association of Marriage and Family Therapists' (AAMFT) *Code of Ethics*.

   A. Student
   B. Client
   C. Professor
   D. Therapist

2. A(n)______________ law regulates who may practice in a state.

   A. Credentialing
   B. Certification
   C. Licensing
   D. Accreditation

3. Therapist ________ is not sufficient reason for bringing forth a malpractice lawsuit.

   A. Ineptitude
   B. Carelessness
   C. Negligence
   D. Scheduling error

4. Protecting a client from unauthorized disclosures by the therapist without prior consent is part of ________.

   A. Information disclosure
   B. Communication privileges
   C. Right to silence
   D. Confidentiality

5. In couple therapy, _______ "owns" the right to waive privilege regarding information obtained during a conjoint session.

   A. The therapist
   B. The husband or the wife
   C. The couple
   D. The court

6. Continuing-education credits (CE credits) earned through an American Association of Marriage and Family Therapists (AAMFT) approved sponsor means that the program is _________.

   A. Sanctioned by AAMFT
   B. Endorsed by AAMFT
   C. Approved by AAMFT
   D. The responsibility of the sponsor

(*See answers next page.*)

1. B) Client

An ethical complaint can be made by a client, but can never be made against a client. Options A, C, and D are all viable targets against whom to file an ethic complaint.

2. C) Licensing

Licensing is the formal recognition by a regulatory agency or body that a person has passed all the qualifications necessary to practice that profession in that state. Typically, licensure requirements include some combination of education, training, and examination to demonstrate competency. The goal of licensure is to ensure that the licensees have the minimal degree of competency necessary to ensure that public health, safety, and/or welfare are protected. Typically, they are granted at the state level; if the individual works in multiple jurisdictions, then they must be licensed in each jurisdiction. Credentialing is a formal process that uses an established series of guidelines to ensure that clients receive the highest level of care from healthcare professionals who have undergone the most stringent scrutiny regarding their ability to practice (A). Accreditation is a public service that aims to improve the quality of educational programs in marriage and family therapy (MFT) and encourage programs' ongoing self-evaluation, development, and improvement (D). Certification is the formal attestation or confirmation of certain characteristics of an object, person, or organization (B). Often, but not always, confirmation is provided by some form of external review, education, assessment, or audit.

3. D) Scheduling error

Scheduling error is merely a therapist mistake, whereas options A, B, and C are all legitimate grounds for bringing forth a malpractice lawsuit.

4. D) Confidentiality

Client confidentiality is the requirement that therapists protect their client's privacy by not revealing the contents of therapy. Options A, B, and C are not proper legal ethical terms.

5. C) The couple

The psychotherapist–client privilege applies not only to individuals participating in one-on-one therapy, but also to groups of individuals participating in couple and family therapy. This means that when there is more than one client participating in therapy, the privilege applies to all clients involved in the therapy. Absent a court order, only the client can waive the privilege. A client has the privilege of refusing to disclose, as well as preventing others participating in the therapy sessions from disclosing, privileged information.

6. D) The responsibility of the sponsor

An organization gains the approval of the AAMFT to sponsor continuing-education programs. The sponsor then becomes responsible for each program. The specific program is not endorsed, sanctioned, or approved by the AAMFT. Only the overall sponsorship is approved by the AAMFT.

7. The American Association of Marriage and Family Therapists (AAMFT) Ethics Committee contacts you about a complaint filed against you by a client. The committee asks for your records related to the client's therapy with you. You should:

A. Cooperate fully with the committee's request
B. Contact the client and obtain a release of information before cooperating
C. Contact the client and attempt to settle the matter informally
D. Request mediation services

8. You share an office with another family therapist. One morning, you arrive early to find your partner having sex with one of her current clients. You should__________.

A. Discuss the matter with your partner later
B. Report the partner to the ethics committee
C. Discuss the matter with the client and explain the option to take action against the therapist
D. Discuss the matter with the client and attempt to get them to sign a release of information so you can pursue a complaint against the therapist, even if the client decides not to

9. A family therapist who has been having marital problems in his personal life notices that during couple therapy with several of his clients, he is tending to agree more with the husband's perspective. He should __________.

A. Explain to his clients the reasons for his countertransference
B. Seek consultation
C. Refer his couple therapy clients to another therapist until he works through his issues
D. Keep doing therapy as usual, as this process is normal and is only occurring in a few of his cases

10. The purpose of state licensing boards is primarily to _________.

A. Educate the public
B. Educate the profession
C. Protect the public
D. Set minimum standards of practice

11. The Health Insurance Portability and Accountability Act (HIPAA) of 1996 applies to _________.

A. All healthcare providers
B. Only healthcare providers who transmit patient information by fax and the internet
C. Only healthcare providers who employ someone, such as billing services, with access to patient information
D. Only healthcare providers who transmit patient information electronically

(*See answers next page.*)

7. A) Cooperate fully with the committee's request

If contacted by an ethics committee in response to a complaint from a client, you must cooperate fully. Confidentiality is not an issue because the committee must obtain a signed waiver of confidentiality from the complainant before it takes any action.

8. B) Report the partner to the ethics committee

Usually, when you know or suspect that a colleague has committed an ethical violation, you attempt to resolve the matter informally by bringing it to his attention. However, if the violation is not amenable to informal resolution, as in this case, you must take further action, such as filing a report to an ethics committee. Of course, you should protect the confidentiality rights of the client, therefore, in your complaint, you would not provide identifying information about the client.

9. B) Seek consultation

Therapists who become aware of personal problems that may interfere with performance in their work should take appropriate measures. In this case, the most appropriate measure would be to seek consultation. Through consultation the therapist may be able to resolve his countertransference issue or be better able to decide what further action to take, for example, suspending work with certain types of clients.

10. C) Protect the public

The state boards derive their authority from the principle of protecting the public. That is the justification for giving examinations, setting requirements for licensure, writing and enforcing regulations, and so on.

11. D) Only healthcare providers who transmit patient information electronically

HIPAA does not apply to all healthcare providers. It only applies to "covered entities"—health plans, healthcare clearinghouses and healthcare providers—who transmit health information electronically. A provider who only communicates information by mail, phone, or fax is not a covered entity. Transmitting information electronically refers to use of the internet and includes receiving health information as well as transmitting information. For example, a provider is a covered entity even if they never transmit information but receive information, such as a description of benefits email, via the Internet. In addition, a provider employing someone who sends or receives patient information on the provider's behalf via the internet is also a covered entity.

12. A 14-year-old girl tells her therapist that she wants to kill herself and that she's been thinking of using her mother's prescription pain pills to overdose. The therapist then tells the client that he will have to tell her parents about her suicide risk. The girl becomes enraged and says that she would not have disclosed the information if she knew that the therapist would tell her parents. The therapist should ___________.

A. Agree not to tell the parents if the girl agrees to a no-harm contract
B. Agree not to tell the parents, but tell them without the girl's knowledge
C. Tell the parents and refer the girl to another therapist because she will probably not be able to trust the therapist again
D. Tell the parents and apologize to the girl for having to do so as part of a therapist's ethical duty and mandated-reporter status

13. Therapists who become sexually involved with their clients ___________.

A. Usually do so because they believe they are in love with the client as a result of the client's unique and desirable characteristics
B. Usually do so as a result of a lack of experience and poor judgment
C. Usually do so to fulfill personal needs resulting from events in their own life
D. Do not show any characteristics that distinguish them from therapists who do not become sexually involved with their clients

14. A marriage and family therapy (MFT) professor is dating a graduate student in his class. Although the student is the same age as the professor and this relationship has not been a distraction to the learning environment or the rest of the cohort, the professor's behavior is _____________.

A. Unethical only if he is engaging in a sexual relationship with the student
B. Unethical regardless of whether he is engaging in a sexual relationship with the student
C. Ethical because there appears to be little potential for harm
D. Ethical as long as it does not violate any university regulations

15. A client tells you that he is planning to shoot his ex-girlfriend. You know that he owns a gun and has a history of violent behavior. You should ___________.

A. Attempt to get him to change his mind
B. Warn the police and attempt to warn the ex-girlfriend
C. Be sure that you maintain the confidentiality of this disclosure
D. Collaborate on a "no violence" contract

(*See answers next page.*)

12. D) Tell the parents and apologize to the girl for having to do so as part of a therapist's ethical duty and mandated-reporter status

According to both ethics and law, a therapist may disclose confidential information without the client's consent to protect the client from harm. This applies to minors and adults alike. In this case, it would most likely be appropriate to inform the girl's parents about her suicide risk. The reasons for this should be explained to the girl and the therapist should apologize for the breach of confidentiality. Given the apparent level of risk involved, it would probably not be sufficient to rely on a no-harm contract (A). It would certainly be inappropriate and countertherapeutic to lie to the client (B). And it may not be necessary to refer the client (C). If handled empathically, it is likely that the girl will come to understand the therapist's reasons for disclosing to the parents and may come to appreciate that her safety was the overriding concern.

13. C) Usually do so to fulfill personal needs resulting from events in their own life

The experts generally agree that therapists who have sexual relationships with their clients are not only exhibiting poor judgment but are also usually suffering from some type of impairment, often related to boundary issues or unfulfilled needs.

14. B) Unethical regardless of whether he is engaging in a sexual relationship with the student

The MFT professor is engaging in a dual relationship with clear potential for harm or exploitation. For instance, the professor's grading of the student may be influenced by his relationship with her. For this reason, his behavior is unethical.

15. B) Warn the police and attempt to warn the ex-girlfriend

In this situation, your client poses a clear and imminent danger of physical violence to an identifiable victim. Regardless of the specific laws in your state, you have a valid reason to breach confidentiality in this case, and warning the police and attempting to warn the victim would be the best way to meet the "duty to protect."

AUDIO PODCAST 16.1
Ethical and Legal Overview
Eli A. Karam
https://bcove.video/3pM9Bgn

AUDIO PODCAST 16.2
Steps in Ethical Decision-Making
Eli A. Karam
https://bcove.video/3ARIWF6

AUDIO PODCAST 16.3
Informed Consent and Confidentiality
Eli A. Karam
https://bcove.video/3KnN039

AUDIO PODCAST 16.4
No Secrets Policy
Eli A. Karam
https://bcove.video/3PNM35e

REFERENCES

American Association for Marriage and Family Therapy. (2001). *Code of ethics*. AAMFT.

American Association for Marriage and Family Therapy. (2015). *Code of ethics*. AAMFT.

American Association for Marriage and Family Therapy. (2017). *Best practices in the online practice of couple and family therapy*. AAMFT.

Association of Marital & Family Therapy Regulatory Boards. (2016). *Teletherapy guidelines*. AAMFT.

Barnett, J. E. (2019). The ethical practice of psychotherapy: Clearly within our reach. *Psychotherapy*, *56*(4), 431–440. https://doi.org/10.1037/pst0000272

Blumer, M. L., Hertlein, K. M., & VandenBosch, M. L. (2015). Towards the development of educational core competencies for couple and family therapy technology practices. *Contemporary Family Therapy*, *37*(2), 113–121. https://doi.org/10.1007/s10591-015-9330-1

Hecker, L (Ed.). (2010). *Ethics and professional issues in couple and family therapy*. Brunner-Routledge.

Hecker, L. L., & Edwards, A. B. (2014). The impact of HIPAA and HITECH: New standards for confidentiality, security & documentation for marriage and family therapists. *American Journal of Family Therapy*, *42*(2), 95–113.

Hudgins, C., Rose, S., Fifield, P. Y., & Arnault, S. (2013). Navigating the legal and ethical foundations of informed consent and confidentiality in integrated primary care. *Family, Systems, & Health*, *31*(1), 9–19. https://doi.org/10.1037/a0031974

Stone, A. A. (1976). The Tarasoff decisions: Suing psychotherapists to safeguard society. *Harvard Law Review*, *90*, 358–378.

Youngren, J. N., & Harris, E. A. (2008). Can you keep a secret? Confidentiality in psychotherapy. *Journal of Clinical Psychology*, *64*(5), 589–600. https://doi.org/10.1002/jclp.20480

PART VII

The Mock Exam

Test-Taking Strategies

17

LEARNING OBJECTIVES

After reading this chapter, you should be able to:

1. Summarize the different types and structure of multiple-choice items on the Association of Marital and Family Therapy Regulatory Boards (AMFTRB) Marital and Family Therapy National Examination
2. Select new test-taking strategies for the AMFTRB examination
3. Review appropriate study time increments to prepare for the AMFTRB examination
4. Use specific test strategies when taking the marriage and family therapy (MFT) practice examination
5. Identify examination questions based on AMFTRB examination domains

INTRODUCTION

What type of standardized test taker are you? People taking tests like the AMFTRB examination often report that they know more than their examination results indicate. Under the pressure of an exam; however, you may choose answers that are a product of guessing rather than of confidence in decision-making. Lack of confidence is often the result of inadequate test preparation or anxiety. Therapists studying for the examination always want to know the best techniques that will assist them in answering questions correctly. First and foremost, you will need to make sure that you are well versed in the exam content reviewed in this text in order to pass the test. Although nothing is a substitute for content knowledge, understanding and applying the following test-taking strategies may also help you succeed on the examination.

THE MULTIPLE-CHOICE ITEM

A multiple-choice question is an objective test item. It is objective because the perceptions or opinions of another person do not influence the correct response. Multiple-choice questions on the AMFTRB examination have four potential answers with only one correct response. The entire multiple-choice question is called an *item*. Each item consists of two parts—the stem and options.

THE STEM

The stem is the initial part of a multiple-choice item designed to present a problem in a clear and concise manner. The stem should contain all the details necessary to answer the question. The stem of an item can be a complete sentence that asks a question. It also can be presented as an incomplete sentence that becomes a complete sentence when it is combined with one of the options of the item. In addition to sentence structure, a characteristic of a stem that must be considered is its polarity. The polarity of the stem can be formulated in either a positive or negative context. A stem with a positive polarity asks the question in relation to what is true, whereas a stem with negative polarity asks the question in relation to what is false. Sometimes stem questions are phrased as clinical situations or vignettes. In these vignette items as seen on the AMFTRB examination, the stems of the questions may be as long as a paragraph and could contain a lot of information that you must analyze before you can choose an answer.

THE OPTIONS

All of the possible answers offered within an item are called *options*. The option that is the best response is the correct answer. The other options are incorrect and keep you from selecting the correct answer. Incorrect options are called *distractors*. Distractors present a challenge to the test takers, forcing them to be very careful in their selections. The typical number of options is four responses, and that reduces the probability of guessing the correct answer while limiting the amount of reading to a sensible level. Options usually are listed by number (1, 2, 3, and 4), lowercase letters (a, b, c, and d), or uppercase letters (A, B, C, and D). An option can be a sentence, can complete the sentence begun in the stem, can be an incomplete sentence, or can be a single word.

IDENTIFY OPPOSITES IN OPTIONS

Sometimes an item contains two options that are the opposite of each other. They can be single words that reflect extremes on a continuum, or they can be statements that convey converse messages. When opposites appear in the options, they must be given serious consideration. One of them will be the correct answer, or they both can be eliminated from consideration. When one of the opposites is the correct answer, you are being asked to differentiate between two responses that incorporate extremes of a concept or principle. When options are opposites, more often than not, but not always, one of them is the correct answer.

IDENTIFY EQUALLY PLAUSIBLE OR UNIQUE OPTIONS

Sometimes items contain two or more options that are similar. It is difficult to choose between two similar options because they are comparable. One option is no better or worse than the other option in relation to the statement presented in the stem. When analyzing options, use the "if → then" technique. Ask yourself, "If I perform this intervention in the option, then what will be the outcome?" In equally plausible options the outcomes frequently are the same or similar. Usually, equally plausible options are distractors and can be eliminated from consideration.

QUESTION TYPES

KNOWLEDGE QUESTIONS

Knowledge questions require you to recall or remember information. To answer a knowledge question, you need to commit facts to memory. Knowledge questions expect you to know terminology, specific facts, trends, classifications, categories, criteria, structures, principles, generalizations, and theories. This basic information is the foundation for thinking critically.

COMPREHENSION QUESTIONS

Comprehension questions require you to understand information. To answer a comprehension question, you must commit facts to memory as well as translate, interpret, and determine the implications of that information. You demonstrate understanding when you translate or paraphrase information; interpret or summarize information; or determine the implications, consequences, corollaries, or effects of information. Comprehension questions expect you to know and understand the information being tested. After you understand basic information, you can identify the significance of data, which is an initial step in critical thinking. The difference between knowledge questions and comprehension questions is that you must know facts to answer knowledge questions, but you must understand the significance of the facts to answer comprehension questions.

APPLICATION QUESTIONS

The application of information demonstrates a higher level of understanding than just knowing or comprehending information because it requires the learner to show, solve, modify, change, use, or manipulate information in a real situation or presented scenario. To answer an application question, you must apply concepts you learned previously to a specific situation. The concepts may be theories, technical principles, rules, procedures, generalizations, or ideas that have to be applied in a presented scenario. Application questions test your ability to use information. The making of rational and reflective judgments, which are part of the critical-thinking process, results in a course of action.

ANALYSIS QUESTIONS

Analysis questions require you to interpret a variety of data and recognize the commonalities, differences, and interrelationships among presented ideas. To answer an analysis question, you must identify, examine, dissect, evaluate, or investigate the organization or structure of the information presented in the question. Analysis questions make the assumption that you know, understand, and can apply information. They then require an ability to examine information, which is a higher thought process than knowing, understanding, or applying information. To study for complex questions, you cannot just memorize and understand facts or identify the commonalities among facts; you must learn to discriminate. Analysis questions often require you to use differentiation to determine the significance of information.

IDENTIFYING AND UNDERSTANDING THE KNOWLEDGE DOMAINS

DOMAIN 1—THE PRACTICE OF SYSTEMIC THERAPY

Domain 1 focuses on knowledge questions surrounding key ideas, terms, and definitions related to general systems theory, cybernetics, and the foundations of the MFT profession (AMFTRB, 2022). For the most part, these questions will primarily be straight-forward knowledge questions that emphasize systemic thinking.

After three sessions, a teenager has stopped smoking marijuana because he is not allowed to drive without a clean drug test. The parents are happy and feel like therapy is no longer necessary since their son has changed his ways. At the conclusion of the session, the teen whispers to the therapist that he plans to go back to smoking after his dad returns the car keys.

The therapist notes that although the family has changed, the change is superficial and has no effect on the fundamental organization of the system. This type of change is referred to as:

A. First order
B. Second order
C. Detouring
D. Accommodation

The correct answer is A. Your basic objective in this Domain 1 question was to know the difference between first-order and second-order change. The question illustrates first-order, or superficial, change.

Option B: There is second-order change when the basic changes made to the structure and functioning of a family system actually alter its fundamental organization: the family's pattern of symptomatic interaction is so fundamentally disrupted that it then ceases.

Option C: This has nothing to do with change. It is a structural family therapy term that refers to conflict between two spouses that is redirected to their child.

Option D: A family therapist would define *accommodation* as a joining technique in which a therapist adjusts to input from a family in order to strengthen the basis from which they can push for change.

DOMAIN 2—ASSESSING, HYPOTHESIZING, AND DIAGNOSING

This domain focuses on how we categorize and make meaning from everything that is reported and observed in the systemic assessment phase of therapy (AMFTRB, 2022). Many of these questions originate from what a systemic therapist would ask in an initial session or intake interview. *Diagnostic and Statistical Manual of Mental Disorders* (5th ed.; *DSM-5*; American Psychiatric Association, 2013) questions, usually in the form of vignettes, abound in this domain.

Janice is a 33-year-old woman who describes herself as being in a major "funk" for the past 4 weeks. She is recently divorced and has gained nearly 30 pounds in the last year since losing her job. Which of the following symptoms would MOST clearly indicate a diagnosis of Major Depressive Disorder for this woman?

A. Sleeplessness, difficulty concentrating, and loss of appetite
B. Loss of interest in normal activities, agitation, and feelings of worthlessness
C. Loss of appetite, agitation, and feelings of worthlessness
D. Weight loss, difficulty concentrating and indecisiveness, and hypersomnia

The correct answer is B. None of the symptoms listed in the answers definitively indicate a major depressive episode, which requires the presence five or more characteristic symptoms for at least 2 weeks. However, the *DSM-5* requires that at least one of the five symptoms must be depressed mood or loss of interest in most or all activities. Of the answers given, only option B includes one of these symptoms and, therefore, is the best answer.

Options A, C, and D do not include depressed mood or loss of interest in most or all activities.

DOMAIN 3—DESIGNING AND CONDUCTING TREATMENT

Domain 3 covers both the establishment of treatment goals and the actual "doing" of family therapy, with questions focusing on how a therapist would conduct treatment depending on the given model or theoretical orientation. Here we see the intervention component of therapy come through in the questions (AMFTRB, 2022).

Aaron and Trish present to couples therapy for an initial session because Trish thinks that Aaron has been working too much lately, and she needs help at home with her two small children. Aaron contends that when he is home, Trish ignores him and appears distant and disconnected. Trish is too tired to interact with him and seems disengaged during the session. You notice dark circles under her eyes, and she appears very thin. When you begin asking her questions, you hear a flat affect in her voice. Regarding your treatment plan:

A. You need to consider individual therapy for Trish now and postpone the couples therapy until later
B. You need to consider talking with Trish's doctor to find out what they have noticed
C. After further assessment, you might want to include appropriate referrals in the early stage of treatment for Trish to determine her physical status, while continuing doing couples therapy
D. You would want to refer Trish for individual therapy and see Aaron and Trish for couples therapy

The correct answer is C. There's enough information in the question to determine that further assessment of Trish is necessary. This is the most appropriate plan of action in terms of treatment planning.

Option A: Trish's physical state needs to be properly assessed before considering individual therapy.

Option B: Although Trish's doctor may be the most recent physician she has seen, further assessment needs to be done to determine the most appropriate referral for Trish.

Option D: Again, further assessment is needed before you can determine the treatment plan.

DOMAIN 4—EVALUATING ONGOING PROCESS AND TERMINATING TREATMENT

Domain 4 explores the mid- to late phases of therapy, including the process and protocols of moving a family system through termination. Beyond just looking at therapy process, this domain looks at measuring client progress and feedback. It expands the lens to include evidence-based practice as well (AMFTRB, 2022).

What is NOT a good reason to terminate therapy?

A. The therapist is unable or unwilling, for appropriate reasons, to continue to provide care
B. The client fails to make adequate progress toward therapy goals
C. When the therapist feels that the relationship with the client is too demanding and overwhelming
D. A conflict of interest is identified after treatment begins

The correct answer is C. It is inappropriate to terminate a client because the therapist feels overwhelmed by the demanding nature of the child. What this situation calls for is consultation to explore why the therapist feels overwhelmed, and how these feelings intersect with the client's issues and patterns in relationships.

Option A: Although there are occasionally appropriate reasons to discontinue care, the therapist should attempt to provide the client with resources and referrals for care elsewhere.

Option B: If a client is not making adequate progress toward therapy goals, it may be time to consider termination or refer them elsewhere.

Option D: This is an acceptable reason to terminate therapy.

DOMAIN 5—MANAGING CRISIS SITUATIONS

These questions are easy to identify as they are mostly vignette based and center around suicidality, homicidality, domestic violence, as well as child and older abuse. These questions may also focus on your legal responsibilities as a mandated reporter and holder of confidentiality, addressing when or when not to include third parties into the system (AMFTRB, 2022).

Michael, a 24-year-old client with a previous history of suicidal ideation and major depressive episodes leaves a voicemail for his therapist, thanking her for everything that she has done and stating that "it's time to end it." and that "this was inevitable." The therapist calls Michael's home and his mother doesn't know his whereabouts, remarking she hasn't seen him in almost 12 hours. There is no release of information allowing the therapist to talk to Michael's mom. What does the law permit in this situation?

A. The law does not permit the therapist to speak to the mother other than to ask whether she knows where Michael is
B. The therapist's duty to protect mandates that she warn the mother and to call the police regarding Michael's threat
C. The therapist is not allowed to breach confidentiality in this situation
D. The therapist may speak to the mother about her concerns about Michael's welfare

The correct answer is D. In an emergency or other situation, family therapists are allowed to contact significant others who are involved in or important to client care, even if no release of information is signed.

Option A: The therapist is allowed to speak to Michael's mom about her concerns for the son because this is an emergency situation.

Option B: This answer appears to resemble "duty to warn" if there is a reasonably identifiable victim being threatened. The therapist could call the police if she thought that they might aid in locating Michael, but the mother is not being threatened in this scenario.

Option C: This is untrue.

DOMAIN 6—MAINTAINING ETHICAL, LEGAL, AND PROFESSIONAL STANDARDS

Domain 6 questions center around ethical decision-making, using the American Association of Marriage and Family Therapists' (AAMFT) *Code of Ethics* (2015) and AAMFT's *Best Practices in the Online Practice of Couple and Family Therapy* (2017) as prime resources. These questions are primarily vignette based, with some straightforward items added into the mix of this domain (AMFTRB, 2022).

Ethical standards would suggest that when a life situation/personal issue makes it impossible for a therapist to continue working with a client, the therapist should ____________.

A. Refer the client to an associate or colleague
B. Refer the client to other therapists who are members of the AAMFT

C. Do termination work with the client in whatever time remains
D. Consider the client's needs and make the most reasonable arrangements for the continuation of treatment with an appropriate professional

The correct answer is D. Only one of these answers is complete, so it is important to read every answer before choosing one. One clue to the best answer was in the words *consider the client's needs*. This is the best answer because it properly identifies a marriage and family therapist's ethical obligation to arrange for alternative services in this circumstance. The AAMFT *Code of Ethics* (2015) states that marriage and family therapists do not abandon or neglect patients in treatment without making reasonable arrangements for the continuation of such treatment (Standard 1.11). Referral is directly mentioned in this answer, and doing the proper termination work is implied by the words *consider the client's needs*.

Option A: Although referral is appropriate, this option is not as complete as the correct answer, and referral doesn't have to be made to an associate or colleague.

Option B: Although referral is appropriate, this is not a complete answer and the therapist does not have to refer to an AAMFT clinical member.

Option C: Although doing termination work is appropriate in this scenario, this response does not mention making a referral.

ADDITIONAL TEST-TAKING STRATEGIES

Use test-taking techniques for every question in conjunction with your knowledge base. When you select an answer based on your knowledge, have confidence in your answer. However, the use of the following test-taking strategies becomes more important when you are unsure of the answer because each distractor that you are able to eliminate will increase your chances of selecting the correct answer.

KNOW (BUT DON'T OBSESS OVER) THE KNOWLEDGE AREAS

This is an examination to assess knowledge of MFT content, so you will need to make sure that you can describe an overview of the key concepts and terms related to each of the of the AMFTRB's knowledge areas (AMFTRB, 2022). Given that the difference between passing and failing the examination almost always is a result of gaps in knowledge, you need to focus the majority of your studying on filling in knowledge gaps or refreshing information previously learned in your training. Although the content is important, you can never fully know everything that will be covered on the examination. Not unlike other standardized examinations that you have taken previously in your academic career, like the Scholastic Aptitude Test (SAT) or Graduate Record Examination (GRE), you cannot judge readiness as knowing everything about the content areas. Remember, the AMFTRB doesn't intend for its for test takers to "know it all" in order to pass. Consistent with others who have passed this examination prior to you, it is completely normal to enter test day without feeling totally ready.

PICK YOUR REVIEW SOURCES WISELY

You need to limit your study materials to this text or other key resources that summarize material, like a family therapy textbook that you used in graduate school. There will be topics that you are asked to know about corresponding to each AMFTRB knowledge area that you may not have previously been exposed to in your graduate program. Our review guide has been designed to provide important information on these areas all in one convenient place. It is challenging enough to digest all of this material; one need not lose time procuring additional outside materials. Remember, you should only seek out additional resources if something in this text is unclear or you feel that you need more than the information included.

BE CAREFUL WITH SAMPLE QUESTIONS AND PRACTICE EXAMINATIONS

Although students like to study from sample test questions (and we have spent much time and effort constructing representative questions of what you are likely to encounter on the actual examination), this is not a complete strategy. Your answers to sample questions provided in these pages may inappropriately influence your decisions on the actual examination when asked about similar topics. For example, you may see an answer that is similar to one that was correct or incorrect on a sample item and you will be more apt or less apt to select it based on this prior experience. Remember, the questions on the "real" AMFTRB National Examination will not be exactly the same as the ones on the practice test, and you must evaluate all four answers independently without any undue bias that may be caused by your practice question experience. Although written by an experienced MFT educator and practitioner, the sample questions that you experience in this text are not going to be on your actual examination, as those items will be constructed by a group of professionals selected by the AMFTRB.

If you have access to sample questions, such as those provided throughout this text, be careful how you digest and process this material. Some of you may be tempted to "sneak a peek" at the answer key with accompanying rationale to see whether you were correct immediately after selecting a response. However, we believe a much better way to use these questions is to pretend that you are taking the actual test—try to simulate actual game conditions and review your responses only after you have completed all items.

After you are done studying the content in the previous chapters (including sample questions at the end of Chapters 2–16) in this book, and think you are ready to take the for our Mock MFT examination, select a 4-hour period during which you can create a quiet environment without interruptions to approximate the actual test-day environment. Answer the questions as you would on the actual examination—using the strategies and having to pick one answer—even if you are not completely sure that it is correct.

STUDY IN TIME INCREMENTS THAT REPLICATE ACTUAL EXAMINATION CONDITIONS

Given that the actual examination is 4 hours long, another strategy is to build up the mental endurance so that you will be able to study and maintain focus for similar amounts of time. Thus, many people find it beneficial to work up to studying in 4-hour blocks of time rather than for a few minutes here and there. Although this may be challenging at the onset, it will be beneficial as test day approaches because you will have the confidence necessary to not lose your concentration and persevere through the examination. With this strategy, if you do not take unnecessary breaks, you will see that you can easily get through 180 questions in the 4 hours allotted. *(This averages out to give you approximately 80 seconds per item if take the entire 4 hours to complete the examination.)* This experience should relieve some of your anxiety about the timed nature of the examination.

DON'T PRIORITIZE MEMORIZATION

Even though we include an extensive glossary in Chapters 2 to 16 and provide a brief overview of model developers to orient you to important terms and figures in MFT, don't turn your precious studying into a memorization exercise of terms and people. The majority of the AMFTRB examination is not designed to test your memory, rather it intends that you choose one of several answers that most directly relates to the topic or is the best option based on your knowledge of the content area. Thus, it is much more important that you understand each of the 70 knowledge areas instead of fixating on memorizing definitions or memorable characters from family therapy's rich history.

EXPLAIN IT IN YOUR OWN WORDS

Often, marriage and family therapists are focused on using model-specific language and other "therapy" jargon that they learned in their training programs without being able to clearly explain in their own words what these concepts and terms actually mean. For practice, try to explain the knowledge areas and classic theories/models to someone who knows little to nothing about MFT and who will ask you lots of questions. This exercise not only helps solidify knowledge acquisition, but also moves you away from the "memorization trap" previously mentioned, while inching you further toward application of the content.

DO IT LIKE THEY DO IT IN THE CLASSROOM, NOT LIKE YOU PERSONALLY DO IT IN THE THERAPY ROOM

The AMFTRB designs this examination to be a test of your knowledge of MFT content. Given that the test questions will be generic and do not take your own professional experience into consideration, you must be careful to avoid biases that emanate from your prior clinical experiences. What we learned in the classroom, in many instances, is not exactly what we would do in the therapy room (Cornille et al., 2003). In fact, the longer we are removed from our graduate school experience, the more our preferred way of working takes precedence over the "textbook" answer that examinations like this one are looking for. Therefore, when selecting an answer, you should base it on the content that you reviewed in the previous chapters and what you learned in the classroom. Asking yourself—"What did I study in this book that relates to this question?" or "Which of the six AMFTRB domains does this question fit in and what do I know about this knowledge area?"—is much more beneficial to you than reflecting on "What would I do in this clinical vignette?" or "How should I handle this situation?" The latter questions tap into your clinical experience and idiosyncratic way of conducting systemic therapy rather than the existing knowledge in a domain that is the basis for selecting the correct answer. Remember, there is only one correct answer for each question. Because everyone has a different therapeutic style, basing your answers on what you personally see or do in the therapy room may lead you to a different response than someone else taking the examination. However, the textbook or existing body of information around the knowledge areas is more consistent, regardless of setting or practice experience.

STAY POSITIVE

Although you may have confidence in your clinical ability as a burgeoning marriage and family therapist, you also may have strong misgivings about an examination that tests something other than therapeutic skill being a major determiner in your professional destiny. You may even have "standardized test PTSD" from an earlier period in your educational history. In addition to earning a master's degree, you have amassed the requisite number of postgraduate clinical and supervision hours—why isn't that enough? Passing the AMFTRB National Examination, however, is a requirement for licensure and seen as a way of determining whether therapists possess the knowledge needed to practice safely and ethically. Just as the ACT and SAT are viewed as yardsticks to measure the ability to perform in college, the AMFTRB examination is seen as a major gauge of essential MFT preparation to successfully practice at various levels. Much like a spouse who predicts failure or has a negative expectation of their significant other, approaching this examination with a poor attitude and resentment about having to take it will handicap you before you even hit "submit" on the first question. Not only is it crucial to approach the examination with a positive attitude, but you should try to visualize it as successfully placing another piece in the professional puzzle that is your therapeutic career. Fit this piece correctly and it will create the path for other pieces to fall into place.

APPLY MFT SKILLS WITHIN THE KNOWLEDGE AREAS

Although there may be some straight recall questions about a knowledge area or a specific family therapy model, it is more likely that many items will be focused on higher level critical thinking skills or on you "applying" information to a specific clinical vignette. In real-life clinical practice, therapists are taught to flexibly modify their therapeutic actions based on many contextual variables impacting the client system. Be careful before you respond; however, as the questions on the examination are about the application of MFT within the knowledge areas. Regardless of the setting in the vignette, you must remember that this knowledge does not change. For example, the core components of responding to a client in a crisis situation (e.g., self-harm/suicidal ideation) are the same no matter what setting the therapist is in (private practice, community mental health, school, or residential) or what modality (individual, couple, or family) is being used. In another example, traditional structure within a treatment plan (history/assessment, presenting problem, goals, interventions used) should always be consistent, even if the model being used to treat the client system may be very different.

THINK NATIONALLY, NOT LOCALLY

The AMFTRB National Examination that you are taking is used for licensure in every state apart from California (Caldwell et al., 2011). Although the correct answer to a question is the same for all therapists taking the examination, laws typically vary on a state-by-state basis. This could confuse some test takers, given responses to situations may be varied in real-life, everyday clinical practice. Therefore, don't think about answering the question in terms of laws that apply in your state of residence.

DON'T BE MISLED BY MFT CATCHWORDS OR PHRASES

Test takers may also be confused when struggling to identify the correct answer from several listed that could all conceivably work in the vignette or scenario. Read the question diligently to determine what the question is actually looking for, noting when the responses are laden with certain phrases that may be red herrings. In these instances, be careful not to make a common mistake such as selecting the answer that has the most MFT friendly language, such as *from a systemic perspective* or *focus on the family interaction*. Although these are important MFT concepts, you need to make sure that these answers fit the scenario or question asked. If you are judging answers solely based on the inclusion of important MFT terms—independent of what the question is really asking—you will often be drawn to an incorrect answer.

PAY ATTENTION TO QUALIFIERS

Qualifiers are words that alter a statement. Look for qualifying words embedded in the questions. These words are sometimes in all CAPS to set them apart. Examples of qualifying words are *best, next, least, most, first,* and *not.* Whenever you see a qualifying word in a question, it is the key to selecting the correct answer from the others and is directly related to the answer. Thus, when you read each of the response choices or answers, you should put the qualifying word in front of it to ensure that you are focusing on what, in this question, is important. You will repeat the qualifying word before reading each answer. By repeating the word before each response choice, you are making sure that you are focusing on what is important when selecting among the answers. Qualifiers also show up in response options, in addition to being featured in the stem. Remember to keep in mind that the answer is usually wrong if it contains absolute words like *all, always, never,* and *none.*

This type of question requires you to put a value on each option and then place them in rank order. If the question asks what you should do first, what the initial action by the therapist should be, or what the best response is, then rank the options in order of importance from one to four, with the most desirable option as number one and the least desirable option as number four. The correct answer is the option that you ranked number one. If you are having difficulty ranking the options, eliminate the option that you believe is most wrong among all the options. Next, eliminate the option you believe is most wrong from among the remaining three options. At this point, you are down to two options, and your chance of selecting the correct answer is 50%. When key words such as *most important* are used frequently, all of the options may be appropriate clinical care for the situation. However, only one of the options is the most important. When all the options appear logical for the situation, reread the stem to identify a key word that asks you to place a priority on the options.

AVOID ADDING UNNECESSARY INFORMATION TO THE QUESTION

Avoid jumping to conclusions or making unsubstantiated assumptions as another common test-taking mistake involves adding unnecessary material to the questions. This is done unconsciously when you mistakenly think of a client system that you have worked with that resembles what is described in a question. Sometimes when this occurs, information related to this real-life client or situation is added to the information that you are considering when selecting the correct response choice or answer, even when it is not actually included in the question. For example, if a man is described as severely depressed, you may inappropriately think that he is a danger to himself because you recently worked with someone who was depressed and contemplating suicide. However, being severely depressed does not necessarily mean that you are posing any danger to yourself. This added information may cause you to choose the incorrect information. Remember, the question has all the information needed to choose the best answer. You should stay with the material in the question and not add information based on your previous clinical experience.

LOOK FOR CLUES IN VIGNETTE QUOTES

Evaluate use of quotation marks throughout the question before considering the response choices, as they are often the keys to selecting the correct answers. For example, a vignette may describe a husband who walks into the first therapy session and states, "I'm only here because my wife threatened to leave me if we didn't try couple's therapy," followed by a question about the *best* MFT response in this situation. Although this question does not explicitly state that it is asking how to best address an unwilling or ambivalent client in a couple system, it is implied by the husband's verbal statement as described in the quoted statement. These words are there for a reason and are usually important clues about knowledge areas being tested or the critical information needed to select between correct and incorrect answers.

WATCH FOR THE THEORETICAL FRAMEWORK NEEDED TO ANSWER THE QUESTION EMBEDDED IN THE STEM

A vignette may ask you to use a particular MFT model or theoretical approach to select the correct response. The framework that you should use is often mentioned in the last sentence before the answers are listed. For example, a case vignette that ends with *using a solution-focused approach, a family therapist should...* requires you to look at the response choices to see which relate to an intervention that is brief, collaborative, and focused on measurable results in which a client can take a very active role. The correct answer would be very different if a therapist, responding to the same case vignette, was asked to use a *transgenerational model.*

DISTINGUISH BETWEEN VERBS

If you are debating among multiple answers, the verb choices can often provide some clues. For example, some answers describe a therapist doing something for a client system that is "active" in nature. These response choices often begin with the word *provide* when the question asks what a therapist acting as the expert should do in a particular situation. Words like *explore* and *engage*, on the other hand, are active verbs that usually indicate that a therapist is relying on a client to serve as an expert or to come up with their own solution. *Ignore* or *wait* may indicate that the therapist is not taking critical information into account or acting when needed. Therefore, you can usually eliminate choices that suggest the therapist do nothing or refrain from taking action because the correct answer will involve the therapist working with the client system to actively work with the problem in the present. Although examining the verb used in the response choices is only one piece of information, it can be a crucial determiner in selecting the best response when two choices look equally viable.

KEEP SAFETY FIRST!

Some questions on the examination want to know what you would do *first* or *next* or to pick out the clinical issue that is *most important* in the vignette. In your real-world clinical practice of MFT such decisions are often somewhat subjective and idiosyncratic to your own therapeutic style. On the actual examination; however, all therapists must select the same correct answer. With this in mind, a therapist should always address health and safety issues before moving on to issues that relate to self-esteem and relationships. Thus, when the question includes the qualifying word *first*, the answers should be considered in light of the health and safety needs of a client system. Issues involving client safety typically take priority over the concept of self-determination.

DETERMINE THE STAGE OF THERAPY THAT THE QUESTION IS REFERENCING

Remember to focus on the particular stage of therapy that the question is referencing. Understanding the goal of each stage and associated tasks is essential, as questions want to make sure that things are happening in the correct order. For example, if the question is about an initial session with a family system, the activities may be centered around joining and engagement. Engagement includes finding out why each member of the client system is there and specifically why they are seeking services now, explaining what to expect in treatment, listening to family members' concerns, and explaining the limits of confidentiality. Including a reference to a specific session in the question is a clue to determine what stage of the therapy process a therapist and client system are in and what activities are appropriate for this stage. Although questions will rarely explicitly state the stage, it can be identified by what has occurred such as *when gathering information on the problem* to indicate assessment or *when developing the contract* to indicate planning. Also, it may be useful to classify response choices into these stages in order to select what comes *first* or *next*.

HIV-POSITIVE QUESTIONS

If a question deals with an HIV-positive client, the therapist should first encourage the client to reveal this information to their partner. If that response is not available, pick the option that encourages the client to implement safe-sex practices or wants the therapist to research state laws regarding duty-to-warn situations.

CULTURAL COMPETENCY

Cultural competency is very important on the examination. This may include linking clients to specific culturally relevant resources as opposed to generic resources. When reviewing vignette questions, remember to assess for the degree of acculturation of each client in the system.

REFLECT ON THE SIGNIFICANCE OF CLIENT AGE STATED IN VIGNETTE

If the age of a client or others is included in a case vignette, it is usually relevant to selecting the correct response choice. If a behavior is age appropriate, a therapist would view this behavior as typical, which would require no special intervention. If the behavior is not age appropriate, however, the therapist may need to do a mental status examination or refer for a psychiatric evaluation. Although you do not need to memorize the exact age at which an individual leaves one stage of development or reaches a milestone, the age can be a useful hint as to where a client is in the life course and what may be expected.

DON'T EXPECT THE "PERFECT ANSWER"

Do not expect the "perfect answer" to be on the test. You must choose the best answer out of the four choices that you are given by eliminating any answers that do not appear to be correct. If more than one response choice appears to be viable, go back and read the question again—looking only at the remaining viable responses. Most questions will probably require a few cycles of this process. Going back to the question each time you are unable to dismiss all but one response choice will assist in selecting the correct answer for that question.

FOCUS ON SYMPTOMS AND DURATION

As you read an examination item related to a client's mental health that is usually a part of Domain 2's diagnosis and *DSM-5* related questions, keep in mind which symptoms the client is experiencing as well as the frequency and duration of those symptoms. For example, *suicidal thoughts for the past month, reoccurring flashbacks, inability to concentrate for the past 6 weeks*, and so on.

IDENTIFY THE QUESTION'S TIME ORIENTATION

Given that examination questions usually focus on the here-and-now actions, be cautious when reviewing potential responses that involve recommending additional sessions to the client in the future, as these options do little to solve the problem right now. More "historical" answer choices may seem viable at first (i.e., concentrating on the client's past history and family-of-origin conflicts), but keep in mind that many test questions are geared toward short-term therapy, not long-term therapy. The exception to this advice is if the question involves a transgenerational or psychodynamic model that involves working historically to resolve constraints from the client's past.

KNOW WHEN (AND WHEN NOT) TO REFER

Choose an answer that involves assessing, questioning, and clarifying the client's situation before you make any decisions such as referring the client to a psychiatrist or other medical doctor. If the therapist does not have the proper training/skills necessary to treat the client, it is the therapist's responsibility not to practice out of their scope of competence and refer the client to someone who does possess that knowledge. For example, if the therapist thinks that it is necessary to administer a certain assessment instrument, but has no experience with this instrument, then they must refer the client to someone who has the specialized training required to administer that test. Watch for questions that involve physical complaints by clients—refer to a physician first to assess for any underlying medical conditions. Be alert for test questions that mention just one physical symptom, perhaps "hidden" in the middle of the question. You must always refer to a doctor even if there is only one physical complaint.

CONCLUSION

Although passing the AMFTRB National Examination is among the most challenging obstacles to overcome in becoming a licensed marriage and family therapist, this chapter has provided test-taking strategies designed to help you reach that goal. How many of these strategies were you already naturally implementing? Which ones will take some time to adapt to? To build confidence while preparing for this examination, you need to know question types, what the question is looking for, and how to rule out distractors and eliminate incorrect responses. Taking tests may not be your favorite activity, but examinations are a necessary part of your professional development. Along with appropriate familiarity with the knowledge areas and examination domains, following these strategies will enhance your ability to perform on test day.

REFERENCES

American Psychiatric Association. (2013). *Diagnostic and statistical manual of mental disorders.* (5th ed.).

American Association for Marriage and Family Therapy. (2017). *Best practices in the online practice of couple and family therapy*. AAMFT.

Association of Marital and Family Therapy Regulatory Boards. (2022). *Handbook for candidates*. Professional Examination Service.

Caldwell, B. E., Kunker, S. A., Brown, S. W., & Saiki, D. Y. (2011). COAMFTE accreditation and California MFT licensing exam success. *Journal of Marital and Family Therapy*, *37*(4), 468–478. https://doi.org/10.1111/j.1752-0606.2011.00240.x

Cornille, T. A., McWey, L. M., Nelson, T. S., & West, S. H. (2003). How do master's level marriage and family therapy students view their basic therapy skills? An examination of generic and theory specific clinical approaches to family therapy. *Contemporary Family Therapy*, *25*(1), 41–61. https://doi.org/10.1023/A:1022506004673

Preparing for Test Day

18

> **LEARNING OBJECTIVES**
>
> *After reading this chapter, you should be able to:*
>
> 1. Identify study techniques that correspond to specific learning styles.
> 2. Assess readiness to take the Association of Marital & Family Therapy Regulatory Boards (AMFTRB) exam.
> 3. Review timeline and day-of-test on-site expectations for the AMFTRB exam.
> 4. Use healthy routines to prepare for the AMFTRB exam.
> 5. Develop coping strategies to combat test anxiety.

INTRODUCTION

Taking the AMFTRB exam can be a very stressful experience for some marriage and family therapists. Although you may feel very competent in the therapy room, preparing for the exam room often feels very different. The surroundings are unfamiliar, your wait time has been significant, you have allotted significant financial resources to get here, and, worst of all, you might have to repeat this whole process if you do not pass. This chapter prepares you for what to expect in the lead up to the exam and on the actual test day, in accordance with guidelines and recommendations set forth by the AMFTRB.

ARE YOU READY?

Many people question whether they know enough content or are prepared to take the AMFTRB exam. You may use the following informal questions as a guide to assess your readiness.

1. *Would you be able to summarize the most relevant points in a brief "mini lecture" on the theory, intervention, or content area of ______________?*
2. *Do you understand the relevancy of the ________content to marriage and family therapy (MFT) clinical practice and how to apply this information when interacting with clients?*
3. *Do you know how the________ content area relates to the assessment and treatment of client systems?*

If you feel that you have the requisite understanding to answer "yes" to those questions after filling in the blanks with the various AMFTRB knowledge areas, you may only need to review quickly by reading through the content in the previous chapters. Although restrictions prevent test takers from divulging the specific question content of the AMFTRB National Examination, there is no better gauge of your readiness for the exam than taking the practice version distributed through AMFTRB's website (www.amftrb.org). Composed of questions that formally appeared on the actual AMFTRB National Exam, this is as close to the real exam as you can get. Although you may take the practice test as many times as you like, you will be charged the full practice test fee of $60.00 each time you register. The 100 questions on each practice test will remain the same each time you take it. Passing scores have often ranged between 64% to 74%, depending on that test's cohort and particular makeup of the exam. Keep in mind that AMFTRB's practice exam will not provide you with answers you got wrong or subsequent explanations, but it will reveal your score in each of the six domains. It is highly recommended that you finish reading this chapter then complete our 180-item, full mock exam prior to purchasing AMFTRB's practice exam.

If you have deficits in the knowledge areas, however, you should mark the sections in this book that correspond to these gaps and go over them in detail so you can get to the point that you have enough familiarity to recall the key concepts and terms. If you have never heard of the concept or recall little about its relevance to MFT clinical practice, do not worry—everyone has gaps in knowledge—this just means that you will have to spend some extra time learning about the topic.

LEARNING STYLE

You will need to determine which learning style fits you best because research demonstrates that individuals perform better on exams if they use study techniques that are consistent with their styles of learning (Pashler et al., 2008). The following are some suggested techniques for each learning style that can help fill in content gaps that may exist.

KINESTHETIC LEARNERS

If you are a kinesthetic learner, you learn best by doing. You benefit from tactile approaches aimed at experiencing. You learn best through hands-on activities because you tend to be naturally active and have lots of energy. You like taking things apart and putting them back together. Physical exercise helps you think clearly, you often need frequent breaks when studying, and the thought of sitting through lectures makes you cringe. When preparing for an exam, try reading while you exercise. Develop a daily meditation practice to help you stay centered and control your attention. Practice controlling your breathing to help you stay calm, relaxed, and focused while you study. Interact with this book by underlining and making notes in the margins. Rewrite your notes onto index cards, as recopying and transferring material in your own words may help you to remember it.

VISUAL LEARNERS

If you are a visual learner, you learn best by seeing and integrating knowledge through the use of diagrams, PowerPoint slides, and charts. Pay special attention to illustrations and graphic material when you study. Color-code your notes with colorful inks or highlighters. Try whiteboarding the key concepts and organizing the information in a way that makes the most sense to you. Learn to map or diagram information. Mapping is a more visual kind of outline. Instead of a making a linear outline of the main ideas of a text, when you map, you make a diagram of the main points in the text that you want to remember. Study in an environment that is away from visual distractions such as television, people moving around, or clutter. Make your study environment as calm and quiet as possible, perhaps using a white-noise machine to drown out distractions Finally, create to-do lists to keep track of topics you need to study further.

AUDITORY LEARNERS

If you are an auditory learner, you learn best by listening. You may be musically inclined and have a good sense of rhythm and enjoy listening to podcasts and audiobooks. Given that taking notes can be distracting or break your attention, you would prefer listening to lectures or asking questions to learn. You often notice the tone someone uses when they tell you something. Studying with background music does not distract you. To prepare for this AMFTRB exam, try treading material aloud to yourself or talk about what you are learning with a friend or study partner. Hearing the information will help you to remember it. Experiment with dictation and audio record notes and play them back on your phone. The podcasts accompanying this text are easy to understand and assist with auditory learning.

PREPARING FOR THE AMFTRB EXAM

1 TO 3 MONTHS BEFORE THE EXAM: ESTABLISH YOUR ROUTINE

Set aside a regular time to study, as preparing for the AMFTRB exam requires consistency, repetition, and practice. Avoiding procrastination and deciding to sit down to study is the most difficult part of the process for many. Your study schedule must be reasonable and realistic. Shorter, more frequent study periods are more effective than long study periods. For most people, 2- to 4-hour study periods with a short break each hour is an effective protocol. Periods of learning must be balanced with adequate rest periods to keep you alert and receptive to new information. It is important to allow your brain time to relax. Take study breaks from time to time so you do not get overworked and do not study right before bed. Take time to rest your mind before trying to rest your body, or you may find it difficult to fall asleep.

The routine should also simulate that of the actual testing environment when studying. Your posture, surroundings, and equipment should be similar to those in the testing environment. Avoid the temptation to study in a reclining chair, on the couch, or in bed. Keep pets in another room, avoid eating, and turn your cell phone off.

Prior to taking the AMFTRB exam, it is important to exercise both body and mind. Frequent exercise, meditation, and visualization not only reduce test anxiety, but also aid in coping with negative personal feelings, emotions, and thoughts about the exam. Put things in perspective. Remind yourself that your upcoming exam is important, but your entire future does not depend on this exam.

Visualize completing the test successfully despite your anxiety. Using vivid images, play the entire "tape" in your mind—from the moment you wake up on the day of the exam to the moment you finish the exam. Using imagery can also help you to establish a state of relaxation. When we remember a fearful event, our heart and respiratory rates increase just as they did when the event occurred. Similarly, when we recall a happy, relaxing period, we can regenerate and recreate the atmosphere and feeling that we had during that pleasant event. Using imagery is not a difficult technique to master. Just let go and enjoy the experience. Position yourself in your chair, close your eyes, and construct an image in your mind of a place that makes you feel calm, happy, and relaxed. At critical times during your exam prep, you can take a few minutes to use imagery to induce the relaxation response. To reduce stress successfully, you must position yourself in control. When you are in control, your test performance generally improves.

Rest is crucial in establishing your routine and for having a clear, strong mind. If you establish good sleep habits, your body and mind will be ready to perform optimally, without the strain of exhaustion. In addition, sleeping well helps you to retain information better, so you are more likely to recall the answers when you explore exam questions.

THE NIGHT BEFORE THE EXAM

Follow your usual routine the night before the AMFTRB exam. Doing a moderate workout early in the evening (5:00 or 6:00) may help you sleep more soundly at night. Eat a light dinner early in the evening. Use the hours before bed to relax quietly. If you are feeling unsettled, remind yourself that a certain level of anxiety is actually helpful to perform your best. And remember you can always use anxiety-control strategies to moderate your anxiety level if it becomes excessive. This is not the time to make changes that may disrupt your balance. If you do not normally stay up late studying or cramming until the wee hours of the morning, do not start this practice the night before the exam. Go to bed at your usual time. Studies have demonstrated that sleep deprivation decreases reaction times and cognitive skills. Proper sleep is paramount to a rested mind and body, which are needed to perform optimally on the exam.

WHEN TRAVELING . . .

If you are traveling to a testing center outside of your home base, ask a friend, your spouse, or significant other to come accompany you if possible. Who would you rather talk to the night before the examination—someone who is as stressed out as you, or someone who is encouraging and has your back? As soon as you learn your exam date, make a reservation to stay in a hotel close to the exam site. You don't want the additional stress of being caught in traffic in a strange town while trying to get to a site you have never been to before. From the hotel, take a drive to the testing center location and know whether any detours or construction will add to drive time—remember, if you show up late, you forfeit your exam spot and must re-register for another date, including paying an additional registration fee. Go inside the building if it is open to acclimate to your surroundings. Call the testing center and ask them questions if you need more clarifying information.

THE MORNING OF THE EXAM

There are several test-day strategies you can employ to maximize your performance on the AMFTRB exam. Try not to change too much about your normal routine on the day of the test. It's important to eat a nutritious breakfast, but if you normally don't eat breakfast at all, consider eating just a protein bar. Do not overdue caffeine or energy drinks, as being stimulated that much may contribute to unnecessary jitters or upset stomach. Drink enough water to stay hydrated but not so much that you need a restroom break 10 minutes into the exam. By allowing yourself extra time to get ready and leave for the testing center, you will eliminate any anxiety that comes with rushing or stressing out about being late.

CHECKING IN AT THE TESTING CENTER

You must reach your destination at the testing center 30 minutes before the scheduled exam time to allow for check-in procedures. Please be aware that if you are late in arriving, you will not be allowed to take the test and will forfeit your exam fee. You must bring a valid and current (nonexpired) form of government-issued identification (ID; e.g., driver's license or passport). The ID should contain a photograph/signature and the name on it must match the name on your scheduling notification. If you are testing outside of your country of citizenship, you must present a valid passport. If your government-issued identification does not display a photograph or a signature, a secondary form of identification may be used, which includes a photograph and/or signature (whichever is missing from the government-issued identification), and your name printed on the identification. The identification documents must be originals in good condition and cannot be bent, frayed, taped, cracked, or otherwise damaged in any way. If you do not provide the appropriate and/or matching identification, you will not be permitted to test. If you still wish to take the exam, you will be required to apply for a re-exam and pay the re-exam fee to take the exam at a later date, when valid identification is available.

Given that exam security is paramount, all personal belongings should be stored in a temporary locker while your ID and key should always remain on your person while at the testing center. You will also undergo a physical security check before being seated at your computer-testing terminal. These inspections will be done again upon return from breaks before you enter the testing room to ensure you do not violate any security protocol. The test center administrator will ask you to raise your pant legs above your ankles, empty and turn your pockets completely inside out, and raise shirt sleeves above your wrists prior to every entry into the test room. You will be required to remove your eyeglasses, hats, and jewelry for close visual inspection. Jewelry outside of wedding and engagement rings is prohibited. Please do not wear other jewelry to the test center. Hair accessories and ties are subject to inspection. Please refrain from using ornate clips, combs, barrettes, headbands, tie clips, cuff links, and other hair accessories as you may be prohibited from wearing them into the testing room and asked to store them in your locker. Violation of the security protocol may result in the confiscation of prohibited devices and termination of your exam.

As a final step in the process, you will be scanned with a metal detector wand prior to entry into the test room. Please remember that the exam is continuously monitored by audio- and video-recording equipment. If you experience any issues while taking an exam, please raise your hand to inform the test center administrator.

Unauthorized personal items may not be brought into the test room. Such items include, but are not limited to:

- Outerwear
- Beverages
- Notebooks
- Electronic devices
- Wallets
- Hats
- Purses
- Watches
- Wearable technology
- Bags
- Food
- Briefcases
- Cell phones
- Medication

If you have a medical condition that requires medication, food, beverages, or similar items, you must obtain an authorization for special accommodations before scheduling your appointment with Prometric.

DURING THE EXAM

If you continue to feel overly anxious, practice the following anxiety reduction-techniques while at your seat:

- Close your eyes.
- Breathe in slowly to the count of seven and exhale to the count of seven.

- Continue this slow breathing until you actually feel your body begin to relax. (Most people find that it takes two to four breathing sequences.)
- Open your eyes and give yourself a positive, very specific self-talk.
- Move your body. Roll your shoulders, stretch your legs.

Design a "break management plan" ahead of time that includes activities like using the restroom, splashing water on your face, taking deep, slow breaths, and grabbing a nutritious snack and water stored in your locker, so you know exactly how to proceed before returning to the test. Remember that the clock on the computer is still ticking when you take a break.

AFTER THE EXAM

At the end of the exam, leave the test center feeling confident. You have done your best, so do not waste time worrying about your performance or wishing you could change anything. Instead, celebrate; you've earned it! Remember that taking the exam is merely another stop on the long journey of clinical practice, coursework, and supervision that culminates in professional licensure. Your supervisors and former professors have endorsed your capabilities as a competent therapist. Your clients have sought out your services, believing you can help them. All of these stakeholders know you are a competent clinician, regardless of the outcome of your exam. An AMFTRB exam score by itself does not prove that you are a good therapist. Clients would not return if you were a bad therapist. The fact of the matter is that you have a proliferation of people who know that you are ready to move onward and upward!

IF AT FIRST YOU DON'T SUCCEED . . .

Yes, taking a licensing exam is a big deal! But it is still just an exam, and not passing the first time does not signify the death of your professional career. The road to licensure is not that much different than other journeys in life and not usually without unexpected delays or even disappointments. Rarely do people get the score that they want the first time taking any standardized test. Therapists often attach too much meaning to whether or not they pass the examination the first time. There are many outstanding therapists who have had to take the test multiple times. Remember that you will be able to retake the examination if you do not pass—this is not your only chance. You will eventually pass, whether it is this time or another, so don't let the test define you. Avoid thinking in "all or nothing" terms.

A reframe on a potential exam setback is that you now have more time to review your weaker knowledge areas so that the next time you take the exam, you will be even more familiar with the test and how it works. Try to figure out why these setbacks are occurring and how you can use this information as feedback for making improvements. You did not get an MFT graduate degree, after all, without some disappointments and challenges. Studying for and passing the exam will also not be easy, but you will be eventually successful if you keep focused and learn from challenges encountered.

If you are having difficulty answering practice questions, it may be useful to try to determine what is causing your problem. You should reexamine the tips outlined in the previous chapter to see what strategies may be helpful in preparing for test taking.

Although test-taking strategies are important, failing the exam is almost always a result of gaps in the MFT knowledge areas (AMFTRB, 2022). The AMFTRB exam is very reliable, so to prevent making similar mistakes on another exam attempt, you should spend time analyzing what is causing the difficulties before trying again; for example, knowledge gaps cannot be filled by simply reviewing the test-taking strategies. Although therapists who have failed the examinations may be anxious to restart the process so that they can catch up, it is worth spending time critically reflecting on the strategies used to study and answer questions so that modifications can be made before retaking the AMFTRB exam.

OVERCOMING TEST ANXIETY

THE PROBLEM

Test anxiety is defined as a feeling of uneasiness or apprehension before, during, or after a test because of worry or fear. People differ in the levels of anxiety they experience. A small amount of anxiety could actually be good for you, as it facilitates performance and can increase achievement by pushing the test taker to do their best. Excessive anxiety, conversely, is deleterious and can interrupt the focus necessary to succeed. As a fight-or-flight response, test-taking anxiety releases excessive adrenaline to the nervous system. This adrenaline causes increased heart rate, shaky hands, loss of focus, and, in extreme cases, even panic attacks (Eum & Rice, 2011). When a test taker "blanks out" on a question, they become flustered enough to either skip the question (praying that the next item is easier) or waste time blankly staring at a question without doing anything.

The mental components of test anxiety include trouble focusing and the inability to remember learned information even with the content you know well. The strain of testing makes it difficult to stay focused for long periods of time, especially on an exam like this one that is upwards of 4 hours long. No matter what the severity—anxiety management is a critical part of every study plan. Ignoring the anxiety that accompanies this exam process is counterproductive. Repeatedly studying the content over and over will not reduce your anxiety. Although it is impossible to fully eliminate it through any of the techniques mentioned in this chapter, you do need to assess whether your anxiety is manageable or if it is interfering so significantly with the learning process that you are freezing or having panic when studying. Extreme anxiety can take a huge mental toll, making it difficult not only to recall test information, but to even understand the test questions and pull your thoughts together. If this is the case, you may need more intensive anxiety-reduction interventions. Although most people can develop their own strategies for anxiety management, others need outside help. Usually, individuals who need the assistance of others are those who have experienced debilitating anxiety in other areas of life prior to taking the examinations (Embse et al., 2018).

COUNTER AUTOMATIC NEGATIVE THOUGHTS ABOUT TEST PERFORMANCE

A positive mental attitude can help you control test anxiety by limiting anxious responses so that you can be a more successful test taker. Operating from a position of strength, this requires practice with thought- stopping techniques that put you in control of your own feelings and behaviors. To be in control of yourself, you must operate from a position of positive self-worth with a feeling of empowerment.

Positive thinking focuses your attention on your desired outcomes. If you think you can do well on the AMFTRB exam, you are more likely to full fill this prophecy.

It is critical that you control your automatic negative thoughts by developing a positive mental attitude. When you say to yourself, "This is going to be a horrible experience. I'll never pass," you begin to predict failure for yourself. After having a thought like this that contributes to anxiety, you need to ask yourself, "Do I have evidence to support this thought, or am I making assumptions? Do I have good reason to be anxious?" Instead of embracing the catastrophic cognition, challenge the automatic negative thought by saying, "This is a ridiculous statement. Of course, I can pass this test. All I have to do is study hard and not panic!" It is crucial that you challenge negative thoughts with realistic counter thoughts. Counter thoughts are valuable because they are objectively based and can be converted into positive actions and feelings, thus placing you in a position of control (Kondo, 1997).

EMBRACE BEHAVIORAL RELAXATION TECHNIQUES

Integrating relaxation techniques into your exam-preparation routine can help you relax before and during the test. Deep-breathing exercises, meditation, and yoga are relaxation techniques to counteract feelings of anxiety and to bring the mind and body back into equilibrium. Progressive muscle relaxation (PMR) is also a practice that anyone can use to alleviate disturbing and disruptive emotional symptoms that arise from test anxiety.

REFLECT ON PAST SUCCESSES

Reflecting on past achievements on standardized tests, as well as triumphs in your academic and burgeoning clinical career can help build confidence and serve as a reminder that success is not out of reach. If you were once successful on an exam, you can be successful again. Reflecting on the behaviors and strategies that influenced your success on a previous exam can help you identify long-term strategies for future success.

CONCLUSION

The strategies described in this chapter are designed to prepare you for test day and increase your mastery over the stress of the AMFTRB exam timeline. When you are able to respond to the testing situation with a sense of calm, you will increase your confidence. Use this guidance in conjunction with the test-taking strategies from the previous chapter and the mock exam in the next chapter to build endurance, provide reassurance, and increase your overall exam effectiveness.

REFERENCES

Association of Marital and Family Therapy Regulatory Boards. (2022). *Handbook for candidates*. Professional Examination Service.

Eum, K., & Rice, K. G. (2011). Test anxiety, perfectionism, goal orientation, and academic performance. *Anxiety, Stress & Coping*, *24*(2), 167–178. https://doi.org/10.1080/10615806.2010.488723

Kondo, D. S. (1997). Strategies for coping with test anxiety. *Anxiety, Stress, & Coping*, *10*, 203–215. https://doi.org/10.1080/10615809708249301

Pashler, H., McDaniel, M., Rohrer, D., & Bjork, R. (2008). Learning styles: Concepts and evidence. *Psychological Science in the Public Interest*, *9*, 105–119.

Embse, N., Jester, von der., D, D., Roy., & Post, J. (2018). Test anxiety effects, predictors, and correlates: A 30-year meta-analytic review. *Journal of Affective Disorders*, *227*, 483–493. https://doi.org/10.1016/j.jad.2017.11.048

PART VIII

Marital and Family Therapy Mock National Examination

Questions

19

1. A young mother contacts a family therapist because of extreme worry and anxiety. The parent is unsure of how to respond to recently finding her 4-year-old touching the body of a 3-year-old from his play group. The parent is disturbed and worried that this action may lead to further problematic behavior. The therapist should:

   A. Explore the mother's feelings about sexuality
   B. Provide psychoeducation and reassure the mother that this is normal behavior for children this age
   C. Contact the other child's parent
   D. Assess for child abuse

2. John, a 40-year-old man, seeks individual therapy for depression. He discloses that his long-term girlfriend, Kim, is physically abusive to him and threatens to leave if he doesn't "snap out of it." The client admits that his depression is a big part of the couple's conflict and he is committed to repairing things with Kim. In addition to discussing a safety plan with John, which of the following interventions should the therapist consider initially?

   A. Find out what John means by "depression"; provide referral to domestic violence resources; identify coping skills
   B. Refer to couples therapy; explore how John has coped with Kim; identify social supports
   C. Explore John's ambivalence about leaving the relationship; encourage client to join a domestic violence support group; refer to a psychiatrist
   D. Find out what John means by "depression"; refer client to an MD; identify his automatic negative thoughts

3. Jason agrees to complete thought records in between sessions with a therapist working from a cognitive behavioral framework. During the subsequent session, when asked about the thought-record homework, Jason laments, "I didn't have time to get it done." The therapist gives the same homework again, and the exact same scenario occurs in the next session as well. How should the therapist respond to the client's lack of follow through?

   A. Interpret Jason's behavior as a sign of resistance
   B. Ask Jason directly what interferes with completion of homework
   C. Remind Jason of the importance of homework
   D. Acknowledge that homework can be difficult, especially for people not accustomed to documenting or writing down their thoughts

4. A therapist is working with a client with a history of voyeurism. The client expresses guilt, remarking he still has strong impulses to act on his thoughts. He has unsuccessfully tried to change his automatic negative thoughts around this behavior. The client tells the therapist that he does not know why he cannot stop these urges. What should the therapist do first?

- **A.** Remind the client that you are a mandated reporter and voyeurism is an invasion of privacy
- **B.** Teach the client to counter automatic negative thoughts around voyeurism
- **C.** Explore the feelings behind the voyeuristic behavior
- **D.** Have the client contract with the therapist to abstain from the voyeuristic behavior while receiving therapy

5. A father explains to the therapist that his family recently survived a major house fire that started when a fire in the fireplace was not properly extinguished. He is concerned, because every time his 5-year-old daughter sees a lit fireplace, she becomes terrified and refuses to sleep in her room. The daughter looks frightened during the initial interview as she clings to her parents. How will the therapist know it is time to terminate with the child?

- **A.** The child is able to express her feelings related to the house fire
- **B.** The child is able to sleep in her room by herself
- **C.** The child no longer becomes terrified when seeing lit fireplaces
- **D.** The child is able to reenact the house fire through play therapy without becoming threatened

6. Tonya, a 32-year-old female with a history of suicide attempts, has previously been in treatment for bipolar disorder. Shortly after stopping her medication, Tonya developed symptoms of mania and began binge drinking. At the request of her roommate, the police took Tonya to the hospital and arranged an involuntary admission in the acute psychiatric unit. The client has all of the following rights *except* the right to:

- **A.** Refuse to engage in therapy
- **B.** Refuse to give permission to the hospital staff to contact her family
- **C.** Keep the record of her admission confidential
- **D.** Leave the hospital whenever she chooses

7. A therapist conducts a support group for single parents with developmentally disabled children. During one group meeting, a member begins to describe how he behaves toward his child when he becomes frustrated. The therapist becomes concerned that these behaviors may constitute child abuse. The therapist should initially:

- **A.** Encourage the member to provide more specific information during the group
- **B.** Remind the group about the therapist's legal obligation to report child abuse
- **C.** Engage the other members in a discussion of what is acceptable behavior
- **D.** Meet with the member individually following group to further assess

8. An family therapist is moving to another city. After assessing the risks and benefits that may be experienced by each client, the therapist offers to continue the therapeutic relationship with several clients through a virtual, confidential online platform. Teletherapy is inappropriate in all of the following situations *except*:

A. A client who has just completed therapeutic goals
B. A client who just lost her spouse
C. A high-functioning client making substantial progress toward goals
D. A client expressing suicidal ideation

9. Dwayne reports feeling listless and unsatisfied in his marriage. The man also describes a loss of interest in things he used to enjoy and trouble staying asleep most nights. Recently, Dwayne also suffered a serious back injury and is currently on disability indefinitely. The therapist should first:

A. Determine when Dwayne's problems first began
B. Refer Dwayne for psychiatric evaluation
C. Obtain a signed release to consult with Dwayne's doctor
D. Refer Dwayne to a physical therapy program

10. Shelia, a married mother with twins, is referred to a therapist for depression. The initial assessment reveals that the client recently experienced the sudden death of her mother, who was caring for her father, who is suffering from early-onset dementia. Subsequently, her father is now under Shelia's care. Shelia's husband has recently lost his job, but they need his paycheck to pay the bills. A strategic family therapist would:

A. Assess family system boundaries
B. Provide clear directives to help change symptomatic behaviors
C. Invite the entire family to the next session in order to assess emotional dynamics of the system
D. Collaborate in problem-solving

11. Systemic approaches are a set of theories that conceptualize an individual's symptoms as arising ______________________________.

A. In the unconscious mind
B. From social oppression
C. When a person is not self-actualized
D. Within family and relational dynamics

12. Conjoint treatment of intimate partner violence (IPV) combines a systemic and ____________ approach.

A. Feminist
B. Behavioral
C. Cognitive behavioral
D. Punitive

13. Diversity can be addressed in treatment tasks by all of the following *except*:

 A. Disregarding the possibility of marginalization and discrimination in the assessment process
 B. Use of humor with teens or men
 C. A more formal, respectful relational style with immigrants
 D. Incorporating spirituality

14. The family life cycle is an example of which kind of system:

 A. Microsystem
 B. Mesosystem
 C. Chronosystem
 D. Macrosystem

15. The routine assessment of clinical outcomes refers to the practice of __________.

 A. Supervision
 B. Systemic assessment
 C. Relational diagnosis
 D. Progress monitoring

16. Psychoeducational programs emphasize all the following, *except*:

 A. Skill building
 B. Psychotherapy
 C. Stress management
 D. Information

17. Research on stress in families with schizophrenic members emphasizes the relationship between ______________ and relapse.

 A. Anxiety
 B. Depression
 C. Phobias
 D. Expressed emotion

18. Mike, a marriage and family therapist, has had a hard time with his finances of late. In addition to buying a home, he has spent a lot on continuing education, professional association fees, and his landlord has substantially raised the rent in his centrally located office. In order to increase revenue, Mike should consider:

 A. Shortening the standard session duration to meet with more clients so he can fit more clients into the work week
 B. Raising the fee only for clients who can afford to pay more
 C. Renegotiating previously reduced fees with ongoing clients
 D. Raising fees as per the policy described in the informed-consent document

19. Strategic therapy, as a problem-oriented therapy, includes all of the following *except*:

A. It involves developing a plan for therapy
B. It can be paradoxical in nature
C. It involves frequently working with a team behind the one-way mirror
D. It prioritizes client insight

20. A mother brings her 5-year-old son, Johnny, to a local mental health agency. The child is having recurrent fantasies of being chased by home invaders and has nightmares of running in terror to escape them. What should the therapist do first?

A. Ask Johnny to describe the fantasies
B. Complete a comprehensive biopsychosocial assessment
C. Refer Johnny for play therapy
D. Tell the mother that these types of fantasies are developmentally appropriate, and the child is developing normally

21. Charlie and Molly have been married for only a year. This is Charlie first marriage, but Molly has been married once before. The have a 6-month-old baby girl together. They seek therapy to deal with blended family issues, specifically behavioral problems involving Molly's three children from a previous marriage. Charlie contends that the children, 10, 11, and 13, blatantly ignore him and do not respect their mother's authority. The couple has had many fights about the "right" way to parent and these children are coming between them. The therapist decides to focus initially on the times when Charlie has thought that the children were respecting their mother's authority and the blended family was starting to cooperate with each other. Which of the following statements should the family therapist make to help Charlie and Molly understand the presenting problem from a systems perspective?

A. "It is difficult to be a stepfather."
B. "The children resent the new baby."
C. "Your marital relationship is being damaged by Molly's children."
D. "You are experiencing a normal adjustment to becoming a stepfamily."

22. Neil, a 23-year-old male, is college educated but currently unemployed and lives at home with his parents. He enters an initial session with variety of severe anxiety symptoms, including a feeling of going crazy, fear about dying, an inability to concentrate, insomnia, irritability, chest pains, shakiness, loss of usual interests, and frequent crying spells. The therapist should first__________.

A. Provide reading material about generalized anxiety disorder
B. Request that a primary care physician prescribe anti-anxiety medication
C. Schedule a family meeting to understand more about Neil's home life and to partner with his parents to help their son
D. Obtain a psychiatric evaluation, including an assessment for medication

23. Mike, Michelle, and their 12-year-old daughter, Stephanie, have been referred to therapy after the tragic loss of their teenage son in car accident last summer. After hearing Mike's insistence that therapy involve only the mother and daughter, the family therapist becomes adamant that without the father's participation, it seems impossible to help the family heal and do the requisite grief work. This is an example of ________.

A. A family enactment
B. The battle for structure
C. Disrupting homeostasis
D. An inverted hierarchy

24. Which of the following statements about defense mechanisms is the *most* accurate?

A. Defense mechanisms are adaptive
B. Defense mechanisms can damage relationships
C. Defense mechanisms are unconscious processes
D. Defense mechanisms originate in childhood

25. Kyler, a fourth grader, is referred by his teacher for therapy with the therapist working in the school. The teacher notes that the boy is often disruptive and inattentive in class, which interferes with his ability to learn. Kyler hasn't been completing his homework. The therapist should first ________.

A. Administer a neuropsychological evaluation
B. Complete an attention deficit hyperactivity disorder (ADHD) symptom checklist
C. Refer Kyler to the school's special education department for an evaluation
D. Have Kyler complete a Beck Depression Inventory

26. Derek is complaining that he has been feeling "depressed" lately. Almost embarrassed, he believes he shouldn't feel this way because everyone tells him he has it "made." In the initial assessment, he notes that he has a loving family, a six-figure job, and wonderful friends. The therapist should first ______.

A. Assess for a history of depression in Derek's family
B. Refer Derek to a psychiatrist for an evaluation
C. Administer the Beck Depression Inventory
D. Clarify what Derek means when he states he feels "depressed"

27. Theresa is one of only three marriage and family therapists in a small rural community. After feeling both frustrated and confused with her client's lack of improvement after several months of therapy, Theresa has decided to consult with another local family therapist. Given the small size of the community, it would be best for Theresa to__________.

A. Convey the minimum amount of information needed to receive guidance
B. Make the best effort at omitting any identifying information about the client
C. Protect the client's anonymity by changing important demographic information
D. Obtain a release from the client because in such a small community the colleague might know Theresa's client

28. Lorna has been seeing the Smith family (Diane, 37-year-old mother; Roy, 39-year-old father; and Kaitlin, 8-year-old daughter) for five sessions. During the last meeting, Kaitlin asks Lorna, "Can I tell you what happened after last session between Mommy and Daddy?" Diane immediately objects by saying, "I don't want to talk about that." The therapist makes several unsuccessful attempts to assist family members in a more open discussion about what's going on at home between sessions. To increase open communication, what should the therapist do next?

A. Remind the family about confidentiality
B. Schedule an individual session with Diane
C. Use circular questioning with all family members
D. Gently challenge Diane in front of her husband and daughter about her avoidance in therapy

29. Leon, a client with a violent history and criminal record, was court ordered for anger management therapy after his most recent legal infraction. In session, he complains he is being lied to by his business partner and doesn't think it will ever end unless he takes drastic measures. He also has a history of major depression and poor relationships with his family of origin. The therapist should first __________.

A. Assess for suicidality
B. Assess for danger to others
C. Administer the Beck Depression Inventory
D. Assess for lethality

30. A recent Bosnian refugee is seen in an emergency room after what is thought to be a severe panic attack. Once it is determined he is physically OK, he is referred to an onsite therapist but declines any further help. All of the following are likely explanations for this refusal *except*:

A. The high incidence of panic disorder within the Bosnian refugee population
B. Possible language barriers
C. Alternative ways to get help available in the culture
D. Cultural stigmas associated with treatment

31. A therapist meets with Cindy, a 13-year-old girl, who has poor attendance and is on the verge of failing seventh grade. Standardized testing explains that Cindy is above average in intelligence but lacks empathy and is at high risk for antisocial behaviors. The therapist completes a social history to _________.

A. Explore Cindy's developmental milestones
B. Understand factors that impact Cindy's behavior
C. Identify Cindy's family support system
D. Assess Cindy's current emotional regulation skills

32. Shayla, a newly licensed couple therapist, begins seeing Dave and Cheri. During the initial assessment, Dave questions Shayla's age, experience, and competence. How should Shayla first address Dave's concerns?

A. Provide Dave with honest information regarding Shayla's credentials
B. Confront Dave about his doubts
C. Ask Dave how he feels about seeking help for his relationship
D. Explain that Shayla has treated a lot of couples in the past

33. Claire and Connor bring their bring their 16-year-old, Connor Jr., to family therapy because the teen questions authority, is exploring his sexual identity, and no longer desires to attend church with the family. Connor Jr. indicates that the parents are overinvolved in his business and that he wants to go to a more liberal church. The therapist should explain to the parents that their son is most likely _________.

A. Seeking to identify with peers
B. Trying to find a personal identity
C. Engaging in a power struggle
D. Disrespecting the parents' values

34. Connie, a licensed marriage and family therapist (LMFT), has been working with Becky for 11 sessions. Although Becky always pays the late fee, Connie notices that on at least seven occasions her client has either canceled appointments at the last minute or been a "no show." Becky describes that all of her significant friendships seem to fade over time but doesn't understand why this keeps happening. An appropriate middle-phase intervention would be to _____________.

A. Point out Becky's disrespectful behavior toward Connie
B. Talk about Becky's friends' lack of care
C. Reformulate treatment goals
D. Relate Becky's attendance behavior in therapy as a parallel process to her behavior in her relationships with friends

35. During a family therapy session with Dr. Dana, the parents of your 17-year-old client, Cindy, reveal that they have been reading their daughter's texts and are aware that she has had sex with several young men. What should the family therapist do first?

A. Confront the parents for reading the texts
B. Remind Cindy that this is her parents' right to read texts
C. Encourage Cindy to respond to her parents' disclosure
D. Schedule an individual session with Cindy

36. A therapist meets with Antonio, a first-generation Italian, who is anxious because his wife is pressuring him to move his older, immigrant mother into an assisted living facility. Antonio's mom speaks little English, and he prefers that she live with them until they are no longer able to care for her needs. The therapist should first _________.

A. Be authoritative and suggest a course of action
B. Survey Antonio's cultural perspective around this issue
C. Invite Antonio's mother and his wife to the next session
D. Address the triangle that exists among Antonio, his wife, and his mother

37. After 2 years of successful therapy with his client Jack, the therapist begins the process of termination. Jack states a lack of readiness and appears to feel rejected by the therapist. What should be included in the ending phase of treatment?

A. Contracting for additional sessions because Jack isn't ready for termination
B. Referring Jack to another therapist or agency
C. Reviewing Jack's strengths and weaknesses
D. Focusing on the therapeutic goals Jack has accomplished

38. Thomas, a16-year-old client with some significant learning disabilities, confides in the therapist that he often gets made fun of by his best friend, Mark, and he doesn't know what to do about it. He doesn't want to lose Mark as a friend, but he wants the verbal insults to stop. To help Thomas deal with this relationship, the therapist should ___________.

A. Document instances of inappropriate behavior between Thomas and Mark
B. Role-play appropriate responses to Mark's behavior with Thomas
C. Confront Mark privately outside of session with Thomas
D. Help Thomas process this and other times when he was made fun of for his learning disabilities

39. Forty-one-year-old Cherie, 43-year-old Dave, and their 14-year-old daughter, Bella, come to family therapy because Bella's school performance is steadily declining. Cherie has a bruise on her cheek and a blackened eye. Further questioning reveals the presence of domestic violence in the family. Bella explains, "My parents love each other, but sometimes they fight. They hit each other, but never hit me or anything." As the session progresses, Dave becomes more and more defensive and begins to yell at Bella about the real reason they are in therapy (her grades) while she is describing her view of her parents' situation. The best course of action clinically would be to ___________.

A. Interrupt current discussion; conduct separate individual assessments with each family member; refer the parents to individual therapists
B. Get up and open the door to the office; refer Dave to anger management therapy; refer Cherie to a support group for battered women
C. Interrupt current discussion; refer Bella to a support group for victims of domestic violence; treat the parents conjointly
D. Get up and open the door to the office; refer parents to individual therapists; make a child protective services report

40. Juliana, a 34-year-old Latina, is referred to a therapist by her neurologist. She reports that 3 months ago she was diagnosed with multiple sclerosis (MS). She shares that her fiancé ended their relationship because he couldn't handle the long-term prognosis of the illness. Juliana has had a hard time focusing, going to work, and sleeping ever since. She reveals, "My friends think I am depressed, but my doctor says it is normal to feel this way after receiving a diagnosis." She appears sad and disheveled. What action should the therapist take first?

A. Provide the client with psychoeducation about how receiving a medical diagnosis can lead to depression
B. Obtain a signed release of information to consult with the neurologist
C. Ask how Juliana views the impact of MS on her mental health
D. Explore how MS is viewed in viewed in Latin culture

41. A therapist is working with a 19-year-old woman who is regularly driven to the sessions by her mother. The mother is also paying for her daughter's therapy. The client's presenting problem is that she feels "smothered" by her overprotective parents. The client indicates that she wants the modality to be individual therapy so that she can healthily separate from her parents. Because she is paying for it but hasn't noticed any progress at home, the mother enters the office at the end of the 10th session and wants a copy of her daughter's records to know what her daughter has been saying in therapy. What should the therapist do?

A. Schedule a joint meeting between mother and daughter to discuss the records
B. Ask the mother to submit this request for records in writing
C. Inform the mother of the requirements for disclosure
D. Explain that records are the property of the agency

42. Carla is the mother of 3-year-old Robbie; she referred to therapy by her obstetrician. She is in the last month of her second pregnancy, and is experiencing episodes of depression with excessive crying, hopelessness, and increasing fear that she will harm her child. The client states that she experienced an episode of major depressive disorder following the birth of Robbie. Her husband works two jobs, leaving her alone at home with her son for around 16 hours a day. The therapist's first priority is to ________.

A. Refer Carla for a medical evaluation
B. Report the situation to the child protective services
C. Schedule a couple session
D. Assess Robbie's safety

43. A therapist receives a phone message from a client's psychiatrist, who has been providing medication monitoring for the client's anxiety. The psychiatrist informs the therapist that the client gave him permission to contact the therapist, and he would like to provide clarification about the client's diagnosis and medication regimen. What should the therapist do first?

A. Call the psychiatrist to inform him that you will request the client sign a release in the next session
B. Call the psychiatrist and request a copy of his release before acknowledging you see the client
C. Call the client to request permission to speak with the psychiatrist
D. Call the psychiatrist to discuss concerns regarding the client's case because he has signed a release

44. A couple presents to therapy seeking better strategies to "fight fairly" and avoid physical altercations. After a careful assessment, the therapist is comfortable treating this couple because their previous fights are categorized as situational violence and not intimate terrorism. Conjoint treatment of this type of domestic violence combines a systemic and ______________ approach.

A. Feminist
B. Behavioral
C. Cognitive behavioral
D. Punitive

45. The therapist is conducting an opening interview with a couple using the Gottman Method to assess for possible danger signs in the couple's communication. Which of the following observable signs is considered one of the Four Horsemen of the Apocalypse?

A. Criticism
B. Neediness
C. Anger
D. Frustration

46. The therapist is embarking on one of the five steps of evidence-based practice to assist her in working with a 54-year-old client with a specific phobia around germs and contamination. The first step the therapist will most likely take is __________.

A. Evaluating the validity and applicability of the research
B. Determining whether the research findings are applicable to her client
C. Developing an answerable question to focus the search for information
D. Evaluating the effectiveness of the practice on the client's case

47. All the following are benefits of monitoring progress throughout the course of therapy *except*:

A. It helps determine when therapy is no longer necessary
B. It helps the therapist make modifications in treatment strategy
C. It helps pinpoint a more accurate diagnosis
D. It helps improve outcomes

48. A behavioral couple therapist who directs a husband to act as if he were on a very first date with his spouse is using the __________ intervention.

A. Love map
B. Paradoxical
C. Blamer softener
D. Caring days

49. Which statement is the most accurate about assessments?

A. Nonstandardized assessments are easy to use with individuals with severe pathology
B. Standardized assessments cost very little and should be conducted weekly
C. Standardized assessments are less reliable and valid than nonstandardized assessments
D. Client self-reports, a type of nonstandardized assessment, are considered less reliable than standardized assessments

50. In a client diagnosed with anorexia nervosa, ________ is the least beneficial in monitoring treatment progress.

A. Weight gain or loss
B. Body image
C. Increased goal-directed behavior
D. Amount of physical exercise and activity

51. Client progress is best measured by assessing client satisfaction and __________.

A. The impact of theory
B. The impact of techniques
C. Clinical outcomes
D. Therapist experience

52. In addition to continually evaluating the progress their client is making, therapists should ________.

A. Experiment with new therapy models
B. Change the treatment plan every 1 to 3 months
C. Monitor their own effectiveness
D. Discuss their client's progress with client's support system

53. __________ is an instrument designed to be an ongoing measure of the therapeutic alliance.

A. The Session Rating Scale (SRS)
B. The Outcome Rating Scale (ORS)
C. Minnesota Multiphasic Personality Inventory (MMPI)
D. Relationship Rating Scale (RRS)

54. Feedback is *not* ___________.

A. Sharing thoughts and feelings about the client
B. Reviewing client progress
C. Sharing impressions about the process between members of a family system
D. Giving the client advice

55. A ________ can institute an involuntary hold for a dangerous client.

A. Parent
B. Law enforcement officer
C. Paramedic
D. Sibling

56. Mike has entered therapy after the recent loss of his house and all his possessions in a house fire. He appears calm, but states that his friends and family are more worried about him than he is. Crisis intervention can only be effective if __________.

A. The client is able to agree to an in-depth analysis of the self in crisis
B. There is a collaborative care team in place
C. The client acknowledges the authority of the therapist
D. The client recognizes he is in a crisis

57. The following statements about suicide are all accurate *except*:

A. Suicide impacts all socioeconomic and ethnic groups
B. Clients who talk about suicide should be assessed for plan and intentionality
C. Talking about suicide increases the likelihood that suicidal clients will follow through
D. Suicide threats may result in involuntary hospitalization

58. Supervisors should not engage in supervisory relationships with friends or family members because of the potential inability to _________.

A. Be clinically helpful
B. Avoid sexual encounters
C. Charge for their services
D. Remain objective

59. A therapist learns that his private-practice suitemate has been having sex with a former client who only completed treatment 6 months ago. The therapist would not __________ in this situation.

A. File an ethical complaint with the American Association of Marriage and Family Therapy (AAMFT)
B. Report the colleague to the state licensing board
C. Try to resolve the issue informally
D. Notify appropriate supervisors

60. Records that _________ do not put a therapist at risk for a potential ethical violation.

A. Have been copied and pasted
B. Are illegible and appear to be out of order
C. Have incomplete data
D. Have been corrected if a mistake was made

61. Therapists who commit ethical infractions are subject to both legal and professional penalties. All of the following are criteria to establish that therapist negligence has occurred *except*:

A. The therapist must have breached an obligation to the client
B. A therapist's intention to harm must be established
C. Damage to the client must be established
D. The harm to the client must be caused by the therapist's error

62. In an opening interview, a client states they are considering gender-affirming surgery, but first needs a letter from a therapist to start hormone therapy. The therapist has no prior experience and isn't comfortable working with transgender clients or this type of letter writing. Given that the therapist believes this is outside his scope of competence, they should __________.

A. Refer the client to a therapist who has experience with this population
B. Write the letter for the client based only on the data obtained from the initial session while accurately portraying their level of experience with this population
C. Co-author a documentation letter with the client and let them educate you on how to best work with a transgender population from a collaborative framework
D. Suggest to the client that they really need to find a therapist who is also transgender

63. The notion that the family must become proactive in making healthy changes in their emotional functioning reflects the experiential concept of __________.

A. Equifinality
B. The battle for initiative
C. Feedback loops
D. Battle for structure

64. It is probable that a client diagnosed in the *Diagnostic and Statistical Manual of Mental Disorders* (5th ed.; *DSM-5*; American Psychiatric Association [APA], 2013) with one of the Somatic Symptom and Related Disorders will have first seen a _______ before making an appointment with a therapist.

A. Spiritual healer
B. Physician
C. Osteopath
D. Registered nurse

65. Managing client transference is best accomplished by___________.

A. Helping the client explore the source of their feelings
B. Self-disclosing your own countertransference to the client
C. Questioning the accuracy of the transference
D. Confronting the client for not dealing with the presenting problem

66. In a client diagnosed with narcissistic personality disorder, ______ are the least helpful in monitoring or evaluating therapy progress.

A. Reports from family members
B. Client self-reports
C. Pre–post results from the Narcissistic Personality Disorder Scale
D. Results from the Narcissistic Personality Inventory

67. Continual client feedback has been found to improve therapy outcome and includes _________.

A. Documentation of global change
B. Therapist progress note data
C. The collection of assessment results
D. A collection of client self-report data

68. The __________ is considered to be the best predictor of eventual therapy outcome.

A. Severity of psychopathology
B. Client's experience
C. Therapeutic technique
D. Therapist's expertise

69. The therapeutic alliance has been found to be a good predictor of ____________.

A. Quick symptom relief
B. Sudden gains in relationship satisfaction
C. When change is going to take place
D. Treatment adherence

70. ____________ does not help therapists in evaluating client progress.

A. The use of a standardized feedback instrument
B. Reviewing treatment goals
C. A formal case review
D. Countertransference analysis

71. Qualitative methods of collecting clinical data do not focus on ________.

A. Observation
B. Focus groups
C. Interviews
D. Likert scales

72. Allen just lost his wife in a tragic boating accident. Which of following symptoms is not associated with his complicated grief?

A. Suicidal thoughts
B. Feeling stigmatized by the loss
C. Isolation from one's support system
D. Maladaptive and intrusive thoughts about the deceased

73. Regarding the security of client records, therapists should not ___________.

A. Review state and federal laws regarding the maintenance and storage of client records
B. Use a password-protected and backed-up storage method for electronic records
C. Only maintain the security of records when taking them home to review
D. Establish agency policies regarding the maintenance and storage of records and ensure that employees follow them

74. If a therapist wishes to consult with a colleague about a particular client case, is it acceptable to disclose the name/identity of the client________.

A. If the appropriate consent has been obtained from the client
B. If the colleague is a licensed mental health professional
C. If they work together in the same agency
D. Never

75. Family therapists practicing telehealth should be most concerned with________?

A. Providing accurate representation of qualifications
B. Monitoring outcomes
C. Not being able to read nonverbal behaviors and responses
D. Avoiding split alliances

76. When working with court-mandated clients, the therapist should not_________.

A. Explain to the client the limitations of confidentiality
B. Discuss the risks and benefits of therapy
C. Inform the client that if they don't want to participate in treatment, they won't force them to because unmotivated clients cannot be helped
D. Explain the client's right to refuse services and the potential consequences should the client choose not to participate in treatment

77. Olson's Circumplex Model of family functioning is based on the intersection of __________.

A. Flexibility and cohesion
B. Enmeshment and disengagement
C. Entropy and negentropy
D. Fusion and differentiation

78. Frieda Fromm-Reichmann's concept, the "________ mother," described a domineering, aggressive, rejecting, and insecure mother who was thought to provide the pathological parenting that produced schizophrenia.

A. Undifferentiated
B. Schizophrenogenic
C. Reactive
D. Symbiotic

79. _____________ refers to the idea of reverting to the norm or "more of the same" feedback, whereas __________________ may be experienced by a family in an escalating crisis such as a fight between parents and a teen.

A. Positive feedback; negative feedback
B. Homeostatic feedback; positive feedback
C. Negative feedback; positive feedback
D. Neutral feedback; positive feedback

80. ____________________ is the concept that refers to when a system restructures its homeostasis in response to positive feedback. During this time, the rules that govern the system fundamentally shift.

A. Second-order change
B. Self-correcting change
C. First-order change
D. Lasting change

81. Tera comes presents for therapy 6 months after the death of her 13-year-old son. She tells you that since this happened, she hasn't been able to eat or work. She can't go into his room and all she wants to do is sleep all day. What should you do first?

A. Have Tera sign a safety plan
B. Assess Tera for suicidal ideation, intent, plan, and access to means
C. Schedule additional sessions and alert Tera's family members immediately
D. Assess for any substance use

82. Mike often shuts down when his fiancée Kimberly becomes distraught and needs his support. In the emotionally focused therapy (EFT) model, withdrawers like Mike tend to avoid their partner's emotional need in order to preserve and protect themselves in the relationship. ________ is a primary emotion that Mike may be experiencing under the surface in relation to Kimberly.

A. Indifference
B. Fear
C. Anger
D. Contempt

83. A couple brings their 16-year-old twins, Eli and Jason, to family therapy. Eli is very boisterous and has a hard time at school, whereas Jason is quiet and on the honor roll. The parents talk about what a great son Jason is and how they wish Eli could be more like his twin, both at home and at school. What would a humanistic–experiential family therapist do?

A. See the twins without the parents to help them build self-esteem without the parents splitting them
B. Talk to Eli about how painful it must be to hear a parent talk badly about him
C. Understand that the family pain comes from the stress of raising two same-age children
D. Prescribe the symptom and suggest that Eli continue to get poor grades by not attempting homework

84. After a dispute over a late session fee, the client has refused to pay their bill, ends therapeutic services, and requests in writing that their records be released to their new therapist in order to continue treatment. The original therapist should____________.

A. Inform the client that their records can only be provided to the new therapist after the outstanding balance has been paid
B. Ask the client to first sign a release of information so that the original therapist can talk to the new therapist about the client's attitude and delinquent payment before they agree to take the case on
C. Ignore the client request until the bill is settled or a proper payment plan is in place
D. Alert the client that their records will be released to the new therapist after a proper release of information has been signed by the client, and then give client advance notice of the steps that will be taken in the original therapist's bill-collection protocol

85. If a client tells you that he had sex with a previous therapist, you should ________.

A. Have the client sign a release of information and report the psychologist to the appropriate ethics committee
B. With the client's permission, contact the therapist yourself
C. Report the therapist to an ethics committee with or without the client's permission
D. Outline the client's rights and options regarding legal action and ethics complaints

86. During a session, a client of yours who you know is HIV positive, casually claims that he has been engaging in unprotected sex. You believe he is telling the truth. Are these sufficient grounds for you to break confidentiality and notify the authorities?

A. Yes, you should always break confidentiality whenever an individual makes a claim like this
B. Yes, if you genuinely believe he is making a truthful statement
C. No, because there is no identified third party who is at risk
D. No, you never break confidentiality under any circumstances

87. A marriage and family therapist is seeing a client who is in therapy as a condition of probation. The client says he wants to terminate therapy. The therapist should ______________.

A. Tell the client that he must stay in therapy
B. Tell the client he can leave if he wishes but explain the legal ramifications of doing so to him
C. Terminate therapy immediately
D. Call the client's probation officer immediately or as soon as possible

88. Juanito, a 10-year-old boy, is referred for family therapy along with his mother, Carlotta. She is at a loss about what to do, reporting that her son is extremely irritable and has explosive outbursts multiple times a week. Carlotta notes that since Juanito's dad was incarcerated 2 years ago, he just seems angry all the time now. Which of the following *Diagnostic and Statistical Manual of Mental Disorders* (5th ed.; *DSM-5*; APA, 2013) diagnoses should be considered for Juanito?

A. Bipolar I
B. Intermittent Explosive Disorder
C. Disruptive Mood Dysregulation Disorder
D. Adjustment Disorder

89. After nearly a year of treatment, totaling 38 sessions, a client abruptly cancels all further sessions via voicemail. The therapist's most appropriate response would be:

A. Call the client to check-in
B. Respect the client's right to self-determination and close the file
C. Ask the client to reconsider, given that all treatment goals have not yet been met
D. Send a letter discussing termination

90. Tim and Jackie have entered couple therapy. They describe that their relationship has not been the same since their youngest child left for college several months ago. Tim stays busy in his workshop late into the evening, while Jackie wishes her husband would join her in front of the TV so that they could spend more time together. How should the therapist proceed during the first session?

A. Conduct an inventory of the couple's attachment style
B. Provide psychoeducation to the couple about life stages
C. Ask Tim and Jackie to practice empathy and describe their experience from their partner's point of view
D. Schedule individual sessions with each member of the couple

91. A Muslim female client enters therapy with the goal of becoming more assertive. After she fails to complete several homework tasks aimed at self-advocacy at home and at work, the therapist asks about her inability to follow through. She indicates she is fearful of initiating change because her culture does not approve of assertive women. Which of the following interventions should be used in this situation?

A. Support the client's efforts to pursue her original goal
B. Reformulate the goals with the client
C. Explore the client's perception of the cultural conflict and constraints around being more assertive
D. Reframe the client's statements as resistance

92. A 30-year-old gay man, Tyler, reveals to the therapist that he was recently arrested for soliciting prostitution. He is currently facing serious legal charges and feels lonely and desperate. Tyler is filled with guilt and shame when thinking about revealing both this news and his sexuality to his siblings and parents. Feeling a greater need to be connected with his people, Tyler wants acceptance from his family of origin. The therapist's best course of action would be to ______________.

A. Contact the man's family
B. Help Tyler develop a support system
C. Reassure Tyler that he does not really need his family if they cannot accept him as he is
D. Refer Tyler to a gay therapist

93. Jeff calls in crisis because he just found out he was terminated from his high-paying executive job. He is obviously very upset and is catastrophizing by making states like "I'll never work again in this industry. I'm doomed!" The therapist knows that in the past, Jeff has had difficulty adapting to unexpected changes in his life, including a breakup with a girlfriend and the loss of a close friend. One of the major goals in this situation is ______________.

A. To identify underlying conflicts as they relate to the crisis
B. To eliminate the problem that triggered the crisis
C. To help Jeff come back to his previous level of functioning
D. To decrease the danger that Jeff poses to himself

94. The "slippery slope" with regard to ethics for therapists __________.

A. Indicates that the therapist is about to get sued
B. Signifies that the therapist has been negligent
C. Often starts with benign boundary crossing
D. Contends that the therapist is sure to get in trouble with an ethics committee

95. In the process of reporting the results of research, a competent and ethical therapist should do all of the following *except*:

A. Provide a discussion about the limitations of the research
B. Describe the possible applications of the data for diverse populations
C. Avoid data distortion
D. Omit discussion of variables that the therapist believes may have skewed the data

96. By using a subtle linguistic shift involving both acknowledgment and validation, the collaborative language therapist introduces the idea of future change in the client's life. This technique is known as _______________.

A. Solution talk
B. Externalizing the problem
C. Possibility talk
D. "Not knowing"

97. You are working with 10-year-old Thomas, a fourth grader who worries about everything, including school performance and his social interactions with peers. As a narrative therapist, how would you respond to your young client's presenting problem?

A. "Thomas, it sounds like you worry more often than you would like."
B. "How did you first meet Mr. Worry, Thomas?"
C. "Thomas, you need to worry more!"
D. "How many times a day do you find yourself worrying and for how long?"

98. The Green Family enters family therapy because their 16-year-old daughter, Tania, has been sneaking out to meet her boyfriend late at night. Thirteen-year-old Linda often tells on her sister, but the parents, Mike and Donna, often ignore Linda and are helpless when it comes to trying to control Tania. As a structural family therapist, what might you do with this family in an opening session?

A. Ask the family to dramatize what happens when they discover Tania has snuck out again; have the family practice a new approach in session; assign homework for everyone
B. Ask Tania how she got to be so successful at sneaking out; encourage Mike and Donna to worry more about Linda and less about Tania
C. Ask the family to dramatize what happens when they discover Tania has snuck out again; intellectualize with Linda about her sister's bad behavior; assign homework to everyone except Linda
D. Tell Tania you didn't always like following parental rules when you were her age either; have the parents focus more on their marriage and dating behaviors than on their oldest daughter's dating behaviors

99. At the end of an opening session with a particularly difficult client who reports low motivation to engage in therapy, the therapist asks, "How will you know when it is the right time not to come to therapy anymore?" By using this question, the therapist is ___________.

A. Using a paradoxical intervention
B. Rolling with client resistance
C. Implementing a solution-focused technique
D. Giving the client an "out" in case they do not want to return for a second meeting

100. Emma and Kevin enter couples therapy with the presenting problem of fighting unfairly. Emma often insults Kevin when she doesn't get to spend enough time with him. Kevin thinks she is jealous of his job and busy work schedule. He also believes she resents him for their relocation to Chicago last year because of his job. Which of the following interventions would a narrative therapist MOST likely use?

A. Highlight unique outcomes, separate them from their fighting through externalization, and look for new ways to narrate their move in way that benefits the couple

B. Ask them to describe a good day, challenge any distorted thinking in their story, and compliment them on coming to therapy

C. Have them act out a fight, map with them the effects that fighting has on their relationship, and suggest bibliotherapy

D. Create a genogram with each of them, look for exceptions to the problem, and suggest they fight at a designated time each day

101. Aaron and Trish come in to see you because they have difficulty controlling their 6-year-old son, Liam. Within minutes of starting the session, Liam has destroyed your office, knocking over furniture and everything on your desk. The parents apologize, but don't intervene to stop Liam's behavior. A behavioral family therapist would set which of the following priorities in the early stage of the family work?

A. Determine the types of rewards that would appeal to Liam as positive reinforcement for good behavior

B. Highlight play therapy techniques for Aaron and Trish to use at home with Liam

C. Help Aaron and Trish develop consistent discipline

D. Extinguish Liam's acting-out tantrums

102. In structural family therapy, scapegoating and overprotection of a child by the mother and father are considered types of __________.

A. Triangulation

B. Detouring

C. Cross-generational coalitions

D. Projections

103. You are working with Jeff, an extremely fearful graduate student who has previously been diagnosed with an anxiety disorder and is currently afraid that his classmates are continually judging him. Using a cognitive approach to treat this client, initial cognitive restructuring will most likely focus on ___________.

A. Reattribution

B. Cognitive rehearsal

C. Thought stopping

D. Decatastrophizing

104. You have been referred a teenager who tragically lost his mother to cancer last month. As he struggles to engage in the opening meeting, you consider sharing how your father died when you were the same age as your client. How could this type of self-disclosure—discussing a personal experience with the death of a parent—help the client?

A. It could create empathy with the client
B. The therapist could treat the client as "expert" and enlist his help
C. The disclosure could create a sense of shared experience between client and therapist
D. It establishes the therapist as an authority on grief issues

105. You are working with a single mother, Victoria, and her aggressive 9-year-old son, Victor. He has a problem with stealing. Your first intervention would be to __________.

A. Assess the behavior that takes place before the stealing occurs
B. Teach Victoria to set up a system that rewards Victor for not stealing
C. Teach Victoria to use appropriate punishment to extinguish the behavior
D. Set up a contingency contract between mother and son

106. Mikey, age 12, refuses to engage in an opening family therapy session. His parents report that his lack of participation and refusal to complete even the most basic of tasks, often highjacks the family's ability to get things done. As a structural therapist, what technique would you use to engage the son in the session?

A. Ignore Mikey until he decides to speak on his own
B. Sit next to Mikey and tell him what he is doing is okay and understandable
C. Direct Mikey to remain silent
D. Instruct the parents to make Mikey talk

107. Client-centered therapy requires the therapist to __________.

A. Be direct but caring
B. Work in the "here and now"
C. Create links between the client's present behavior and past experience
D. Let the client arrive at their own decisions and insights

108. From a systems perspective, family behavior that helps to minimize deviation and maintain the family stability, is referred to as ______________.

A. Mimesis
B. The family projection process
C. Negative feedback
D. Positive feedback

109. Childhood sexual abuse may produce either sexual acting out or sexual inhibition in a man during adulthood in his intimate relationships. This illustrates the concept of __________.

A. Equifinality
B. Positive feedback
C. Equipotentiality
D. Negative feedback

110. According to Bowen, "triangles" form in families in order to ______________.

A. Establish boundaries
B. Establish power
C. Decrease fusion
D. Reestablish homeostasis

111. A Native American client with self-confidence issues would most likely be comfortable with a therapist who __________.

A. Incorporates traditional tribal medicine
B. Works from a humanistic–existential perspective
C. Is primarily cognitive behavioral
D. Expands the system to include other family members

112. Mike is a 24-year-old who lives at home with his parents. He is very shy and uses gaming as an escape. Although he longs to be in a romantic relationship, Mike doesn't think anyone could love him, He wants to use therapy to build confidence in talking with others. How can the therapeutic relationship help Mike to interact in a more authentic way to help with his relationship goals?

A. By practicing self-disclosure and trying on new types of interacting
B. By identifying automatic negative thoughts
C. By practicing thought stopping and building skills
D. By eliminating avoidance habits

113. In a family in which the mother and daughter are enmeshed, a structural family therapist would intervene by ___________.

A. Instructing the family to demonstrate a problem situation, having them exchange roles, assigning homework to practice the new way of relating
B. Instructing the family to demonstrate a problem situation, having them replay the situation while the therapist spatially separates the mother and daughter, assigning homework to practice the new way of relating
C. Spatially separating the mother and daughter, having them demonstrate a problem situation, letting the father suggest a different solution
D. Asking the mother and father to change roles as they demonstrate a problem situation, having the daughter describe a better solution, then designing homework to reinforce the new pattern

114. A marriage and family therapist with psychodynamic training views family problems arising from ___________.

A. Intrapsychic conflicts within individual family members
B. An inflexible family structure that constrains the family from transitioning to the next stage of the family life cycle
C. A transgenerational transmission process
D. An unbalanced ledger

115. A therapist is seeing a family who is having challenges adapting to the growing financial demands of private school and travel club soccer. Instead of exploring the problems in detail, the therapist asks, "When is this problem not a problem?" The purpose of this question is to ___________.

A. Reframe the situation in a more positive way
B. Identify exceptions as a resource for positive change
C. Challenge the family's dominant story around money
D. Restructure the family's cognitions around money

116. A structural family therapist instructs an enmeshed mother and her adolescent son to sit on opposite sides of the couch, pointing out the mountain of pillows between them. This intervention would be described as _________.

A. Mimesis
B. An enactment
C. Creating intensity
D. Boundary making

117. __________would be an appropriate early-stage intervention for a Bowenian therapist working with a high-conflict, emotionally volatile young married couple.

A. Detriangulating
B. Teaching behavior exchange and communication skills
C. Helping each partner to reconnect with their families of origin
D. Helping each partner identify their triggers and learn how to think before reacting

118. A widowed mother seeks family therapy because she feels out of control with her teenage twin sons. One son tries to parent his mother by critiquing her financial decisions and giving her unsolicited advice on wardrobe choice, whereas the other boy is overly distant and attempts to spend as much time as possible away from the home with friends and other extended family. The mother just wants to be in control of her home and family again. _________is the model of family therapy that would most likely be recommended for this system?

A. Cognitive behavioral therapy
B. Bowen family systems
C. Internal family systems
D. Structural

119. Aaron and Trish avoid talking to each other about the lack of physical intimacy in their marriage by venting to their 18-year-old daughter Cindy about their partner's inability to initiate sex. This is an example of ___________.

A. Displacement
B. Enmeshment
C. Fusion
D. Triangulation

120. Bella, a 16-year-old honors student, is attending therapy to deal with academic pressures. She comes from a high-achieving family, and she is expected to go to any Ivy League school, like both of her parents before her. During your discussion, she reveals that her 42-year-old college prep tutor forced her to have sex with him last month. However, she is careful to add, she feels perfectly safe now. You should ________________.

A. Report the abuse
B. Not report the abuse because Bella is not in any danger
C. Have Bella report the abuse
D. Investigate the possibility of abuse, but only report if you determine that Bella is currently in danger

121. A strategic family therapist is most likely to use which of the following therapeutic techniques when intervening with a couple who complain that they are constantly arguing with each other?

A. Obtain a detailed history from each partner
B. Ask the couple to identify the benefits they obtain from arguing
C. Tell the couple to argue for at least 2 hours each evening
D. Work individually with the partner who is most differentiated

122. Which of the following "referral situations" is unethical?

A. Your client needs educational testing
B. You feel the client would be better served by a gay therapist, especially since you do not agree with the client's gay lifestyle
C. Your client wants a therapist who has a background in the armed services
D. Your client has schizophrenia, and you feel that someone with more expertise in that area would be more effective

123. An anxious mother brings in her 14-year-old son, who was recently hospitalized for anxiety following the divorce of his parents. The mother is overwhelmed by guilt, attributing the divorce to her son's declining mental health. Bowen would most likely describe the boy's behavior as exemplifying ___________________.

A. The family projection process
B. An emotional cutoff
C. The function of the symptom
D. Enmeshment

124. On an assessment, it is ________________.

A. Necessary to list referral sources only if they are related to treatment issues
B. Necessary to list referral sources
C. Optional to list referral sources
D. Not necessary to list referral sources

125. A strategic therapist tells a client who wants to quit overeating that he should keep all of his food outside of his home in a place that is accessible only by walking for more than 20 minutes. This is an example of which of the following paradoxical techniques?

A. Reframing
B. Symptom prescription
C. Ordeal
D. Pretend technique

126. You have been working with Kenny, an alcoholic client, weekly for the last 4 months. Kenny has not progressed in treatment and is still drinking regularly. The best treatment approach here would be to ________________.

A. Discharge Kenny because of failure to progress
B. Implement an abstinence contract and refer to Alcoholics Anonymous
C. Refer Kenny to a higher level of care
D. Refer Kenny to a substance abuse specialist

127. Keith has just been diagnosed with stage 4 pancreatic cancer. Which of the following is *least* useful as a first intervention with a client who has just found out that he has terminal cancer?

A. Utilize crisis intervention techniques
B. Help Keith confront death
C. Help Keith gain access to medical resources
D. Process with Keith his feelings in the wake of receiving the diagnosis

128. Janet, a 32-year-old woman who you have only been seeing for a few weeks, comes to her previously scheduled appointment appearing distraught, disheveled, and disorganized. She reports being raped about 7 hours sago while out walking her dog. Because Janet knew she had time scheduled with you later in the day, she has not yet notified the police or been to the emergency room. Which of the following would you *not* include as an immediate intervention?

A. Find Janet a group for survivors of rape
B. Validate Janet's feelings and provide essential psychoeducation about expected emotional reactions
C. Help Janet restore a sense of safety
D. Immediately arrange for a medical referral

129. Brandon, a client with no previous history of violent behavior, is severely disturbed about the recent breakup with his girlfriend. He walked in on her having sex with her sociology professor. Brandon blames the failure of the relationship on the professor and tells you that he feels like killing him. Brandon reports tracking him for the last week and could easily surprise the professor at his home because he lives alone. Given this information, what is a therapist required to do in this situation?

A. Maintain Brandon's confidentiality since he has no history of violent behavior and provide crisis intervention
B. Refer Brandon to a physician or psychiatrist for medication to manage these symptoms and then monitor the situation closely
C. Hospitalize Brandon to stabilize him and protect the professor
D. Take reasonably necessary steps in an effort to protect the college professor

130. The therapist is performing a suicide evaluation of Tammy, a 36-year-old woman who reports feeling depressed and having morbid thoughts about dying. What does your initial assessment need to include to determine Tammy's current level of risk?

A. Tammy's level of impulse control and whether her judgment is impaired at this time
B. Tammy's level of depression and social support
C. Tammy's coping skills and whether they are adequate for handling the current situation
D. Tammy's plan for committing suicide

131. A therapist is seeing a 17-year-old girl for individual therapy. During the third session, she reveals that sometimes she cuts herself on her legs (where no one can see) when she's feeling stressed or overwhelmed. The *first* thing the therapist should do is ________________.

A. Develop a safety plan with her
B. Contact her parents, as this is a safety issue and they must be informed
C. Refer her to a psychiatrist for a medication evaluation
D. Refer her to a physician, as working with self-injurious clients is out of a therapist's scope of practice

132. ________________ is a framework used to establish how families respond to stressful events and crises.

A. ABC-X Model of Family Stress
B. The McMaster Model
C. Olson's Circumplex Model
D. The Beaver's System Model

133. All of the following are barriers that limit the adoption of standardized progress measures into the everyday practice of systemic therapy *except*:

A. Clients may feel uncomfortable with rating their therapist in their presence
B. There is a lack of knowledge by therapists and dissatisfaction with specific characteristics of monitoring measures
C. An organization may not feel that the measures fit with their needs
D. The data are not clinically useful

134. The ethical principle of beneficence refers to ___________.

A. Faithfulness to the promises made
B. The obligation to act fairly
C. The responsibility to do good
D. The responsibility to do no harm

135. The first thing a therapist should do during the ethical decision-making process is to _________.

A. Identify the problem
B. Follow their initial instinct
C. Implement a course of action
D. Generate potential courses of action

136. ___________ should *not* be documented in the progress notes in a termination session.

A. The therapist's personal opinions about the client
B. Any continuity-of-care needs and plans
C. The reasons for termination
D. The client's reaction to the ending

137. Which one of the following would be considered a contraindication to family therapy?

A. The family is experiencing severe domestic violence that has not been brought under control
B. A family member's symptoms are manifestations of problems in the family system
C. A family member has been diagnosed with a terminal illness
D. Previous family therapy has been unsuccessful

138. Mike, a marriage and family therapist, is referred a case in which the father has sexually abused both of his sons. Mike has his own trauma history of having been sexually abused by his uncle when he was a child. Mike should ______________________.

A. Not accept the referral, as Mike will likely experience countertransference that will negatively impact treatment
B. Accept the referral as long as the client is willing and able to commit to treatment
C. Consider his effectiveness in being able to treat this client
D. Refer the father to an intensive outpatient program, as they are proven more effective than individual treatment

139. For the past year, Leslie has been taking victim referrals from the violent crimes unit of the local police department. Lately, she's been feeling increasingly depressed, has been withdrawing from friends and colleagues, and has begun having nightmares. This therapist is likely experiencing ______________________.

A. Burnout
B. Vicarious traumatization
C. Posttraumatic stress disorder (PTSD)
D. Negative countertransference

140. As part of her opening-session routine, Kim makes a point of asking all her new client to notice what has changed with their presenting issue since making the initial phone call for the appointment. This is most representative of a ____________therapist.

A. Solution-focused
B. Cognitive behavioral
C. Narrative
D. Strategic

141. In postmodern therapies, *constructivism* refers to the idea that ____________________.

A. Categories of knowledge and reality are not necessarily constructed by social relationships and interactions
B. The way we expect to experience the world alters how we feel about it and how we act
C. How we know reality is intimately regulated by how we feel about it
D. The process of constructing knowledge regulates itself, and because knowledge is a construct rather than a compilation of empirical data, it becomes possible to know the extent to which knowledge reflects an ontological reality

142. Linda, a Bowenian therapist, conducts an initial family interview with the Johnson family. Overall, the family is exhibiting a high degree of fusion. Although the mother, father, and two older siblings present with high levels of anxiety and the inability to stay calm around each other, the youngest daughter, however, remains calm and appears to be more differentiated than the others. Linda will likely choose to work with ________________.

A. The least differentiated family member
B. The most differentiated family member
C. All family members as a group
D. All family members in individual therapy until they reach a similar level of differentiation

143. Contextual family therapy posits that family members develop problems or distress when ____________________.

A. The family system is rejecting and abandoning
B. The context of the family encourages enmeshment
C. The self is not integrated with the subparts
D. There is a lack of trust and caring in the family system

144. Tony receives a rather harsh critique from his boss at work. At home, later that evening, he is sarcastic and argumentative with his wife, Monica, for no apparent reason. Tony's behavior toward Monica is an example of ____________________.

A. Sublimation
B. Dissociation
C. Displacement
D. Rationalization

145. A practitioner of Masters and Johnson's behavioral sex therapy is *least* likely to agree with which of the following statements:

A. The "identified patient" in therapy is the partner with the sexual dysfunction
B. The sexual response cycle consists of four phases
C. Sensate focus bans intercourse at the beginning of therapy
D. There is no difference between vaginal and clitoral orgasms

146. The role of therapist is __________ in collaborative family therapy.

A. The expert on the therapeutic process
B. A co-learner along with the client
C. An ethical partner in the therapeutic process
D. Part of the reflecting team with the client

147. Michelle's paranoid schizophrenic client, Jaime, requests access to her therapy records to figure out what the therapist has been saying about her "behind her back." Michelle refuses her request after determining it would be damaging to Jaime's well-being if she were to see the records. Jaime claims that "they are my records and I have the right to look at them." In this case the records belong to ______.

A. The client
B. The therapist
C. The client and the therapist share ownership of the record
D. The state licensing board

148. You helped a couple who was on the brink of divorce rebuild their marriage. At Christmas, you receive an expensive framed work of art from the couple with a card thanking you for a "job well done." You should _______________.

A. Accept the gift
B. Refuse the gift
C. Return the artwork to the store where they bought it
D. Donate the artwork to a charitable organization

149. You are working with a challenging couple and have come to a gridlocked position in the therapy. Your suitemate is an excellent clinician and sees more couples than anyone else in town. If you decide to consult with a colleague about the "therapeutic impasse" you are having with this client system___________.

A. It is necessary to advise the couple of the consultation
B. It is necessary to get permission from each member of the couple to discuss confidential information with the consultant before doing so
C. It is unnecessary to get permission from the couple to discuss confidential information with the consultant as long as their identity is not revealed to the consultant
D. It is unnecessary to get permission from the couple to discuss confidential information with the consultant as long as only relevant information is discussed during the consultation

150. As a newly licensed therapist, what is the most important thing for to evaluate before accepting a referral?

A. Scope-of-practice issues
B. Your training and experience
C. The client's disorder
D. The motivation level of the client

151. Your client died suddenly, and now her 25-year-old son would like a copy of her records so he can understand more about her mental state at the time of her death. Who will decide whether you can make your records available to him?

A. The executor of the client's will
B. The client's lawyer
C. You, as the client's therapist
D. The client's husband

152. Mike, a marriage and family therapist, is just starting his private practice and has made an arrangement with another successful therapist to pay her $50.00 for each new client she refers to Mike. This is ________________.

A. Ethical as long as the arrangement is agreeable to Mike and the other therapist
B. Ethical as long as the clients are informed of this policy at the beginning of therapy
C. Unethical because it represents a "multiple relationship"
D. Unethical if the payment is only for the referral

153. You are seeing Tina and Tom, but they cannot afford to pay for your therapy services. Tina is a masseuse and asks whether she can trade her services for therapy. You should____________________.

A. Inform them that it would be unethical and begin a discussion about sliding-scale fees
B. Acknowledge their struggle and accept the arrangement
C. Refer them to a financial counselor and discontinue therapy
D. Refer them to a sliding-scale clinic

154. Advising a client about a legal action in a divorce proceeding would be outside the scope of ______________, whereas providing eye movement desensitization and reprocessing (EMDR) therapy when not adequately trained would be considered to be outside of the scope of ________________.

A. Competence; practice
B. Practice; competence
C. Practice; administering
D. Training; education

155. You are one of only a few marriage and family therapists in a small rural community. Your neighbor asks whether you will see her teenage daughter for therapy. She owns and operates a store in town where you shop. How should you best respond to her request?

A. You decide to give the neighbor a referral because you don't want your potential dual relationship to possibly contaminate her daughter's therapy
B. You agree to see the daughter and, without saying anything, go to the store on the other side of town to avoid dual relationships with the family
C. You are not concerned about dual relationships under these circumstances and decide to take the case because you don't want the family to have to drive 20 miles to the closest clinic where they could see another therapist
D. You consider whether your relationship with the neighbor will affect the potential therapeutic relationship with the family and decide whether to take on the case accordingly

156. Which statement about ethical and legal issues is most accurate?

A. Legal issues are seldom consistent with ethical standards
B. Marriage and family therapists should always consider legal issues as secondary to their association's ethical code
C. Ethical issues seldom overlap with legal issues
D. Ethical issues often overlap with legal issues

157. Lacy comes to therapy because her work takes priority over her marriage. Her fuse is short around her passive husband, and she is unsure whether she wants to stay in his marriage. How would a Bowenian therapist approach this case?

A. See Lacy alone and work to de-triangulate the work from the marriage
B. See the couple and process unresolved issues that perpetuate the tension in the marriage
C. See Lacy alone and promote differentiation of thoughts and feelings
D. See the couple and promote level communication and a work–life balance

158. In strategic family therapy, "prescribing the symptom" can ________________.

A. Undermine the family's resistance to change
B. Change the meaning of a situation by changing the way it is perceived
C. Relabel the symptom
D. Increase differentiation among members of the family

159. Tom, a 32-year-old police officer, was referred to therapy after his partner died in his arms after a shooting that Tom feels responsible for. He has become withdrawn in his marriage and other relationships. He is having difficulty functioning at work. As a cognitive behavioral therapist, what would you most likely think Tom's problems are a result of?

A. A distortion of reality based on incorrect premises and assumptions
B. Chronic anxiety leading to a high level of emotional reactivity
C. An exaggerated feeling of inferiority and an insufficiently developed feeling of community
D. An inability to experience contradictory feelings leading to distortion of perception

160. Bipolar II Disorder is distinguished from Bipolar I Disorder by the requirement of the presence of which of the following for Bipolar II Disorder?

A. Manic and major depressive episodes
B. At least one psychotic episode
C. Hypomanic and major depressive episodes
D. Two or more major depressive episodes

161. Behavior that is overly dramatic, reactive, intensely expressed, and perceived by others as shallow and superficial is characteristic of _________ personality disorders?

A. Borderline
B. Schizotypal
C. Obsessive-compulsive
D. Histrionic

162. For a *Diagnostic and Statistical Manual of Mental Disorders* (5th ed.; *DSM-5*; APA, 2013) diagnosis of Delirium, a person must exhibit a disturbance in ___________ plus at least one other disturbance in cognition.

A. Attention and awareness
B. Psychomotor functioning
C. Receptive and expressive language
D. Executive functioning

163. Deb brings her 16-year-old son, Isaac into your office. She reports he is losing weight and now just spends all of his time in his room instead of with friends. You notice that Isaac appears agitated and somewhat confused and is sweating and has dilated pupils. When he speaks, he runs on in an animated way, but is virtually incoherent and hard to follow. What is the most likely diagnosis for Isaac?

A. Cannabis Intoxication
B. Schizophrenia
C. Stimulant Intoxication
D. Bipolar I Disorder

164. For the past year, 41-year-old Randy has had extreme difficulty maintaining an erection. Although he occasionally gets them in the morning upon waking up, he cannot achieve an erection at any other point in time. He has no known medical conditions or substance use issues to speak of. He is very worried and embarrassed by this problem. What would be the most likely *Diagnostic and Statistical Manual of Mental Disorders* (5th ed.; *DSM-5*; APA, 2013) diagnosis?

A. Erectile Disorder
B. Orgasmic Disorder
C. Premature Ejaculation
D. Hypoactive Sexual Desire Disorder

165. Which of the following statements regarding progress notes related to treatment plans is the most accurate?

A. Progress notes show gains made toward specific therapeutic goals and objectives
B. Progress notes are used primarily as a memory aid
C. Good therapy progress notes follow a predetermined format
D. Progress notes reflect the treatment plan's implementation as well as provide indicators for needed changes in the plan as therapy progresses

166. Which of the following statements about client goals is the *most* accurate?

A. It is the client's responsibility to both generate and measure goal progress
B. Client goals should be quantified and broken down into measurable objectives
C. Goals are set collaboratively with the client, stated in both realistic and positive terms, and reviewed regularly throughout the course of therapy
D. The therapist sets the goals for the client based on the diagnosis and measures reduction in symptoms as a clinical indicator of progress

167. Although there is compelling evidence that monitoring and feedback can improve client outcomes, this practice is ______________.

A. Common among private practitioners
B. Underutilized by private practitioners
C. More common in private practice than in agency settings
D. Determined by therapeutic modality

168. A feminist family therapist would do all of the following *except:*

A. Strive for an egalitarian relationship
B. Empower underrepresented voices
C. Emphasize traditional assessment and diagnosis
D. Encourage clients to set their own goals

169. You have been conducting cognitive behavioral couples therapy with newlyweds, Jules and Jordan, for 18 sessions. They entered therapy having very different ideas about how a marriage should work. How would the therapist know when it is time to terminate therapy?

A. Jules and Jordan have learned how to communicate without arguing
B. The stated time limit set for therapy has expired
C. Jules and Jordan have altered their unrealistic ideas and expectations about their marriage
D. Jules and Jordan can draw healthy boundaries with their parents

170. During an opening session with a defiant teen, Jack, the client refuses to talk. His parents only told him about going to therapy a few hours before the first session. Which of the following interventions should you attempt to engage Jack?

A. Sit in silence with Jack for the remainder of the session
B. End the session and tell Jack to return when he is more comfortable discussing his concerns
C. Use empathic statements in an attempt to understand Jack's silence
D. Explain to Jack that the silence is counterproductive

171. Noting your own observation about a client's emotional state on a mental status exam refers to the ____________ domain?

A. Behavior
B. Insight
C. Mood
D. Affect

172. ____________ is the most objective way to test whether the therapy has been successful in modifying a client's personality.

A. Direct observations in session
B. A pre- and post-treatment Minnesota Multiphasic Personality Inventory-2 (MMPI-2)
C. Review the goals of therapy
D. Change in symptomology as indicated in your records

173. Your client is the victim of a date rape. In addition to individual trauma work, when would you send her to a group for trauma survivors?

A. When the crisis is abated since it is too overwhelming at first
B. Right away, because emotions are best contained in a group setting
C. It does not matter; only the skill of the group therapist is important
D. In the middle stage of therapy

174. According to the Outcome Rating Scale (ORS), asking clients how they are functioning in terms of school, work, or friends reflects the ________________ area of the instrument?

A. Overall
B. Interpersonally
C. Socially
D. Career

175. A therapist is called to a hospital emergency room to assist with a mother who was brought in with her 15-year-old son who had just died of a heroin overdose. The mother, who has no history of mental illness, is refusing to let go of her son and insists that the doctors are not doing enough to save him. How should the therapist approach this case?

A. Ask the doctors to sedate the mother while her son's body is removed
B. Allow the mother to let go of her son in her own time
C. Admit the mother to the psychiatric unit
D. Involve family members in helping to reorient the mother

176. A therapist has been treating an 8-year-old child who was physically abused by a cousin who is 20 years old. The therapist learns that the older cousin recently moved back into the house after losing a job. The therapist is told that the family was given permission by social services to allow the older cousin back into the home. Ethically, the therapist should first:

A. Schedule a joint session with the victim and the perpetrator
B. Contract with the victim to report any further abuse
C. Develop a safety plan for the victim
D. Appeal the decision made by social services and request removal of the perpetrator from the house

177. Your client, Maureen, often vents about the stress associated with taking care of her 90-year-old mother. The client says that she decided last week not to allow her mother to receive any phone calls or visits from friends, because contact with other people upsets her mother and makes her harder to manage. The client says that isolating her mother in this way has helped keep the tension down in the home. What should you do?

A. Assess Maureen's coping strategies since there are better ways to handle this problem
B. Assess for elder abuse by asking Maureen questions and arranging to evaluate her mother
C. Report elder abuse based on the information Maureen has shared
D. Ask Maureen to bring her mother in so that you can assess the nature and structure of their interactions

178. When performing a suicide assessment, which of the following people would most concern you?

A. Cindy, an unmarried white female who has threatened to cut her wrists
B. Barry, an unemployed, divorced 72-year-old male who had tried to overdose on aspirin and bourbon in the past
C. Joe, a middle-aged male who is currently very depressed and has access to sleeping pills
D. Connie, a married 30-year-old female who expresses a sense of hopelessness and says she has thought about buying a gun

179. Larry meets with a licensed marriage and family therapist for help with his anger over his partner's extramarital affair. During the initial session, Larry states he has a "plan to get even and make her pay the ultimate price" for what she did to him. What should the therapist do first?

A. Notify Larry's partner of the verbal threat
B. Remind Larry of the limits of confidentiality
C. Obtain a history of Larry's previous violent behaviors
D. Seek further clarification of Larry's statement

180. Pete is referred to you following a noticeable decline in his job performance. During the opening assessment, Pete talks about his traumatic childhood, physical abuse by his parents, and two divorces. His girlfriend is cheating on him and he attributes his recent job problems to his chaotic relationship with her. He acknowledges drinking alcohol several times a week to help him relax but does not feel it is a problem. The therapist should initially clarify:

A. His potential job loss
B. His childhood physical abuse
C. His substance use
D. His problems with his relationship

REFERENCES

American Psychiatric Association. (2013). *Diagnostic and statistical manual of mental disorders* (5th ed.).

Answers With Rationales

20

1. **B) Provide psychoeducation and reassure the mother that this is normal behavior for children this age**
   Sexual curiosity is a normal part of development for children. Discussing feelings about sexuality (A) would be an important step, but only after providing psychoeducation to the parent about normal development. If the therapist provides psychoeducation to the parent regarding normal behaviors and the parent in turn provides additional information that points to abnormal behaviors or experiences, then options C and D may be appropriate. Until that were to happen, however, the actions described in options C and D would be considered overreactions based on the limited information presented. *(Domain 3-1)*

2. **A) Find out what John means by "depression"; provide referral to domestic violence resources; identify coping skills**
   It sufficiently addresses all points presented in the vignette. When working with domestic violence (DV), we are to create a safety plan, refer to DV resources, and identify/strengthen coping skills. This client mentions depression; thus it is clinically necessary to assess for it. Option B is incorrect because it may be clinically premature to do therapy with couples when DV is present. Option C is incorrect because John did not express ambivalence, we do not have enough information for a psychiatric referral, and as therapists we provide DV resources, not encourage clients to take advantage of specific ones. Option D is incorrect because it is not evident at this juncture that John needs medical attention, and option A better accounts for all necessary steps. *(Domain 2-1)*

3. **B) Ask Jason directly what interferes with completion of homework**
   Meeting Jason where he is at in a neutral, curious way is the most appropriate way to approach this situation. Interpreting Jason's behavior as a sign of resistance may be an overreaction, so option A is incorrect. Reminding Jason of the importance of homework might come across as shaming and judgmental, so option C is out. Acknowledging that homework can be burdensome (D) is not as helpful when working to increase homework compliance. *(Domain 4-1)*

4. **C) Explore the feelings behind the voyeuristic behavior**
   Without an understanding of the internal feelings underlying the behavior, and the secondary gain it provides for the client, treatment will not be effective. Option A is more confrontational and will not address the underlying causes of the behavior or help change the behavior. The client is saying that option B is not working. Option D is not going to be effective unless both the therapist and the client understand the feelings behind the behaviors. *(Domain 3-2)*

5. **C) The child no longer becomes terrified when seeing lit fireplaces**
One of the ways to determine that it is time to terminate is when the client is symptom free. Because this client's presenting complaint is around lit fireplaces, once the little girl is no longer terrified of them, it would be time to terminate. *(Domain 4-2)*

6. **D) Leave the hospital whenever she chooses**
A person who is involuntarily hospitalized does not have the choice to leave the hospital, but rather is released by hospital personnel only after an evaluation and observation shows the patient is safe to self and/or others. During involuntary hospitalization a person has the right to (A) refuse treatment, (B) decline having family contacted, and (C) keep records of admission confidential. *(Domain 5-1)*

7. **D) Meet with the member individually following group to further assess**
The nature of the disclosure dictates that the therapist meets individually with the group member instead of in front of the group. When a group member discloses information that relates to safety concerns, such as abuse or suicidality, further exploration of the disclosure should not be done in the group setting (A). This allows the therapist to properly assess the client and avoid potentially shaming the client. It may be appropriate, in the future, to review confidentiality and reporting requirements (B) and to discuss acceptable behaviors (C), but these steps would occur only after the therapist assesses the group member individually. *(Domain 5-2)*

8. **C) A high-functioning client making substantial progress toward goals**
Higher functioning clients, those able to cope with day-to-day issues, would be most appropriate for this type of therapy. It would be more appropriate to terminate with clients completing their treatment prior to moving (A). The other clients (B) and (D) are in a crisis and would not be appropriate clients for this form of therapy. Instead, they should be referred to a local therapist. *(Domain 6-1)*

9. **A) Determine when Dwayne's problems first began**
This question is asking what the therapist should do first. The therapist should first take a history of Dwayne's problems. The therapist should obtain a signed release to speak with the client's doctor (C) and in the future could refer Dwayne for psychiatric evaluation (B), but only after taking a history. Referring Dwayne to a physical therapy program (D) is not clearly indicated in the vignette as an appropriate referral and the therapist should consult with the doctor to discuss this type of referral due to the client's stated health history. *(Domain 2-2)*

10. **B) Provide clear directives to help change symptomatic behaviors**
A strategic therapist is directive and would not (A) help a client prioritize goals, but rather would be the one to set the goals. Option A would have been the correct answer if the theoretical model was structural instead of strategic. Option D is wrong because a strategic therapist would not collaborate in problem-solving, nor would they (C) be concerned with emotional dynamics. *(Domain 1-1)*

11. **D) Within family and relational dynamics**
Option A would point to a more psychoanalytic perspective, whereas option B is representative of a social justice framework; option C in Maslow's hierarchy of needs, is the highest level of psychological development. *(Domain 1-2).*

12. **C) Cognitive behavioral**
Cognitive behavioral therapy (CBT), in the context of IPV, includes interventions that are designed to reduce partner violence by identifying and changing the thought processes leading to violent acts and teaching partners new skills to control and change their behavior. Option A would empower the female victim but would not be a good choice for conjoint treatment, option B lacks the important cognitive components, and option D would be a bad choice, as it would further stigmatize the client system. *(Domain 3-3)*

13. **A) Disregarding the possibility of marginalization and discrimination in the assessment process**
Increasing diversity requires paying attention to ways minority clients may feel marginalized and discriminated against in traditional assessment procedures. All other choices (B, C, and D) address different components of diversity in the assessment process. *(Domain 2-3)*

14. **C) Chronosystem**
All the options are all levels of Bronfenbrenner's ecological systems theory, but *chronosystem* describes the pattern of environmental events and transitions over the life course, as well as changing sociohistorical circumstances. *(Domain 2-4)*

15. **D) Progress monitoring**
Clinical progress monitoring is the formal assessment of treatment outcomes that mental health clinicians routinely engage in. It is beneficial for the client and the therapist in monitoring treatment progress. *(Domain 4-3)*

16. **B) Psychotherapy**
Psychoeducational programs help people better understand mental health conditions and contain skill building (A), stress management (C), and information (D) components. Although psychotherapy may contain some psychoeducation, it can be short-term (a few sessions)—dealing with immediate issues, or long-term (months or years)—dealing with long-standing and complex issues. (*Domain 1-3*)

17. **D) Expressed emotion**
Expressed emotion (EE) contributes to an adverse family environment, which includes the quality of interaction patterns and nature of family relationships among the family caregivers and patients of schizophrenia and other psychiatric disorders. *(Domain 2-5)*

18. **D) Raising fees as per the policy described in the informed-consent document**
Ethically, therapists must disclose their fees and the basis on which they are computed at the beginning of treatment. From the outset of treatment, clients need to understand when, why, and how their fees could be raised. Option A could harm clients in order to benefit the therapist financially, which is unethical. Option B would be considered unethical because the therapist would be exploiting wealthier clients. And, finally, option C could cause harm to clients unable to pay the re-negotiated fee. *(Domain 6-2)*

19. **D) It prioritizes client insight**
Options A, B, and C are all hallmarks of a strategic approach to family therapy, whereas option D is hallmark of psychodynamic approaches to therapy. *(Domain 1-4)*

20. **B) Complete a comprehensive biopsychosocial assessment**
While asking for descriptions from the child (A) and making referrals for play therapy (C) may be appropriate at a later point, these actions should only be implemented after a comprehensive assessment. Plus, asking Johnny to describe the fantasies (A) might trigger an intense fear response, so we need assess his coping mechanisms first. Without conducting a comprehensive assessment, the therapist does not have enough information to tell the mother that the child is developing normally (D). *(Domain 2-6)*

21. **D) "You are experiencing a normal adjustment to becoming a stepfamily."**
This response normalizes developmental tasks of blending families without pathologizing other members of the system. *(Domain 1-5)*

22. **D) Obtain a psychiatric evaluation, including an assessment for medication**
Although options A, B, and C may be appropriate later on in the treatment, given the severity of symptoms that Neil presents with, it would be most prudent to first get a psychiatric evaluation before proceeding. *(Domain 2-7)*

23. **B) The battle for structure**
According to Carl Whitaker, the battle for structure manifests itself over who will attend the therapy meeting. When families "elect" to attend therapy without a particular family member, they are not only deciding to go against the therapist's request, they are also sending a message about who is control of the treatment. *(Domain 1-6)*

24. **C) Defense mechanisms are unconscious processes**
This question is asking about the most accurate thing to remember about defense mechanisms. By definition, a defense mechanism is always an unconscious behavior or thought (C), whereas options A, B, and D may only be accurate in certain situations. *(Domain 1-7)*

25. **C) Refer Kyler to the school's special education department for an evaluation**
Kyler's symptoms are possible signs of a learning disability; therefore, a school evaluation would be the best answer. It would not be appropriate for the therapist to administer testing without the requisite training (A), and there is nothing mentioned in the scenario that points to the child being depressed (D). A school evaluation will include checking for ADHD (B). *(Domain 2-8)*

26. **D) Clarify what Derek means when he states he feels "depressed"**
There is very little information provided to the therapist in this scenario. Although Derek says he feels depressed, there is not sufficient evidence given to determine whether he meets the clinical criteria for depression or if that word holds a different meaning for him. Therefore, the therapist needs to gather additional information from Derek regarding his symptoms, experiences, and understanding of "feeling depressed" before proceeding with any other intervention. Options A through C might be appropriate interventions if the client's understanding of "feeling depressed" matches a clinical diagnosis of depression, but we cannot make that determination without further clarification. *(Domain 2-9)*

27. **D) Obtain a release from the client because in such a small community the colleague might know Theresa's client**
If a therapist does not disclose the identity of a client, a release from the client is unnecessary. If a therapist practices in a small rural area where the likelihood of anonymity is low, it would be appropriate for the therapist to obtain a release before consulting.

Making an effort to omit identifying information (B) and conveying the minimal amount of information (A) do not sufficiently protect a client's confidentiality. Altering a client's demographic information (C) could prevent the therapist from understanding cultural issues that may be influencing the therapy. *(Domain 6-3)*

28. **C) Use circular questioning with all family members**
Because a more open discussion was unsuccessful, the therapist is going to help family members communicate by providing specific questions to answer. Circular questioning is a technique that can be used to open up the conversation and explore differences among family members, which is the next step the therapist should take. Reminding the family about confidentiality (A) is not indicated at this time as a next step. Talking with Diane individually (B) would be counter to opening family communication. Option D could be harmful to Lorna's relationship with Diane, split the therapeutic alliance, and cause the client to further shutdown in future sessions. *(Domain 3-4)*

29. **D) Assess for lethality**
Assessing for lethality is the most complete answer as it encompasses the possibilities of both suicide and homicide—both are called for due to client's violent history and stated depression. Assessing for suicidality only (A) would potentially miss any homicidal tendencies, whereas assessing for danger to others (B) would exclude a suicide assessment. Administering the Beck Depression Inventory (BDI; C) could be done at some point but is not currently a priority due to possible risks. *(Domain 5-3)*

30. **A) The high incidence of panic disorder within the Bosnian refugee population**
There is no evidence to support the fact that anxiety is highly prevalent with this ethnic population. Even if it is, it would not provide an adequate explanation as to why the client is refusing treatment. In comparison, options B, C, and D are all possible explanations for such refusal. *(Domain 5-4)*

31. **B) Understand factors that impact Cindy's behavior**
The therapist needs to understand what is impacting Cindy's behavior in order to identify issues to be addressed in therapy. Gathering a social history would provide the therapist with a comprehensive understanding of environmental factors that influence the Cindy's behaviors. Option C is only one component of a client's social history. Developmental history (A) and emotional regulation skills (D) are not included in a client's social history. *(Domain 2-10)*

32. **A) Provide Dave with honest information regarding Shayla's credentials**
This question is asking what Shayla should do first. Providing the client with honest information regarding credentials would help build transparency and help build the alliance with the client. After sharing information, Shayla could ask Dave how he feels about seeking help (C) as well as explain her history of working with couples (D). Confronting clients (B) is not an intervention used in the early stages of therapy and could be detrimental to the alliance. *(Domain 3-5)*

33. **B) Trying to find a personal identity**
Connor Jr.'s actions represent a normative developmental stage of separating and establishing a separate identity. There is nothing in the stem to indicate that the problem here has to do with peer identification (A). Although this could be seen as a power struggle, this is just a small component of the parent/child dynamic (C). Because Connor Jr. is not

rejecting church attendance, but simply wants to find a different church, this indicates that he is not disrespecting parental values (D). *(Domain 3-6)*

34. **D) Relate Becky's attendance behavior in therapy as a parallel process to her behavior in her relationships with friends**
The scenario indicates that Becky is unaware of the impact of her behavior on her friendships. Relating Becky's therapy attendance behavior to her behavior with friends is an appropriate intervention and it addresses the client's lack of awareness. *(Domain 3-7)*

35. **C) Encourage Cindy to respond to her parents' disclosure**
Cindy's parents violated her privacy. She should be provided with an opportunity to react to this disclosure and process with her parents how it affects her. *(Domain 3-8)*

36. **B) Survey Antonio's cultural perspective around this issue**
It is always important for the therapist to understand the cultural context of a clients' situation. This holds true regardless of what theoretical orientation guides the therapist's work. It would be premature to suggest a course of action (A) so early in the therapy, and options B and D could be done after addressing the cultural context. *(Domain 3-9)*

37. **D) Focusing on the therapeutic goals Jack has accomplished**
It is common for clients to lose sight of the reason for treatment (symptom reduction and improvement of functioning). It is therefore important to remind the client what brought them to treatment and stay focused on goal completion when preparing for termination. *(Domain 4-4)*

38. **B) Role-play appropriate responses to Mark's behavior with Thomas**
Given that Thomas indicates that he does not know what to do, the therapist should assist the client in developing important self-advocacy skills and role-playing would help to achieve this task. Documenting inappropriate behavior (A) would not directly help the client. Confronting Mark privately is not possible since he is not part of the client system (C). Helping Thomas process this and other instances of mistreatment (D) would not empower Thomas or provide him with the skills needed to handle this issue with Mark. *(Domain 3-10)*

39. **A) Interrupt current discussion; conduct separate individual assessments with each family member; refer the parents to individual therapists**
When there is a history of domestic violence (DV) and the situation becomes heated in the session, the first thing a therapist can do to manage the situation is to call a time-out and interrupt the current discussion. Because this is still in the assessment stage, the presence of DV calls for separating family members and conducting individual assessment. Couples therapy is not recommended for couples when there is active DV and a lack of safety for the victim. Option A contains all of the correct options. There is not enough information to suspect child abuse (D). Treating the couple conjointly may be contraindicated (C). Opening the door would only be necessary if the interruption technique did not work (B). *(Domain 5-5)*

40. **C) Ask how Juliana views the impact of MS on her mental health**
The best place to start would be by asking Juliana her views of the presenting problem. In addition to being diagnosed with MS, the client has ended a significant romantic relationship and had a lot of other changes over the past few months that are also likely to

affect her mental health. Option A sides with the doctor's view of the problem without taking into account the other issues Juliana mentioned. Option B could be done at some point, but not when the therapist is initially connecting with the client. Option D could also be done at some point once the therapist has properly assessed how the client views her situation. *(Domain 2-11)*

41. **C) Inform the mother of the requirements for disclosure**
The therapist must protect the adult client's confidentiality and would need consent from the client prior to sharing information with the mother. The therapist would be breaking confidentiality by scheduling a meeting with the mother since the client is over 18 and has indicated that she wants individual therapy (A) or releasing records based on the mother's written request (B). Explaining that the records are the property of the agency (D) does not accurately address this situation. *(Domain 6-4)*

42. **D) Assess Robbie's safety**
The therapist's priority in this case is to assess the safety of the child. Because the client was referred for therapy by her doctor, it would not make sense to refer her for a medical evaluation (A). The therapist does not have enough information to make a report (B). A session with the couple may be important later on but would not be the initial priority (C). *(Domain 5-6)*

43. **B) Call the psychiatrist and request a copy of his release before acknowledging you see the client**
Legally, in order to release or exchange information about a client you need to have a written release, which should be done without acknowledging you see the client. Calling the client and receiving a verbal consent would not be sufficient, thus (C) is incorrect. You could do option A; however, it is time-consuming. Option D is incorrect since the therapist would be breaking the client's confidentiality without possession of an original or copy of the written release. *(Domain 6-5)*

44. **C) Cognitive behavioral**
The practice includes interventions that are designed to reduce partner violence by identifying and changing the thought processes leading to violent acts and teaching clients new skills to control and change their behavior. *(Domain 1-8)*

45. **A) Criticism**
Gottman's research suggests that criticism is the least destructive of the Four Horsemen, but is damaging nonetheless. Criticism is an assault against your partner and is designed to tear down the other partner. Criticism is most often packaged in "you always" or "you never" statements. *(Domain 1-9)*

46. **C) Developing an answerable question to focus the search for information**
The first step in the evidence-based practice (EBP) process is to identify the clinical problem or question for which you are seeking evidence. Asking a focused and relevant question about your client's situation will inform your search. *(Domain 3-11)*

47. **C) It helps pinpoint a more accurate diagnosis**
Therapists usually make a diagnosis only at the onset of therapy, while progress measures can be used continually during therapy. *(Domain 1-5)*

48. D) Caring days
Caring days is a behavioral couple therapy behavioral exchange technique in which couples act as if they care about their spouses, regardless of the other's actions. *(Domain 1-10)*

49. D) Client self-reports, a type of nonstandardized assessment, are considered less reliable than standardized assessments
Nonstandardized measures are less reliable and valid than standardized measures, however, the advantage is that they are less costly and can be used during each session if necessary to monitor ongoing progress. *(Domain 2-12)*

50. C) Increased goal-directed behavior
Increased goal-directed behavior or energy is symptomatic of mania rather than an eating disorder. *(Domain 4-6)*

51. C) Clinical outcomes
Client progress is best indicated by improvements in clinical functioning as well as what the client perceives as contributing to success in therapy. *(Domain 4-7)*

52. C) Monitor their own effectiveness
Therapists should continually monitor their own effectiveness as professionals and take steps to improve when necessary. *(Domain 4-8)*

53. A) The Session Rating Scale (SRS)
The SRS was developed to measure elements of the therapeutic alliance, including the quality of the relational bond, the degree of agreement between the client and therapist regarding goals, and client and therapist agreement regarding the tasks of therapy. *(Domain 4-9)*

54. D) Giving the client advice
Therapist feedback is the direct sharing of thoughts, feelings, and impressions about the client system. It is not advice giving, which may limit clients in self-determination and making their own decisions. *(Domain 4-10)*

55. B) Law enforcement officer
When someone makes threats of self-harm or suicide, law enforcement officers are legally allowed to force that person into medical care. Police and medical providers only commit clients against their will with the client's best interests in mind, not as an arbitrary punishment. *(Domain 5-7)*

56. D) The client recognizes he is in a crisis
Crisis intervention offers immediate, intensive, and brief professional assistance to people who have had a traumatic experience. The purpose is to help an individual cope and return to a previous level of physical or emotional functioning without being at risk of endangering self or others. This short-term professional support attempts to deal with the immediate crisis or problem. Prompt and focused interventions help prevent the development of a serious long-term disability. Crisis intervention also encourages the development of new coping skills to help the individual function more effectively. *(Domain 5-8)*

57. C) Talking about suicide increases the likelihood that suicidal clients will follow through

There is no research that suggests that talking to individuals about suicide increases their chance of committing suicide. In fact, talking about it provides an opportunity for individuals to express concerns, thoughts, and feelings about any possibility related to harming oneself. *(Domain 5-9)*

58. D) Remain objective

Supervisors should be mindful about boundaries and multiple relationships. *(Domain 6-6)*

59. C) Try to resolve the issue informally

If an apparent violation has substantially harmed, or is likely to substantially harm, a person and is not appropriate for informal resolution or is not resolved properly, further action should be taken depending on the situation, such as referral to state or national committees on professional ethics, state licensing boards, or appropriate agency or institutional authorities. *(Domain 6-7)*

60. D) Have been corrected if a mistake was made

The client's record must be kept in a professional way. This means that charts must be up to date and case notes need to be kept logical, neat, legible, and organized. Sloppiness, altered information, blank spaces, and out-of-sequence notes will have a negative impact on credibility. *(Domain 6-8)*

61. B) A therapist's intention to harm must be established

A therapist can still be found guilty of negligence even if they did not intend to hurt the client and felt that they were acting in the best interest of the client. *(Domain 6-9)*

62. A) Refer the client to a therapist who has experience with this population

While making a referral may be the correct immediate response, it will be incumbent on the therapist to get additional training and knowledge about providing services for LGBT clients in the future in order to expand scope of competence. *(Domain 6-10)*

63. B) The battle for initiative

Experiential therapists in Carl Whitaker's approach must allow the family to win the battle for initiative, which requires them, as opposed to the therapist, to be responsible for making changes. *(Domain 1-11)*

64. B) Physician

Disorders with prominent somatic symptoms constitute a new category in the *DSM-5* called "Somatic Symptom and Related Disorders." These include the diagnoses of Somatic Symptom Disorder, Illness Anxiety Disorder, Conversion Disorder (Functional Neurological Symptom Disorder), Psychological Factors Affecting Other Medical Conditions, Factitious Disorder, Other Specified Somatic Symptom and Related Disorder, and Unspecified Somatic Symptom and Related Disorder. All of these disorders share a common feature: the prominence of somatic symptoms associated with significant distress and impairment. Individuals with disorders with prominent somatic symptoms are commonly encountered in primary care and other medical settings but are less commonly encountered in outpatient psychotherapy practices. *(Domain 2-13)*

65. A) Helping the client explore the source of their feelings
Transference is the redirection of feelings and desires retained from the past toward a person in the present. Increasing self-awareness of transferences provides an opportunity to make behavioral changes. *(Domain 3-12)*

66. B) Client self-reports
Given the nature of the ego syntonic nature of this diagnosis, self-reports tend to be less reliable than a standardized measure or reporting by family members. *(Domain 4-11)*

67. D) A collection of client self-report data
Continual client feedback, also known as *routine outcomes monitoring*, *progress monitoring*, or *feedback-informed treatment*, refers to the collection of self-report data (e.g., symptoms, well-being, and the therapeutic alliance) from clients on a regular basis. Client feedback can then be interpreted against standardized metrics. This allows a therapist to compare a client's progress to an expected, or ideal, rate of change. Continual client feedback has been found to improve therapy outcome and detect problems that lead to dropout. *(Domain 4-12)*

68. B) Client's experience
The client is the single most potent contributor to the successful outcome in therapy. Research suggests that the majority of client change that occurs in therapy happens earlier rather than later in the treatment process; therefore, early improvement, specifically, the client's own experience of meaningful change in the first few visits, is emerging as one of the best predictors of eventual treatment progress. In fact, therapeutic relationships in which no improvement occurs by the third visit do typically result in an improvement over the entire course of therapy; clients who did not experience improvements by the third visit are twice as likely to drop out of treatment than those who report progress. *(Domain 4-13)*

69. D) Treatment adherence
The therapeutic alliance has been found to be a good predictor of treatment adherence and positive outcomes across a range of client diagnoses and treatment settings. A positive relationship between the therapist and the client is based on trust and confidence and often leads to a good working alliance in which the therapist and client system can agree on tasks, goals, and bonds of therapy. *(Domain 4-14)*

70. D) Countertransference analysis
Countertransference occurs when a therapist transfers misplaced thoughts and feelings from their own history to a client in therapy and can be harmful if unrecognized. *(Domain 4-15)*

71. D) Likert scales
Qualitative methods include interviews, observation, focus groups, textual or visual analysis, and meetings, whereas Likert scales are considered quantitative. *(Domain 4-16)*

72. B) Feeling stigmatized by the loss
The symptoms of complicated grief include maladaptive thoughts and behaviors related to the deceased, continuous emotional dysregulation about the death, social isolation, and suicidal ideation. *(Domain 5-10)*

73. C) Only maintain the security of records when taking them home to review
Therapists must ensure that records and documentation kept in any medium are secure and that only authorized persons have access to them. *(Domain 6-11)*

74. A) If the appropriate consent has been obtained from the client
When seeking consultation about a particular client case, unless the client has given their specific consent for you to discuss their situation with another professional, it is unethical for a therapist to reveal any identifying information about the client while discussing the case. *(Domain 6-12)*

75. C) Not being able to read nonverbal behaviors and responses
While practicing telehealth, family therapists must be aware of certain issues and ethics, such as security of client information, potential breaches of confidentiality, reduced ability to protect clients or warn others of potential danger, difficulties reading nonverbal behaviors, and the potential for client misunderstanding of written communications. *(Domain 6-13)*

76. C) Inform the client that if they don't want to participate in treatment, they won't force them to because unmotivated clients cannot be helped
When working with mandated clients, therapists discuss the limitations to confidentiality prior to starting therapy. This includes the type of information and with whom that information is shared. Therapists also discuss any potential consequences should a mandated client refuse therapeutic services. *(Domain 6-14)*

77. A) Flexibility and cohesion
The Olson Circumplex Model conceptualizes flexibility, cohesion, and communication skills as three central variables that define family interactions and suggests that balanced levels of cohesion and flexibility are most conducive to healthy family functioning. *(Domain 2-14)*

78. B) Schizophrenogenic
The term *schizophrenogenic mother* is a negative stereotype found in the psychiatric literature of the 1950s through to the 1970s. It posits that the schizophrenic is painfully distrustful and resentful of other people, due to the severe control and early rejection they experience from maternal figures. *(Domain 1-12)*

79. C) Negative feedback; positive feedback
According to family systems theory, families strive for a sense of balance or homeostasis. Negative feedback loops help to maintain homeostasis. Positive feedback loops, in contrast, are patterns of interaction that facilitate change or movement toward either growth or dissolution. *(Domain 1-13)*

80. A) Second-order change
First-order change is not as sustainable as second-order change, which is the fundamental rewriting of the system's underlying rules. *(Domain 1-14)*

81. B) Assess Tera for suicidal ideation, intent, plan, and access to means
Tera is showing significant signs of depression, so assessing for suicide would be the next step. The client has not stated that she feels suicidal, so having her sign a safety plan skips an important step of self-harm assessment. Alerting Tera's family, unless she

becomes acutely suicidal and is at imminent risk to herself, would violate her confidentiality. Although assessing for substance use could be part of your interview with Tera, it is not the best answer available here. *(Domain 5-11)*

82. **B) Fear**
Fear is the only primary emotion in the response options. Options A, C, and D are all secondary emotions. Secondary emotions are unconscious attempts to avoid experiencing the more vulnerable feelings, known as *primary emotions*, activated by a comment or situation. The EFT therapist creates a safe environment to help the couple reveal and constructively respond to each other's primary emotions. *(Domain 1-15)*

83. **B) Talk to Eli about how painful it must be to hear a parent talk badly about him**
Satir focused a lot on communication between family members and commenting on how the parents talk about their sons in front of them is one way of introducing communication styles, as well as the concept of "family pain" inhibiting emotional growth and health. Paradoxical interventions are not reflective of humanistic–experiential therapy. *(Domain 3-13)*

84. **D) Alert the client that their records will be released to the new therapist after a proper release of information has been signed by the client, and then give client advance notice of the steps that will be taken in the original therapist's bill-collection protocol**
According to the American Association of Marriage and Family Therapists *Code of Ethics* (2015), marriage and family therapists should never withhold records under their immediate control that are requested and needed for a client's treatment solely because payment has not been received for past services. Therapists should also give reasonable notice to clients with unpaid balances of their intent to seek collection by agency or legal recourse. When such action is taken, therapists will not disclose clinical information. *(Domain 6-15)*

85. **D) Outline the client's rights and options regarding legal action and ethics complaints**
Reporting the client's previous therapist without the client's permission would constitute an unauthorized breach of confidentiality. If you had a waiver of confidentiality, you could make the report yourself, but you can't "have the client sign a waiver"—this implies that you may be placing undue pressure on the client to do something he does not want or is not ready to do. In this situation, your best option would be to outline the client's rights and options and let him decide whether to take legal action or file a complaint with an ethics committee. *(Domain 6-16)*

86. **C) No, because there is no identified third party who is at risk**
The issue of confidentiality for clients who have tested positive for HIV or have AIDS, when they engage in risky sexual behavior, is a complicated issue. In this question, based on the comments made by your client, you do not have sufficient grounds to break confidentiality. A disclosure is only permitted if (a) there is an identifiable third party who is at risk, (b) the third party is unaware they are at risk, and (c) the client has refused or is not considered reliable to inform the third party. *(Domain 6-17)*

87. **B) Tell the client he can leave if he wishes but explain the legal ramifications of doing so to him**
In these situations, the marriage and family therapist must process how the client's decision may impact his probation status. Thus, before proceeding with termination, the

therapist should ensure that the client understands what legal sanctions he may face if he does not stay in therapy. *(Domain 4-17)*

88. **C) Disruptive Mood Dysregulation Disorder**
Disruptive Mood Dysregulation Disorder is defined by a predominantly irritable/angry mood and extreme outburst. It must be diagnosed by age 10. It is a new diagnosis in the *DSM-5* meant to address what was considered an overdiagnosis of Bipolar I in children. Option B is wrong because Intermittent Explosive Disorder only involves tantrums but does not have the persistent anger/irritability. Option D is wrong because the timeline exceeds 6 months from the stressor. *(Domain 2-15)*

89. **A) Call the client to check-in**
The abrupt termination warrants further inquiry by the therapist. Respecting the client's self-determination (B) or sending out a letter regarding termination (D) may be appropriate actions, but only after attempting to gather more information. Asking the client to reconsider (C) is not called for and makes the decision more about the therapist's needs than the client's. *(Domain 4-18)*

90. **B) Provide psychoeducation to the couple about life stages**
The first thing for the therapist to do when the couple presents with a life- stage issue is to provide psychoeducation and normalize their experience and feelings (B). All other interventions might come into play once the source of conflict is understood, and proper assessment is completed. *(Domain 2-16)*

91. **C) Explore the client's perception of the cultural conflict and constraints around being more assertive**
Exploring the client's perception of the cultural conflict would allow the therapist to address the client's expressed concerns and start where the client is. Supporting the client's efforts to pursue her original goal (A) and reframing the client's statements as resistance (D) ignore the perceived impediments to achieving the goals. Renegotiating the goal with the client (B) would be premature and should not be considered until after the cultural component is explored. *(Domain 3-14)*

92. **B) Help Tyler develop a support system**
The key points in this question are that the client is facing a serious legal issue, is lonely and desperate, and that his family doesn't know he is gay. He lacks and, therefore, needs social support. Although it might be appropriate at some point to explore his options regarding his family, it is more important initially to help him develop some type of support system. *(Domain 5-12)*

93. **C) To help Jeff come back to his previous level of functioning**
This is a question about crisis intervention. Crisis intervention helps an individual or family to deal with a specific current crisis. One of the goals of crisis intervention is to help the client return to the previous level of functioning. Crisis intervention does not attempt to deal with options A or B. Although distraught, we have no reason to believe Jeff is a danger to himself (D). *(Domain 5-13)*

94. **C) Often starts with benign boundary crossing**
The "slippery slope" often starts with benign boundary drifts before a violation occurs. Subtle boundary violations generally occur for several reasons. The first is a lack of

understanding of boundaries in general. The second is that the therapist is not in touch with their own boundaries. Third, the therapist may not understand a particular client's boundaries. Finally, the therapist may make incorrect assumptions about a client's ability to communicate when a boundary has been crossed. *(Domain 6-18)*

95. **D) Omit discussion of variables that the therapist believes may have skewed the data**
When a researcher mentions variables, they should make an effort to describe all variables that had any possibility of skewing the data. *(Domain 6-19)*

96. **C) Possibility talk**
Encouraging possibility talk is a specific intervention used by collaborative language therapists. Although collaborative language therapy uses similar interventions, solution talk (A) is a solution-focused technique. Externalizing the problem (B) is a narrative technique and not knowing (D) is another technique in collaborative language therapy. *(Domain 1-16)*

97. **B) "How did you first meet Mr. Worry, Thomas?"**
Asking, "How did you first meet, Mr. Worry" is an example of the use of externalization. This language separates Thomas from the problem of his worry. Suggesting that Thomas needs to worry more (C) takes a paradoxical approach. Narrative therapists do not use paradoxical interventions. This concept is more reflective of strategic therapy. *(Domain 1-17)*

98. **A) Ask the family to dramatize what happens when they discover Tania has snuck out again; have the family practice a new approach in session; assign homework for everyone**
Asking the Green family to dramatize what happens when they discover Tania "sneaking out" is a description of an enactment, a common structural intervention used to see how a family interacts. Having the family practice a new approach in session is a common way to reinforce structural gains with the family. Finally, assigning homework for everyone is part of Minuchin's directive approach. He would not ask a family to create their own homework. *(Domain 1-18)*

99. **C) Implementing a solution-focused technique**
Solution-focused therapists, working to frame things in a future-oriented way, begin using solution talk from the outset of therapy to both cast the client into a world in which the problem has been resolved and to help set achievable goals. *(Domain 1-19)*

100. **A) Highlight unique outcomes, separate them from their fighting through externalization, and look for new ways to narrate their move in way that benefits the couple**
Narrative therapists highlight unique outcomes to describe moments when the problem is not a problem. They believe it is important to externalize clients from their perception of the problem, and they look for new stories to circulate with the client. *(Domain 1-20)*

101. **C) Help Aaron and Trish develop consistent discipline**
Developing consistent parental disciplining techniques is an intervention from which all parents can benefit, particularly these clients. This needs to happen early on so that these demoralized parents can take back the leadership in their family life with their son. *(Domain 1-21)*

102. B) Detouring
As articulated by Minuchin, detouring occurs when the tension between husband and wife is reduced through the attention they pay to the child. This attention can involve either blaming the child for the family's problems (scapegoating) or overprotection of the child who is identified by them as ill or weak. Triangulation (A) doesn't work here as it refers to a situation in which the child's loyalty to one parent means rejection of the other parent. *(Domain 1-22)*

103. D) Decatastrophizing
Although all of these cognitive interventions are plausible, some techniques are better suited to certain disorders, especially as initial interventions. Decatastrophizing is particularly useful for clients like Jeff with an anxiety disorder because they tend to overestimate the risk and consequences of perceived danger. *(Domain 1-23)*

104. C) The disclosure could create a sense of shared experience between client and therapist
A therapist's self-disclosure should occur only with the goal of serving a therapeutic purpose for the client. A therapist wants to empathize with the client, not create empathy toward the therapist. *(Domain 6-20)*

105. A) Assess the behavior that takes place before the stealing occurs
This question asks what you would do first. Identifying the conditions (antecedents, consequences) that are maintaining the target behavior is a standard behavior modification process. It requires asking the client system to identify the personal triggers for losing control before setting up a behavioral modification program to help them. The other options—B, C, and D—are standard in behavioral parent-training techniques that could be useful later on in the therapy. *(Domain 2-17)*

106. B) Sit next to Mikey and tell him what he is doing is okay and understandable
This is the only option that involves structural technique, an example of joining. The other options are strategic in nature. *(Domain 1-24)*

107. D) Let the client arrive at their own decisions and insights
Client-centered therapy places the client as the expert of their own inner processes, decisions, and insights. It is a nondirective approach, which de-emphasizes advice-giving and being directive on the part of the therapist. *(Domain 1-25)*

108. C) Negative feedback
In cybernetics, the information exchanged between family members can act as either positive or negative feedback. Negative feedback is corrective and helps the system return to or maintain its steady state. Thus, a "negative feedback loop" helps to minimize deviation and thereby maintain the family's stability. Option D, positive feedback, increases deviation from a steady state and, therefore, disrupts the family system's homeostasis. *(Domain 1-26)*

109. C) Equipotentiality
The question illustrated is a clear example of equipotentiality, which is a general systems theory concept proposing that one cause (childhood sexual abuse) may produce different results (acting out or sexual inhibition). Option A is the opposite of this, positing that different causes can produce the same results. *(Domain 1-27)*

110. D) Reestablish homeostasis
According to Bowenian theory, triangles help reduce tension and increase stability and, thereby restore homeostasis. *(Domain 1-28)*

111. B) Works from a humanistic–existential perspective
Choosing the best answer requires you to have some knowledge of Native American culture. Most traditional tribal spiritual practices involve telling stories, experiencing intense emotions, guided imagery, and/or meditation. These are most consistent with humanistic–existential therapy. This orientation is also present-oriented, which is another reason it is a good choice. The majority of Native Americans are not actively involved in traditional healing practices (A), cognitive behavioral therapy (C) may be too directive, and there is no indication that family therapy is needed here (D). *(Domain 3-15)*

112. A) By practicing self-disclosure and trying on new types of interacting
The question is asking specifically how the therapeutic relationship could help Mike with his relationship goals. Mike needs help both with practicing self-disclosure and trying on new types of relating. These other interventions, though good, do not target his goal in the same direct way. *(Domain 3-16)*

113. B) Instructing the family to demonstrate a problem situation, having them replay the situation while the therapist spatially separates the mother and daughter, assigning homework to practice the new way of relating
Although all of these are possible answers, option B is the best. The structural therapist sets up an enactment before boundary making with the family. A response that mentions homework or follow-up is also better than one that does not. Structural therapists would be relatively directive, assigning the homework, rather than asking clients to come up with assignments on their own. *(Domain 1-29)*

114. A) Intrapsychic conflicts within individual family members
If you didn't know the right answer to this question, it might have been helpful to first eliminate the answers that you know are wrong; for example, you might have been able to choose option A by process of elimination if you recognized the theories associated with other answers. Psychoanalytic family therapists view family dysfunction as the result of intrapsychic conflicts within individual family members. Their primary goal in treatment is to modify the personality of individuals in the family so that family members can relate to one another on the basis of their current situation rather than on the basis of the past. Option B is associated with structural family therapy, option C with Bowen, and option D references contextual family therapy. *(Domain 1-30)*

115. B) Identify exceptions as a resource for positive change
Asking clients to search for exceptions to their financial problem is an intervention associated with solution-focused therapy. If the clients can identify and describe fully those times or situations in which their problem is less severe or nonexistent, this can suggest certain things that the clients can do to create more of these "nonproblem" experiences around money. When clients can identify situations in which things go well for them, these situations can become resources or models for change. Challenging the dominant story around money is an intervention from narrative therapy (C), whereas option D is derived from cognitive behavioral therapy. *(Domain 1-31)*

116. D) Boundary making
Although all responses are from structural family therapy, option D is the clear choice. Boundary marking is a technique that regulates the permeability of boundaries separating a subsystem. By reinforcing separateness in the mother–daughter dyad, the structural therapist is fostering each person's autonomy. *(Domain 1-32)*

117. D) Helping each partner identify their triggers and learn how to think before reacting
Before this couple can learn to communicate better, they need to be able to reduce emotional reactivity. Identifying triggers and thinking things through before emotionally reacting need to occur first. Detriangulating is an important middle-stage intervention for Bowenian therapists (A). Teaching communication skills is an important early- and middle-stage intervention (B), but D is a better choice for an early intervention. Helping the couple reconnect with their families of origin is a late-stage Bowenian intervention (C). *(Domain 1-33)*

118. D) Structural
Structural family therapists measure dysfunction based on boundaries and how family members adapt to different stressors. In functional families, family members are flexible and easygoing. The vignette describes enmeshment and diffuse boundaries between the mother and her one son who is overinvolved in her business. In healthy systems, the parents hold the authority. They decide what's best for their children, and instill healthy, clear boundaries. In dysfunctional systems, like this one, children seem to run the house by calling the shots and making the rules, and parents may fall helpless to their demands. In this vignette, the mother just wants to be the leader of the executive subsystem, or parental hierarchy. *(Domain 1-34)*

119. D) Triangulation
In efforts to describe family processes that extend beyond the dyadic level, the idea of triangulation is one of the more robust theoretical concepts that has emerged. Triangulation can occur in a variety of ways, but always involves a pair of family members incorporating or interjecting a third family member into the mix. Triangulation is seen in the cross-generational coalitions that can develop within families, a concept that Minuchin has linked to the development of maladjustment in children. *(Domain 1-35)*

120. A) Report the abuse
This question is about child abuse reporting obligations. The important information in this case is that Bella is a 16-year-old victim of child sexual abuse. Regardless of the girl's current safety, she is still a minor and, therefore you are mandated to report the abuse. Option C can be easily eliminated. When you know of or reasonably suspect child abuse, your reporting obligation is your own and can never be turned over to another person. You have enough information for a "reasonable suspicion" and, further, your duty is to report, not to investigate. Child protective services will take care of the investigation. And, again, the girl's current safety is irrelevant. She is a minor who has reported being abused, so you must make a report. *(Domain 5-14)*

121. C) Tell the couple to argue for at least 2 hours each evening
This is an example of "prescribing the symptom,"—directing the clients to do more of the problem behavior to show that the client has voluntary control over it. *(Domain 3-17)*

122. B) You feel the client would be better served by a gay therapist, especially since you do not agree with the client's gay lifestyle

Therapists refer based on scope-of-practice or competence issues, not value-laden issues. Referring a gay client to a gay therapist based on your values could risk the client feeling abandoned or discriminated against. *(Domain 6-20)*

123. A) The family projection process

The family projection process results in a child developing less adaptive coping skills under the stress that the parents are experiencing, which in this case is manifested by a suicide attempt. Option C offers a strategic term, whereas enmeshment (D) is derived from structural family therapy. *(Domain 1-36)*

124. B) Necessary to list referral sources

A therapist should indicate on an assessment whether or not there is a referral source. If so, the assessment should include the full name, address, and phone number of the person or agency that provided the referral. *(Domain 2-17)*

125. C) Ordeal

In this situation, overeating becomes less appealing to the client because of the amount of work (walking for 20 minutes) it will take to engage in the behavior. The ordeal forces the client to perform an unpleasant or inconvenient act in order to engage in the target behavior, which is what this question describes. *(Domain 3-18)*

126. C) Refer Kenny to a higher level of care

Referring an alcoholic client to a higher level of care like an intensive outpatient or inpatient program would be an appropriate intervention because the client is not able to abstain with just individual therapy. If Kenny has been in therapy for 4 months, this is a sufficient amount of time for the client to demonstrate that he can control his drinking on his own. Discharging a substance-abusing client because of failure to progress would be appropriate when the client has not remained abstinent, has not attended Alcoholics Anonymous (AA) or other referral resources, and has not successfully completed detoxification or inpatient treatment. This is not the best choice here because the question does not indicate that all of the other interventions have been offered to the client and the client has not followed through with treatment recommendations. Referring the client to a substance abuse specialist would be an early-stage intervention. It is not something you would do after working with a client for 4 months. *(Domain 4-19)*

127. B) Help Keith confront death

In most cases, a client who has just been notified that he has terminal cancer will not be ready to confront death. The first part of treatment involves letting the client know he has some time left to accomplish the things he wants to get done. People who have just been diagnosed with a terminal illness are in a state of crisis and may exhibit a range of responses, from numbing to strong affective expressions. The goal of the first stage of therapy should be to help the client handle his diagnosis and gain control of his feelings. This goal is accomplished by using crisis-intervention techniques. It is also important to make sure the client is linked to appropriate medical resources. *(Domain 5-15)*

128. A) Find Janet a group for survivors of rape
Encouraging Janet to join a support group is an important response, but this would occur after the immediate crisis has been contained. Janet is in crisis. Components of crisis intervention with rape victims in the acute phase include a medical evaluation, validation of feelings, providing information about expected emotional reactions and practical problems that need immediate resolution, building her self-esteem, and reassuring her that it was not her fault. *(Domain 5-16)*

129. D) Take reasonably necessary steps in an effort to protect the college professor
The Tarasoff ruling indicates that you are mandated to breach this client's confidentiality. It is irrelevant that the client has no history of violent behavior. Hospitalization is an option when the client is dangerous, rather than a requirement. The requirement is to take reasonable and necessary steps in an effort to protect the identifiable potential victim. Because this question asks what the marriage and family therapist is "required" to do, you need to focus on something that is mandated in this situation rather than on other measures the therapist might take. This option describes a therapist's obligation under the Tarasoff law. Brandon has verbalized a serious threat of physical harm against a specific person (i.e., he has thought about "killing" the professor) and seems to have developed a plan for how to carry out his threat. *(Domain 5-17)*

130. D) Tammy's plan for committing suicide
Suicide risk evaluations include both direct and indirect assessments. In the direct assessment, question the client directly, emphasizing specific factors that have been linked to an elevated, more imminent suicide risk. Explore whether the client has communicated an intent or wish to commit suicide; whether the client has a specific suicide plan; whether the client has the means to enact the plan; and, if the client has a plan and the means, whether the client's plan is relatively lethal. Although options A, B, and C are all important, they are all more indirect forms of assessment of suicide risk. *(Domain 5-18)*

131. A). Develop a safety plan with her
Formulating a safety plan with her would be the first step the therapist would take. Most cutters are not suicidal and use cutting as a way of self-soothing and dealing with strong emotions. Setting a specific timeframe during which she will agree not to harm herself, as well as helping her identify alternative behaviors in which to engage when she feels the desire to cut, would be important initial treatment interventions. Although options B, C, and D may be alternatives in the future, these options would not be your initial response. *(Domain 5-19)*

132. A) ABC-X Model of Family Stress
The development of the ABC-X Model resulted from the emergence of concepts such as family resilience. The ABC-X Model is a framework used to establish how families respond to stressful events and crises. The McMaster Model defines the primary function of a family to be providing an environment that supports the family's ability to accomplish three types of tasks: basic, developmental, and hazardous tasks. Olson's Circumplex Model distinguishes among three dimensions of family functioning: cohesion, flexibility, and communication. The Beaver's Systems Model describes family functioning in terms of two dimensions: competence and style. *(Domain 2 18)*

133. D) The data are not clinically useful

Routine outcome monitoring is an effective tool used to help clinicians identify whether a given client is at risk for a negative outcome or on track to experience benefit. Research to date has demonstrated that routine outcome monitoring and feedback significantly reduces deterioration and dropout rates in routine psychological treatment. *(Domain 4-20)*

134. C) The responsibility to do good

Beneficence is one of the four principles that ethical codes are based on. A therapist who abides by ethical principles of beneficence is acting in a manner that does the greatest good possible. *(Domain 6-21)*

135. A) Identify the problem

When making an ethical decision, the therapist should first identify the dilemma by gathering as much information as possible. The therapist can ask whether this is a legal, professional, ethical, or clinical problem and then seek out proper consultation. The therapist could also determine whether the problem is due to something the therapist may or may not be doing, if it has to do with the client, or maybe with the policies and procedures of the agency the therapist belongs to. The key is for the therapist to be clear, objective, and specific in defining the ethical dilemma. *(Domain 6-22)*

136. A) The therapist's personal opinions about the client

When therapy is finished and the termination is mutually agreed upon, the following should be documented: the reasons for termination, the client's reaction to the ending, any continuity-of-care needs and plans, any referrals, any unfinished issues. *(Domain 4-21)*

137. A) The family is experiencing severe domestic violence that has not been brought under control

In cases where the couple or family have ongoing and current relationship violence or aggression, therapy may be ill-advised or seriously contraindicated, as this could pose a safety issue. In those cases, it may be best to seek individual therapy with a therapist trained to work with relationship aggression or refer to a domestic violence shelter. All of the other options include indications to family therapy. *(Domain 2-19)*

138. C) Consider his effectiveness in being able to treat this client

Mike should first consider how effective he could be with this client. Mike's effectiveness would depend on the personal therapy/healing work he has done, his clinical experience working with this population, and his ability to appropriately manage possible countertransference issues that may arise. Making this referral, without ever having met the client, would be premature. *(Domain 6-23)*

139. B) Vicarious traumatization

Therapists experiencing burnout often display apathy and cynicism, whereas Leslie's symptoms look more like vicarious traumatization. This is common among therapists who work with traumatized clients. The symptoms can be similar to PTSD. It is important for therapists to recognize what is happening and seek the necessary support and consultation. *(Domain 6-24)*

140. A) Solution-focused

Solution-focused therapists believe clients have all the skills necessary to heal when they enter therapy. This belief is demonstrated by the pre-session change question that assumes clients benefit from their decision to seek help. *(Domain 3-19)*

141. B) The way we expect to experience the world alters how we feel about it and how we act

Constructivism is the theory that says learners construct knowledge rather than just passively take in information. As people experience the world and reflect on those experiences, they build their own representations and incorporate new information into their pre-existing knowledge. Constructivism holds that since knowledge is a construct it is not possible to know the extent to which knowledge reflects reality. Although constructivism is most closely associated with postmodern systemic models, such as solution-focused and narrative therapy, it is best viewed as a "meta-theory" that encompasses many late 20th-century developments in psychotherapy. *(Domain 1-38)*

142. B) The most differentiated family member

According to Bowen, a high degree of fusion is the source of family dysfunction. Therefore, the goal of Bowenian therapy is to help family members become less fused, or more differentiated. Bowenians sometimes work with the most differentiated family member in individual sessions. *(Domain 1-39)*

143. D) There is a lack of trust and caring in the family system

Ivan Boszormenyi-Nagy, the developer of contextual family therapy, emphasizes the ethical environment of the family. Nagy postulates that trust, mutual support, fairness, accountability, and loyalty are key to the healthy family system, and symptoms develop when there is a lack of caring or trust. Option B is referring to structural therapy, whereas option C is referring to the internal family systems (IFS) model. *(Domain 1-40)*

144. C) Displacement

Defense mechanisms are unconscious distortions of reality, which are used to reduce anxiety and, on a deeper level, to keep unwanted unconscious impulses out of awareness. Three of the options list defense mechanisms, so to answer this question you need to understand how displacement could be manifested. Tony's behavior is an example of displacement. He has unconsciously redirected an emotional response from a dangerous or threatening object (his boss) to a substitute object that is less threatening to his ego (his wife). Sublimation (A) is a defense mechanism and a type of displacement but is not what has occurred in this question. Sublimation occurs when a person redirects an unacceptable impulse into a socially desirable activity. By contrast, displacement occurs when the impulse is redirected to a person or object, rather than an activity. Dissociation (B) is a process whereby thoughts or memories that produce anxiety are cut off from consciousness. Rationalization (aka *intellectualization*) occurs when a person interprets or explains their behavior in a way that makes it seem more rational, logical, or socially acceptable. *(Domain 1-41)*

145. A) The "identified patient" in therapy is the partner with the sexual dysfunction

A therapist relying on the techniques of Masters and Johnson would not agree that the "patient" or focus of treatment should be the dysfunctional partner. Instead, the therapist would focus on the relationship. The unit of treatment is the couple, so both partners would be given information about the human sexual response and permission to enjoy their sexuality. *(Domain 1-42)*

146. **B) A co-learner along with the client**
The collaborative approach pioneered by Harlene Anderson and Harry Goolishian views therapist and client as "conversational partners" who engage in "dialogical conversation" to explore the client's problems. The therapist takes a position as "co-learner" with the client in order to understand the client and their unique perspective. The therapist's stance is of "not knowing" and considers the client to be the "expert" on their own life, and as the therapist's "teacher." The therapist's expertise lies in his ability to create the kinds of conversations and experiences that pull forth the client's inner resourcefulness and wisdom. *(Domain 3-20)*

147. **B) The therapist**
The records always belong to the therapist. The client can request a copy of their record and see it if the therapist determines it would not be detrimental, but the record is always the property of the therapist. Neither a state board, nor a client owns the record. *(Domain 6-25)*

148. **B) Refuse the gift**
The primary concern should be what is in the best interests of the clients. Generally, therapists consider small gifts or tokens of appreciation to be acceptable but do not accept expensive gifts. This action is most in line with acting in the best interests of your clients. You should not accept an expensive gift from the couple because it might lead to problems in your relationship with them in the future. You would want to explain to the family why you are refusing the gift in a clear but sensitive way. *(Domain 6-26)*

149. **C) It is unnecessary to get permission from the couple to discuss confidential information with the consultant as long as their identity is not revealed to the consultant**
Note that supervision and consultation are treated differently. When receiving supervision, your supervisor must know the client's name, because the supervisor is responsible for the work that you do with the client. Consultation involves no such requirement. This is consistent with the requirements of the American Association of Marriage and Family Therapist's (AAMFT) *Code of Ethics* (2015). *(Domain 6-27)*

150. **A) Scope-of-practice issues**
All of these are important considerations, but only one always determines whether or not a marriage and family therapist should accept a client. The referral must fall within marriage and family therapy (MFT) scope of practice. You may take on a case when you have had only some experience or education in handling the presenting issue, but you would, of course, need to seek supervision or consultation from someone else in the field who has the needed experience. *(Domain 6-28)*

151. **A) The executor of the client's will**
This a straightforward situation that is governed by laws related to privilege. The person designated as executor in the deceased client's will is holder of the privilege, and they can decide whether to claim or waive the privilege with regard to your records and testimony. *(Domain 6-29)*

152. **D) Unethical if the payment is only for the referral**
The American Association of Marriage and Family Therapist's (AAMFT) *Code of Ethics* (2015) prohibits marriage and family therapists from offering or accepting remuneration for referrals except when the amount paid represents the actual costs of the referral

(e.g., the costs of copying and forwarding the client's file or consulting with the therapist about the referred client). Paying a predetermined fee just for the referral is not consistent with this requirement. *(Domain 6-30)*

153. A) Inform them that it would be unethical and begin a discussion about sliding-scale fees
It is unethical to enter into dual relationships with clients when they are avoidable. Although bartering with clients is not completely unethical, it has the potential to create a dual relationship and should be avoided when possible. These clients may benefit from a referral to a financial counselor, but this answer choice does nothing to educate your clients and ignores the possibility of a mutually agreeable sliding-scale fee. *(Domain 6-31)*

154. B) Inform them that it would be unethical and begin a discussion about sliding-scale fees
Advising a client about legal action would be considered to be outside of the scope of practice. *Scope of practice* refers to the legally defined boundaries of a therapist's professional practice. A therapist performing EMDR therapy on a client without being adequately trained in that area would be considered to be outside of the therapist's scope of competence. *Scope of competence* refers to the limits of what a therapist is qualified to do based on education, training, and experience. *(Domain 6-32)*

155. D) You consider whether your relationship with the neighbor will affect the potential therapeutic relationship with the family and decide whether to take on the case accordingly
You have not established that this is an avoidable dual relationship. Considering whether or not your relationship as a customer at her store and whether your relationship as neighbors will affect the therapeutic relationship is important. You may feel comfortable being a customer and the daughter's therapist, because being a customer is a straightforward relationship. On the other hand, depending on the type of relationship you have with her as her neighbor, it might not be appropriate. *(Domain 6-33)*

156. D) Ethical issues often overlap with legal issues
Many ethical issues faced by family therapists involve legal issues, such as confidentiality rights of clients and certain legal limitations of confidentiality. *(Domain 6-34)*

157. C) See Lacy alone and promote differentiation of thoughts and feelings
Seeing Lacy alone and promoting differentiation of thoughts and feelings is a common Bowenian early-stage goal and it addresses her confusion about where she wants to go in her marriage. *(Domain 3-21)*

158. A) Undermine the family's resistance to change
The goal of prescribing the symptom is to help family members change their dysfunctional rules. Symptom prescription is thought to create the possibility of unbalancing the family system, making the family more available for change. This is the purpose of prescribing the symptom, which involves asking the family to continue or even exaggerate what it is doing in order to undermine the family's resistance to changing that behavior. Prescribing the symptom results in a therapeutic double-bind—it forces the client to either give up the symptom or admit that it is under voluntary control. *(Domain 3-22)*

159. A) A distortion of reality based on incorrect premises and assumptions
Tom's problems are a result of a distortion of reality based on an incorrect assumption—his core belief that he is somehow responsible for his partner's death. Chronic anxiety that leads to a high level of emotional reactivity is a Bowenian concept (B). An exaggerated feeling of inferiority and an insufficiently developed feeling of community is an Adlerian concept (C). An inability to experience contradictory feelings leading to a distortion of perception describes the object-relations concept of splitting (D). *(Domain 2-20)*

160. C) Hypomanic and major depressive episodes
It is straightforward if you know the *Diagnostic and Statistical Manual of Mental Disorders* (5the ed.; *DSM-5*; APA, 2013). The presence of hypomanic and depressive episodes is required for the diagnosis of Bipolar II Disorder but not Bipolar I Disorder. The diagnosis of Bipolar II Disorder requires the presence of at least one major depressive episode (not two or more), and Bipolar I Disorder may or may not include one or more major depressive episodes. *(Domain 2-21)*

161. D) Histrionic
This question describes key symptoms of histrionic personality disorder. Behavior that is overly dramatic and reactive, intensely expressed, and perceived by others as shallow and superficial characterizes histrionic personality disorder. Other features of this disorder include excessive emotionality and attention-seeking and various disturbances in social relations, such as a lack of consideration for others and excessive demands for reassurance. *(Domain 2-22)*

162. A) Attention and awareness
A diagnosis of delirium requires a disturbance in attention and awareness and at least one additional disturbance in cognition, such as impaired memory, disorientation, impaired language, deficits in visuospatial ability, or perceptual distortions. Although one would expect executive functioning to be impaired during delirium, the diagnosis requires a disturbance in attention and awareness. A disturbance in psychomotor functioning or in receptive and expressive language is not required for a diagnosis of delirium. *(Domain 2-23)*

163. C) Stimulant Intoxication
Isaac is exhibiting symptoms that are consistent with stimulant intoxication: dilated pupils, perspiration, agitation, confusion, and increased talkativeness. If intoxicated on cannabis, he would likely be overly relaxed or spaced out. Isaac also does not appear to be hallucinating or showing any other signs of schizophrenia. *(Domain 2-24)*

164. A) Erectile Disorder
A diagnosis of erectile disorder requires the presence of at least one of three symptoms (marked difficulty in obtaining an erection during sexual activity, marked difficulty in maintaining an erection until completion of sexual activity, and/or marked decrease in erectile rigidity) on all or almost all occasions of sexual activity. Symptoms must have persisted for at least 6 months and cause clinically significant distress. *(Domain 2-25)*

165. D) Progress notes reflect the treatment plan's implementation as well as provide indicators for needed changes in the plan as therapy progresses
Progress notes can indicate when a technique isn't working well and which other options might work better. The treatment plan will need to be adjusted over time, and progress notes guide you in that process. *(Domain 4-22)*

166. C) Goals are set collaboratively with the client, stated in both realistic and positive terms, and reviewed regularly throughout the course of therapy
The client and therapist collaborate to set the goals, and although it is primarily the therapist's responsibility to track progress, it is best to also include the client in the process. *(Domain 4-23)*

167. B) Underutilized by private practitioners
Despite compelling evidence that monitoring and feedback can improve client outcomes, available data suggest that this practice is rare in clinical settings due to resistance from clinicians, lack of training, unwillingness of clients to complete measures, and a concern about the economic and political motives for use. *(Domain 4-24)*

168. C) Emphasize traditional assessment and diagnosis
A feminist family therapist approach would not emphasize traditional assessment and diagnosis. To avoid pathologizing client's problems, feminist therapists do not use traditional labels to describe feelings and behaviors. These therapists acknowledge the power differential that is inherent to the therapist–client relationship, but attempt to minimize it, and strive for an egalitarian relationship. Feminist therapists also avoid blaming women for their current problems, and place emphasis on the woman's strengths. *(Domain 4-25)*

169. C) Jules and Jordan have altered their unrealistic ideas and expectations about their marriage
Couples cognitive behavioral therapy (CBT) focuses on challenging automatic dysfunctional thoughts about the partner. Therapy can successfully conclude when Jules and Jordan replace their irrational belief systems about marriage with realistic ideas and expectations and find new ways to relate by practicing communication and problem-solving skills. *(Domain 4-26)*

170. C) Use empathic statements in an attempt to understand Jack's silence
As a marriage and family therapist (MFT), your initial task is to engage the client. The client's silence is most effectively addressed by acknowledgment of how the client might be feeling; therefore this option is the best choice. *(Domain 4-27)*

171. D) Affect
Affect refers to the emotional state that clinicians observe, as opposed to *mood*, which refers to what clients report in terms of how they feel. *(Domain 4-28)*

172. B) A pre- and post-treatment Minnesota Multiphasic Personality Inventory-2 (MMPI-2)
This question asked for the most "objective" way to test the effectiveness of therapy in changing a personality characteristic of a client; the word *objective* is important as is the goal of the therapy. The MMPI-2 is a structured personality test. It includes a number of scales that assess characteristics such as social introversion, hysteria, depression, masculine/feminine interests, and psychopathic deviation. It is considered to be a valid and reliable test. Note that, of the four choices, this is the only objective measure. *(Domain 4-29)*

173. A) When the crisis is abated since it is too overwhelming at first
The ability to assess the proper timing for referral to a group is very important for a therapist. The group process can be very beneficial for certain issues, especially for survivors of trauma. You probably eliminated options B and C pretty quickly. This is the best answer among the choices given. The traumatic events surrounding the date rape may be too emotionally laden for group process. The statement, "emotions are best contained

in a group" is wrong. Emotions are best contained in individual sessions where the focus is concentrated on one person. *(Domain 4-30)*

174. C) Socially
The ORS asks clients to rate how well they have been doing over the previous week in terms of personal well-being (individually); family and relationships (interpersonally); work, school, or friendships (socially); and their general sense of well-being (overall). *(Domain 4-31)*

175. B) Allow the mother to let go of her son in her own time
The mother is engaging in denial, which is the first stage of grieving. Allowing the mother to let go of the son in her own time (B) would allow the mother to engage in this stage of grief. Asking the doctor to sedate the woman (A) or admitting the woman to the psychiatric ward (C) would be overreactions based on the information provided in the stem. The therapist could choose to involve family members (D), but only at a later stage. *(Domain 5-21)*

176. C) Develop a safety plan for the victim
Given that the minor's safety is the main objective, the development of a safety plan should take priority. Option A is out because it is contraindicated to have a victim and a perpetrator in the same session. This is something that could happen in the future when safety concerns are fully addressed. Options B and D could be done, but enhancing the child's safety is foremost. *(Domain 5-22)*

177. C) Report elder abuse based on the information Maureen has shared
The isolation of an older person is a form of elder abuse that family therapists are required to report to authorities. The law requires you to report even a reasonable suspicion of such abuse. Assessing the client's coping strategies would be appropriate. Fulfilling your legal obligation to report elder abuse, however, is your priority in this case (A). You don't need to assess the issue of elder abuse further. The daughter's report is enough to arouse a reasonable suspicion of elder abuse and, therefore, you must file a report. Once law enforcement or adult protective services (APS) agency receives the report, an APS unit will collect information to determine whether to intervene or dismiss the report. If the report is substantiated, APS will obtain information about the maltreated elder and her family and determine what types of treatments and services would most effectively resolve the family's abuse-related problems. *(Domain 5-23)*

178. B) Barry, an unemployed, divorced 72-year-old male who has tried to overdose on aspirin and bourbon in the past
Barry's risk factors are age, gender, marital status, and previous attempt. *(Domain 5-24)*

179. D) Seek further clarification of Larry's statement
It is important to clarify what Larry means by his statement to "get even" before deciding on the next steps. If the client means divorcing and getting as much as possible in a settlement, that is one thing, but if the client means physically harming the partner, the therapist will need to address it differently. *(Domain 5-25)*

180. C) His substance abuse
The potential issue of substance abuse must be addressed as an underlying issue before dealing with the other issues presented. Once substance abuse is addressed, the therapist can focus on the client's potential job loss (A), childhood abuse (B), and problems with his relationship (D). *(Domain 5-26)*

REFERENCES

American Association of Marriage and Family Therapists. (2015). *Code of ethics*. Author.

American Psychiatric Association. (2013). *Diagnostic and statistical manual of mental disorders* (5th ed.).

Index